W9-CPO-096

CHOOSING STUDENTS

HIGHER EDUCATION ADMISSIONS TOOLS FOR THE 21ST CENTURY

CHOOSING STUDENTS

HIGHER EDUCATION ADMISSIONS TOOLS FOR THE 21ST CENTURY

Edited by

Wayne J. Camara
Ernest W. Kimmel
The College Board

LEA LAWRENCE ERLBAUM ASSOCIATES, PUBLISHERS
2005   Mahwah, New Jersey   London

Lawrence Erlbaum Associates, Inc., Publishers
10 Industrial Avenue
Mahwah, New Jersey 07430

Cover design by Sean Sciarrone

Library of Congress Cataloging-in-Publication Data

Choosing students : higher education admissions tools for the
21st century / edited by Wayne J. Camara, Ernest W. Kimmel.
    p.   cm.
Includes bibliographical references and index.
ISBN 0-8058-4752-9 (cloth : alk. paper)
    1. Universities and colleges—United States—Admission.
I. Camara, Wayne J. II. Kimmel, Ernest W.
LB2351.2.C54 2004
378.1'61'0973—dc22   2003062651

Printed in the United States of America
10 9 8 7 6 5 4 3 2 1

Contents

Preface

Although colleges and universities have long cherished their right to choose the students they will teach, the manner in which they make those choices is under intense scrutiny during the first decade of the 21st century. Gone are the days when it was widely assumed that higher educational institutions act for the public good. Students, parents, legislators, litigators, and judges have challenged both particular admissions decisions and the process by which those decisions were made by colleges, graduate, and professional schools. This scrutiny of the way in which each institution chooses its students occurs in the context of increasingly severe competition among students for admission to those institutions that are perceived to be "best." Admission to higher education has become both the perceived and the real gateway to success in the American economy and society. As President Bollinger points out in the opening chapter of this volume, this scrutiny of the admission process also occurs in the context of unparalleled competition among institutions to be perceived as best. National and regional rankings by the media have become the scoreboard of higher education. Winning "the gold" becomes the obsession of higher education—and those who make admission decisions are held responsible for producing a "winning" entering class.

A subtext of the debate over how universities make admission decisions is a concern for fairness. Yet there is no consensus over the meaning of *fairness* in the distribution of educational opportunities. Parts of American society argue that fairness requires that members of gender, racial, language, or ethnic groups be provided access to educational opportunities in proportion to their representation in the general population—or in the applicant pool.

Others, however, argue that fairness means that each individual is judged on his or her qualities, abilities, or past achievements in comparison with all other applicants, without regard to gender, race, ethnicity, or other personal characteristics. Still others, typically university administrators, maintain that any selection process must recognize that institutions have a wide variety of needs that give reasons for choosing some students because they are promising athletes or musicians, because they are the offspring of alumni, faculty, or major contributors, or because they have some unique experiences or talents that will create a diverse freshmen class.

A debate on the admissions process almost invariably involves a debate about the tools used in the admissions process. Most admission decisions are made using tools that have been around for 50 years or more: teacher grades from the previous level of education; scores on standardized tests; essays allegedly written by the applicant; recommendations by harried teachers or professors who may or may not really know the applicant. Teacher grades, from the previous level of the education process, are criticized for reflecting behaviors other than academic performance (e.g., attendance) and/or for being too tightly "bunched" at the top of the scale and, thus, providing little information for differentiating among candidates. The current admissions tests are criticized as being too narrow, or insufficiently responsive to high-school curriculum. Essays and recommendations are thought to provide little reliable information. This volume seeks to broaden the debate about the attributes of the candidates that are valued in making admissions decisions as well as the tools used in the admission process to assess those attributes. Significant attention is given to finding new variables that may have less of a disparate impact on poor or racial/ethnic students, as well as reliably measuring a broader range of talents and skills related to college success.

Running throughout this volume is the recognition that the initial debate needs to be on what we, as a society, mean by *college success*. Too often, academic success has been operationally defined as a high grade point average (GPA) or some other indicators. What additional criteria can be used to represent those other attributes that higher education claims to develop? Contributors to this volume provide useful suggestions on ways to improve current admissions practice; others argue for new constructs and measures of those constructs, as well as providing conceptual models for developing such new measures. Still other contributors deal with the implications for higher education of the ubiquitous state-defined academic standards and their related assessments. This volume is best read as part of an ongoing conversation about the purposes of higher education and the many factors than can, and, perhaps, should, enter into decisions about choosing students.

In chapter 1, Lee Bollinger provides a university president's reflections on the nature of competition in higher education and the role that admissions testing has come to play in that competition. Robert Laird, the former Director of Undergraduate Admissions for the University of California–Berkeley, provides, in chapter 2, a view from within the process. He highlights both the struggle over the definition of fairness and the extraordinary efforts required to fairly evaluate large numbers of applicants. In chapter 3, Ernest Kimmel, formerly an Executive Director of Test Development at the Educational Testing Service, describes the group of students who will be seeking to enter higher education during the next 10 years or so and points out that most of the projected growth is among Hispanic and Asian young people. He analyzes a number of factors that could affect the number who apply and raises the question of whether universities will be prepared to move beyond current practices to meet the needs of this more diverse population of students. Wayne Camara, Vice-President for Research at the College Board, argues in chapter 4 that it is fruitless to develop preadmission measures of additional characteristics if those measures are going to be judged solely on their ability to predict academic success; new criteria of college success are needed. In chapter 5, Camara draws on research in the occupational, as well as in the educational, arena to highlight promising nonacademic attributes.

Paul Sackett, a psychologist whose work has focused on issues of fairness in recruitment and selection in work settings, provides, in chapter 6, a sobering analysis of the challenging tradeoffs between performance and diversity. In chapter 7, Warren Willingham, a veteran researcher on issues of admissions and college outcomes, reports on some of the limits and promises of the ways in which grades are assigned. Robert Linn, a distinguished researcher in the field of educational measurement, provides a thoughtful critique of current practices in chapter 8.

Robert Sternberg, a major voice in shaping contemporary conceptions of intelligence as developed expertise, examines in chapter 9 ways of broadening both our concept and our measurement of cognitive abilities. William Sedlacek, a long-time advocate of considering multiple factors in evaluating students, especially those from racial/ethnic or other nontraditional backgrounds, makes the case in chapter 10 for using noncognitive measures in the selection process. Neal Schmitt, Frederick Oswald, and Michael Gillespie provide, in chapter 11, insight into the measurement of additional performance criteria, as well as variables that might predict these criteria. In chapter 12, Patricia Etienne and Ellen Julian describe the motivation of the Association of American Medical Colleges to broaden the set of predictors used in choosing medical students as well as the developmental process to create measures of certain personal characteristics of applicants. Peter Pashley, Andrea Thornton, and Jennifer Duffy report, in chapter 13, the multiple ways in which law schools have sought to select diverse student bodies. They describe ongoing research seeking to model the selection of an entering class with optimal characteristics that meet the goals of the institution. In chapter 14, Isaac Bejar describes a program of research and development to make the process of designing and creating assessments more systematic. These efforts draw heavily from the cognitive sciences and recent developments in computing and in natural language processing.

The concluding chapters of this volume explores the implications for college admissions of the school reform efforts that have occurred in almost every state. Stanley Rabinowitz, in chapter 15, examines the similarities and differences between the use of assessments in secondary school and the information needs of the postsecondary system. In chapter 16, Michael Kirst reports on the lack of coherence in content and assessment standards between higher education and the K–12 system. He argues that the failure to bring the expectations of these two levels into alignment will continue to confuse students and schools as well as result in students who are poorly prepared for higher education. Based on his extensive involvement in helping Oregon's secondary and postsecondary systems bring their expectations into alignment, David Conley, in chapter 17, concludes this volume by providing a constructive model for helping assess what students know and can do in relationship to the expectations of both levels of the system.

ACKNOWLEDGMENTS

We want to thank the College Board and its president, Gaston Caperton, for sponsoring the January, 2002, conference, New Tools for Admission to Higher Education, at which many of the ideas in this book were presented initially. Each of the contributors to this volume has brought his or her expertise to bear on the question of improving the ways in which higher education institutions choose students. We thank them for their willingness to share their ideas and their patience in persevering through the various challenges of creating a volume such as this. We also want to thank Robert Majoros and Helen Ng of the College Board staff for their many efforts, large and small, to move this volume from idea to reality. Finally, the encouragement and help of Lane Akers and Bonita D'Amil at Lawrence Erlbaum Associates have been critical to this enterprise.

—*Wayne J. Camara*
—*Ernest W. Kimmel*

I

Diversity in
Higher Education

1

Competition in Higher Education and Admissions Testing

Lee C. Bollinger

Columbia University

Higher education in the United States seems always to generate public controversy, and today is no exception. Just in the past 10 years, for example, we have seen enormous public attention and debate about the rising costs for students attending colleges and universities (e.g., Troutt,1998), about the proper scope of freedom of speech and debate on our campuses, that is, the debate over "political correctness" (e.g., American Civil Liberties Union [ACLU], 1996), and about the proper role of the government in funding basic science at our research universities (e.g., Atkinson, 2000). Although none of these controversies has vanished entirely, all have become more subdued, even if only momentarily. Other issues, however, have emerged to take their place on the national center stage. For example, there are new debates over the role of universities in stem cell research and cloning (e.g., Association of American Universities [AAU], 2002)—and about tracking foreign students after September 11th (e.g., Committee on Education and the Workforce, 2002).

The most important contemporary debate by far—and, in all likelihood, the most important of the past several decades—is the constitutional and

3

policy controversy over what we misleadingly have come to call "affirmative action": the effort to achieve racial and ethnic diversity on our campuses by considering race and ethnicity as factors in the admissions process (e.g., AAU, 2002; American Council on Education [ACE], 1995; D'Souza, 1991; Hankins & David, 1996).

Interestingly, other controversies, albeit of somewhat lesser moment, also involve admissions policies. One notable controversy is the current debate over the utility and social effects of the SAT®.[1] More recently, the policy of early admission has been added to the list of current contested topics. Indeed, all one has to do is stand back just a little from our system of colleges and universities, and instantly one gets a sense of how every facet of higher education can quickly become a matter for public scrutiny. It is important to recognize, however, that most of these discrete controversies arise out of much more fundamental issues for higher education. Many of the specific disputes related to admissions are actually symptomatic of a much more profound issue facing colleges and universities, one that deserves clarification and attention, and that is the increasingly pernicious competition in higher education generally.

Much of the current debate regarding higher education admissions relates to the merits of SAT I®. The President of the University of California, Richard Atkinson, brought this issue to the forefront of national attention by proposing that the SAT I no longer be required for admission to the University of California (UC) system (Atkinson, 2001a, 2001b). He has proposed that it be replaced with some group of SAT II® or other achievement-oriented tests— that is, with tests that evaluate how well students have mastered specific subjects taught in high school. He has done this, Atkinson says, because the SAT I pursues a futile and harmful goal of measuring an individual's "aptitude," or some general mental capacity. In his words:

> Aptitude tests such as the SAT I have a historical tie to the concept of innate mental abilities and the belief that such abilities can be defined and meaningfully measured. Neither notion has been supported by modern research. Few scientists who have considered these matters seriously would argue that aptitude tests such as the SAT I provide a true measure of intellectual abilities. Nonetheless, the SAT I is widely regarded as a test of basic mental ability that can give us a picture of students' academic promise. (Atkinson, 2002, p. 32)

President Atkinson cites recent analyses of the predictive validity of the SAT I showing that it adds little to that already provided by achievement tests and grades (Geiser & Studley, 2001). But his principal criticism is that

---

[1]SAT®, SAT I®, and SAT II® are registered trademarks of The College Board.

this particular standardized test has unfortunate and distorting consequences in our educational system, both at the high school and at the college levels. He argues that this general testing of "aptitude" diminishes the significance of regular high school courses and leads high schools and students to waste valuable educational time in fruitless "prepping" for this kind of test (Atkinson, 2002). Perhaps the most grievous injury of the SAT I, in President Atkinson's eyes, is that it undermines the ability of America's colleges and universities to fulfill their responsibility in a democratic society to judge students "on the basis of their actual achievements, not on ill-defined notions of aptitude" (2002, p. 32). We should instead, he insists, employ tests in our admissions processes that "have a demonstrable relationship to the specific subjects taught in high school" (p. 34) so that students can use the tests to assess their mastery of those subjects. Above all, Atkinson (2002) argues, we should "employ admissions processes that look at individual applicants in their full complexity and take special pains to ensure that standardized tests are used properly in admissions decisions" (p. 34). Atkinson (2002) concludes:

> It is not enough to make sure that test scores are simply one of several criteria considered; we must also make sure that the tests we require reflect UC's mission and purpose, which is to educate the state's most talented students and make educational opportunity available to young people from every background. (p. 35)

This is a helpful debate to have, and there is much to be said on all sides of this debate about the merits of the SAT I. Is this really a test that purports to measure innate intellectual capacity? Or is it a test of some important intellectual capacities (just as important as, say, U.S. history) that can be learned and improved upon over time, perhaps even by mastering what we regard as regular subjects and courses? Unfortunately, The College Board seems not to have had a consistent message on these matters. In an introductory letter to an SAT brochure, the President of The College Board, Gaston Caperton, writes: "[E]ven though we've published literally millions and millions of copies of sample SATs, the rumor persists that the SAT measures something mysterious. Nothing could be farther from the truth" (College Board, 2001, p. 3). What it measures may not be mysterious, but it is not simple, either. Nor has it been static. At one time, the College Board defined the SAT as an aptitude test, and it was asserted that the test was not subject to coaching. Then it was no longer called an aptitude test, but a test of reasoning skills (College Board, 2000, 2001); it was no longer the Scholastic Aptitude Test, but simply the SAT, which did not stand for anything (Atkinson, 2001b) — at least the A was not to stand for anything.

The College Board acknowledges that the test is coachable, but not nearly as coachable as some of the commercial "coaches" claim that it is (Powers & Camara, 1999). But it is, the College Board asserts, eminently teachable—indeed, they emphatically argue that it is not too coachable, but highly teachable. On this point they are probably right; the best way to do one's best on the SAT is to be a good student—not to try to cram, but to be a good student over the long term. Be an adept, careful, subtle, insightful reader. Develop quantitative skills to solve real-world problems. Read as much as you can, write a lot, learn to use language effectively, take hard courses, and solve problems in and out of school. Think critically! That's the best way to maximize one's performance on the SAT.

And, yet, one would be hard pressed to make the case that that is how the world sees and responds to the SAT. One hears, anecdotally to be sure, that many, many schools "teach to the test," which means they focus on improving vocabulary alone and practicing on sample tests. This is so despite all the attention that is focused on the SAT, despite the high stakes that the students and their parents invest in the test results, and despite the efforts of the Educational Testing Service and the College Board. Schools, educators, teachers, and students seem not to have a sense of the pedagogical rationale for the test and the verbal and mathematical skills that the test seeks to measure.

It would help a great deal, therefore, if students more clearly understood that the skills that the SAT I seeks to test (the intellectual capacities themselves, not merely vocabulary) can be learned over an extended period of time. That might serve to mitigate the sense of hopelessness and despair—a sense of inherent unfairness, an unfair test reinforcing an unfair world. Importantly, the way we go about selecting young people ought to nurture a sense of hope, not of hopelessness. It is this still too widely pervasive perception that the SAT I is an aptitude test that troubles President Atkinson most—the perception that it is a test, to a large degree, of "nature"—a test of something that these students can do little or nothing about. President Atkinson (2002) noted that his proposal to change to using SAT II scores "tells students that a college education is within the reach of anyone with the talent and determination to succeed" (p. 35). In other words, for him, the proposal to move from SAT I to SAT II has to do with the desire to give all students a sense of possibility, a sense of hope.

The fact that, for whatever reason, so many people continue to see the SAT I as an aptitude test works to the detriment of the SAT I and to the detriment of students' education. The analogy section of the SAT has been the focus of special criticism from many. One reason that it is vulnerable to the skepticism and criticism of laymen and others is simply that the analogy questions sound odd or strained. Analogies are rare enough in our everyday lives and common speech, and parallel analogies such as those found on the test (A is to B as Y is to Z) are very rare indeed; they are simply not the way we usually think or speak.

The perceptions and the consequences of those perceptions, therefore, ought to be of critical concern to us as educators and as those responsible for administering the public trusts of colleges and universities (private as well as public). It seems likely that virtually all students today know their SAT scores, in the same way that 35 years ago every 18-year-old male knew his draft number. And despite the fact that the SAT was not created to discriminate between a 1560 and a 1540, it is clear which score most students and parents would much prefer. From miniscule and even meaningless numerical differences, great meaning is extracted—suggesting that the system in which the SAT I is situated yields significant distortions in things we value.

Do leaders in higher education grasp the implications of the extraordinary, and highly unexpected, public response to this critical speech by the President of the University of California? University presidents are not customarily listened to so keenly. President Atkinson himself was astonished. "I was unprepared," he says with evident understatement, "for the intense public reaction" (2002, p. 31) to his remarks before the American Council on Education on the SAT I. Both the *Washington Post* and *The New York Times* carried the story on their front pages (Fletcher, 2001; Schemo, 2001). This remarkable public response to the question of whether to use the SAT, coupled with what is evident to anyone who observes the annual college admissions process—namely the frenzied concern with SAT scores—raises the question of whether the use of the SAT I is really, in fact, the issue. The SAT has become a symbol of, or, in the language of literary criticism, the objective correlative, that is the object directly correlated to the emotion (Eliot, 1920)—all the anxieties and concerns, fears and frustrations involved in today's college admission system. The underlying issue is not, in fact, the test, but rather the nature, character, and degree of the competition now endemic in the college admissions process, and in higher education generally.

Projecting all of our anxieties onto the SATs is reminiscent of society's focus about 10 years ago on the rising cost of higher education. There was no question that cost was, and is, a real and large concern (Johnstone, 2001). Costs have been going up faster than the consumer price index (CPI), although, as has been pointed out on many occasions, what universities do and what they pay for is far different than the cost of living incurred by the average urban dweller (which is what the CPI measures). The issue of cost was overladen with concerns and anger about other issues. Many of these issues had to do with the widening cultural gap between academia and the nation as a whole: (a) a loss of confidence in the academy; (b) a concern about political correctness; (c) a sense that there was an excessive emphasis on research; (d) a diminution of the value of teaching; (e) a focus on graduate education at the expense of undergraduate education; and (f) a feeling that faculty were underworked and overindulged. It is always important to respond to underlying issues and not simply to the articulated one, whether it be cost or the SATs.

And the more fundamental issue facing higher education today is the seemingly endlessly rising sense of competition—or a particular kind of competition—among applicants and students, and among selective colleges and universities. Although one of the most significant changes in American higher education over the past half century is the increase in the number of high-quality colleges and universities (some, after all, like the University of California at San Diego, did not exist 50 years ago), the number of students desiring to attend these schools has simply increased more dramatically. There are more high-school students, and a higher proportion of them than ever before are concluding that a high-school education is not enough. That should not come as a surprise given the hard fact that one's material and immaterial prospects in life improve exponentially with every degree obtained beyond high school (see Carnevale & Desrochers, 2002).

But the numbers only tell part of the story (as is always true of numbers). There is a greater and growing sense that which college or university one attends (ranked on some scale of a presupposed hierarchy of quality or prestige) matters enormously. There is a greater sense of education being a commodity than there has been before. There is more affluence coupled with a concern that everyone's child attend the "best" school. One can purchase the right house, the right cars, and many of the amenities of life, but admission to the right college or university is not something you can simply purchase. And the school one attends is not like a social club, which one can quit and join another; rather it is one's alma mater, a mark that, for better or worse, one carries for life. All the effects and consequences of this need to attend the right college are plain for anyone to see; the standard is becoming "spare no expense" to seize every possible advantage in the admissions game. There is the urgent sense, in other words, that which college one attends will, as Robert Frost (1969) says, although ambiguously, make "all the difference" (p. 105). Within this worldview, standardized test scores are the one thing that one can look to, at the end, to enhance one's competitiveness. Because they are clear, crisp, and numerical and not subjective, it is natural, therefore, for SAT scores to become the principal lightning rod for admissions anxiety.

The problem—the large and fundamental problem—is that we are at risk of it all seeming, and becoming, more and more a game. What matters is not so much the education but the brand. In this world, we seek clarity everywhere in the competitive struggle. It is no wonder, then, that numerical rankings like those of *U.S. News and World Report* (2002) should emerge to guide tens of thousands of parents and young people in the game. And it is no wonder that the rankings should depend increasingly on numerical and quantifiable data as well. And it is no wonder that selective colleges and universities should themselves adjust their behavior over time, to some extent, to improve their status on the rankings and thereby improve their attractiveness to potential students. The size of a class, for example, might be determined not by educational concerns, but rather, by which size yields the highest average standardized test scores. Or students with no hope of getting in are nevertheless encouraged to apply, in order to improve the apparent "yield" of the institution. Other examples abound, unfortunately.

The tentacles of this way of thinking have the potential to reach into every corner of our general understanding of intellectual and artistic life. Colleges and universities, to be sure, should not be immune from the stimulation of competition. Enormous improvements, on matters we rightly care about, can occur because people—applicants, students, faculty, and others—can walk away and go elsewhere. But not all forms of competition are equal, and there will always be the risk of a downward spiral in an atmosphere that values the wrong things, such as maximizing the average test score or the average number of points scored against a football opponent, or admitting applicants with powerful advocates rather than students who show the promise of making the best use of the institution's resources. We must never forget that much of what makes colleges and universities special, and over the long run, socially important, is both fragile and counterintuitive in a democratic, free-market system.

A specific observation and concern illustrates the main point of this essay. One of the most negative aspects of the "game" atmosphere of college admissions is the sense of individual entitlement that grows naturally out of this process, the sense that says, "If I have achieved these things and these scores, relative to my competitors, I deserve to be treated accordingly." Each person, this way of thinking says, should be compared—should be ranked—against every other person and treated as "an individual." The upshot of this logic is pressure toward homogenization within our institutions instead of diversity.

This is a large subject and one tied intimately to the current debates about the constitutionality and the educational wisdom of affirmative action. Of deepest concern is the inability of some in our society to appreciate the importance—the educational and, indeed, the democratic importance—of learning and thinking in a diverse, heterogeneous environment. Higher educational institutions have not done a good job of articulating their theories of education and of explaining how those educational theories relate to their admissions policies. Educational leaders have done an insufficient job in making the case for any admissions policy other than admitting the best and the brightest students we can find—however that is defined (but not uncommonly by reference to SAT scores). A great benefit of the current debate over affirmative action is that it has permitted educators to appreciate and to argue for the benefits that flow from diversity of all kinds, not just racial and ethnic diversity. We have been able to situate racial and ethnic diversity at the core of a liberal education, which is where it properly belongs.

The best way to make the case for diversity is to turn to Shakespeare's art and its unquestioned inclusion in a liberal education. Why does everyone subscribe to the centrality of Shakespeare? It is partly, as many have observed over the centuries, in Shakespeare's uncanny genius for being able to cross into different characters' minds. Within a few lines, within a few minutes of a play, one has the distinct impression of encountering a particular human being, one who thinks and feels and reacts in unique ways. That capacity for empathy is, in large part, what exposure to diversity in an educational context involves— the opportunity to come to a greater understanding of others' points of view and how their life experiences might have caused them to be who they are and to form the opinions they hold. Racial diversity is particularly important because race remains the "American dilemma" (see Myrdal, 1962). But it is also particularly important because grappling with race is a powerful metaphor for crossing sensibilities of all kinds, and crossing sensibilities is part of the core of Shakespeare's genius and of a great education.

The debates going on today about the validity and broader consequences of standardized tests that measure generalized abilities, such as the SAT I, are very important. In that debate, however, it is critical that we look at and consider the ways in which such tests affect societal attitudes about education and, even most importantly, that we consider how these specific debates over SATs are symptomatic of a set of underlying concerns. Higher education faces a fundamental issue involving the character of competition. This issue involves admissions, but touches many other aspects of higher education. Not all competition is bad, by any means, but some can fuel a distorted and oversimplified self-conception of what "quality" in education and research entails. It would be a great pity if one of the harsh consequences of that tendency toward competition were the misunderstanding and elimination of our proud history of educational diversity in all its forms.

REFERENCES

American Civil Liberties Union. (1996). *Racist speech on college campuses.* Retrieved April 30, 2003, from http://www.aclu.org/library/aahate.html

American Council on Education. (1995). *Making the case for affirmative action in higher education.* Washington, DC: Author.

Association of American Universities. (2002). *AAU statement on human cloning.* Washington, DC: Author.

Atkinson, R. C. (2000, September 28). Why federal funding for basic research is important. *San Diego Union-Tribune,* p. B.11.2.

Atkinson, R. C. (2001a, February). *Standardized tests and access to American universities.* The 2001 Robert H. Atwell Distinguished Lecture, 83rd Annual Meeting of the American Council on Education. Washington, DC. Available at http://www.ucop.edu/pres/prespeeches.html

Atkinson, R. C. (2001b, Spring). Rethinking the SAT. *The Presidency,* p. 20.

Atkinson, R. C. (2002, Winter). Achievement versus aptitude in college admissions. *Issues in Science and Technology,* p. 32.

Carnevale, A. P., & Desrochers, D. M. (2002, April). The missing middle: Aligning education and the knowledge economy. Paper commissioned for *Preparing America's Future: The High School Symposium.* Sponsored by the Office of Vocational and Adult Education, U.S. Department of Education in Washington, DC. Retrieved February 18, 2003, from http://www.ed.gov/offices/OVAE/HS/carnevale.doc

College Board. (2000). About the SAT program. In *College Board Program Handbook, 2000.* New York: Author.

College Board. (2001). *What does the SAT® measure and why does it matter?* New York: Author.

Committee on Education and the Workforce (2002). Hearing before the Subcommittee on 21st Century Competitiveness and the Subcommittee on Select Education of the Committee on Education and the Workforce, House of Representatives, 107th Congress, Second Session. *Homeland security: Tracking international students in higher education — Progress and issues since 9/11* (Serial No. 107–79). Washington, DC: U.S. Government Printing Office.

D'Souza, D. (1991). Sins of admission. In *The affirmative action & diversity project. A web page for research.* Retrieved April 29, 2003, from http://aad.english.ucsb.edu/aa.html

Eliot, T. S. (1920). Hamlet and his problems. In *The sacred wood: Essays on poetry and criticism* (pp. 95–103). London: Methune.

Fletcher, M. A. (2001, February 17). Key SAT test under fire in Calif. University president proposes new admission criteria. *The Washington Post,* p. A1.

Frost, R. (1969). The road not taken. In *The poetry of Robert Frost* (p. 105). New York: Henry Holt & Co.

Geiser, S., & Studley, R. (2001). *UC and the SAT: Predictive validity and differential impact of SAT I and SAT II at the University of California.* Oakland: University of California, Office of the President.

Hankins, E., & David, T. (1996, Nov./Dec.). Racial division is enhanced by notions of "diversity." *The University Review.* Retrieved April 30, 2003, from http://www .utexas.edu/review/affirmative_action.html

Johnstone, B. (2001, Spring). The worldwide shift of higher education costs from governments and taxpayers to parents and students. CCGSE *Newsletter, 4,* 2. Retrieved April 22, 2003, from http://www.gse.buffalo.edu/ DC/CCGSE/vol4_iss1/p.2.htm

Myrdal, G. (1962). *An American dilemma: The Negro problem and modern democracy.* New York: Harper & Row.

Powers, D. E., & Camara, W. J. (1999). *Coaching and the SAT I* (College Board research note No. RN–06). New York: The College Board.

Schemo, D. J. (2001, February 17). Head of U. of California seeks to end SAT use in admissions. *The New York Times,* p. A1.

Troutt, W. E. (1998, January). *Straight talk about college costs and prices: Letter of transmittal.* Washington, DC: National Commission on the Cost of Higher Education. Retrieved April 20, 2003, from http://www.eriche.org/government/transmittal. html

U.S. News & World Report. (2002, September 23). America's best colleges 2003. *U.S. News & World Report.* Retrieved from http://www.usnews.com/usnews/edu/college/ cohome.htm

2

What Is It We Think We Are Trying to Fix and How Should We Fix It? A View From the Admissions Office

Robert Laird

Former Director of Undergraduate Admissions
University of California–Berkeley

On June 23, 2003, the U.S. Supreme Court upheld the use of race and ethnicity in university admissions in *Gratz v. Bollinger* and *Grutter v. Bollinger.* In so doing, the Court reaffirmed the fundamental importance of equal access to higher education in this country, particularly access to the most selective public and private colleges and universities, but those decisions also carry with them significant obligations and responsibilities for institutions that wish to consider race and ethnicity in their admission processes. Many of the proposals in this book may well contribute to improved admissions policies and processes that colleges and universities are beginning to redesign in light of the Court's decisions. In order for the various proposals presented in this book to truly make sense, however, we need to understand how selective admission currently works and, especially, to understand the differences in the admission processes used by most selective private colleges and universities compared to those used by most selective public institutions.

The simplistic, often clumsy, admission processes used by many selective public universities are often the result of three factors. First, many selective public universities have not been selective for very long, and, second, most of them became selective relatively quickly without much experience or time to plan careful, sound selection processes. This was certainly true, for example, at Berkeley. Although now one of the most selective public universities in the country (fall 2003 freshman admission rate: 23.9%), Berkeley did not become selective until fall 1973. Until that year, the campus admitted every UC-eligible freshman applicant who applied on time. It took many years and a number of political and legal confrontations before Berkeley began to develop the sophisticated, individualized freshman selection process that was finally put into place for fall 1998.

Third, we need to understand that the admissions operations at large public universities compete for budget money with a great many other internal constituencies, many of which—faculty research, for example—have much higher standing in an institution's priorities. The staggering, and increasing, volume of freshman applications exacerbates this competition. For fall 2003, Berkeley received more than 36,900 applications—and that was only the fourth highest volume within the UC system after UCLA, UC San Diego, and UC Santa Barbara. Managing a huge number of applications on what is often a very limited budget—and, therefore, with a small staff—has forced many public universities to find simple ways to sort applicants and make decisions on them. Consequently, many public universities have relied on numerics—perhaps grade point average (GPA) or SAT I score or a formula that combines those two items or other variables—to admit their entire freshman class or to admit some students, place others in a reading pool, and to deny other students, all without ever looking at an individual's application. For many years, most observers just sort of shrugged their shoulders and said, "What do you expect? It's a large public U." In the last few years, however, many state taxpayers have come to regard the admission of their children to their flagship public university as an entitlement. And, as admission to selective colleges and universities, both public and private, has become a national obsession, the admissions policies and practices of many public universities have been widely criticized as clumsy, impersonal, and, most telling of all, unfair.

At the same time, most selective private colleges and universities have treated their applicants as individuals, reading each application at least twice, including applicant essays, letters of recommendation, and, often, interview write-ups. In most cases, these institutions make careful, individual decisions about each applicant based on the information at hand and the professional judgment of the admissions staff. If there is a criticism of such practices, it is that such a process is "subjective," that the results cannot in some way be quantified or verified.

In addition to widespread confusion about these two basic approaches, some in the field merely want to identify new, quantifiable, variables for use in formulaic ways. They may argue that "Formulas are fine; it's just that we do not include enough variables." The temptation is to take most, or even all, of the variables considered in such a process and combine them into some sort of *uber*-formula so that a computer can make the admission decision. That is a fundamentally flawed approach. Rather, we need to ask the question "What obligations, if any, do selective public and private colleges and universities have to their applicants and their families?" One answer from the public universities, often driven by severe budget restrictions, clearly has been "Very little." Both public and private institutions, however, do have an obligation to treat each of their applicants as individuals, to review each applicant fully and individually, and to measure both academic and nonacademic achievements against the opportunities and challenges faced by each individual.

The use of formulas or indices to make "automatic" admission decisions is clearly unsound. So are application reading processes that use "binary" review and/or scoring, in which an applicant is judged in an absolute way to either have or not have a particular achievement or quality—that is, a process in which an applicant gets, say, 150 points for "leadership" or "hardship" or "community service" or gets 0 points, with no gradations between the absolutes.

Any proposal for admission practices in the 21st century must be based on a consensus on the purposes of admission policies, especially those used in selective colleges and universities. We need to decide whether we think the purpose of an admission process—not just the purpose of standardized tests in an admission process but the purpose of the entire process itself—is to reward students for their work up to the point they file their college applications, or whether it is to select students who will do their best at a particular college or university in the future, whether we measure that best by first-year college grade point average, 4-year or 6-year graduation rates, intellectual excitement and curiosity brought to the classroom and residence hall, leadership both in college and after, or service to others both in college and after. In addition, any discussion of admission practices has to confront the role of both public and private colleges and universities—often stated quite explicitly—as social equalizers that provide opportunities to students from disadvantaged backgrounds including, most especially, low-income students and African Americans, Latinos, and Native Americans. The long-term answer to the question of admission policy goals may well be a combination of those possibilities. At the very least, however, we should be conscious and clear about what it is we are doing and why we are doing it. Currently, that is often not the case.

A SIGNIFICANT SHIFT IN THE DIRECTION OF SELECTIVE ADMISSIONS: THE OFFICE FOR CIVIL RIGHTS (OCR) AND THE USES OF STANDARDIZED TESTS

When the University of California Board of Regents passed SP-1 in July 1995 ending the use of affirmative action in UC admission and the voters of California followed in November 1996 by passing Proposition 209, supporters of affirmative action sharply increased their criticism of the SAT I and attacked the University's use of both the SAT I and credit for Advanced Placement (AP®)[1] classes in its freshman admission policies. The most focused of these attacks was through a lawsuit filed in February 1999 against UC Berkeley (*Castañeda v. Regents of the University of California*, 1999).

Much of the legal reasoning and the criteria for acceptable uses of standardized tests in *Castañeda* came from an unofficial set of guidelines that was being pushed hard in the mid-1990s by the Office for Civil Rights in the U.S. Department of Education. About six years ago, John Hayes III and Theresa Fay-Bustillos began appearing at national and regional admissions conferences and meetings to articulate what they argued were the acceptable uses of the SAT I and other standardized tests. Hayes was an attorney in the Kansas City office of OCR and Fay-Bustillos was an attorney (now vice president) for the Mexican American Legal Defense and Education Fund (MALDEF). Although these acceptable-usage criteria had never been circulated publicly by OCR and had not been formally approved by any government office, Hayes and Fay-Bustillos clearly gave the impression that colleges and universities would be held accountable to these standards.

Attorneys for the plaintiffs in *Castañeda* seized on their arguments and included them as part of their legal reasoning in their lawsuit, although at the time those criteria had no apparent legal standing. OCR finally issued the guidelines officially in draft form in May 1999. There was a very strong reaction against that draft by admission officers and, not surprisingly, the College Board and the Educational Testing Service. As Hebel (2000) noted in *The*

---

[1] Advanced Placement®, Advanced Placement Program®, and AP® are registered trademarks of the College Board.

Chronicle of Higher Education, "many college officials viewed the document as an attempt to discourage them from using standardized tests" (p. A31). A much gentler version was issued as a second draft in December 1999, and a third draft appeared in July 2000, very similar to the second, but now called *The Use of Tests When Making High-Stakes Decisions for Students.* Perhaps equally important, the document was subtitled *A Resource Guide for Educators and Policymakers.* The public comment period ended in mid-August 2000, and the U.S. Department of Education issued the final version on December 15, 2000 (U.S. Dept. of Education, Office of Civil Rights, 2000) The term *Resource Guide* was puzzling, and exactly what legal standing these guidelines might have on policy and legal decisions became an open and very important question.

Although admissions officers around the country were very resentful of the heavy-handed way that OCR went about pushing its ideas, some very good things came out of subsequent exchanges among all of the parties with vested interests in the issue. Although the legal standing of the OCR criteria were uncertain, they certainly forced—or should have forced—college and university admissions officials to reexamine not only their use of tests but also the purposes of their admissions policy and the role that an individual student's circumstances and context should play in an evaluation of that student's accomplishments both in school and outside school. OCR was accurate in its determination that some tests with very important consequences for students were, and are, being used irresponsibly and with unfair consequences for some students. This is especially true when those tests have differential outcomes by race and family income and where those tests are used in rigid selection formulas with no regard for the individual circumstances of each student.

The high-water mark for the OCR effort to influence the use of standardized tests in high-stakes educational decisions came in March 2000 when the late Senator Paul Wellstone introduced *The Fairness and Accuracy in Student Testing Act* (2000). MALDEF issued a press release in support of the bill with a testimonial from Fay-Bustillos. This bill, however, was not taken up during the 2000 or 2001 sessions of Congress. As of November 2002, it was still in the Senate Health, Education, Labor, and Pensions Committee. With the death of Wellstone and the change in Senate leadership, it is likely that it will never be considered.

Right Between the Eyes

From mid-1999 until George W. Bush took office, it looked as if the OCR high-stakes testing guidelines, buttressing OCR's theory of "disparate impact," were going to change the way K–12 and colleges and universities used standardized tests in important and major ways. In late April 2001, however, the U.S. Supreme Court, in deciding a case called *Alexander v. Sandoval,* put a bullet right between the eyes of OCR. In that decision, the Court ruled that private citizens must prove intent to discriminate on the part of public colleges and other state agencies in order to successfully challenge the use of instruments, such as standardized tests, that have a disparate impact regarding race or ethnicity (Savage, 2001). In a single stroke, the court eviscerated OCR's carefully developed legal reasoning that disparate impact, even absent intent to discriminate, was sufficient grounds to challenge such instruments.

The Court's decision in *Alexander v. Sandoval* had an immediate impact. In December 2001, in a letter to Florida Governor Jeb Bush, civil rights groups challenged the criteria used by the state of Florida to award its merit-based scholarships, called Bright Futures (Selingo, 2001). The criteria combine GPA with specific minimum cut-off scores on the SAT I or ACT®.[2] As Selingo noted in *The Chronicle of Higher Education,* only 3% of the top scholarship winners were African American, compared to 14.4% of the test takers. Almost certainly as a result of *Sandoval,* however, the language of the complaint was relatively muted and, most notably, the letter did not raise the possibility of a legal challenge to the scholarship criteria.

It is likely that the decision in *Sandoval* will prove a major setback in the struggle toward a fairer and more equal society for minority groups and women. But, in a kind of bitter irony, *Sandoval* gutted the *Castañeda* lawsuit against UC Berkeley, which was subsequently settled in 2003 almost entirely in the university's favor. It also ended a highly visible lawsuit, called *Cureton v. NCAA,* in which African American athletes challenged the NCAA's use of rigid SAT I cut-offs to determine freshman eligibility for intercollegiate college athletics (Hawes, 2001).

What Selective Public and Private Colleges and Universities Should Be Doing

A number of the proposals in this book seem promising, but no matter which of these proposals may ultimately be implemented in admissions policies and practices around the country, there are many things that college and universities—especially those that are selective—should be doing already. The balance of this chapter identifies these policies and practices. In spite of the effects of *Sandoval* on the disparate impact argument, many of the other OCR principles in *The Use of Tests When Making High-Stakes Decisions for Students*

---

[2] ACT® is a registered trademark of ACT, Inc.

remain quite sound, and the first four items are taken directly from those OCR guidelines.

1. An Institution Should Have a Clear Statement of Purpose for Its Admission Policy.   Although it may seem painfully obvious to an outside observer, the need for a clear statement of purpose or set of goals for a college or university's admission policy has not always been clear to admission directors, senior administrators, and faculty. Policymakers should pay particular attention to the functions of standardized tests in such a statement. A central purpose of the SAT I, for example, is to improve the prediction of first-year college GPA. If an institution's process uses the SAT I, but there is no reference to first-year college GPA in its policy, the institution has an obligation to explain in its statement of purpose exactly what function the test plays in its process beyond serving as a handy separator.

Not only should an institution have such an admission policy statement but that statement should be tied directly to the university's mission statement. The actual admission policy should flow directly from both the university's mission statement and the admission policy's statement of purpose. In crafting its admission policy statement of purpose, there are a number of purposes or goals that an institution might consider including:

- To enroll a class that will most benefit from the institution's curriculum and faculty;
- To enroll a freshman class with the most distinguished high-school academic records;
- To enroll a class that will reflect the racial and ethnic diversity of the state;
- To enroll a freshman class that will be the most engaging to teach in the classroom;
- To enroll a freshman class that will go on to serve the community, the state, and the nation;
- To enroll a freshman class that will bring the greatest distinction to the university after graduation;
- To enroll a class that will earn the highest collective freshman GPA;
- To enroll a freshman class that will have the highest 4-year (or overall) graduation rate;
- To enroll a freshman class that will support the institution financially after graduation;
- To enroll a freshman class with the highest possible test score averages.

There are many universities that have an implied statement of purpose in their admission policies but have never formally crafted such a statement as an independent document. It seems eminently reasonable to ask institutions to have such a statement. How can a university know if its admission policy is successful unless it knows what that policy is supposed to achieve? At the same time, however, it's a little scary to think that a federal court could at some point pass judgment on such a statement and the methods for evaluating it. That situation seems increasingly possible, given the degree to which admission policies are being challenged in court.

2. An Institution Should Use Appropriate Criteria in Its Admission Process. An institution should use a range of criteria in its selection process, and these criteria should be directly tied to its admission policy statement of purpose. They should certainly include high school (and college, if appropriate) courses completed, grades in those courses, and test scores—if a campus has a clear set of reasons for using test scores and does not use them in formulas or indexes that automatically admit or reject applicants. Selection criteria should also include intellectual curiosity and accomplishment, extraordinary talent, leadership, service to others, motivation, tenacity, and demonstrated ability to overcome hardship. In every instance where it is legal to do so, these criteria should include race and ethnicity, as permitted under *Grutter v. Bollinger* (2003).

None of these criteria should be viewed as static or absolute entities. That is, courses taken, for example, should be assessed against what was available in each applicant's high school, and this assessment should include any information provided by the applicant or the school regarding access to courses, especially advanced-level courses. Such information could include restrictive tracking policies or cases where demand for a particular course clearly outstripped the number of spaces offered by the school or the cancellation of courses for such reasons as budget cuts, even though such courses might still be shown on a school's list of courses offered. Colleges and universities should include on their applications a question that asks if there were any circumstances that affected the pattern of courses undertaken by the applicant.

Institutions should avoid using criteria in ways that treat applicants as groups and that treat all members of such groups as exactly the same—not just on the basis of race and ethnicity, which the Supreme Court outlawed in *Gratz v. Bollinger* (2003), but also on the basis of zip code, high school, leadership, achievement, or hardship. Admission processes that award points for specific achievements and personal qualities and then add up the point totals are almost always clumsy and distorting. Giving all applicants who have shown leadership, for example, the same 150 points masks the differences in achievement and responsibility between a student who has been president of two school clubs and the student who has served as an elected representative to the local school board. Giving all students at a particular high school 300 points as "disadvantaged" without considering the wide variation in circumstances that are bound to exist from one student to another even within a particularly disadvantaged high school is careless and imprecise.

3. *If an Institution Assigns Formal Weights or Values to Its Admission Criteria, It Should Be Sure That Such Weights or Values Are Reasonable.* As with the word *appropriate* in number 2, *reasonable* is an arguable term. Nevertheless, it is certainly possible to recognize unreasonable weights—a process, for example, in which test scores are the overwhelming determinant. It is also possible to develop empirically derived weights through the application of multiple regression analysis to various selection criteria. Although these criteria appear to have a more solid analytical foundation that more judgmentally assigns weights, they often make it very difficult for a college or university to explain its admission policy to the public—and to other interested parties, including legislators and attorneys. There is also the danger of a kind of tunnel vision with empirically derived weights; that is, there is the risk that the statisticians who develop such weights may become preoccupied with statistical differences that may matter to them but not in the broader context of a freshman applicant pool.

Embedded in this issue of weights is a very thorny question: Are there limits to the weights that should be given to individual criteria, especially standardized test scores and honors or AP courses? If so, who sets those limits and on what basis? In one sense, it is almost impossible to imagine that a court would rule in an area that has traditionally been seen as a prerogative of academic freedom. Justice Powell, writing in *Regents of the University of California v. Bakke* (1978), cited a faculty's right to choose whom it would teach as a fundamental tenet of academic freedom. Justice O'Connor's opinion for the majority in *Grutter v. Bollinger* (2003) also gives great deference to colleges and universities.

4. *An Institution Should Regularly Evaluate Its Individual Criteria and Its Aggregated Criteria to Determine if They Are Achieving the Goals Attributed to Them and to the Admission Policy in the Statement of Purpose.* The OCR guidelines say that an institution should have conducted validity studies on the individual criteria it uses to select students in order to determine if those criteria do what they are supposed to do. This is a reasonable guideline and one for which the ACT and SAT organizations provide help to colleges and universities. How do you know that the individual criteria are contributing to the overall goals of the admission process? It may be that there are limits to the precision with which such validity studies may be done, but an institution should be obligated to do the best analysis it can on its selection criteria. The University of Michigan decisions emphasize this point in regard to the use of race and ethnicity.

5. An Institution Should Not Use Formulas or Rigid Raw Numeric Cutoffs in Its Process.

Enough publicity has been given to the inappropriateness of using test scores as a single criterion or using sharp cutoffs on indices combining multiple criteria in what OCR has called high-stakes decision making. Nevertheless, there are lots of selective institutions, both public and private, that use numeric formulas to separate applicants within their admission process. Although Berkeley dropped its use of an index seven years ago, at least two other UC campuses still use that same index or one that is very similar. Other large selective public and private universities also use indices of one kind or another to sort applicants.

There are at least two difficulties with an index like that formerly used by Berkeley (GPA × 1000 plus SAT I and 3 SAT II scores). The first of these is that changes in freshman applicant pools over time can distort the original values reflected in that index. Berkeley dropped the academic index in 1998 because, as its applicant pool became more and more competitive, huge numbers of applicants were bunched near or at the 4.0 GPA mark. That meant that they all got 4,000 points—or very close to that—on the GPA portion of the index. The only thing that separated them from each other, then, was their test scores.

The second difficulty with indices or numerical cutoffs is the effect that measures with disparate impact may have on different groups of applicants. The Supreme Court's decision in *Alexander v. Sandoval* (2001) notwithstanding, there remains the fundamental issue of fairness in the use of tests. Because average test scores vary by race and by family income and parental education levels, the index worked against students whose first language was not English, students from low-income families, and students who were African American, Chicano/Latino, or Native American. The Berkeley admissions office could compensate for this disadvantage by giving preference in other parts of the process to economic disadvantage and, until fall 1998, race and ethnicity. Nevertheless, prior to 1998, Berkeley used the index to determine admission for some freshman applicants without reading their files and to assign other applicants to our reading pool. A difference of just 10 points in an applicant's index score, therefore, might have made a big difference in that applicant's chances for admission. The faculty admissions committee recognized that the index was distorting the freshman admission process at Berkeley and rightfully eliminated it.

There is also the trap of being seduced by a really elaborate formula that employs a lot of variables and gives the illusion of great precision—a temptation that often arises when the faculty chair of an admissions committee is a mathematician or statistician. And there is the related danger of believing that by adding to an index an explicit number of points for specific criteria further on in the review process, an institution has mitigated the damage done by the original use of its index. In many cases, however, hundreds of students will already have been dropped out of the review because of their basic index scores and therefore never receive the benefit of those added points.

It is easy to call for no formulas or raw numeric cutoffs in selective admissions, and such a call may seem to ignore the harsh financial realities in the institutional funding of admissions operations. The use of formulas is almost always tied to the need to manage large volumes of applications with a small staff and limited financial support from the senior administration. This creates a sharp tension between ideal practices and workload realities including the individual institution's financial support for the admissions process. On those campuses where increased money is being devoted to admissions, it is likely that almost all of those increases are going to outreach, marketing, and recruitment, rather than to increasing the professional admissions reading staff. The appropriate use of "numerics"—individual standardized test scores, extra grade points for advanced-level courses, and formulas—is going to get a lot of attention in the next few years. Formulas that do not account for differences in opportunity or applicant background are going to be—and deserve to be—increasingly under attack.

6. An Institution Should Read as Many Individual Applications as Possible. This guideline follows directly from guideline 5. Reading applications is labor intensive and therefore expensive, but it is also the way to make the best-informed decisions possible, and it engages admissions officers, faculty, and other readers in important and valuable ways. Perhaps most important, reading individual applications is the cornerstone of an admission process that considers race and ethnicity following the O'Connor opinion in *Grutter v. Bollinger* (2003).

It is fundamentally important to such reading processes that (a) there be careful training and norming of readers, (b) that such training continue throughout the reading process, (c) that individual reader outcomes be tracked and adjusted where necessary, and (d) that the entire process be carefully evaluated when it is completed. Every application should be read by at least two different readers, and the second reader must not know the evaluation(s) or score(s) assigned by the first reader. There has to be a carefully thought-out process for resolving disparities in reader scores on the same application, and there will almost certainly have to be formal tie-breaking procedures if, at the end of the process, an admissions office ends up with more applicants with the same score than there are admissions spaces remaining. Electronic technology means that an institution can provide lots of information to readers, have them enter scores electronically, track both individual and reader-group scores, and track both individual and reader-group reading volume every day of the cycle. Reader reliability and validity must be evaluated very carefully, and readers who cannot or will not embrace the agreed-on normative values of the process must be dropped. It is important to emphasize that reading individual applications without formulas or even fixed weights does not mean wild and random subjectivity.

Senior budget officers on large campuses may continue to resist large increases in funding for admissions in order to create such a process, especially as state budgets—and therefore public university budgets—continue to decline. At Berkeley, for example, the decision to read every application at least twice required an additional $197,000 in that first year (it is important to remember that the application volume at Berkeley is significantly greater than at almost any other university in the country). That is a lot of money, but for that amount, Berkeley got an admissions process that made much better informed decisions about applicants, was perceived as very fair, built considerable goodwill among applicants and their families, and gave the campus increased political and legal protection. And whatever the cost of reading all applications, Justice O'Connor emphasized in *Grutter v. Bollinger* (2003) that administrative burden or expense are not acceptable excuses for failing to conduct an individual review of each applicant if an institution considers race and ethnicity in its admission process.

7. An Institution Should Consider an Applicant's Context in Assessing His or Her Achievements.   Given the huge disparities in opportunities offered to American youngsters, it is crucial to assess a student's achievements against her or his circumstances. That does not mean just language history, family income, and parental education levels, especially in the evaluation of standardized test scores, although these three items are fundamentally important. It means understanding as much as possible about the individual student's circumstances as well as her family, school, and community circumstances. And it does not mean automatically rewarding applicants who have faced difficult circumstances. It means measuring their achievements against those circumstances. It means acknowledging the qualities of responsibility and dependability in a student who cares for younger siblings every day after school as much as for the student who is a leader in school activities. It means acknowledging that an applicant has done all that she could have done if she took the only two AP courses offered in her high school—and did well in them.

8. *An Institution Should Learn All It Can About the High Schools That Provide Its Applicants.* Admissions officers are often quick to describe a high school as "outstanding" or "poor" or "a real disaster," but we should be suspicious of these easy judgments. Often, such judgments are based on impressions from a 2-hour school visit or from reading three or four applications from a school. Colleges and universities, however, can build profiles of high schools using databases that are widely available. At Berkeley, we asked the staff in the UC Office of the President to help us with such a project seven years ago. Analysts there put together data elements from the California State Department of Education, the UC systemwide database, and the Enrollment Planning Service of the College Board to get us started. The Berkeley admissions staff then added to the *Profiles* and took them to a remarkable level of sophistication.

One section of UC Berkeley's High School Profile focuses on the school's curriculum and includes the number of honors courses offered, the number of AP courses offered, the percentage of graduates completing the UC college-prep course pattern, and the state percentile rank for that completion rate. A second section includes graduation rates, the percentage of graduates taking AP exams, the percentage of AP exams taken on which students make scores of 3 or higher, the state percentile rank for that percentage, the average verbal, math, and composite scores on the SAT I, the average SAT I score for applicants to UC from this school, and the percentage of students taking the SAT I. A third section includes average parental income for the school, the percent of students who are Limited English Proficient, the percentage of students on Aid to Families with Dependent Children, and the percentage of students eligible for free federal meal programs. The profile also includes the number of applicants to Berkeley from the preceding year and the number and percentage of those applicants admitted.

The Berkeley *Profile* also shows the individual applicant's academic and demographic information and calculates a percentile ranking on each of those variables for that applicant compared to all of the other current applicants from that high school and, in a separate column, compared to all applicants in that year's freshman applicant pool.

Berkeley, however, has only partial answers to four really important questions:

1. Does a particular high school track students and, if so, how?
2. How many seats are available in honors/AP courses compared to the demand for those seats?
3. Were all of the courses on a high school's course list actually offered that year?
4. Were there conflicts in the high school's master schedule that prevented a student from taking advanced level courses?

It is important to know the answers to these questions in order to understand why a particular student may not have taken honors/AP courses in a school that offers—or appears to offer—a significant number of them. Five years ago, the UC Berkeley admissions office began sending an annual questionnaire to each California high school to gather this information. It is an imperfect process, but we learned a great deal of useful information about many high schools.

If colleges and universities around the country agree on the value of such profiles, it ought to be possible to design and build those profiles for each state, perhaps by a state department of education working with a group of admissions directors, rather than having each campus build a separate—and, therefore, very expensive—set of profiles for its own use.

9. An Institution Should Track the Performance of the Graduates of Each High School Who Enroll at That Institution and Consider That Information in Evaluating Applicants.   For each feeder high school, an institution should track mean first-year GPA, 1-year persistence rates, mean GPA at graduation, and 6-year graduation rates for all admitted students. It may also be helpful to calculate the mean GPA differential between high school GPA and both first-year GPA and GPA at graduation. In calculating such data items, an institution has to pay careful attention to the number of students included in such calculations. Obviously, the fewer students from a particular high school, the more variation there may be from year to year. It is also important to note the distribution of students by major. There is considerable evidence that college and university grading practices in engineering and the sciences are significantly more stringent than in the humanities and social sciences. (Ramist, Lewis, McCamley, 1990; Ramist, Lewis, & McCamley-Jenkins, 1994; Strenta & Elliott, 1987; Willingham, 1985). It is also important to remember that variables measured over 6 years are based on students who may have had very different opportunities and circumstances than applicants from the same high school 6 years later. Equally important, the longer the time span for a tracked variable, the more likely it is that immeasurable intervening events may have affected the outcomes.

It is also important to recognize that such comparative information is only part of the information that, in an ideal world, admissions officers would have. Parents, in particular, often believe that if their sons and daughters had just gone to Oakland Tech (where I happen to have gone to high school) or Hayward High, or some other so-called weak high school, they would have had much higher GPAs and therefore been admitted to Berkeley. Students, however, are often less worried about the differences between high schools than affronted by students from their own high schools who deliberately took classes from the easiest teachers. Gathering information on the grading practices of individual teachers and knowing from which teachers in a particular school an applicant had taken courses would add a significant degree of fairness to selective admissions but, in almost every case, is not a realistic possibility.

10. An Institution Should Develop, to the Extent Possible, Verification Procedures for Information Supplied by Applicants.   Admissions officers and policymakers have increasingly begun to worry about the advantages affluent students have in their access to expensive test preparation and to private college admissions counselors who advise and "package" (their word) applicants to colleges and universities. Selective colleges and universities need to think carefully about the possibility of adding a question to their application that asks if the applicant paid for a commercial test preparation course and, if so, which one. Additional questions might ask whether an applicant had professional help on the application other than from his school counselor and, if so, the name of that person/service, much as the 1040 form asks a taxpayer for the name of any professional tax preparer used. These items would provide important contextual information about an applicant.

Schevitz (2000) reported that Duke University took the first step in this direction by asking applicants on its fall 2001 application if they had help on their application essays. Duke did the same thing for its fall 2002 applicants. Brownstein (2002) attempted to assess the 2-year experiment. In this article, Christoph Guttentag, the director of undergraduate admissions at Duke, speaks candidly and worries realistically about the degree of honesty among applicants to Duke and among college applicants in general.

An even more serious problem is the issue of falsified information and plagiarized or purchased application essays. This is a difficult and vexing problem for admissions officers in selective colleges and universities even to begin to measure, and there is no simple solution to it. The Internet has made cheating on college application essays much easier for students and much more difficult for admissions officers to identify with certainty. It used to be that our staff could read books like *Essays That Worked* (Curry & Kasbar, 1990), and we would all recognize instantly the "In a way, I am like an uprooted tree" essay when we saw it. It is also not difficult—at least in some instances—to identify an essay written by someone else (an overzealous parent or a private college admissions counselor) because the voice and tone of the essay do not fit a 17- or 18-year-old. The Internet, however, has made available thousands and thousands of very good essays actually written by real 17- and 18-year-olds, and, in general, the broader or more open-ended a university's essay topic(s), the easier it will be to find an essay from another source that will serve.

It may be possible for an institution to build or buy the technical capacity to scan through Web sites offering application essays and then apply a key-word/key-phrase screen to all of the application essays the institution receives or to subscribe to one of the Web-based plagiarism detection services such as plagiarism.com. Such a process, however, would require that all applications be submitted electronically or that the admissions office scan all handwritten essays into its computer system so that the essays could then be put through the screening program. Checking essays in this way would be cumbersome, time-consuming, and expensive. In January 2003, the University of Michigan and the University of Texas announced that they would require proctored essays beginning with fall 2005 freshman applicants as a way to control outside help on applicant submissions (Bartlett, 2003).

There are two other areas where cheating may benefit an applicant. The first is the section of the application usually called something like "Honors, Awards, and Activities." The second deals with personal and family circumstances. Some private colleges require that the college counselor in a high school sign off on the list of honors, awards, and activities provided by each applicant. In California, where there are many very large high schools and lots of high schools with no counselors, such a practice would probably be ineffective. Other colleges and universities require that an applicant submit documentation for such claims, but that is cumbersome and, in some cases, difficult or impossible for applicants to do. In addition, students who are really computer savvy can produce their own documentation and make it look remarkably authentic.

Lying about personal and family circumstances is also an area of vulnerability for selective institutions, especially in states that have ended affirmative action in their public universities—California, Florida, and Washington. In these states, admissions policies tend to place even heavier emphasis on socioeconomic disadvantage and other kinds of hardship than when affirmative action was permitted. A student may lie about family income or under-state the level of education attained by his parents. An admissions office can cross-check income information with the financial aid office, assuming that low-income students will also have applied for aid. Although such a verification process can be cumbersome and imprecise, it may be necessary to add this step to an admissions review. The truth is, however, that students may be tempted to lie about other circumstances as well, including the death of a parent—or both parents or the entire family—the hardships of immigration to this country, or the presence of a debilitating condition or illness in oneself or one's parents. These kinds of claims are very difficult to verify, especially for applicants from large public high schools.

In general, admissions officers give the public impression that we recognize falsification and plagiarism regularly and with ease. This, frequently, is a bluff, based on the relatively few essays that are obviously someone else's work—that is, the clumsy cheaters. I would bet that we got fooled regularly at Berkeley, but it is impossible to say how often. The way that we would catch most of the perpetrators is that they would brag to their fellow students about how slick they were and other students would turn them in. In such cases, we would then write or call the applicant and politely ask questions and, in some case, ask for documentation. We did the same thing with cases of suspected falsification of race or ethnicity prior to Proposition 209.

The UC system, as one example, has depended on the section at the end of the application that applicants must sign: "I certify that all the information provided in my application is accurate and that I am the author of the attached personal statement. I understand that the University of California may deny me admission or enrollment if any information is found to be incomplete or inaccurate." This is a weak tool for ensuring the honesty of the applicant.

In November 2002, the UC systemwide faculty admissions committee finally announced (Board of Admissions and Relations With Schools, 2002) that UC would conduct random verification checks of honors, activities, and personal and/or family circumstances listed by freshman applicants on their UC applications. This was an important and valuable step in ensuring the integrity of the UC admissions process, particularly because UC does not require letters of recommendation from high-school teachers and counselors. Because of the huge number of California students who apply to UC, requiring letters of recommendation would cause a furor in California high schools, imposing an enormous burden on already overworked teachers and, especially, counselors. It is not uncommon for large California high schools to have 300 or more applicants to the UC system—and many of the most disadvantaged high schools have no counselors at all to write such letters.

Next to requiring proctored application essays and verifying applicant information, the most effective thing a university can do to limit cheating is to offer applicants very specific, focused essay topics and to change those topics every year. The UC system has adopted this format for fall 2004 applicants. No more "favorite figure in history or literature" or "discuss some national or international issue of concern to you" kinds of topics. In addition, one small part of the problem is that most colleges and universities do not say what kinds of outside help are or are not permissible when a student completes her application, other than the kind of vague statement just quoted from the UC application. College and university application forms should include a carefully crafted statement from the faculty admissions committee or the dean or director of admission saying clearly what kinds of help and how much of it are allowed within the boundaries of personal integrity, fairness, and ethical behavior.

Most college freshman applicants are honest and ethical in the completion of their applications. The UC faculty announcement of the new verification process included a report that UC San Diego had sampled 437 of its fall 2002 freshman applicants and had found that only one of those students had been unable to provide the necessary supporting evidence. Further evidence that most students are honest in the preparation of their applications is the repeated observation of admissions officers from around the country that applications, especially the essays, are often thrown together carelessly. Cheating is not as much of a problem as are missed opportunities. That is, so many students either do not take the application process seriously enough, wait until the last moment to write their essays, or do not know how to write about themselves effectively, so that they fail to include information that might influence the decision. But, because so many students do no more than an adequate job presenting themselves in their applications, students who cheat effectively have all that much more advantage in the admission process.

Finally, colleges and universities are part of this cheating problem. Stecklow (1995) revealed that a number of colleges and universities deliberately submitted falsified data to U.S. News and World Report in order to improve their rankings in the U.S. News and World Report college-rankings issue. Many colleges and universities have also adopted early decision plans in order to boost their standing in the U.S. News and World Report. In late 2000, both the University of Wisconsin and the University of Idaho were caught doctoring photographs in order to present racially diverse groups of students in recruitment publications. Many colleges and universities, including Berkeley until a year ago, routinely attempt to "buy" National Merit Scholars in order to be able to brag about their numbers.

The national debate over the SAT I instigated by UC President Richard Atkinson (2001), the Supreme Court decisions in *Grutter v. Bollinger* and *Gratz v. Bollinger* (2003), and the subsequent focus on rethinking the tools of the admission process provide a remarkable opportunity for admissions policymakers and everyone else interested in selective admissions to have a thoughtful, complex, and creative discussion about what selective admission means, how it is conducted, and how it might be improved. Many of the approaches in this book may very well strengthen admission processes in both public and private colleges and universities. At the same time, it is crucial to understand what does not need fixing and to pay careful attention to the time and budget pressures that, to a very large extent, drive what really happens in an admissions office once all of the applications have poured in and the real work begins.

REFERENCES

Atkinson, R. C. (2001, February 18). *Standardized tests and access to American universities.* The 2001 Robert H. Atwell Distinguished Lecture, delivered at the 83rd Annual Meeting of the American Council on Education, Washington, DC. Retrieved January 28, 2003, from www.ucop.edu/ucophome/commserv/sat/speech.html

Alexander v. Sandoval., S. Ct. 99–1908 (2001).

Bartlett, T. (2003, January 16). Universities of Michigan and Texas will require applicants to take a writing exam. *The Chronicle of Higher Education.* Retrieved March 1, 2003, from http://chronicle.com/daily/2003/01/2003011602n.htm

Board of Admissions and Relations With Schools. (2002). *First-year implementation of comprehensive review in freshman admissions: A progress report from the board of admissions and relations with schools.* Oakland: University of California Academic Senate.

Brownstein, A. (2002, March 1). Duke asks applicants if they got help on essays, and most say they did. *The Chronicle of Higher Education,* p. 35.

Castañeda v. Regents of the University of California. Lawsuit filed on February 2, 1999, in U.S. District Court, San Francisco, by the Lawyers Committee for Civil Rights et al., on behalf of eight plaintiffs.

Curry, B., & Kasbar, B. (Eds.). (1990). *Essays that worked: 50 Essays from successful applicants to the nation's top colleges.* New York: Fawcett Book Group.

The Fairness and Accuracy in Student Testing Act, S. 460, 107th Cong. (2000).

Gratz v. Bollinger, 123 S. Ct. (2003).

Grutter v. Bollinger, 123 S. Ct. (2003).

Hawes, K. (2001, August 27). NCAA's day in court. *The NCAA News.* Retrieved March 1, 2003, from http://www.ncaa.org/news/s001/20010827/active/3818n04.html

Hebel, S. (2000, July 14). Little is changed in latest draft of Education Department guidelines on standardized tests. *The Chronicle of Higher Education,* p. A31.

Ramist, L., Lewis, C., & McCamley, L. (1990). Implications of using freshman GPA as the criterion for the predictive validity of the SAT. In W. Willingham, C. Lewis, R. Morgan, & L. Ramist (Eds.), *Predicting college grades: An analysis of institutional trends over two decades* (pp. 261–288). Princeton, NJ: Educational Testing Service.

Ramist, L., Lewis, C., & McCamley-Jenkins, L. (1994). *Student group differences in predicting college grades: Sex, language, and ethnic groups* (College Board Rep. No. 93–1). New York: College Entrance Examination Board.

Regents of the University of California v. Bakke., 438 U.S. 265 (1978).

Savage, D. (2001, April 25). Supreme Court scales back part of the '64 Civil Rights Act. *The Los Angeles Times*, p. A.1.

Schevitz, T. (2000, December 25). College hopefuls padding admission forms. *San Francisco Chronicle*, p. A1.

Selingo, J. (2001, December 21). Civil rights groups blast Florida's use of SAT scores in awarding scholarships. *The Chronicle of Higher Education*, p. A18.

Stecklow, S. (1995, April 5). Cheat sheets: Colleges inflate SATs and graduation rates in popular guidebooks. *The Wall Street Journal*, p. A1.

Strenta, A. C., & Elliott, R. (1987). Differential grading standards revisited. *Journal of Educational Measurement*, 24(4), 281–291.

U.S. Department of Education, Office of Civil Rights. (2000). *The use of tests as part of high-stakes decision making for students: A resource guide for educators and policymakers*. Washington, DC: Author.

Willingham, W. W. (1985). *Success in college: The role of personal qualities and academic ability*. New York: College Entrance Examination Board.

3

Who Is at the Door?
The Demography
of Higher Education
in the 21st Century

Ernest W. Kimmel

Executive Director, Retired
Educational Testing Service, Princeton, NJ

Since early in the development of the United States, widespread access to education and knowledge has been a cherished goal of the American society. The United States has led the world in creating a universally available elementary and secondary school system. In the second half of the 20th century, access to postsecondary education was greatly expanded. This chapter tries to bring together information from a variety of sources to answer the question of who will be seeking to enter the higher education system during the early years of the 21st century. The chapter concludes by examining a number of factors that may impact the projected numbers of those seeking higher education.

The broad shifts in the composition of the population of the United States are widely covered in the popular press. We read of population shifts to the west and south; we see endless stories about the aging Baby Boomers; the U.S. Census Bureau (2003) reports that Latinos are now the largest minority group in the United States. During the 20th century, the U.S. population shifted from a majority of men to a majority of women. The average age went from under 23 to at least 35. In every decade of the century, the west grew faster than the other regions of the country. At the beginning of the 20th century, one of every eight residents was of a race other than White; at the end of the century, one of every four residents was non-White (Hobbs & Stoops, 2002).

One of the areas of most dramatic change is in the level of education of the populace. In 1910, 13.5% of the 25 and older population had completed 4 years of high school (Snyder, Hoffman, & Geddes, 1997, Table 8). By 2000, 84% of the 25 and older population had attained that level (Newburger & Curry, 2000, Table 1). In 1940, 5.5% of the men and 3.8% of the women in the 25 and over population had 4 or more years of college. By 2000, the comparable figures were 27.8% of the men and 23.6% of the women. These extensive gains in educational level are even more remarkable in view of the growth of the total population from about 76 million in 1900 to over 281 million in 2000 (Hobbs & Stoops, 2002, Fig. 1.1).

NATIONAL OUTLOOK FOR THE FUTURE

High school graduates are projected to increase from 2.8 million in 2001 to just over 3 million in 2012 after peaking at 3.2 million in 2008–2009 (Gerald & Hussar, 2002, Table 23). The projections of high-school graduates done by the Western Interstate Commission for Higher Education (WICHE; 1998) estimate that the peak will occur in the years 2007–2008. "The significant rise in the number of graduates reflects the increase in the 18-year-old population over the projection period, rather than changes in the graduation rates of 12th-graders" (Gerald & Hussar, 2002, p. 53). Undergraduate enrollment is projected to grow from 12.9 million in 2000 to over 15 million in 2011 (National Center for Education Statistics [NCES], 2002, Table 5-1). The total enrollment in all degree-granting institutions is projected to increase from 15.4 million in 2001 to about 17.6 million in 2012 (Gerald & Hussar, 2002, Table 10). This 14% overall increase is driven by the projected increase of 14% percent for men and almost 20% for women in the traditional college-age population of 18- to 24-year olds. This substantial increase in the "Baby Boom echo" cohort will more than offset the slowing growth in older student populations. Figure 3.1 illustrates the continued growth in younger students while the enrollment of over 35 women grows by only 6% and the number of enrolled men in this older cohort declines.

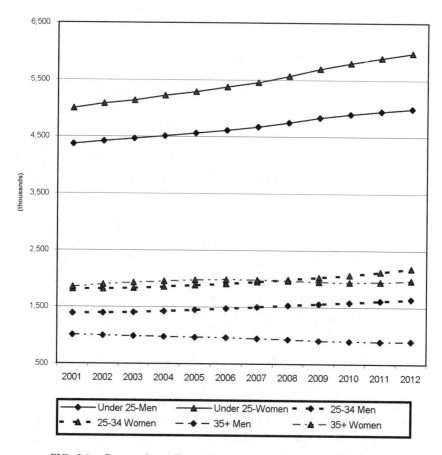

FIG. 3.1. Projected enrollment by gender and age 2001–2012. (Data from Gerald & Hussar, 2002.)

Nationally, the number of full-time students is projected to grow much faster than the number of part-time students. The number of full-time women students is projected to grow by over 20% during the 2001–2012 period while the number of full-time men students increases by about 13%. The number of part-time men and women students is projected to grow by 10% or less (Gerald & Hussar, 2002, Table 11).

All sectors of higher education are projected to grow significantly. Enrollments at 2-year public institutions are projected to grow by about 12% during the 2001–2012 period. Enrollments at 4-year publics, 4-year privates, and 2-year privates are all projected to increase by 15%–16% during this period. Private institutions are projected to increase their share of total enrollments very slightly by 2012, accounting for 23.4% of enrollments compared with 23.2% of enrollments in 2001 (Gerald & Hussar, 2002, Tables 15–18).

Nationally, the number of undergraduates is projected to grow by 15% by 2012, from 13.3 million in 2001 to about 15.3 million in 2012. The enrollment of women will continue to grow faster than men, 17.2% versus 12.1%. Graduate and professional enrollments are projected to grow just over 11%. At this postbaccalaureate level, the enrollment of women also continues to grow faster than the enrollment of men. The graduate school enrollment of women is projected to grow by 14.6% while male enrollment grows by less than 7%. In first professional degree programs, a 17.1% increase in the number of women is projected, in contrast to a 6.4% growth for men (Gerald & Hussar, 2002, Tables 19–21).

However, college and university administrators should not assume that these projected increases will ensure full enrollments. Nor should faculty assume that current academic programs will meet the needs of those students who enroll. Those knocking on the college door are not evenly distributed geographically, nor are they necessarily prepared to meet the current academic expectations of many colleges and universities.

THE REGIONAL AND STATE PICTURE

The broad national trends just described will not occur evenly across the country. The changes in student populations will differ considerably among regions and states. The WICHE (1998) study of projected high school graduates observed:

> While the vast majority of states will experience growth in the number of high school graduates into the early years of the new century, a few states will not. In every region, at least one state is projected to have fewer (high school) graduates in 2011–12 than it did in 1995–96. (p. 17)

In addition to the WICHE study that projected high-school graduates by state, type of secondary school, gender and race/ethnicity, the National Center for Educational Statistics (Gerald & Hussar, 2002) projected the number of public high school graduates by state to 2011–2012. The two studies project similar percentage growth in each region from 2000–2001 to 2011–2012. At the state level, however, the two sets of projections vary considerably. The projected numbers and percent change for each region and state are shown in the Appendix.

Table 3.1 clusters states by their projected percentage change in high school graduates. The table classifies states by the more conservative (least change)

TABLE 3.1

Where Will the Growth Occur? Projected Changes
in High-School Graduates Between 2001 and 2012

Significant Growth +10% or greater	Modest Growth +2% to +10%	Little Change ±2% or less	Modest Loss −2% to −10%	Significant Loss −10% or more
42% of 2001 graduates	14% of 2001 graduates	30% of 2001 graduates	< 9% of 2001 graduates	5% of 2001 graduates
Arizona	Colorado	Alabama	Hawaii	District of Columbia
California	Connecticut	Alaska	Iowa	Louisiana
Florida	Delaware	Arkansas	Kansas	Maine
Georgia	Maryland	Idaho	Missouri	North Dakota
Illinois	Massachusetts	Indiana	Montana	Oklahoma
Nevada	New York	Kentucky	Nebraska	South Dakota
New Jersey	Tennessee	Michigan	Vermont	West Virginia
North Carolina		Minnesota	Wisconsin	Wyoming
Texas		Mississippi		
Virginia		New Hampshire		
		New Mexico		
		Ohio		
		Oregon		
		Pennsylvania		
		Rhode Island		
		South Carolina		
		Utah		
		Washington		

Note. Author's analysis of data from WICHE (1998) and Gerald and Hussar (2002).

figure of the two projection studies. There are 10 states that both studies project to grow by 10% or more during the 2001–2012 period. Many of these are populous states; together they accounted for about 42% of the 2001 high-school graduates. With the exception of New Jersey, none of them "exports" more than 30% of their college-attending graduates (Morgan, 2002, Table D). Only Florida and Virginia receive as many as 25% of their first-year enrolled students from other states.

The high-school graduates of another seven states are projected to grow by at least 2% during this period. These eight states accounted for about 14% of the 2001 graduates. About 45% of the college-attending graduates of Connecticut go out of state for their first undergraduate year. Out-of-state graduates account for more than 25% of the first-year undergraduate enrollment in four of these states (Colorado, Connecticut, Delaware, and Massachusetts).

The relatively modest growth of in-state high-school graduates may be offset by the in-migration of students from other states.

Using the more conservative projection of change, 18 jurisdictions will experience little change in the number of high-school graduates. Together, these states accounted for 30% of the 2001 graduates. It should be noted that the two projection studies have important differences for some of these states. Alaska and New Hampshire send about 50% of their college-attending graduates out of state, but this only accounts for a few thousand first-year students per year. More than 25% of the first-year undergraduate enrollments of five of these states (Idaho, Minnesota, New Hampshire, Rhode Island, and Utah) come from other states.

Eight states, scattered across the four regions, are projected to see decreases in the range of 2% to 10%. These states accounted for less than 9% of the 2001 graduates. Of these states, Vermont is the only state with substantial in-and-out migration; almost 50% of the college-attending graduates leave the state, but over 50% of the first-year enrolled students come from other states.

Another eight jurisdictions (including the District of Columbia) are projected to have declines of greater than 10%. This will have little impact on the national picture because, combined, they accounted for only 5% of the high-school graduates. Out-of-state students account for 30% or more of the enrolled students in the District of Columbia, North Dakota, and Wyoming. Both Maine and the District of Columbia send significant proportions of their college- attending graduates to other states.

RACIAL AND/OR ETHNIC PARTICIPATION IN EDUCATION

Much of the growth in high-school graduates and in undergraduate enrollments is projected to come from racial and/or ethnic populations. Based on the WICHE (1998) study, the number of Hispanic high-school graduates in 2012 will be almost 1½ times the number in 1995—adding over 300,000 graduates. During the same period, Asian American high school graduates will grow by 95%, adding about 95,000 graduates. There will be about a 25% increase in the number of African American graduates, with about 75,000 more graduating in 2012 than did in 1995. By 2012, there will be slightly fewer White high-school graduates than in 1995, a decrease of about 7,000 graduates.

On a national basis, the proportion of White graduates will decrease by almost 13 percentage points. Ten states will experience decreases of between 15 and 38 percentage points in the share of White high school graduates between

1995 and 2012. Nevada will experience the greatest decrease in the proportion of White graduates. Their lost share will be filled by Hispanic, and to a lesser extent, Asian American graduates. A similar pattern of shifting racial and/or ethnic proportions is expected in Arizona, California, Florida, Georgia, Oregon, and Washington. Arkansas is projected to experience a decreased proportion of African American graduates as well as White students while Hispanic students increase their share of high school graduates. The decrease in the proportion of White graduates in Oklahoma is projected to be offset by increases in the share of Hispanic and Native American graduates. In Rhode Island, Hispanics will substantially increase their share of high school graduates while African Americans will have a slightly higher proportion of graduates.

Carnevale and Fry (2000) projected undergraduate enrollments to 2015 by state and racial and/or ethnic group. The national picture is similar to the patterns already described for high school graduations. The Hispanic undergraduate enrollment in 2015 is projected to be about 1 million students greater than it was in 1995, an increase of over 70%. The number of Asian American undergraduates is projected to increase about 85%, or over 600,000 students by 2015. Carnevale and Fry (2000) projected an increase from 1995 to 2015 of about 500,000 White undergraduates, or just under 6%. During this same period, African American undergraduates are projected to increase by about 23% or 395,000 more students.

The growth in Hispanic and Asian American undergraduates is highly concentrated in a few states. California accounts for 49% of the projected growth in Asian American undergraduates and 36% of the projected growth in Hispanic students. Florida, Illinois, New Jersey, New York, and Texas will also have large increases in the number of Hispanic undergraduates. Together with California, they will account for almost three quarters of the anticipated Hispanic growth. Large increases in the number of Asian American students are expected in Massachusetts, New Jersey, New York, Texas, and Washington. Including California, these six states account for about 70% of the increase in the number of Asian American students.

The projected increase in African American students is spread more widely among the states. The largest increases are projected in Texas, Georgia, Florida, and Maryland, accounting for about 37% of the total increase.

The number of White undergraduates is projected to increase in some states while decreasing in others. Texas, Florida, California, Washington, North Carolina, Arizona, Colorado, Utah, and Georgia are projected to have increases of 30,000 or more White undergraduates, while New York, Pennsylvania, Ohio, West Virginia, and Michigan are projected to have decreases of 10,000 or more.

TABLE 3.2

Change in Proportion of Undergraduate Students from Each Racial/Ethnic Group—1995–2015

	African American	Asian American	Hispanic	Other	White
Alabama	−0.2	+0.4	+0.6	−0.4	−0.4
Alaska	+0.1	+11.2	+3.3	−4.2	−10.5
Arizona	+0.2	+0.6	+7.0	+1.7	−9.6
Arkansas	−1.0	+0.4	+1.3	—	−0.8
California	−1.5	+7.0	+6.9	—	−12.3
Colorado	+0.7	+1.4	+3.9	+0.7	−6.7
Connecticut	+1.7	+2.0	+4.2	+0.6	−8.4
Delaware	+3.1	+0.8	+2.2	—	−6.1
District of Columbia	−7.4	+1.9	+3.1	−1.9	+4.2
Florida	+0.7	+0.5	+8.2	—	−9.4
Georgia	+4.1	+0.8	+0.9	—	−5.8
Hawaii	−0.3	+2.7	+1.8	—	−4.3
Idaho	+0.2	+0.6	+3.0	+1.7	−5.4
Illinois	−0.2	+2.1	+4.4	—	−6.4
Indiana	+0.9	+0.7	+1.4	—	−3.0
Iowa	+1.1	+1.3	+1.1	—	−3.6
Kansas	+1.1	+0.9	+3.0	+0.4	−5.3
Kentucky	+0.8	+0.4	+0.8	—	−1.9
Louisiana	+2.4	+1.0	+2.1	—	−5.5
Maine	+0.1	+1.2	+0.9	—	−2.1
Maryland	+3.2	+2.5	+3.4	—	−9.1
Massachusetts	+1.6	+4.6	+4.1	—	−10.3
Michigan	+1.4	+1.2	+1.4	−0.5	−3.5
Minnesota	+2.0	+3.0	+1.6	—	−6.7
Mississippi	+0.6	+0.4	+0.6	−0.5	−1.2
Missouri	+1.1	+0.4	+1.2	−0.1	−2.7
Montana	+0.1	+0.7	+1.7	+2.7	−5.1
Nebraska	+1.2	+0.9	+2.2	—	−4.3
Nevada	+0.5	+1.9	+8.4	+0.3	−11.1
New Hampshire	+0.2	+1.1	+0.9	+2.8	−5.0
New Jersey	+0.8	+4.1	+5.5	—	−10.4
New Mexico	−0.2	+0.2	+4.7	+2.4	−7.2
New York	−0.3	+3.7	+4.5	—	−8.0
North Carolina	+1.3	+0.8	+0.8	−0.7	−2.2
North Dakota	+0.6	+0.5	+0.9	+2.7	−4.6
Ohio	+2.3	+1.0	+1.0	—	−4.3
Oklahoma	+2.3	+0.9	+2.5	—	−5.7
Oregon	+0.3	+2.0	+3.4	—	−5.6
Pennsylvania	+1.5	+1.6	+1.8	+0.1	−5.0

(Continued)

TABLE 3.2 (continued)

	African American	Asian American	Hispanic	Other	White
Rhode Island	+1.2	+2.3	+6.4	—	−9.9
South Carolina	−0.3	+0.5	+0.7	—	−0.9
South Dakota	+0.4	+0.5	+0.4	+3.1	−4.4
Tennessee	+1.9	+0.4	+0.6	—	−2.9
Texas	+0.6	+1.3	+5.1	+0.5	−7.5
Utah	+0.3	+1.5	+2.2	+1.2	−5.2
Vermont	+0.4	+0.7	+1.9	—	−2.9
Virginia	+2.1	+2.9	+2.6	—	−7.5
Washington	−0.1	+3.9	+3.5	—	−7.3
West Virginia	+0.4	+0.8	+1.0	—	−2.1
Wisconsin	+2.1	+2.6	+1.4	—	−6.1
Wyoming	+0.1	+0.7	+4.0	+0.9	−5.7
National	+0.4	+3.0	+4.7	+0.1	−8.2

Source: Carnevale and Fry (2000) Appendix B.

There will be noticeable changes in the relative proportions of undergraduate students from different racial and/or ethnic groups in several states as shown in Table 3.2. Nationally, the proportion of White undergraduates is projected to decrease by slightly over 8 percentage points between 1995 and 2015. In five states, the proportion of White students is projected to decrease by 10 or more percentage points. In California, Asian Americans and Hispanics will each increase their share of the undergraduate population by about 7 percentage points. Nevada will see a substantial gain in the proportion of Hispanic students and a small gain in the proportion of Asian Americans. In Alaska, Asian Americans are projected to increase their share of undergraduates by over 11 percentage points, while Hispanics will gain about 3 points. Hispanics and Asian Americans will each expand their share of the student population by 4 to 6 percentage points in New Jersey. In Massachusetts, Hispanics and Asian Americans are each projected to gain over 4 percentage points while the proportion of African Americans increases by somewhat less than 2 points.

ENVIRONMENTAL FACTORS THAT MAY AFFECT ACTUAL ENROLLMENTS

Although those who developed the projections of high-school graduates and college enrollment attempted to account for a variety of factors that may affect the behavior of students and their families, changes in various social policies as well as the general political–economic situation may also affect the number and kind of students who actually enroll in college during this period.

High School Standards and Graduation Policies

In the 20 years since the release of A Nation at Risk (National Commission on Excellence in Education, 1983), every state has engaged in some form of "educational reform" that has had the goal of raising the standards of what is expected of every student in American schools. The implications of those efforts are discussed in chapters 15, 16, and 17. The enactment of the No Child Left Behind Act of 2001 (2001) sets testing requirements for each state, again with the intention of raising the standards for students attending public schools. Although intended to help students be better prepared for life, career, and further education, these efforts may have the effect, at least in the short term, of reducing the numbers of students who do graduate from high school. As with so many other factors, the impact is likely to be greatest on children from disadvantaged homes, disproportionately from non-White racial and/or ethnic groups.

In a recent analysis of the impact of high-stakes tests and high-school graduation exams across all states, Amrein and Berliner (2002) reported "that there is inadequate evidence to support the proposition that high-stakes tests and high school graduation exams increase student achievement" (p. 57). More troubling is their finding that academic achievement, as measured by ACT, SAT, and AP scores, declined after the implementation of high school graduation exams. Amrein and Berliner (2002) concluded that their "analyses suggest that high stakes tests and high school graduation exams may tend to inhibit the academic achievement of students, not foster their academic growth" (p. 58).

Betts and Grogger's (2000) study of the effects of raising grading standards made clear that such higher standards may help some students at the expense of others. Using the High School and Beyond data, they estimated the impact of higher grading standards on student achievement as measured by a 12th grade test and on educational attainment as measured by high-school graduation rate and college attendance. In contrast to the Amrein and Berliner (2002) study, these analyses suggested "that higher grading standards are associated with higher 12th-grade test scores, on average" (p. 11). However, Betts and Grogger (2000) also found that:

> Thus grading standards have different effects on students at different locations in the distribution of educational achievement. Higher grading standards have somewhat more than twice the effect on test scores at the top quartile of the

distribution than they have at the median or bottom quartile. Thus higher standards may contribute to greater inequality in the distribution of educational
achievement. (p. 13)

Overall, Betts and Grogger (2000) found that higher grading standards had
no significant effect on educational attainment although there is a suggestion
that higher standards could lead to slight decreases in high-school graduation.
When they examined this effect by race they found that "For both blacks and
Hispanics, however, grading standards have negative and significant effects on
high school graduation" (p. 19).

These recent studies do suggest that the current spate of changes to school
standards, including high-stakes testing, may impact the numbers of students
eligible to enter higher education. In particular, the educational reforms may
have a negative impact on the number of African American and Hispanic students who graduate from high school and demonstrate adequate achievement
on admissions tests such as ACT and SAT. Because so much of the projected
increase in enrollments is from the Hispanic population, many of those projected to be seeking higher education may not graduate from high school or be
prepared for the academic demands of college.

Perceived Economic Value of College

The educational credentials of the nation's workforce have grown substantially
since 1959. At the same time, employers have increased the skill requirements
expected of workers in the increasingly office-centered economy. Carnevale
and Rose (1998) found that "College-educated workers are gaining ground
while all others are experiencing real income losses" (p. 18). A subsequent
study (Carnevale & Desrochers, 2002) found that "the wage premium for
college-educated workers, compared with high school educated workers, has
increased by almost 70 percent since the early 1980s in spite of the fact that
the supply of college-educated workers has increased by 60 percent over the
same period" (p. 2). In looking to the future, Carnevale and Desrochers (2002)
argued that "there is every reason to believe that the demand for college-
educated workers will continue to grow along with the income divide between
those who have some postsecondary education and those who do not" (p. 2).
Their study further projects a net deficit in workers with at least some college
education as the Baby-Boom generation retires. These economic incentives
are likely to encourage more students to seek entry into postsecondary education—causing the actual enrollments to surpass the projections. Whether the
students are successful in that pursuit will depend, in large measure on the

success of the K–12 school system in preparing a larger share of the age cohort to "meet the high standards that provide access to postsecondary education, training, and good jobs" (Carnevale & Desrochers, 2002, p. 18).

State Budgets

The media are full of stories about the dire financial situation of most states. Historically, during times of financial stringencies for the states, higher education has taken bigger reductions than any other major spending category (Gold, 1995). During the current economic slowdown, substantial cuts for higher education are being announced with each new state budget. Many of the cuts have been in the range of 12%. Yet these cuts coincide with a time of projected enrollment increases. Callan (2003) observes that:

> The students who make up these growing high school graduating classes are concentrated heavily in the south and west and in states where the child poverty rate is high. They are the poorest as well as the most ethnically and racially heterogeneous generation of students to appear on the doorstep of American higher education. (p. 2A)

His observations are congruent with the data presented earlier in this chapter.

The public institutions, which enroll over 80% of the nation's college students, have responded to these cuts as they have in previous recessions, by sharply increasing tuition. Trombley (2003) found that "Tuition and mandatory fee charges at four-year public institutions rose in every state, startlingly so in some cases. . . . Community college tuition and mandatory fees rose in all but two states" (p. 1A). The American Association of State Colleges and Universities' (AASCU; 2002) survey of public 4-year institutions found that "undergraduate tuition and fees . . . rose by 9.1 percent for 2002–2003, the largest single-year increase in almost a decade" (p. 1). A study conducted prior to the latest round of budget cuts, concluded:

> Regarding affordability, we know that state support of public colleges and universities has increased; that these increases have not been commensurate with the rising costs of providing higher education; that the largest portion of these costs has been borne by students and families through increases in tuition; and that tuition is increasingly financed by student borrowing. Our conclusion regarding the affordability of a college or university education is this. Americans are losing ground. (National Center for Public Policy and Higher Education, 2002, p. 9)

The impact of the reduced state appropriations and the resulting tuition hikes will impact most heavily upon the poor and racial and/or ethnic minorities—

the very segments of the population that are projected to drive the increased enrollments.

Financial Aid

In the 1999–2000 academic year, more than one half of the 16.5 million undergraduates received some type of financial aid from federal, state, institutional, or other sources. Forty-four percent of all undergraduates received grants, averaging $3,500, and 29% received student loans, averaging $5,100 (Berkner, Berker, Rooney, & Peter, 2002). The National Center for Public Policy and Higher Education study (2002) found that "Federal and state financial aid to students has not kept pace with increases in tuition" (p. 6) and that "More students and families at all income levels are borrowing more than ever before to pay for college" (p. 7). There have been increases in federal and state financial aid, but they have not kept pace with the increased costs, especially of tuition. For example, in 1986, the average Pell grant was about 98% of tuition at public 4-year colleges; by 1998, the average Pell grant would cover less than two thirds of tuition at a public 4-year college (Callan, 2002, p.15, Fig. 4).

Federal financial aid has shifted away from grants during the past 20 years. In 1981, loans accounted for 45% of federal student aid; in 2000, 58% of federal student aid was in the form of loans. "A higher percentage of low-income students borrow, and borrowing is a much greater burden on low-income students and parents" (National Center for Public Policy and Higher Education, 2002, chap. 1). This financial aid factor, so closely tied to state budget priorities, seems likely to most severely impact the poor and racial and/or ethnic students who are projected to swell college enrollments. AASCU's (2002) study reported that

> the price of college attendance at four-year public institutions, as a percentage of family income, has remained relatively steady for middle and high income families since the early 1980s. However, student charges as a percentage of family income escalated significantly for low-income families throughout the 1980s and early 1990s. (p. 4)

This trend is bound to re-emerge during the current spate of tuition hikes and to serve as a damper on enrollment in higher education.

Immigration and International Students

International students have been an important element of enrollment management at some institutions. In late 2002, the Institute of International

Education (IIE; 2002b) released figures that showed that the international student enrollment in U.S. colleges and universities increased by 6.4% in 2001–2002. These students would have been in the United States before the September 11, 2001 terrorist attack. However, a survey done by IIE (2002a) a year after the attack indicated wide variation among campuses in the continued presence of international students, with over one half reporting steady or growing enrollments but 42% reporting declining enrollments. Although the number of students from many Islamic countries remained the same, there were notable drops from countries like Saudi Arabia and the United Arab Emirates. It seems likely that heightened concern about security may impact international student enrollment during the next several years. As new policies are implemented that require more stringent screening of visa applicants, the number of international students may be radically reduced.

SUMMARY

This chapter has portrayed the projected growth in high-school graduates and higher education enrollments until the early part of the second decade of the 21st century. Those projections indicate that most of the growth will be concentrated in a few states and that Hispanic and Asian students will comprise a significant portion of the growth. A number of environmental factors that have the potential of impacting enrollments, some in a positive direction, others in a negative, were identified. In seeking to understand future enrollments, an individual institution will need to study the referenced projections in detail and evaluate the impact on its policies and practices of the environmental factors noted. However, even if the projections prove reasonably accurate, institutions need to recognize that many of the incoming students will be from backgrounds that, historically, have left them ill-prepared for the demands of higher education. Each college and university needs to evaluate how its academic programs and student services will need to change to meet the needs of the students who are on the doorstep.

APPENDIX

Projected Number of High School Graduates in 2001 and 2012

	NCES Public*	WICHE Public**	WICHE Nonpublic**	WICHE Total**
Alabama				
2001	36,660	39,384	4,700	44,084
2012	35,500	39,300	4,574	43,874
Alaska				
2001	6,750	6,970	177	7,147
2012	6,700	6,514	133	6,647
Arizona				
2001	39,550	39,531	2,499	42,030
2012	52,910	48,650	5,033	53,683
Arkansas				
2001	26,760	27,575	1,410	28,985
2012	25,780	27,431	1,359	28,790
California				
2001	320,100	289,503	30,367	319,870
2012	382,500	330,898	35,989	366,887
Colorado				
2001	40,090	40,764	2,923	43,687
2012	47,140	43,429	3,869	47,298
Connecticut				
2001	31,260	30,569	5,793	36,362
2012	36,670	33,149	6,183	39,332
Delaware				
2001	6,680	6,516	1,687	8,203
2012	7,100	6,679	1,885	8,564
District of Columbia				
2001	2,670	2,551	796	3,347
2012	1,600	2,348	585	2,933
Florida				
2001	109,020	113,055	14,850	127,905
2012	135,580	128,909	18,680	147,589
Georgia				
2001	62,250	71,219	10,154	81,373
2012	74,990	82,517	15,747	98,264
Hawaii				
2001	9,780	11,386	2,657	14,043
2012	9,410	12,363	2,463	14,826
Idaho				
2001	15,740	16,417	624	17,041
2012	15,810	17,779	744	18,523

	NCES *Public**	WICHE *Public***	WICHE *Nonpublic***	WICHE *Total***
Illinois				
2001	111,610	110,972	14,466	125,438
2012	130,660	125,466	15,004	140,470
Indiana				
2001	57,130	60,939	4,207	65,146
2012	58,220	61,906	4,551	66,457
Iowa				
2001	33,970	35,069	2,078	37,147
2012	31,790	31,701	1,861	33,562
Kansas				
2001	29,850	29,653	1,655	31,308
2012	27,530	27,571	2,013	29,584
Kentucky				
2001	37,620	38,257	3,488	41,745
2012	42,200	38,378	3,670	42,048
Louisiana				
2001	37,840	37,577	9,112	46,689
2012	33,320	32,642	8,342	40,984
Maine				
2001	12,410	13,392	2,304	15,696
2012	10,750	11,074	2,280	13,354
Maryland				
2001	48,410	49,880	7,700	57,580
2012	53,000	53,544	9,092	62,636
Massachusetts				
2001	54,400	53,316	11,124	64,440
2012	56,690	56,919	10,586	67,505
Michigan				
2001	91,390	94,351	10,040	104,391
2012	93,580	96,812	10,213	107,025
Minnesota				
2001	58,500	58,686	3,581	62,267
2012	55,830	58,195	3,391	61,586
Mississippi				
2001	23,970	22,922	3,755	26,677
2012	22,780	23,350	3,794	27,144
Missouri				
2001	54,370	54,557	6,384	60,941
2012	52,610	53,661	5,677	59,338
Montana				
2001	10,700	11,605	543	12,148
2012	8,810	10,356	659	11,015
Nebraska				
2001	19,880	20,509	2,091	22,600
2012	18,240	19,094	2,065	21,159

	NCES Public*	WICHE Public**	WICHE Nonpublic**	WICHE Total**
Nevada				
2001	14,910	14,374	567	14,941
2012	24,900	24,230	968	25,198
New Hampshire				
2001	12,110	12,894	2,245	15,139
2012	12,500	12,224	2,045	14,269
New Jersey				
2001	75,940	72,590	11,416	84,006
2012	93,910	83,380	15,225	98,605
New Mexico				
2001	17,790	17,311	1,691	19,002
2012	15,730	17,652	1,719	19,371
New York				
2001	142,330	148,779	25,978	174,757
2012	146,370	160,077	26,154	186,231
North Carolina				
2001	63,330	64,148	4,168	68,316
2012	75,970	75,406	5,846	81,252
North Dakota				
2001	8,400	8,692	519	9,211
2012	6,100	6,639	430	7,069
Ohio				
2001	110,530	112,549	13,253	125,802
2012	108,220	110,984	13,292	124,276
Oklahoma				
2001	36,940	38,126	1,366	39,492
2012	32,800	34,684	1,234	35,918
Oregon				
2001	30,030	30,856	2,622	33,478
2012	30,050	33,004	3,123	36,127
Pennsylvania				
2001	115,420	117,202	16,608	133,810
2012	118,320	117,316	15,231	132,547
Rhode Island				
2001	8,560	8,774	1,416	10,190
2012	9,280	8,929	1,361	10,290
South Carolina				
2001	29,360	35,048	3,554	38,602
2012	32,840	33,401	4,219	37,620
South Dakota				
2001	8,810	9,457	980	10,437
2012	6,870	8,310	1,072	9,382
Tennessee				
2001	39,750	49,052	6,658	55,710
2012	41,710	55,426	7,423	62,849

	NCES Public*	WICHE Public**	WICHE Nonpublic**	WICHE Total**
Texas				
2001	210,690	197,226	13,939	211,165
2012	243,560	216,803	15,962	232,765
Utah				
2001	31,160	31,548	690	32,238
2012	30,590	32,765	710	33,475
Vermont				
2001	6,840	6,929	640	7,569
2012	5,580	6,095	859	6,954
Virginia				
2001	66,310	65,756	6,140	71,896
2012	81,030	73,406	7,311	80,717
Washington				
2001	57,520	54,227	3,606	57,833
2012	58,780	60,447	4,374	64,821
West Virginia				
2001	18,290	18,781	749	19,530
2012	15,620	16,669	804	17,473
Wisconsin				
2001	59,490	59,569	4,662	64,231
2012	56,670	57,896	4,226	62,122
Wyoming				
2001	6,240	6,690	198	6,888
2012	4,640	5,060	180	5,240

*Data from Gerald and Hussar (2002). **Data from WICHE (1998).

REFERENCES

American Association of State Colleges and Universities. (2002). *Student charges and financial aid.* Washington, DC: Author. Retrieved February 20, 2003, from www .aascu.org/student_charges03/default.htm

Amrein, A. L., & Berliner, D. C. (2002). *The impact of high-stakes tests on student academic performance: An analysis of NAEP results in states with high-stakes tests and ACT, SAT, and AP test results in states with high school graduation exams.* Retrieved February 17, 2003, from http://www.asu.edu/ educ/epsl/EPRU/document/EPSL-0211–126-EPRU.pdf

Berkner, L., Berker, A., Rooney, K., & Peter, K. (2002, Fall). Student financing of undergraduate education: 1999–2000. *Education Statistics Quarterly.* National Center for Education Statistics. Washington, DC: U.S. Office of Education.

Betts, J. R., & Grogger, J. (2000). *The impact of grading standards on student achievement, educational attainment, and entry-level earnings* (Working Paper No. 7875). Cambridge, MA: National Bureau of Economic Research.

Callan, P. M. (2002). *Coping with recession* (Report No. 02–2). San Jose, CA: National Center for Public Policy and Higher Education.

Callan, P. M. (2003, Winter). A different kind of recession. In *College affordability in jeopardy: A special supplement to National Crosstalk*. San Jose, CA: National Center for Public Policy and Higher Education. Retrieved February 19, 2003, from www.highereducation.org/reports/affordability_supplement/

Carnevale, A. P., & Desrochers, D. M. (2002, April). The missing middle: Aligning education and the knowledge economy. Paper commissioned for *Preparing America's Future: The High School Symposium* sponsored by the Office of Vocational and Adult Education, U.S. Department of Education in Washington, DC. Retrieved February 18, 2003, from http://www.ed.gov/offices/OVAE/HS/carnevale.doc

Carnevale, A. P., & Fry, R. A. (2000). *Crossing the great divide: Can we achieve equity when Generation Y goes to college?* Princeton, NJ: Educational Testing Service.

Carnevale, A. P., & Rose, S. J. (1998). *Education for what? The new office economy: Executive summary.* Princeton, NJ: Educational Testing Service.

Gerald, D. E., & Hussar, W. J. (2002). *Projection of education statistics to 2012* (NCES 2002–030). National Center for Education Statistics. Washington, DC: U.S. Department of Education.

Gold, S. D. (Ed.). (1995). *The fiscal crisis of the states: Lessons for the future.* Washington, DC: Georgetown University Press.

Hobbs, F., & Stoops, N. (2002). *Demographic trends in the 20th century* (Census 2000 Special Rep., Series CENSR-4), U.S. Census Bureau. Washington, DC: U.S. Department of Commerce.

Institute for International Education. (2002a). *The impact of September 11 on international educational exchange.* New York: Author. Retrieved February 19, 2003, from http://www.iienetwork.org

Institute for International Education. (2002b). *Open doors 2002.* New York: Author. Retrieved February 19, 2003, from http://www.iienetwork.org

Morgan, F. B. (2002, Spring). Fall enrollment in Title IV degree-granting postsecondary institutions: 1998. *Education Statistics Quarterly.* National Center for Education Statistics. Washington, DC: U.S. Office of Education.

National Center for Education Statistics. (2002). *The condition of education 2002* (NCES 2002–025). Washington, DC: U.S. Department of Education.

National Center for Public Policy and Higher Education. (2002). *Losing ground: A national status report on the affordability of American higher education* (Rep. No. 02–3). San Jose, CA: Author. Retrieved February 20, 2003, from www.highereducation.org/reports/losing_ground/

National Commission on Excellence in Education. (1983). *A nation at risk: The imperative for educational reform.* Washington, DC: U.S. Department of Education.

Newburger, E. C., & Curry, A. E. (2000). *Educational attainment in the United States (Update): March 2000* (Current Population Rep. P20–536). U.S. Census Bureau. Washington, DC: U.S. Department of Commerce.

The No Child Left Behind Act of 2001. (2001). P. L. 107.110 (107th Congress), p. 115, STAT. 1425.

Snyder, T. D., Hoffman, C. M., & Geddes, C. M. (1997). *Digest of education statistics, 1997* (NCES 98–015). National Center for Education Statistics. Washington, DC: U.S. Department of Education.

Trombley, W. (2003). The rising price of higher education. In *College affordability in jeopardy: A special supplement to National Crosstalk*. San Jose, CA: National Center for Public Policy and Higher Education.

U.S. Census Bureau. (2003, January 21). *Resident population estimates of the United States by race and Hispanic or Latino origin: July 1, 2001, and April 1, 2000.* Washington, DC: United States Department of Commerce.

Western Interstate Commission for Higher Education (WICHE). (1998). *Knocking at the college door: Projections of high school graduates by state and race/ethnicity 1996–2012.* (Jointly published with The College Board). Boulder, CO: Author.

4

Broadening Criteria of College Success and the Impact of Cognitive Predictors

Wayne J. Camara
The College Board, New York

What does it mean to be successful in college? Is college success the same for each institution? Do academic departments within the same institution define success differently? Do individual students and their parents have similar or differing views of what constitutes college success? This book explores a range of additional predictors that might supplement the traditional measures used in admissions today—the SAT or ACT, high school grades, college application, student statement and/or essay, and letters of recommendation. Each year, college administrators, faculty, the media, and policymakers lament the fact that the admissions process places so much emphasis, both perceived and real, on so few measures. The authors of many of the following chapters describe past and future research on additional predictors that might offer some utility in college admissions, whether that utility is viewed as incremental validity (or predictive accuracy), increased diversity, identification of special talents, or the broadening of the factors considered in making such important decisions.

This chapter contends that we cannot evaluate new predictors of college success until we first define college success. We will not be successful in broadening the range of prediction tools used in college admissions if we cannot understand the multidimensional nature of college success. Currently, the term *college success* is misused and exploited to represent the particular value or view of an individual or group toward higher education. Educators have described college success in the same global manner in which employers speak of job performance. Often, college success is defined as academic success, measured by grades and GPA. The assumption is that one such general factor can capture almost all of the variance associated with both performance in education or at work and the variance among predictors used in each setting.

However, college success is similar to job performance in that neither is unidimensional. Performance in educational and employment settings is composed of many facets or dimensions that are often quite distinct. Campbell, McCloy, Oppler, and Sager (1993) postulated three main dimensions of proficiency that apply to educational performance: declarative knowledge (facts, principles, self-knowledge); procedural knowledge and skill (knowledge and skill of how to accomplish the work, cognitive skill, interpersonal skill, etc.) and motivation (level of effort, persistence), as well as a taxonomy of eight performance components that may or may not be present in all situations (specific task proficiency, general proficiency, communication, effort, discipline, peer and team performance, supervision and leadership, and management and administration).

There are many factors associated with college success and performance that extend beyond traditional academic success and achievement. Teamwork, adapting to rapidly changing environments, leadership, using and adapting to new technologies, and working in a diverse environment are among the meta-trends in the global work environment (Campbell, Kuncel, & Oswald, 1998). Because these may be the types of skills and abilities that employees will need, many educators and business leaders have asserted that these skills and abilities should be a central feature of any admissions system. This model of admissions would value performance that reflects the demands of the work environment. Other models for admissions decisions advocate for valuing students' ability to benefit from college, students' potential to contribute to society, or the extent that students have overcome adversity (Bowen & Bok, 1998; College Board, 1999). Academic performance is not the only dimension of college success, and grades are not the only criterion measure (Willingham, 1985).

Willingham (1985) described several studies that attempted to quantify how faculty and students define college success. Some of the factors found across studies were intellectual growth, personal growth, ethicality, ability to communicate, leadership, and ability to analyze problems and master new concepts. Gillespie, Kim, Oswald, Ramsay, and Schmitt (2002) searched through educational objectives and mission statements from 35 colleges to identify criteria that institutions explicated. Over 170 separate statements were clustered into 12 factors:

1. knowledge, learning, mastery of general principles;
2. continuous learning, intellectual interest, and curiosity;
3. artistic and cultural appreciation and curiosity;
4. multicultural tolerance and appreciation;
5. leadership;
6. interpersonal skills;
7. social responsibility, citizenship, and involvement;
8. physical and psychological health;
9. career orientation;
10. adaptability and life skills;
11. perseverance; and
12. ethics and integrity.

Clearly, there is substantial support from research and anecdotal evidence that college success is a complex construct that must be viewed quite broadly. There are a number of distinct components to college success that may differ in terms of their antecedent behaviors and covariation with other variables.

CRITERIA FOR COLLEGE SUCCESS

A criterion, in an admissions or selection context, generally refers to a dependent variable or outcome measure. The criterion is a measure of the desired outcome and is what is used to evaluate the validity and utility of the predictors. Freshman and cumulative grade point average (GPA) have been the most popular criterion measures used in admissions decision research, with individual college course grades, college graduation, and persistence appearing in a respectable number of studies (Camara & Echternacht, 2000). Freshman GPA (FGPA) and cumulative GPA (CGPA) principally measure general cognitive performance or outcomes and probably measures only the first of the 12 factors of college success identified by Gillespie et al. (2002); they clearly are not a suitable outcome measure for many other factors related to college success. College grades also, in large part, measure this same general cognitive factor, as well as domain specific knowledge and skills (e.g., foreign language, writing). GPA and grades may reflect motivation, effort, attendance, growth, and behavior to some extent, but differences in grading practices across teachers, courses, and institutions make it difficult to quantify this multidimensionality in a consistent form (Camara, Kimmel, Scheuneman, & Sawtell, 2003). Persistence and graduation have been used as criteria in a number of studies (Burton & Ramist, 2001).

In recent years, there has been renewed attention to the "criterion problem" in industrial and organizational psychology. The problem had long been thought to be associated with the difficulty of finding a good, predictable criterion. It is actually a problem of definition both at the conceptual and the operational level. Guion (1998) stated "improved prediction cannot be expected without firm understanding of what we want to predict" (p. 111). This situation applies to higher education as well. Colleges and universities develop educational objectives and mission statements that describe the values of that institution, the types of students it is seeking, and the "value added" that it hopes to impart to students who attend the institution. Yet there is variation across colleges in terms of which factors they value, the relative weight given each factor, and the extent to which these factors are observable and measurable. Different stakeholders also vary significantly in which components of undergraduate college performance they would judge as most critical (Campbell et al., 1998). It is difficult to find consensus on the definition of some of the factors associated with college success such as ethics and integrity, artistic curiosity, and multicultural appreciation and tolerance. It may be even more difficult to measure and observe these factors in a consistent manner across all students or applicants.

The most common validation criterion measure, GPA, is, at best, a proxy for long-term criteria such as success in employment or success in graduate school. Research in both education and employment contexts has established that general cognitive ability, as measured by tests such as the SAT, is a significant predictor across a range of performance dimensions (Camara & Echternacht, 2000; Campbell et al., 1998; Schmidt, Ones, & Hunter, 1992; Willingham, 1985). However, additional components of undergraduate performance that might improve admissions, placement, and retention decisions have been largely ignored.

Colleges and universities describe college success and the student performance associated with college success in terms of a broad and multidimensional concept. Operationally, however, they continue to use a unidimensional concept—academic success—as the criterion. GPA remains the only consistent outcome measure easily available in multicollege validation studies for a variety of reasons. First, until recently, few campuses maintained any type of relational database on students. It is still common to find applicant files (which contain data on predictors) in the admissions office, whereas GPA is held in a separate database, and data on courses completed, course titles, and persistence are retained in yet a third database, all of which may be housed in separate departments. The time and labor required to merge files is well beyond the means of the admissions and enrollment management departments that have the primary interest in admissions research. The College Board, as well as ACT and other organizations that conduct admissions testing, offers free validation studies to institutions. It has always been difficult to persuade colleges to participate in such studies, and only a very small fraction of all 4-year colleges participate in these studies or make available a local validation study conducted at their campus. Of those institutions that do participate, over 90% provide only FGPA. In 1994–1995, when a major revision was made to the SAT, a substantial effort was undertaken to recruit colleges to participate in a national validation study. Only 23 colleges out of more than 50 that were contacted agreed to participate. Of these, only seven provided course-level data (Bridgeman, McCamley-Jenkins, & Ervin, 2000). Between 1996 and 2002, a total of 987 validity studies were conducted on the SAT and other predictors through the College Board's institutional validity service. Of these, 282 were routine studies initiated by colleges, and only 12 colleges provided course-level data. Validity studies are typically requested by a college's admissions office. Acquiring course-level data requires additional cooperation, above and beyond that needed to obtain FGPA, from the college registrar's office. To include course grades in such studies, the admissions office is dependent on the registrar's office and a programmer to extract course grades and match them to admissions data (M. Rosenthal, personal communication, March 18, 2003).

The Association of American Universities (AAU) directed an effort to identify the content and cognitive skills students need for success in entry-level college courses. Over 400 faculty from 20 universities participated in a study to identify the knowledge and skills for university success in specific academic domains (e.g., math, English, science). The resulting "Standards for Success" provides both a research-based list of the content and cognitive skills that faculty define as essential for success, and a framework for a national conversation about college success skills (Conley, 2003)

Many educators, policymakers, and other stakeholders have called for broader measures for admissions decisions and complained about the importance placed on admissions tests and high-school GPA, yet when college GPA is the sole criterion used to validate predictors and evaluate utility, there is little incentive to develop alternative measures that may relate to dimensions of college success for which there are no outcome measures or data available from colleges. The standards movement in K–12 education has employed a very familiar acronym to argue for changes in educational assessment— WYTIWYG—what you test is what you get. The notion that tests shape school curriculum, teacher instruction, and what students learn when high stakes are attached to the results is reasonably supported by research (Linn, 1999). A similar analogy applies to new predictors. If additional criteria of college success are valued and measured, if these criteria are distinct from current criteria that emphasize grades, and if measures (subjective or objective) of these criteria are available on students, then there will be an impetus to invest in the research and development needed for a broader range of predictors that measure these distinct performance dimensions.

The current lack of other outcome measures must change if we are serious about developing new predictors. In this volume, Schmitt, Oswald, and Gillespie (chap. 11) discuss biographical data and situational judgments tasks; Sternberg (chap. 9) proposes measures of practical knowledge and creativity as supplements to analogical reasoning; and Sedlacek (1998; chap. 10) describes additional noncognitive measures that could offer some utility to admissions decisions. However, in each instance, research conducted to explore the efficacy of these new predictors primarily relied on FGPA, because it was the only readily available criterion measure on student performance across institutions. Any new predictor measure will continue to be evaluated in terms of its incremental validity over existing measures, but the new measures proposed in this book have their greatest promise among other performance dimensions such as creativity, leadership, persistence, and citizenship. Initial pilot research on several of these measures shows some promise for admissions when FGPA is the criterion (Friede et al., 2003; Sternberg & the Rainbow Collaborators, 2003); however, the lack of other noncognitive measures of college performance is a major obstacle to both the scientific efforts and the academic and economic incentives needed to sustain a long-term commitment to the needed research. As Stricker noted in 1993, it is unrealistic to expect noncognitive measures to contribute to predicting academic performance beyond what can be accomplished with the SAT and high school grades.

BROADENING CRITERION MEASURES OF COLLEGE SUCCESS

Virtually all colleges and universities would agree that measures of academic accomplishment are of relevance to their educational mission, and admissions tests, high school GPA, and the rigor of academic coursework serve a central and important role in assembling a freshman class. However, there are many other desired outcomes from a college education that are less related to academic success. Research on personal qualities conducted in the 1980s identified four areas of achievement (Willingham, 1985):

- Scholarship (college GPA and departmental honors);
- Leadership (both elected and appointed positions);
- Significant achievements (scientific, artistic, athletic, communications, entrepreneurial);
- Institution's judgment (faculty nominations).

Approximately 3,700 freshmen who were still enrolled at nine colleges and universities 4 years later (75% retention rate) were the subjects in a comprehensive study of personal qualities conducted by the Educational Testing Service (ETS) and the College Board. Scholarship, leadership, and achievements were correlated moderately (.25 to .35). College GPAs for these students continually rose each year from about 2.8 in the freshman year to 3.1 in the senior year. A central question in this study was whether there is supplemental information over and beyond the SAT and high-school grade point avaerage (HSGPA) that can help identify successful college students. A variety of measures of the four performance domains were used, and together they improved prediction of the most successful students by 25%. These additional measures improved prediction of leadership and accomplishments by 65% and 42%, respectively, but only increased prediction of scholarship by 7%.

Perhaps the most relevant example of a comprehensive, multiyear research and development effort undertaken to improve selection is work sponsored by the U.S. Army Research Institute for the Behavioral and Social Sciences (ARI) from the early 1980s to the mid-1990s known collectively as Project A. This project and several follow-up projects, some of which are still under way, involve the development and evaluation of an array of predictor and criterion measures for a broad range of jobs in the U.S. Army (Campbell & Knapp, 2001). The goals of the criterion development research were to describe the dimensions of performance in a job as comprehensively as possible, using job analysis techniques, and to develop multiple measures of each performance factor. The research examined components of performance that were associated with entry level recruits and second-term enlistees, as well as those associated with specific jobs and contextualized institutionwide factors (Borman, Campbell, & Pulakos, 2001; Campbell, McHenry, & Wise, 1990). A wide range of criterion measures were developed and tried out as part of this research. The criterion measures that appear most amenable to modification for higher education include:

1. Rating Scales—Both institutionwide and job-specific rating scales were developed, where supervisors (or trainers) would rate employees on a number of specific dimensions of performance as well as two global ratings (i.e., overall effectiveness and potential for successful performance in the future). Additional scales of leadership and supervisory and/or management performance were also developed;

2. A Performance Prediction Scale—supervisors were asked to predict future performance in adverse conditions;

3. Archival Performance Records—performance records maintained on a database;

4. Self-Reported Indices of Performance—a questionnaire asking about accomplishments, courses completed, awards, and other significant events during service;

5. Job History Questionnaire—a means to assess the frequency and recency of performing different tasks;

6. Situational Judgment Tests—examinees are asked to indicate the most and least effective responses to various situations they might encounter;

7. Job Satisfaction Scale—assesses satisfaction with work, supervisors, co-workers, the institution, and contextual factors.

Academic dimensions of performance are well represented in the current admissions measures used in higher education, and additional domain specific skills (e.g., foreign language, calculus) or cognitive skills (e.g., metacognition, study skills) could potentially be assessed with additional assessments or inventories. Many remaining performance dimensions related to temperament, adaptation to different situations and experiences, attitudes and interests, behavioral intentions, past experiences, traits, and accomplishments would be more appropriately captured through rating scales, questionnaires, and situational judgment tests. Self-reported data on performance accomplishments at work and student achievements in school (e.g., GPA, courses completed, grades) have been shown to be highly reliable and accurate (Freeberg, Rock, & Pollack, 1989; Knapp, Campbell, Borman, Pulakos, & Hanson, 2001). Self-reported HSGPA and rank are only slightly less predictive of college grades than actual GPA and rank reported by high schools, and student assessment of their mathematical ability correlates highly with math grades and SAT math scores (Donlon, 1984). There is legitimate concern that self-report data could be distorted if it were used in high-stakes decisions. Efforts to verify self-reported grades and accomplishments may be required in such instances, and research has shown that when elaboration is required or implied, socially desirable responding decreases (Schmitt & Kunce, 2002).

Rating Scales

There may be several opportunities to collect performance information from others during a typical undergraduate education. Friede et al. (2003) found utility for peer and self ratings for a variety of academic outcome dimensions on behaviorally anchored rating scales (BARS). Peer ratings correlated moderately with FGPA (.31), several dimensions from a biodata instrument (leadership, perseverance, citizenship), and absenteeism (−.14). Self-ratings had a low correlation with FGPA (.12), modest correlation with absenteeism (−.19), but as expected, higher correlations with other self-report data collected from biodata, situational job inventories (SJIs), and personality measures due to same-source bias. Peer and self-ratings were largely uncorrelated, suggesting that ratings may sample different aspects of the same constructs, and both ratings were uncorrelated with ACT and SAT scores. The prediction of peer ratings was substantial (adjusted $R = .35$); the highest correlations were observed with those social and interpersonal dimensions that peers may most readily observe.

To make them usable as outcome measures in the future, considerable research is needed on these several promising techniques. Self-ratings on such performance dimensions as domain-specific proficiency, temperament, future plans, frequency, importance, and satisfaction with various experiences and performances should be explored. Peer ratings may have utility in social and interpersonal dimensions of performance but may also suffer bias if ratees select their peer raters as was done here. Ratings by residence hall directors appear useful in capturing disruptive performance dimensions and conscientiousness, but may also be unavailable for large numbers of undergraduates who live off campus or are less familiar to their hall director. Structured faculty rating scales may be promising in capturing domain-specific knowledge and skills, and other performance dimensions such as conscientiousness and effort. As with other ratings, bias could be a problem if students select the faculty to complete ratings, if faculty are not familiar with ratees, or if rater training is not provided. Success in future settings, whether work environments or graduate school is an important outcome criterion for undergraduates. Additional research examining the extent that raters can reliably and accurately anticipate future behavior is needed before measures of these dimensions are used, yet they may be among the most defensible and valued performance dimensions to include.

Archival Records

As already noted, access to a rich and centralized college student database is, perhaps, the single most important condition to expanding the breadth of how college success is defined and measured. A multidimensional outcomes database is a necessary condition for validating noncognitive predictors on any large-scale basis. Colleges and universities, and the national associations that support them, such as the College Board, the American Council on Education, and the National Association of College Admissions Counselors, often collaborate to create institutional relational databases that capture such data as student course grades, course titles, persistence, time to degree, honors and recognition, participation in any preparatory or remedial programs, or other criterion measures. This same approach could be used to establish a national clearinghouse that would collect and manage multidimensional outcome data for participating institutions in a manner that protects student and institutional privacy but permits researchers to access data for cross-institutional research on new performance dimensions and predictors. Each institution can advance such an ambitious research agenda by matching student records and databases and conducting or participating in validation efforts with multiple criteria that extend beyond GPA. Persistence, defined as students who complete freshman year and return as sophomores, graduation (in a specified amount of time, e.g., 4, 5, or 6 years), and credits completed are measures that should be readily available for validation studies at any 4-year institution. Persistence and graduation are dichotomous variables that will have limited utility in validating new measures, but credits completed and absenteeism, even when measured by self-report ratings, have proved useful in undergraduate performance studies (Friede et al., 2003).

Undergraduate History, Activities, and Experience

A number of studies have described the relationship between specific educational experiences during graduate and undergraduate education and entrance into specific graduate programs and careers (Camara & Baum, 1993; Campbell et al., 1998). Self-reported historical and experience inventories that inquire about college courses completed, grades, research projects, team work, and other extracurricular and work activities could serve as criterion measures, and may actually be more accurate than data housed in archival records (Knapp et al., 2001). Given the lack of data on student performance dimensions in colleges, self-report history and experience scales may offer the most immediate opportunity for expanding the performance domain related to college success.

Several other important dimensions should be considered in determining the performance domain for college success. First, industrial–organizational psychology devotes considerable attention to the distinction between task-specific criteria and global criteria of performance. For example, Project A identified both task-specific criterion dimensions that applied to specific jobs as well as Army-wide dimensions associated with effective soldiers. The project demonstrated that different predictor combinations have different relationships with different criterion measures (Wise, McHenry, & Campbell, 1990). Students do not enter jobs, but they do enter specific majors and take different kinds of courses requiring both general-task knowledge and domain-specific knowledge. Undergraduate curriculum is most similar during students first and second year of college, which is one reason that FGPA is an appropriate and useful criterion measure for academic success in college (Camara & Echternacht, 2000). However, as students take more advanced courses, there are greater differences in the subject domain, in the knowledge, skills, and abilities (KSA) required, and in the desired performance outcomes. Listening, speaking, writing, and reading in a foreign language are skills that are of great importance to students majoring in foreign languages, whereas critical reading in English and analysis of text and relationships are of greater importance to students majoring in literature or philosophy. Similarly, subject-specific skills associated with engineering may be quite different from the KSAs required in nursing. College performance, like work performance, includes both subject-specific task requirements and more generalized cognitive requirements (e.g., critical reading, writing, reasoning). Ramist, Lewis, and McCamley-Jenkins (1993) demonstrated that gender and an academic composite level[1] were related to course-taking patterns among freshmen. Students in the high academic composite level were much more likely to take advanced courses, such as calculus and laboratory sciences, than students in the low composite level. Research has demonstrated that SAT verbal, SAT mathematics, and HSGPA have different relationships when grades in specific courses serve as the criterion (Bridgeman et al., 2000; Ramist et al., 1993), suggesting that different cognitive skills may be emphasized in different majors.

A second important performance dimension is the distinction between academic performance and noncognitive performance. This is similar to the distinction in analyses of work performance between task-specific behavior and contextual activities. Distinctions between these two performance domains, which have been described in the work setting (Borman & Motowidlo, 1993),

---

[1]Combining students across colleges and then dividing students into three composites—high, medium, and low—based on a combination of their high school rank and SAT scores.

can easily be applied to the college setting. Contextual performance of college students is distinguished from task-performance in similar ways:

- Task performance is related to specific technical or cognitive skills or the "can do" aspect of performance, whereas contextual performance often relates to persistence, volunteering, effort, following and supporting rules and procedures, and cooperating with others, or the "will do" aspects of performance.
- Task performance relates to academic knowledge skills and abilities required for success in academic performance (e.g., course grades), whereas contextual performance relates to predisposition and volition.
- Task performance usually varies between different academic areas and course requirements, whereas contextual activities are common to many or all courses, majors, and institutions.

A MODEL OF UNDERGRADUATE COLLEGE SUCCESS

Predictors derive their importance and relevance by their ability to predict the criteria of interest to colleges and universities. Broadening the criteria space requires a more comprehensive model of college success. This might be modeled after the work of Campbell et al. (1993) in organizations and Campbell et al. (1998) in graduate schools. Components of graduate school performance in psychology proposed by Campbell et al. (1993) include:

1. Independent research accomplishment;
2. Using content knowledge expertly;
3. Expert use of research and data analytic methods;
4. Oral and written communication;
5. Exhibiting sustained, goal-directed effort;
6. Being an effective team member; and
7. Carrying out leadership/management functions.

Several of these functions, such as using content knowledge expertly, oral and written communication, sustained and goal directed effort, and being an effective team member may be just as relevant to undergraduate success. Note that most of these could be classified as contextual activities. Other behaviors related to undergraduate success could include:

1. Acquiring information;
2. Critical reading and listening skills;
3. Commitment and involvement in activities or disciplinary area;
4. Computer skills and Web navigation;
5. Attendance and conscientiousness;
6. Academic accomplishment; and
7. Purposeful behavior and planning for the future.

Cognitive tests such as the SAT and ACT are most relevant for cognitive criteria of academic accomplishment such as college grades and GPA. A variety of noncognitive predictors would be more relevant to many of the other criteria. Noncognitive performance criteria in education may have less adverse impact (and smaller subgroup differences) than cognitive criteria such as FGPA and CGPA. The development of a performance model of college success must also delineate the appropriate weights for different facets of performance. Such weighting could reflect the specific values and mission of each institution or could be developed through a collaborative approach among many similar institutions. Without a broader model of college success and the development of objective criteria to measure this domain, admissions will remain narrowly focused on cognitive predictors such as grades and test scores for predicting and evaluating college success—defined as academic accomplishment.

EXISTING PREDICTORS
OF COLLEGE SUCCESS

Figures 4.1 and 4.2 illustrate the relative importance placed on the most frequently used admissions measures by 4-year public and private institutions from 1979 to 2000 (Breland, Maxey, Gernard, Cummings, & Trapani, 2002). Colleges indicated the importance of different factors on their undergraduate admissions policies and practices using a 5-point rating scale.[2] High-school grades and rank continue to be viewed as the most important factor in admissions, with admissions test scores a consistent second. Public institutions appear to place increasing importance on the rigor of high-school courses, whereas private institutions have consistently viewed course rigor as important. All other factors, such as essays, recommendations, interviews, and portfolios appear

---

[2] 5 (*single most important factor*), 4 (*very important factor*), 3 (*moderately important factor*), 2 (*a minor factor*), and 1 (*not considered*).

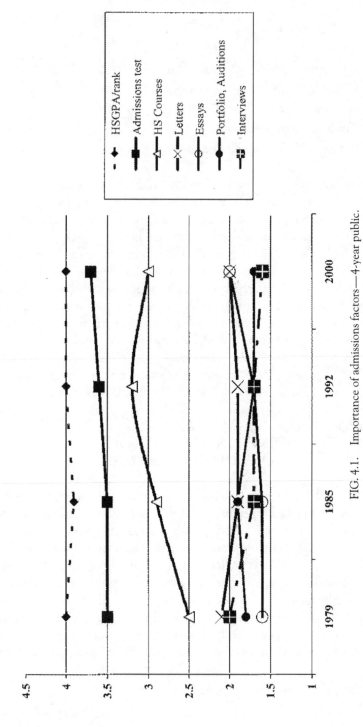

FIG. 4.1.   Importance of admissions factors—4-year public.

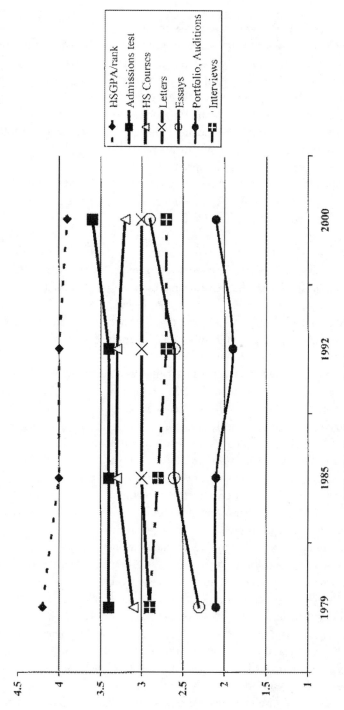

FIG. 4.2. Importance of admission factors—4-year private.

Legend:
- HSGPA/rank
- Admissions test
- HS Courses
- Letters
- Essays
- Portfolio, Auditions
- Interviews

substantially less important for most public institutions. There are exceptions at some institutions and for specific programs such as music and art. Private institutions report the importance of essays as increasing slightly in recent years. The other factors are given more weight at the privates than at public institutions but substantially less weight than GPA, test scores, and course rigor. These findings are not surprising and reflect the differences between public and private institutions in size, number of applicants, and resources. The private colleges responding to this survey were significantly smaller than the public institutions and were more likely to employ comprehensive or holistic admissions reviews of applicants. HSGPA or class rank has continued to be consistently important for both private and public colleges over the years while admissions tests have increased slightly in importance in recent years. The pattern or rigor of high-school coursework (as well as AP course enrollment, not shown) have been moderately important factors for admissions. Letters of recommendation, essays, and interviews have been a minor factor for private colleges and even less important for public institutions. Interestingly, student essays have increased in importance for private 4-year colleges since 1985. Portfolios and auditions are typically used for selective programs in the arts, although students applying to other majors will often submit a collection of work.

Table 4.1 illustrates the extent to which existing admissions measures address some of the most frequently identified outcome constructs or performance factors associated with college success. High-school grades and GPA provide the broadest overall predictor of college success because they may reflect a range of different factors such as effort, class participation, conscientiousness, and attendance. However, grades and the resulting GPA are limited by the level of subjectivity associated with the grades themselves, the grading standards, and the nonacademic factors that are incorporated into the measure. Other nonstandardized predictors, such as letters of recommendation, student essays, and self-reported data from the application may or may not address some of the other temperament and interest factors associated with college success. For example, a student essay or teacher recommendation may illustrate or describe a student's social responsibility, artistic curiosity, or career orientation in some detail. However, the absence of such discussion on another student's statement or faculty recommendation does not necessarily indicate a lack of these traits or characteristics.

Comparable information on methods used in employment selection is more difficult to come by and may not represent all types of organizations. A 1996 survey of employment testing by the American Management Association (in Sharf & Jones, 1999) found that 28% of members used cognitive ability tests, followed by 20% who used managerial assessments and personality tests. Cognitive ability tests and personality tests were most likely to be used in the public sector and least likely to be used in nonprofit organizations. Tippins and Wunder (1997) surveyed Fortune 100 employers and reported that onsite interviews were used by virtually all organizations. Resumes (including an evaluation of education and experience) were the second most frequent measure, used by 71% of employers. Campus interviews and tests were each used by 40% of employers and background checks and references were used by 36% and 28%, respectively. Twenty-five percent of employers reported using college GPA in hiring decisions.

ADDITIONAL COGNITIVE MEASURES

Reasoning tests, such as the SAT, achievement tests, high-school GPA, and high-school course grades measure general cognitive abilities, reasoning abilities, and may cover subject-specific knowledge and skills. Although there are a variety of ways to measure general cognitive skills or achievement, there is a limit to the incremental validity to be gained by including additional predictors of the same general construct. Sternberg (1997), among others, suggested that broadening the measured predictors beyond such analytical skills offers a greater promise of enhancing prediction than continuing efforts to improve and refine the same cognitive predictors that have been used for decades.

Snow (1999) described a need to both broaden and deepen admissions measures in ways that are valuable and useful to both individuals and institutions in higher education. He stated that:

> ... breadth means expanding the spectrum of cognitive, conative and affective aptitudes that are assessed ... promoting increased diversity in the talents and personal qualities that get considered and developed in higher education. Depth means gaining a deeper, and richer description and understanding of the psychology of the constructs being assessed. (p. 132)

Sternberg (1985) proposed a theory of triarchic intelligence that suggested the most successful learners are those who demonstrate a balance of analytical, creative, and practical abilities. *Analytical abilities* are measured on tests like the SAT and ACT and are assessed by traditional cognitive ability tests of reasoning and problem solving. *Creative abilities* are reflected in the generation of novel solutions and approaches. *Practical abilities* are akin to everyday intelligence needed to solve daily problems encountered at school, at work, and in life. An important component of practical abilities is tacit knowledge that enables individuals to adapt to, select, and shape real-world environments.

TABLE 4.1

College Admissions Predictors and Constructs

Construct	College Admission Predictors								
	SAT V	SAT M	SAT W	Ach. Tests	HSGPA	HS Grades	Essay	References	Application
Verbal Reasoning	★				▣	▣			
Math Reasoning		★		→	▣	▣			
Writing			★	→	▣	▣			
Oral Communication						→			
English Language Proficiency	▣		▣	→	▣	▣			
General Knowledge	★	★	★		★	★			
Subject-Specific Knowledge				★		★			
Visual-Spatial Abilities									
Meta-cognition								→	
Creativity									
Idea Generation									
Contextual Performance					★	★			
Self Management								→	

Effort and Motivation

Perseverance

Intellectual Curiosity

Conscientiousness

Leadership

Artistic Curiosity

Career Orientation

Multicultural Appreciation/Tolerance

Interpersonal Skills

Teamwork

Social Responsibility & Involvement

Athleticism

Ethics & Integrity

Physical & Psychological Health

Class Participation

Attendance

Note. ✭ covers domain; ▣ partially covers domain; ✦ inconsistent coverage (may cover domain in some situations)

Such knowledge reflects the practical ability to learn from experience and to apply this knowledge to value-based situations (Sternberg & Hedlund, 2002). Tacit knowledge is typically measured with situational judgment inventories (Chan & Schmitt, 1997). The College Board supported a research study that examined the incremental utility and validity of several measures of triarchic abilities with college freshmen (Sternberg et al., 2003). This study is described in detail in chapter 9.

Admissions tests largely represent two of several cognitive ability factors—crystallized intelligence and/or achievement and, in a more limited fashion, fluid-analytic intelligence and/or abstract reasoning. Snow (1999) proposed three additional factors that could be added to the cognitive spectrum of admissions tests: visual-spatial-perceptual ability, a broader measure of fluid reasoning, and idea generation.

Visual-Spatial-Perceptual Ability

Visual or spatial ability actually includes several different abilities such as mechanical reasoning, visualization, and spatial orientation. *Spatial aptitude* has been defined as the ability to think visually of geometric forms and to comprehend two-dimensional representations of three-dimensional objects (U.S. Department of Labor, 1970). A number of large testing programs include one or more measures of spatial ability. For example, the space relations test from the Differential Aptitude Tests requires test takers to visualize an object from different perspectives and identify the correct pattern. The General Aptitude Test Battery (GATB) includes similar subtests that comprise a spatial aptitude measure (Anastasi & Urbina, 1988). Assembling objects, a measure of spatial visualization, was added to the Armed Services Vocational Aptitude Battery (ASVAB) in 2001, and an earlier form of the test included a Space Perception subtest. Spatial abilities may also be assessed with paper-form board tasks, paper-folding tasks, object rotation, mazes, coding, and other performance tasks that incorporate visual–motor, dexterity, fine-motor skills, or other special abilities. Often these tests are speeded, and large gender differences are common on spatial ability measures (Anastasi & Urbina, 1988). Gender differences vary by the type of spatial task, and are small to nonexistent on spatial visualization tasks such as the Assembling Objects test of the ASVAB, and largest on mental rotation tasks in three dimensions (Linn & Peterson, 1985). When combined with other ASVAB subtests and Project A measures, six spatial tests formed a single and distinct factor (Russell & Peterson, 2001). The spatial ability tests of Project A correlated with job-performance criteria, but added only between .01 to .03 incremental validity above the cognitive ability measures (McHenry, Hough, Toquam, Hanson, & Ashworth, 1990). There is evidence that spatial abilities relate to specialized skills and achievements in such fields as architecture, medicine and engineering, but add little to the prediction of college grades (Snow, 1999).[3] In addition, the prevalence of sub-stantial gender differences in many spatial measures and the lack of direct rel-evance to general criteria of college success would likely make such measures unacceptable except for specialized fields such as medicine and engineering. Similarly, Field Dependence, as measured on tests such as the Group Embed-ded Figures Test, correlates with grades in science and mathematics, though not with FGPA, and accounts for additional variance beyond the SAT Math test and high-school grades (Witkin, Moore, Goodenough, & Cox, 1977). At the undergraduate level, however, specialized field or major-dependent mea-sures have less utility than they do for graduate school admissions because most freshman students are admitted to an institution, not to a major.

Fluid Reasoning

This construct is closest to inductive reasoning and involves flexible, adap-tive, abstract, and inferential reasoning in novel learning and problem-solving situations. Snow (1999) acknowledged that this construct is present in the SAT Reasoning Test, but argued that purer measures should be developed. He suggested reasoning and problem-solving tasks in context—that is, in the knowledge and problem domains that will be used in college. Snow envisioned simulations that require students to learn new and challenging materials in simulated learning contexts. Ackerman's (1987) distinction between consis-tent and inconsistent tasks parallels the distinction between crystallized and fluid intelligence in many ways. Fluid tasks often involve nonverbal or perfor-mance tasks such as block design, finding embedded figures, or unscrambling words and sentences, but they need not be content free. In fluid or inconsistent tasks, novelty and adaptation are the principle requirements, and the same response patterns and transfer of cognitive strategies will not work. However, developing contextualized fluid tasks that are broad enough to be relevant to all students, irrespective of interests and majors, is a major challenge. Addi-tionally, such tasks have been criticized as unauthentic and unrealistic (Snow, 1999).

---

[3] Zwick (2002) noted that the SAT did attempt to include a test of spatial ability in 1930 but apparently dropped it because it was not useful in predicting college grades.

Idea Generation/Creativity

Idea generation is a component of creativity and is clearly a valued ability in most areas of higher education (Snow, 1999). Several tests include measures of idea generation that are distinct from broader measures of creativity. Sternberg (1985) demonstrated that measures of creative intelligence go beyond measures of analytical ability provided by tests like the SAT and ACT. Two types of creative measures were employed in the study described in chapter 9, which examined the validity and differential prediction of triarchic abilities over admission test scores (Sternberg & the Rainbow Collaborators, 2003).

Other cognitive constructs have also been proposed and studied to different degrees. Specific aptitudes or abilities have also been studied in research and employment. Kobrin, Camara, and Milewski (2002) reported that SAT II Subject Tests add little incremental validity in predicting college performance above and beyond that accounted for by the SAT I. Schmidt (2002) noted that special aptitude tests are often redundant with general cognitive ability tests and that these abilities and aptitudes would be more variable across jobs and academic disciplines. Everson (in press) describes the influence of modern cognitive psychology on admissions testing and notes that assessments must now tell us more about *what* students know and *how* they learn. He proposes incorporating measures of learning strategies, prior knowledge, and metacognitive abilities with more traditional measures of content knowledge and abilities. A number of cognitive dimensions relevant for assessing the processes students undertake for learning have been proposed; these include knowledge representation, mental models, and metacognition (Glaser, Lesgold, & Lajoie, 1985). The Motivated Strategies for Learning is a measure of self-regulated learning that has been used to predict academic performance (VanderStoep, Pintrich, & Fagerlin, 1996). At present, measures of cognitive processes appear more relevant for diagnostic assessment and learning than for summative assessment, such as in admissions. Cognitive diagnostic assessment, combined with traditional knowledge tests, would appear to have value and utility for college placement. The information would both inform the institution and student about appropriate course placement and provide an instructional roadmap for learning strategies to address any weaknesses or to facilitate new learning.

Admissions testing emerged from practical needs and was evaluated primarily on empirical grounds until very recently (Everson, 1999). Snow (1999) argued that we must start by broadening predictors. As more diverse aptitudes and talents are used in admissions decisions, they may be more fully recognized as goals of higher education. However, there are several problems with such an approach. First, there may not be universal agreement across higher education about the value and usefulness of some aptitudes and talents. Second, assessment instruments will continue to be evaluated primarily on empirical grounds such as predictive validity. Unless appropriate criteria are available, we could not evaluate the utility of predictors that are less related to academic success in college. Third, is it appropriate for testing organizations to determine which aptitudes and talents should be recognized as goals across higher education or should institutions of higher education determine these? In the past 10 years, educational reforms have promoted assessments in K–12 as a vehicle to reform instruction and pedagogy, yet these efforts have largely stalled and have not had the desired impact in higher education (Linn, 1999).

CONCLUSION

College success has been described broadly in college handbooks, their mission statements, and in academic discussions for decades. Gillespie et al. (2002) found over 170 statements that partially define the mission and objectives of 35 colleges for their undergraduate education. In practice, however, higher education largely defines college success in terms of college grades, most often in terms of FGPA.

There are many more important outcomes of an undergraduate education that are valued by colleges and their students. Campbell and colleagues (1993) have proposed a multidimensional model of job performance in organizations and made a first attempt at defining a similar model of graduate school performance (1998). Undergraduate college success can similarly be conceived of as a multidimensional model involving academic accomplishments, as well as growth, achievement, and accomplishments in cross-disciplinary skills (e.g., communications) and nonacademic areas.

Admissions tests have evolved from very practical needs for an efficient and valid mechanism to sort and select among the increasing numbers of college applicants during the last third of the 20th century. Today the tests have retained their efficiency and validity, but there is increased realization that college success should be defined by factors in addition to academic performance. Therefore, predictors beyond cognitive measures are required. High-school grades suffer from restriction of range that dramatically reduces their utility and validity for applicants at the most competitive colleges. The disparities of grading standards and policies, as well as level of course rigor, affect the interpretation of grades across high schools. Admissions tests and grades continue to serve as the most important measures for both private and public institutions for the past 30 years (Breland et al., 2002). In the search for additional predictors, some colleges are increasingly giving more weight to course rigor; yet as with grades, this measure suffers from subjectivity and inconsistency. In addition, student access to rigorous courses may create another hurdle for students attending poorer and smaller high schools.

Additional measures of cognitive skill have been proposed, yet given the relatively high-validity coefficients found when admissions tests are used in conjunction with high-school grades, there is little room left for incremental improvements when college grades serve as the sole criteria. There have been increasing discussions of the importance of graduation and persistence, as well as other potential dimensions of college success, yet research focuses almost solely on FGPA.

Chapters throughout this volume describe a variety of alternative predictors and new models for admissions that offer hope for a broader measure of college skills. Chapter 5 describes research on alternative predictors from both education and the workplace. Leaders in higher education need to collaborate with researchers to develop the evidence needed to broaden predictors of college success by demonstrating the value of measuring broader criteria of college success. Such a research agenda requires hard work, multiple studies, and a large investment in time and effort by major universities to define and develop the variety of outcome performance measures needed to stimulate research that can broaden predictors and diversity in higher education.

REFERENCES

Ackerman, P. L. (1987). Individual differences in skill learning: An integration of psychometric and information processing perspectives. *Psychological Bulletin, 102,* 3–27.

Anastasi, A., & Urbina, S. (1988). *Psychological testing* (7th ed.). Upper Saddle River, NJ: Prentice-Hall.

Borman, W. C., Campbell, C. H., & Pulakos, E. D. (2001). Analyzing job performance measurement. In J. P. Campbell & D. J. Knapp (Eds.), *Exploring the limits in personnel selection and classification* (pp.157–180). Mahwah, NJ: Lawrence Erlbaum Associates.

Borman, W. C., & Motowildo, S. J. (1993). Expanding the criterion domain to include elements of contextual performance. In N. Schmitt & W. Borman (Eds.), *Personnel selection in organizations* (pp.71–98). San Francisco: Jossey-Bass.

Bowen, W. G., & Bok, D. (1998). *The shape of the river.* Princeton, NJ: Princeton University Press.

Breland, H., Maxey, J., Gernard, R., Cummings, T., & Trapani, C. (2002). *Trends in college admissions: A report of a survey of undergraduate admissions policies, practices, and procedures.* ACT, AIR, College Board, Educational Testing Service, National Association of Collegiate Admissions Counselors.

Bridgeman, B., McCamley-Jenkins, L., & Ervin, N. (2000). *Predictions of freshmen grade-point average from the revised and recentered SAT I reasoning test* (College Board Research Rep. No. 2000–1). New York: The College Board.

Burton, N., & Ramist, L. (2001). *Predicting success in college: SAT studies of classes graduating since 1980* (College Board Research Rep. No. 2001–01). New York: The College Board.

Camara, W. J., & Baum, C. (1993). *Developing careers in research. Knowledge, attitudes and intentions of recent doctoral recipients in psychology: A discriminant analysis.* (Final Rep. 92MF04400101D). Rockville, MD. National Institute of Drug Abuse.

Camara, W. J., & Echternacht, G. (2000). *The SAT I and high school grades: Utility in predicting success in college* (College Board Research Note No. RN–10). New York: The College Board.

Camara, W. J., Kimmel, E., Scheuneman, J., & Sawtell, E. (2003). *Whose grades are inflated?* (College Board Research Rep. No. 03–04). New York: College Board.

Campbell, J. P., & Knapp, D. J. (2001). *Exploring the limits in personnel selection and classification.* Mahwah, NJ: Lawrence Erlbaum Associates.

Campbell, J., Kuncel, N. R., & Oswald, F. L. (1998, April). *Predicting performance in graduate school: The criterion problem.* Paper presented at the annual meeting of the Society of Industrial and Organizational Psychologists, Dallas, TX.

Campbell, J. P., McCloy, R. A., Oppler, S. H., & Sager, C. E. (1993). A theory of performance. In N. Schmitt, & W. Borman (Eds.), *Personnel selection in organizations* (pp. 35–70). San Francisco: Jossey-Bass.

Campbell, J. P., McHenry, J. J., & Wise, L. L. (1990). Modeling job performance in a population of jobs. *Personnel Psychology, 43,* 313–333.

Chan, D., & Schmitt, N. (1997). Video-based versus paper-and-pencil method of assessment in situational judgment tests; subgroup differences in test performance and face validity perceptions. *Journal of Applied Psychology, 82,* 143–159.

College Board. (1999). *Toward a taxonomy of the admissions decision-making process.* New York: Author.

Conley, D. (2003). *Standards for success methodology for developing knowledge and skills for university success.* Unpublished memorandum.

Donlon, T. (1984). *The College Board technical handbook for the Scholastic Aptitude and Achievement Tests.* New York: College Board.

Everson, H. T. (1999). A theory-based framework for future college-admissions tests. In S. Messick (Ed.), *Assessment in higher education: Issues of access, quality, student development and public policy* (pp. 113–130). Mahwah, NJ: Lawrence Erlbaum Associates.

Everson, H. T. (in press). Innovation and change in the SAT: A design framework for future college admissions tests. New York: Routledge-Falmer.

Freeberg, N. E., Rock, D. A., & Pollack, J. (1989). *Analysis of the revised student descriptive questionnaire: Phase II predictive validity of academic self report* (College Board Research Rep. No. 89–8). New York: College Board.

Friede, A., Gillespie, M., Kim, B., Oswald, F., Ramsay, L., & Schmitt, N. (2003). *Development and validation of alternative measures of college success.* (Final report available from The College Board, New York).

Gillespie, M., Kim, B., Oswald, F., Ramsay, L., & Schmitt, N. (2002). *Biodata and situational judgment inventories as measures of college success: Developing and pilot testing phases.* (Interim report available from The College Board, New York).

Glaser, R., Lesgold, A., & Lajoie, S. (1985). Toward a cognitive theory for the measurement of achievement. In D. Klahr & K. Kotovsky (Eds.), *Complex information processing: The impact of Herbert A. Simon* (pp. 269–282). Hillsdale, NJ: Lawrence Erlbaum Associates.

Guion, R. M. (1998). *Assessment, measurement, and prediction for personnel decisions.* San Francisco: Jossey-Bass.

Knapp, D. J., Campbell, C. H., Borman, W. C., Pulakos, E. D. & Hanson, M. A. (2001). Performance assessment for a population of jobs. In J. P. Campbell & D. J. Knapp (Eds.), *Exploring the limits in personnel selection and classification* (pp. 181–235). Mahwah, NJ: Lawrence Erlbaum Associates.

Kobrin, J., Camara, W. J., & Milewski, G. (2002). *The utility of the SAT I and SAT II for admissions decisions in California and the nation* (College Board Research Rep. No. 2002–6). New York: College Board.

Linn, R. L. (1999). Implications of standards-based reform for admissions testing. In S. Messick (Ed.), *Assessment in higher education: Issues of access, quality, student development, and public policy* (pp. 73–90). Mahwah, NJ: Lawrence Erlbaum Associates.

Linn, R. L., & Peterson, A. C. (1985). Emergence and characterization of sex differences in spatial ability: A meta-analysis. *Child Development, 56,* 1479–1498.

McHenry, J. J., Hough, L. M., Toquam, J. L., Hanson, M. A., & Ashworth, S. (1990). Project A validity results: The relationship between predictor and criterion domains. *Personnel Psychology, 42,* 335–354.

Ramist, L., Lewis, C., & McCamley-Jenkins, L. (1993). *Student group differences in predicting college grades: Sex, language and ethnic groups* (College Board Research Rep. No. 93–01). New York: College Board.

Russell, T. L., & Peterson, N. G. (2001). The experimental battery: Basic attribute scores for predicting performance in a population of jobs. In J. P. Campbell & D. J. Knapp (Eds.), *Exploring the limits in personnel selection and classification* (pp. 269–306). Mahwah, NJ: Lawrence Erlbaum Associates.

Schmidt, F. L. (2002). The role of general cognitive ability and job performance: Why there cannot be a debate. *Human Performance, 15,* 187–210.

Schmidt, F. L., Ones, D. O., & Hunter, J. E. (1992). Personnel selection. *Annual Review of Psychology, 43,* 627–670.

Schmitt, N., & Kunce, C. (2002). The effects of required elaboration of answers to noncognitive measures. *Personnel Psychology, 55,* 569–577.

Sedlacek, W. E. (1998). Admissions in higher education: Measuring cognitive and noncognitive variables. In D. J. Wilds & R. Wilson (Eds.), *Minorities in higher education 1997–98. Sixteenth annual status report* (pp. 47–71). Washington, DC: American Council on Education.

Sharf, J. C., & Jones, D. P. (1999). Employment risk management. In J. Kehoe (Ed.), *Managing selection in changing organizations: Human resource strategies* (pp. 371–385). San Francisco: Jossey-Bass.

Snow, R. E. (1999). Expanding the breadth and depth of admissions testing. In S. Messick (Ed.), *Assessment in higher education: Issues of access, quality, student development and public policy* (pp. 132–140). Mahwah, NJ: Lawrence Erlbaum Associates.

Sternberg, R. J. (1985). *Beyond IQ: A triarchic theory of human intelligence.* New York: Cambridge University Press.

Sternberg, R. J. (1997). *Successful intelligence.* New York: Plume.

Sternberg, R. J., & Hedlund, J. (2002). Practical intelligence, g, and work psychology. *Human Performance, 15,* 143–160.

Sternberg, R. J., & Rainbow Collaborators. (2003). *The rainbow project: Enhancing the SAT through assessments of analytical, practical and creative skills.* (Final report available from The College Board, New York).

Stricker, L. J. (1993). *Usefulness of noncognitive measures in the College Board's Admissions Testing Program.* Unpublished paper.

Tippins, N., & Wunder, S. (1997, April). *Entry-level management and professional selection: Best and most common practices (Are they the same?).* Workshop presented at the meeting of the Society for Industrial and Organizational Psychology, St. Louis, MO.

U.S. Department of Labor. (1970). *Manual for USES General Aptitude Test Battery.* Washington, DC: U.S. Department of Labor, U.S. Employment Service, Employment and Training Administration.

VanderStoep, S. W., Pintrich, P. R., & Fagerlin, A. (1996). Disciplinary differences in self-regulated learning in college students. *Contemporary Educational Psychology, 21,* 345–362.

Willingham, W. W. (1985). *Success in college: The role of personal qualities and academic ability.* New York: College Board.

Wise, L. L., McHenry, J., & Campbell, J. P. (1990). Identifying optimal predictor composites and testing for generalizability across jobs and performance factors. *Personnel Psychology, 43,* 355–366.

Witkin, H. A., Moore, C. A., Goodenough, D. R., & Cox, P. W. (1977). Field-dependent and field-independent cognitive styles and their educational implications. *Review of Educational Research, 47,* 1–64.

Zwick, R. (2002). *Fair game: The use of standardized admissions tests in higher education.* New York: Routledge-Falmer.

5

Broadening Predictors
of College Success

Wayne J. Camara
The College Board, New York

Research on predicting college performance focuses on the relationship of a criterion measure with either (a) tests, such as the SAT, or (b) any other predictor. There are many more studies of the former than the latter. Correlations between the SAT Verbal and Math composite with first-year college grade point average (FGPA) range from .44 to .62 (Hezlett et al., 2001). Studies show that the SAT accounts for over 30% of the variance in FGPA and an increment of about .07 to .1 over high school grade point average (HSGPA; Bridgeman, McCamley-Jenkins, & Ervin, 2000; Ramist, Lewis, & McCamley-Jenkins, 1993). Similarly, median multiple correlations between FGPA and the four ACT scores were .43 across 129 recent institutional validity studies (Maxey, 2001). Predictive validity coefficients of tests for graduate and professional are generally .3 to .4, and often exceed the validity of undergraduate GPA (Zwick, 2002). A recent meta-analysis of the predictive validity of the SAT I included approximately 3,000 studies, involving over 1 million students. The study found that this test is a valid predictor of performance early in college, with multiple correlations of SAT I Verbal and Math composite with FGPA ranging from .44 to .62 (Hezlett et al., 2001). This same study found that the SAT I is also a valid predictor of academic performance later in college (e.g., graduation, cumulative GPA) with multiple correlations ranging from the mid-30s to the mid-40s.

The story is the same for cognitive ability tests in employment screening. Schmidt and Hunter (1998) provided a historical review of research on cognitive ability tests that consistently demonstrated the highest validity for both entry-level and advanced positions across a wide range of jobs and settings, and proposed a special status for tests because of their strong theoretical and empirical foundations as the single best predictor of job performance. In their meta-analysis, they reported a validity coefficient of .51 for cognitive ability tests, accounting for about 25% of the variance in job performance. Goldstein, Zedeck, and Goldstein (2002) noted that there are two possible reactions to such consistent and overwhelming support for cognitive tests. The "case closed" approach acknowledges that cognitive tests are strong predictors of human behavior, which is incredibly complex and influenced by many factors, and ceases efforts to find additional predictors. The second possible reaction is to look for additional predictors, especially noncognitive predictors that are likely to have a low correlation with cognitive tests and may account for some of the additional 70% or 75% of unexplained variance in college success or job performance, respectively. There has been no shortage of theories or proposals for additional measures to supplement cognitive measures (admissions tests and grades). Research on noncognitive measures appears to be the most promising avenue to pursue at this time if one is interested in incremental validity, constructs that are most distinct from widely used cognitive measures, and different distributions of test takers on a wider range of abilities. However, research on noncognitive predictors is limited and often involves only small scale studies with samples of students from a single institution

A wide range of additional measures or factors have been used or proposed for college admissions. There are five general domains for such measures: (a) cognitive measures, (b) temperament, (c) personal qualities/experiences, (d) applicant characteristics, and (e) other factors. Table 5.1 illustrates these five predictor domains and specific measures. Cognitive measures include tests such as the SAT and ACT, measures of specific skills or achievement (e.g., SAT II Biology, Test of English as a Foreign Language [TOEFL]), state exit exams, and local placement or admissions tests.

High school grades, such as GPA or weighted GPA,[1] and class rank are also measures of cognitive ability. However, academic rigor or the intensity of courses completed in high school is the best predictor of attaining a bachelor's

---

[1]Many colleges report weighting GPA where honors or AP courses are given additional weight. Colleges also may recompute HSGPA excluding nonacademic courses.

degree, with the highest level of math courses completed having the greatest weight (Adelman, 1999; colleges give additional weight to grades in honors or advanced placement (AP) courses). Many specify a minimum number of academic courses required in total and specific subjects (e.g., English, mathematics, laboratory science, foreign language). Academic rigor is rarely quantified because the availability of honors and AP courses differs across schools and access to rigorous courses differs substantially across high schools. Because of the extreme variation in course offerings, grading patterns, grading policies and/or systems, and the competitiveness of the student body, it is difficult to evaluate a transcript without contextual information. These and other existing cognitive measures have been discussed in chapter 4. The next section briefly reviews some alternative measures potentially related to college success, their promise and limitations.

Noncognitive measures encompass a wide variety of constructs and measures. Temperament, personality traits, and self-appraisals comprise one broad category. Personal experiences and biographical data are a related but distinct domain of noncognitive measures. Applicant characteristics are traits associated with a student's background characteristics, such as state of residence, gender, race and/or ethnicity, and economic status. Finally, other factors include a variety of characteristics about the high school one attended and other contextual factors.

This chapter focuses on those noncognitive attributes that fall in the "Temperament/Personality" and the "Personal Qualities/Experiences" domains. However, before discussing those categories, it is important to comment briefly on the last two categories of predictor domains illustrated in Table 5.1: applicant characteristics, and other factors. Both of these categories represent a range of potential predictor measures that reflect different values in making admissions decisions. Eight models or classification schemes have been proposed to represent differing philosophical perspectives about admissions decisions among higher educational institutions (College Board, 1999). For each model, criteria such as potential to benefit (for enrollment at the institution and completion of college), overcoming adversity, or potential to contribute (to society, the community) are highly valued, whereas for other models, capacity to perform and prior accomplishments are more highly valued. Applicant qualities, such as gender, ethnicity and/or race, age, residence, military service, or ability to pay (financial need) are often used in assembling a freshmen class but would be difficult to use in a mechanistic fashion. Contextual factors, associated with the size, demographics, rigor, and competitiveness of attending high schools are also considered to some extent in comprehensive admissions processes but little research has been conducted on these factors as they relate to college

TABLE 5.1

Predictor Domains in College Admissions

Cognitive Measures			Noncognitive Scales	Personal Qualities/ Experiences and Biographical	Applicant Characteristics	Other
Tests	*HS Grades*	*HS Courses*	*Big 5 Personality Traits*	*Personal Qualities*	• Race/ethnicity	*High School Characteristics*
General Ability/ Reasoning	• Rank	• AP/IB	• Conscientiousness	• Letters of recommendation	• Economic disadvantage	• Quality of high school (e.g., number of AP/IB courses, percentage of students attending college, average SAT/ACT scores)
• SAT I	• GPA	• Honors	• Agreeableness	• Resume	• State/country of residence	
• ACT	• GPA in specific courses	• Carnegie units (CU)	• Openness	• Communication with counselors and teachers/counselor evaluation	• Health statement/physical exam	• Location of high school
Specific Ability	• Grade trajectory	• College preparatory	• Extraversion	• Portfolios/auditions	• Ability to pay/ need for financial aid	*Contextual Factors*
• SAT II: Subject Tests	• Weighted GPA	• Rigor and distribution	• Neuroticism	• Essay/personal statement	• Religion	• Institutional priorities
• TOEFL			*Self-Report*	• Interview	• Gender	• Competitiveness of applicant pool (number and quality of applicants)
• State mandated HS exit tests			• Positive self-concept	*Biographical/Experience*	• Disability	
• Minimum competency tests			• Realistic self-appraisal	• Academic honors	• Age	
			• Understands and deals with racism	• Special projects or research	• Full/part-time status	
			• Prefers long-range goals to short-term goals	• Extracurricular activities	• Declaration of major/professional diversity	
			• Successful leadership experience	• Leadership activities		
			• Community service	• Community service		
			• Knowledge acquired or in a field			

- Locally developed or admin. tests
- Placement tests (writing, reading, math)

Qualities Looked for on Application
- Motivation/initiative
- Follow through
- Moral and ethical character
- Compassion, empathy and social consciousness
- Communication skills
- Understanding of interdisciplinary study
- Intellectual curiosity
- Interest in others

- Art, athletic, music, theater, or science accomplishments
- Employment/work experience
- Fluency in another language
- Disciplinary record
- Life experiences (travel, cultural)

- Veteran/military service
- College transfer credit
- Development (fund-raising) prospects

Effect on the Individual
- Ability to benefit
- Overcome life challenges

- Early decision cycle

Other
- Legacy/Alumni recommendation
- Provost's discretion
- Nomination by U.S. representatives, congressmen, or senators (military academies)
- Random selection (lottery for those meeting minimum eligibility requirements)

success. Research on school level factors has often shown that within-school differences are greater than between-school differences. A school's economic advantage has been found to be a significant predictor of student academic performance and discrepancies between SAT scores and high-school GPA, although most of the variability between performance on these two measures is related to within-school factors (Kobrin, Milewski, Everson, & Zhou, 2003).

TEMPERAMENT, PERSONALITY, AND SELF-APPRAISAL

Personality or temperament scales measure the "will do," measures of bio-graphical experiences measure the "have done," whereas cognitive measures tap the "can do" aspects of academic and job performance. There is a range of self-report instruments that have been widely used in education to assess non-cognitive domains. The Noncognitive Questionnaire (NCQ) was developed to both assess experiential or conceptualized intelligence attributes that are likely to be more predictive of success for nontraditional students (Sedlacek, 1996, 1998). Sedlacek defines nontraditional students as those who have not received a White, middle or upper-middle class, male heterosexual, Eurocen-tric experience as their basic socialization prior to college entry (see p. 179, this volume). Several studies have been conducted with the NCQ that demon-strate adequate scale reliability and varying degrees of correlation with college success (e.g., GPA, retention, and graduation). However, there is substantial inconsistency across studies in terms of the relationship between specific scales and criterion measures, and results appear to be somewhat sample-dependent. The NCQ, as with many other measures of temperament, personality, or self-appraisal, appears easily fakable, which would appear to be a limitation if used in a high-stakes environment.

Most research on interests and values has involved small samples and a variety of criterion measures. General findings are that interests predict occu-pational membership and tenure and values are predictive of job satisfaction. Interests, values, and preferences are manifestations of personality, but dis-tinct from measures derived from personality tests and biodata. In general, stability of scores on such measures is substantially lower for adolescents than adults, and is also related to the time interval between testing. Gender differ-ences are commonly found in interests and values. These differences often necessitate the use of male or female scoring keys and normative tables for many standardized instruments (Dawis, 1991). Research has also shown that student self-reports of academic abilities and talents are significantly related to academic performance in college, but do not generally provide any incremental validity beyond direct cognitive measures of these abilities (Freeberg, Rock, & Pollack, 1989).

Extensive empirical support has been shown for the Big Five model as a unified theoretical and parsimonious framework for the study of personality in different settings with different populations (Costa & McCrae, 1994; Digman, 1997). The five personality factors are:

- Neuroticism—level of stability versus instability;
- Extraversion—tendency to be assertive, sociable, energetic, and outgoing;
- Openness—disposition to be curious, open to new and unconventional situations, and imaginative;
- Agreeableness—disposition to be cooperative, supportive, easy to get along with;
- Conscientiousness—disposition toward purposeful, determined, and goal-directed behavior.

In the past 20 years, there has been an impressive body of research demonstrating the validity of personality measures in predicting job performance criteria, and adding incremental validity beyond cognitive ability measures (Judge, Higgins, Thorensen, & Barrick, 1999; Ones, Viswesvaran, & Schmidt, 1993). Recent research has also shown that personality measures predict academic criteria such as GPA and absenteeism (Lounsbury et al., in press; Paunonen & Nicol, 2001). The criterion used is extremely important as research shows different personality traits relate to different performance and academic criteria, and ethnic and racial differences are generally minimal. Hough (1998) examined the relationship between personality constructs and criterion constructs and reported that achievement is the single best personality construct in predicting job proficiency, training school success, educational success, and counterproductive behavior. Achievement (tendency to strive for competency in work, set high standards) and adjustment (emotional stability, high stress tolerance) correlate .29 and .20, respectively, with educational success.

McHenry, Hough, Toquam, Hanson, and Ashworth (1990) reported the validity for six different predictor composites with five criterion measures of soldier performance in Project A. Table 5.2 provides the validity coefficients for these measures after correction for restriction of range and adjustments for shrinkage. A biographical and temperament/personality inventory, the Assessment of Background Life Experiences (ABLE), included scales measuring four constructs related to military performance: achievement orientation,

TABLE 5.2

Project A Validity Coefficient for Five Job-Performance Factors
and Six Predictor Domains

	Predictor Domain[a]					
Job Performance Factor	General Cognitive Ability (k = 4)[b]	Spatial Ability (k = 1)	Perceptual-Psychomotor Ability (k = 6)	Temperament/ Personality (k = 4)	Vocational Interest (k = 6)	Job Reward Preference (k = 3)
Core technical proficiency	.63	.56	.53	.26	.35	.29
General soldiering proficiency	.65	.63	.57	.25	.34	.30
Effort and leadership	.31	.25	.26	.33	.24	.19
Personal discipline	.16	.12	.12	.32	.13	.11
Physical fitness and military bearing	.20	.10	.11	.37	.12	.11

[a]Corrected for range. [b]k is the number of predictor scores.

dependability, adjustment, and physical conditions. Results demonstrate that this instrument was the best in predicting three of the five criteria: effort and leadership, personal discipline, and physical fitness and military bearing, with achievement orientation contributing the most toward predicting effort and leadership and dependability the best predictor of personal discipline. Interestingly, the vocational interest measure was superior to the ABLE in predicting core technical proficiency and general soldiering proficiency, but no predictor added more than .02 above the cognitive ability composite, ASVAB. The greatest amount of incremental validity above ASVAB was contributed by the temperament/personality composite for the later three criteria. These four measures added .11 to the validity for predicting effort and leadership, .19 for predicting personal discipline, and .21 to the validity for predicting physical fitness and military bearing. It is clear that when the criterion space is expanded to include contextual variables that are distinct from general cognitive ability, temperament and personality measures are useful additions to the predictor battery (Hough, 1998). Etienne and Julian (chap. 12, this volume) summarize some of the practical obstacles to the use of traditional personality measures in selective admissions.

Faking or intentional response distortion has been a major concern with personality inventories. Hough (1998) cited previous research showing that people can and do fake their responses, but that the decrease in validity is marginal. However, the risks of faking are significantly higher if such measures are developed for undergraduate admissions, both because of the national scope and attention placed on admissions, and the prevalence of coaching firms. An even greater challenge to personality or temperament measures would be their social acceptability and perceived relevance to admissions. Personality measures have been viewed less favorably by job applicants than cognitive ability tests, which in turn are viewed less favorably than interviews, performance tests, and biodata (Steiner & Gilliland, 1996).

PERSONAL QUALITIES/EXPERIENCES/ BIOGRAPHICAL DATA

What a person has accomplished in school and life provides important information about future performance and accomplishments. Because there is consistency in one's behaviors, attitudes, and values, measures of these factors should predict such future experiences. Research on biodata has demonstrated that it is successful in predicting a range of criteria related to job performance and that the criterion variance predicted is not redundant with variance predicted by other measures (Mount, Witt, & Barrick, 2000; Muchinsky, 2003). According to Mitchell (1994), biodata has the potential of "improving the validity and fairness of personnel selection programs, while at the same time decreasing the adverse impact of those programs" (pp. 486–487). Biodata scales have also been shown to predict military performance. The work orientation and leadership scales correlated .40 and .33, respectively, with observed performance (Ford, Knapp, Campbell, Campbell, & Walker, 2000). Research in education has shown that accomplishments early in one's school career (e.g., high school) predict accomplishments in the later stages of one's school career (e.g., college) and even after leaving college, with minimal overlap with other predictors such as admissions tests, high-school grades, personality, and interest measures (ACT, 1973; Stricker, Rock, & Bennett, 2001). Willingham and Breland (1982) reported that empirically keyed biographical inventories and nonacademic accomplishments are correlated with academic and nonacademic criteria in college. Empirical keying approaches have generally been replaced by more construct-oriented scoring keys, and items on biodata inventories are often indistinguishable from those on personality tests (Schmitt, Jennings, & Toney, 1999).

The Personal Qualities Project conducted between 1978 and 1984 is still the most ambitious attempt to determine the relationship between 140 predictors and 27 criterion measures of college success (Willingham, 1985). Of the 4,814 freshmen at nine universities who participated in the study, 3,676 (76%) were still enrolled in the fourth year. The study examined the following predictors taken from the student application and admissions folder:

- Application—interviewed, sent work sample, aid applied for, aid offered, and so forth;
- Academic Achievement—high school rank, SAT or ACT scores, valedictorian, academic composite, academic honors;
- Personal Achievement (5-point ratings by research staff based on application information)—community activities, athletic achievement, leadership, creative talent, work level, personal statement, teacher references, and so forth;
- Background—age, ethnicity, state of residence, distance from home, school size, parental education, parental occupation, alumni ties, and so forth;
- College Ratings (scored 0–1, if present)—talent in music, art, literary pursuits, athletics; overcame hardships, significant work experience, rich experiences, important school or community ties, academic rating, educational goals, practical skills, leadership training, and so forth;
- Students' Reasons for Applying—academic reputation, academic program, location, school advice, social atmosphere, and so forth;
- Educational/Career Interests—degree plans, intended major, statement, career interest, and so forth;
- Freshman Experience and Performance (data collected during freshman year)—spring semester goals, FGPA, peer nomination, and so forth.

The 27 criterion measures included traditional criteria such as GPA (first-, second-, third-, fourth-year and CGPA), persistence to senior year, time to graduation, and admission to a graduate or professional program. In addition, 10 areas of accomplishment were classified as scholarship, leadership, or special accomplishments (e.g., artistic and communications). Forty-four percent of students did not receive credit for any of these accomplishments, while 30% received credit for scholarship, 35% received credit for leadership, and 24% received credit for special accomplishments. Scholarship, leadership, and special accomplishments were moderately correlated ($r = .25$ to $.35$) with nearly half the students in any one group also represented in each of the two other success groups.

High school rank and SAT scores were by far the best predictors of academic success in college, with high school rank a somewhat superior predictor of college honors and SAT scores a somewhat better predictor of departmental honors. The inclusion of four additional measures adds only .03 to the prediction of lower and upper level college GPA beyond what high-school rank and SAT provided. A composite criteria of college success was developed at each college by a faculty committee that identified successful students. Once high-school performance and SAT scores were considered, four additional measures added to the prediction of college success: (a) follow-through (persistent effort and achievement in several extracurricular activities), (b) high school honors, (c) well-written essays, and (d) strength of high-school essays. Together, these four measures accounted for an additional 25% of variance above SAT and high-school grades in identifying students that college faculty members perceive as most successful. These measures also made substantial incremental contributions when special accomplishments and leadership were the criterion measure, but increased the prediction of scholarship by only 7%. It is also worth noting that scholarship was much more predictable than other criteria ($R^2 = .61$ vs. .33 to .45 for the other three criterion measures). Follow through, a rating of two instances of multiyear involvement in an activity with achievement and advancement, had the largest regression weight among all six predictors for leadership and special accomplishment, and the second largest weight for students most likely to be successful.

Stricker (1993) proposed development of a variation of biodata inventories for graduate and undergraduate admissions. He proposed standardized measures that would identify students with unusual talents or accomplishments in a variety of areas (e.g., leadership, arts, science, social service). He noted that biodata have greater validity than personality tests, are more acceptable because items concern factual matters, making them less intrusive than personality tests, and are perceived as fairer because the behaviors are under an examinee's control. To minimize attempts at faking or response distortion, he proposed asking students to report factually verifiable information in a combination of multiple-choice and open-ended items. Gillespie, Kim, Oswald, Ramsay, and Schmitt (2002) developed a biodata inventory composed of multiple-choice questions about students' previous experiences and activities, as well as 21 items that required elaboration. Elaborated items have been shown to lower scores on biodata instruments in employment settings (Schmitt & Kunce, 2002). An example of a biodata item requesting elaboration follows (Gillespie et al., 2002):

In the past 6 months, how often did you read a book just to learn something?
   a. never
   b. once
   c. twice
   d. three or four times
   e. five times or more
If you answered b, c, d, or e, please list the books you read (do not list over five).

During the period from 1979 to 2000, approximately 75% to 85% percent of 4-year private colleges reported that motivation, leadership experiences, community or church involvement, extracurricular activities, and compatibility have often or sometimes been treated as important factors in admissions (Breland, Maxey, Gernard, Cummings, & Trapani, 2002). About 40% to 57% of 4-year public institutions similarly view these as often or sometimes important factors in admissions.

A major concern with using personal qualities, experiences, and biodata is their susceptibility to distortion by a student who is motivated to present his or her best side. Intentional response distortion has been found to occur more frequently with job applicants than with job incumbents (Kluger, Reilly, & Russell, 1991). Zwick (2002) argued that if Sedlacek's Noncognitive Questionnaire (NCQ) were actually used in admissions, several items appear easy to fake, such as "I want a chance to prove myself academically" or "My high school grades don't really reflect what I can do." Applicants are able to exaggerate their qualifications and experiences to appear more qualified, and coaching leads to even greater score inflation, and a reduction in validity in some instances (White, Young, & Rumsey, 2001). Items that are verifiable, objective, and appear relevant to college success would be the least susceptible to faking. However, using any of these standardized measures in large-scale undergraduate admissions presents unique challenges that have not been encountered at the same scale in employment selection. Self-report inventories generally have one or two forms, and items could be easily compromised if they were standardized on a nationally available inventory. The impact of coaching and deceptive practices would need to be considered. In education, cognitive ability tests have similarly been viewed as less favorable than grades and records of accomplishments, but Gillespie et al. (2002) reported that college students in all ethnic and racial groups were less favorable about biodata and situational judgment inventories than either grades or admissions test scores.

SITUATIONAL JUDGMENT INVENTORY (SJI)

The SJI, which poses hypothetical situations or problems and asks the respondent to choose or rate among possible response options, was also developed for the Gillespie et al. (2002) study. SJIs are highly contextualized tasks, and unlike personality tests and biodata instruments, they are almost always multidimensional and not pure measures of traits, accomplishments, or past experience (Borman & Motowildo, 1993; Chan & Schmitt, 1997). SJIs possess moderate levels of validity with job performance, above and beyond general cognitive ability, a high degree of face validity and acceptability, and are relatively easy to develop and administer (Clevenger, Pereira, Wiechmann, Schmitt, & Harvey, 2001).

In a recent study (reported in chap. 11, this volume) of biodata and SJIs conducted with college freshmen, criteria such as FGPA and class attendance were correlated with the following 12 dimensions of college success that had been identified from statements of college goals and mission statements (Gillespie et al., 2002): knowledge, continuous learning, artistic appreciation, multicultural tolerance, leadership, interpersonal skills, community involvement, physical and psychological health, career orientation, adaptability, perseverance, ethics, and integrity. These were correlated with a number of traditional criteria, for example, FGPA, and several newly developed predictors. Empirically keyed biodata scales exhibited low correlations with admission test scores; biodata and SJI scales offered significant incremental validity over admission test and personality tests in predicting FGPA ($R^2 = .061$ for biodata, .039 for SJIs, and .082 for both combined) and absenteeism ($R^2 = .098$ for biodata, .117 for SJIs, and .170 for both combined). Several biodata scales also did reasonably well in predicting class attendance ($r = .15$ to .31). In the same study, the relationship of these predictors to the same 12 dimensions of college involvement and an overall measure of college involvement was examined (Friede et al., 2003). Biodata added incremental validity to the prediction of commitment and involvement for 9 of the 12 dimensions.

A variation of SJIs, where students rated six options for handling a difficult video-based situation or problem, was also a component of the cross-college study conducted by Sternberg and colleagues (2003). This measure alone correlated .14 with FGPA, but was only marginally significant in predicting FGPA in combination with two paper-based measures of practical abilities. Sternberg et al. (2003) notes that high school grades may already capture much of the practical skills contained in such measures, and nonacademic criteria may be more successful.

INTERVIEWS, PERSONAL STATEMENTS
AND RECOMMENDATIONS

Colleges use a variety of other predictors such as personal interviews, student statements, and school recommendations. These methods are addressed only briefly in terms of enhancements that could increase their utility for admissions. An interview is optional for many colleges and appears to be used to encourage students to visit the campus and learn more about the institution, and as a general measure of student interest (Rigol, 2003). These interviews are often referred to as "informational" interviews, in contrast to admissions interviews that are used for evaluative purposes. A smaller number of colleges encourage students to participate in an evaluative interview as part of the admissions process, and some competitive or specialized programs (e.g., nursing or architecture) require interviews, often with faculty members.

Evaluative interviews are generally unstructured and serve two purposes (Breland et al., 2002). First, they provide the admissions officer an opportunity to directly observe a rather limited sample of behavior manifested during the interview. Because admissions is concerned with both attracting and selecting students, interviews are generally conducted by a single interviewer, and attempts are made to reduce stress on the student. Second, even evaluative interviews often devote substantial time to "selling" the institution to the student and providing information. Unstructured interviews provide an opportunity to convey information about an institution, its values, and climate (Dipboye, 1997). However, admissions officers can clearly evaluate a student's interest in the institution, a student's academic and nonacademic goals, oral communication and listening skills, and general demeanor during informal interviews. Questions can also clarify ambiguous or unclear entries on an application. Willingham and Breland (1982) reported that coming to campus for an interview did not enhance the probability of admissions for students, but in some colleges, those few students who succeeded in having an outstanding interview did get a clear preference. They also found that 4 years later, there was no evidence that these students performed any better than predicted with high-school rank and SAT scores on any of four criteria (scholarship, leadership, special accomplishments, or students selected as most successful).

Personal statements are required by increasing numbers of colleges and universities, with supplemental essays generally required for consideration for honors programs and special scholarship programs (Rigol, 2003). Wickenden (1982) noted that such statements serve two purposes in undergraduate admissions: to permit elaboration of some particular important aspects of a student's life (e.g., overcoming adversity, special talent, or life experiences) and as an indication of writing ability. Personal statements are typically open prompts that permit a student a choice of topics on which to write. For example, the personal statement from the common application in 2002–2003 asked for a 250–500 word essay on any of five topics:

1. *Evaluate a significant experience, achievement, risk you have taken, or ethical dilemma you faced and its impact on you.*

2. *Discuss some issues of personal, local, national, or international concern and its importance to you.*

3. *Indicate a person who has had a significant influence on you, and describe that influence.*

4. *Describe a character in a fiction, an historical figure, or a creative work (as in art, music, science, etc.) that has had an influence on you.*

5. *Topic of your choice.*

Colleges differ in how the personal statement is evaluated. At some institutions, the statements are evaluated holistically, with guidelines similar to those used in scoring essays in tests such as SAT II: Writing. Rigol (2003) notes that at least one institution from her study of admissions practices has a separately trained group of readers who evaluate essays apart from the overall application review. An example of criteria used to score a personal statement follows:

Instructions to readers: The essay should be judged on mechanics, style, and content. Your ratings for this category should reflect the writer's ability to organize his/her thoughts in relation to the topic answered. Short answer responses from elsewhere in the application may also be considered in this rating.

1. *Short—No effort, inarticulate, poor grammar.*

2. *Superficial—Token effort. May be grammatically sound, but has no substance, no insight into the writer.*

3. *Typical essay—Effort and sincerity evident. No masterpiece, but obvious thought put into essay. While it may not be unique or special, writer comes across as interesting.*

4. *Very well written—Flows. Person may write about the typical topics but does it better than most. Does something a little different or creative and does it well. Essay enables you to get to know the applicant better.*

5. *Extremely well written—Creative, original, memorable. You want to share it with the rest of the staff.* (Rigol, 2003, p. 30)

Willingham and Breland (1982) reported that students whose personal statements were especially well written obtained FGPAs that were slightly higher than predicted from SAT scores and class rank, with similar results found with respect to the content (as opposed to the writing quality). Nearly 60% of students participating in a study of graduate admissions admitted receiving help in editing and revising their personal statements, with 34% receiving moderate or substantial help. Thirty-six percent revealed they received assistance in drafting their statements, and only 38% said they receive no assistance of any kind (Powers & Fowles, 1997). The correlation between personal statements and GRE test essays was .15, showing that the two writing samples are not equivalent. The test essay had substantially higher correlations than the personal statement with most outcome measures (e.g., average grade in writing courses, grade on most recent writing assignment, documentable accomplishments in writing, professor-graded writing sample, etc.). These findings suggest that the addition of an essay on the SAT or GRE may increase the predictive validity of those tests, but may be of little utility in verifying the writing skills found in the personal statement. Powers and Fowles (1997) concluded that "personal statements may not be trustworthy indicators of writing skill because they represent contributions other than just those of applicants" (p. 84). Although the personal statement may provide some unique information about applicants, its validity as an indicator of writing skills still needs to be established. Willingham and Breland's (1982) conclusion that personal essays have rarely been used for predicting college success in any formal validation study remains relevant today.

Although providing a choice of topics to students is both less threatening and more likely to elicit information on important personal qualities and experiences of students, it only increases the difficulty of comparing essays across students in any quantitative or standardized manner. Research conducted on AP examinations demonstrated that differential difficulty among topics masks the effects of examinee choice and that there is a substantial amount of variation around these averages (Allen, Holland, & Thayer, 2003). Differences in topic difficulty, as well as the interaction of topic and student, are sources of unwanted variance that must be considered when comparing student performance across different topics or tasks.

Standardizing topics, eliminating choice, providing training to readers, and asking students to what extent they had assistance in drafting and revising their statements are all suggestions that could increase the validity of the personal statement, but they may reduce student spontaneity and elaboration of their own interests and personal qualities. In summary, personal qualities serve a useful purpose in providing admissions officers with insight into the applicant as a student and person. Additional attempts to increase the validity and utility of such predictors might be better devoted to creating additional measures.

Letters of recommendation and personal statements have been consistently viewed as moderately important (more important than interviews, state of residence, and portfolios, but less important than HSGPA and admissions test scores for undergraduate admissions; Breland et al., 2002). There have been few studies of school recommendations and references. One study found that school references correlated with lower and upper division college grades at .14 and .13, respectively, but added little to the prediction after high-school grades and SAT scores were considered (Willingham, 1985). In employment testing, Muchinsky (2003) states that references are "one of the most commonly used and least valid predictors" (p. 124). Correlations ranging from −.10 to .29 were found between recommendations and supervisor ratings across several occupational areas, and recommendations from relatives, human resources, and co-workers had the lowest correlations (Mosel & Goheen, 1959). Restriction of range is a significant problem with such measures because applicants (both to college and to the work world) select their references, and it is not surprising to find most letters to be highly positive.

THE IMPACT OF USING MULTIPLE MEASURES ON VALIDITY, DIVERSITY, AND ACCEPTABILITY

There is a substantial body of research demonstrating that using admissions test scores in combination with a measure of high-school grades (HSGPA or rank) produces higher validity coefficients than using either measure alone (Bridgeman et al., 2000; Kobrin, Camara, & Milewski, 2002; Noble & Sawyer, 2002; Ramist et al., 1993; Willingham, 1998; Zwick, 2002). Whitney (1989) offered some general conclusions about the validity of admissions predictors:

> at the undergraduate level for general-admissions purposes, both prior academic record and admissions-test scores are useful in predicting college grades, with neither consistently better than the other. The combination of scores and prior grades yields more accurate predictions of college grades than does either alone. (p. 520)

Additional predictors have substantially less impact on validity coefficients once high school performance and admissions tests are employed. Research has shown that the addition of three SAT II subject tests adds between .00 and .03 to the validity coefficient once SAT I and HSGPA are considered for each ethnic and/or racial group (Kobrin et al., 2002). Similar results emerge when non-cognitive predictors are used. Results from the personal qualities study (Willingham, 1985) demonstrated that the addition of high-school honors courses, follow through, personal statements, and school references only increased the multiple correlation by .03 above high school rank and SAT scores. As noted earlier, the inclusion of several additional predictors only increased the multiple correlation between ASVAB and military performance by .02 (McHenry et al., 1990). The predictive utility of new measures and noncognitive predictors will likely be limited as long as cognitively loaded performance (e.g., GPA) is used as the sole criterion. For example, productive follow through was found to be substantially inferior to the SAT and high-school grades in predicting college success in the Personal Qualities Study, yet it did provide incremental validity over these measures when used in combination (Willingham, 1985). Alternative predictors such as biodata, SJIs, personality tests, or student essays are more effective in accounting for additional variance when a wider band of criterion measures, including accomplishments, is employed (Campbell, Kuncel, & Oswald, 1998; Gillespie et al., 2002; McHenry et al., 1990).

If additional measures have limited utility in improving prediction with currently available criteria, why has so much effort been devoted to research on expanding predictors in education as well as employment selection? One very salient reason for the enthusiasm in pursuing alternative predictors has been the prospect that they may increase diversity. Ethnic and racial differences are repeatedly observed in scores on standardized knowledge, skill, ability, and achievement tests. African American and Hispanics score, respectively, approximately one standard deviation and two thirds of a standard deviation lower than whites (J. E. Hunter & R. F. Hunter, 1984; Pulakos & Schmitt, 1996; Sackett, Schmitt, Ellingson, & Kabin, 2001; Zwick, 2002). Similar differences are found on performance assessments in education (Camara & Schmidt, 1999; Dunbar, Koretz, & Hoover, 1991; Linn, Baker, & Dunbar, 1991). Differences between ethnic and racial groups are found on high-school and college grades, although the magnitude of the differences, especially for high-school grades, are somewhat smaller than those on cognitive ability tests (Camara & Schmidt, 1999; Willingham, 1998). Hough, Oswald, and Ployhart (2001) reported that although measures of general cognitive ability in industry have the same standardized mean-score differences, measures of some cognitive constructs have somewhat smaller differences. For example, differences between African Americans and Whites on tasks of memory, mental processing speed, spatial ability, and quantitative ability are noticeably smaller.

A variety of predictors used in education and employment screening have been shown to exhibit less subgroup differences than cognitive ability tests and still have a moderate correlation with relevant performance outcomes (Ryan, Ployhart, & Friedel, 1998; Sackett & Wilk, 1994; Schmitt, Rogers, Chan, Sheppard, & Jennings, 1997; Sedlacek, 1998). Standardized differences ranging from $d = .15$ to $.25$ have been found in several studies of personality tests, biodata, and interviews (Hough et al., 2001). Despite the fact that many cognitive ability tests produce three to five times the adverse impact found in many noncognitive measures, most research has focused on supplementing, rather than substituting, tests results with these measures.

Several studies have attempted to quantify the reduction in adverse impact when multiple measures having substantially less adverse impact are used with cognitive ability tests. Sackett and Wilk (1994) examined the simple effects of combining a test with a large subgroup difference (i.e., SD of 1, $d = 1.0$) and a second predictor on which no subgroup difference existed ($d = 0.0$). If these two predictors were equally valid and uncorrelated with each other, the subgroup difference resulting from an equally weighted predictor composite would be .71, not .50 as many might anticipate. Schmitt et al. (1997) used meta-analysis to estimate validities and subgroup differences for biodata, personality, structured interviews, and cognitive ability tests. They found that when all four measures were used, adverse impact occurred except when the vast majority of applicants were admitted. However, as each subsequent predictor was added, the reduction in d decreases, reaching a point of diminishing return. The addition of three measures with low subgroup differences enhanced the overall validity but had a less than dramatic impact on subgroup differences, and in some situations, the subgroup differences could exceed that of the cognitive test alone (see chap. 6, this volume).

Combining a cognitive test with a noncognitive predictor having substantially less adverse impact could result in a predictor composite having a larger difference than either predictor because it reflects a more reliable measure of the underlying construct (Sackett et al., 2001). When predictors are combined, subgroup differences are generally more likely to be reduced when the additional predictors have a high validity, low or no correlations with the cognitive test, and little or no subgroup differences.

CRITERIA FOR ADMISSIONS MEASURES

A large number of alternative predictors and measures have been suggested by educators and researchers throughout this volume and in other venues. However, any thoughtful discussion of additional predictors should be reviewed against criteria that can be used to evaluate their utility, appropriateness, and

TABLE 5.3

Suggested Criteria for Evaluating Admissions Measures

Commission on New Possibilities (1990)	Willingham (1985)	Ford et al. (2000)
✓ Predictive validity	✓ Predictive validity	✓ Criterion-related validity
✓ Content relevance	✓ Content relevance	✓ Reliability
✓ Instrctional relevance	✓ Scoring consistency	✓ Consistency in adminis-
✓ Reliable	✓ Content fair to all groups	tration and scoring
✓ Scoreable	✓ Fair to disabled students	✓ Test fairness
✓ Fair	✓ Administrative feasibility	✓ Utility
✓ Practical and usable	✓ Generalizable	✓ Useful for prediction
✓ Efficient for delivery in	✓ Reasonable costs	✓ Operational costs
scores	✓ Coachable	✓ Face validity/applicant
✓ Generalizable	✓ Acceptable	acceptable
✓ Versatile	✓ Group difference similar	✓ Group score differences
	to criterion measures	✓ Differential validity
	✓ Differential item function-	✓ Resistance to
	ing not a problem	compromise
	✓ Development feasibility	✓ Construct validity
	✓ Ethical constraints (no	✓ Consequential validity
	deception)	✓ Generality
	✓ Content fair	
	✓ Minimize risks (untested	
	methods)	
	✓ Education value	

promise for higher education. Chapter 4 focused on expanding the available criteria of college success. However, there are other predictor characteristics to be considered. In 1990, a blue ribbon commission issued a report entitled *Beyond Prediction* that outlined a set of recommendations for changes to the SAT testing program, which included proposed criteria for evaluating changes or additions to the SAT (Commission on New Possibilities for the Admissions Testing Program, 1990). They proposed the following criteria for any admissions predictor: (a) predict college success, (b) content and instructionally relevant, (c) reliable and scoreable, (d) fair, (e) practical, efficient, and able to be delivered in high schools, (f) generalizable, and (g) versatile and usable. These criteria appear to emphasize the objective and practical aspects of any predictor. Willingham (1985) developed a more extensive list of criteria for evaluating the utility of predictors of college success that recognizes the importance of the criteria proposed by *Beyond Prediction*, but adds criteria such as acceptability, group-score differences, coachability, administrative feasibility, developmental feasibility, ethical constraints, costs, risks, and educational value. Some of these criteria are of greater concern when examining some of the new measures or predictors that have been proposed for higher education. Finally, Ford, Knapp, J. P. Campbell, R. C. Campbell, & Walker (2000) identified 15 criteria for assessment instruments and methods for 21st-century soldiers and noncommissioned officers, which included many of the aforementioned factors, but added resistance to compromise (measure cannot be easily leaked to or faked by examinees), consequential validity, generality (measures a broad construct), and discriminability (measure has sufficient score range and variance). Table 5.3 provides an overview of these proposed criteria for evaluating predictors.

REFERENCES

ACT. (1973). *Assessing students on the way to college—Technical report for the ACT Assessment program* (Vol. 1). Iowa City, IA: ACT.

Adelman, C. (1999). *Answers in the Tool Box: Academic intensity, attendance patterns and bachelor's degree attainment.* Washington, DC: U.S. Department of Education, Office of Educational Research and Improvement.

Allen, N., Holland, P., & Thayer, D. (2003). *Measuring the benefits of examinee selected questions.* Manuscript in preparation.

Borman, W. C., & Motowildo, S. J. (1993). Expanding the criterion domain to include elements of contextual performance. In N. Schmitt & W. Borman (Eds.), *Personnel selection in organizations* (pp. 71–98). San Francisco, CA: Jossey-Bass.

Breland, H., Maxey, J., Gernard, R., Cummings, T., & Trapani, C. (2002). *Trends in college admissions: A report of a survey of undergraduate admissions policies, practices, and procedures.* ACT, AIR, College Board, Educational Testing Service, National Association of Collegiate Admissions Counselors.

Bridgeman, B., McCamley-Jenkins, L., & Ervin, N. (2000). *Predictions of freshman grade-point average from the revised and recentered SAT I Reasoning test* (College Board Research Rep. No. 2000–1). New York: The College Board.

Camara, W. J., & Schmidt, A. E. (1999). *Group differences in standardized testing and social stratification* (College Board Research Rep. No. 99–5). New York: The College Board.

Campbell, J., Kuncel, N. R., & Oswald, F. L. (1998, April). *Predicting performance in graduate school: The criterion problem.* Paper presented at the Society of Industrial and Organizational Psychologists, Dallas, TX.

Chan, D., & Schmitt, N. (1997). Video-based versus paper-and-pencil method of assessment in situational judgment tests; Subgroup differences in test performance and face validity perceptions. *Journal of Applied Psychology, 82,* 143–159.

Clevenger, J., Pereira, G. M., Wiechmann, D., Schmitt, N., & Harvey, V. S. (2001). Incremental validity of situational judgment tests. *Journal of Applied Psychology, 86,* 410–417.

College Board. (1999). *Toward a taxonomy of the admissions decision-making process.* New York: Author.

Commission on New Possibilities for the Admissions Testing Program. (1990). *Beyond prediction.* New York: The College Board.

Costa, P. T., & McCrae, R. R. (1994). Stability and change in personality from adolescence through adulthood. In C. F. Halverson, Jr., G. A. Kohnmstamm, & R. P. Martin (Eds.), *The developing structure of temperament and personality from infancy to adulthood* (pp. 139–155). Hillsdale, NJ: Lawrence Erlbaum Associates.

Dawis, R. V. (1991). Vocational interests, values and preferences. In M. D. Dunnette & L. M. Hough (Eds.), *Handbook of industrial & organizational psychology* (2nd ed., Vol. II, pp. 833–871). Palo Alto, CA: Consulting Psychologists Press.

Digman, J. (1997). Higher order factors of the Big Five. *Journal of Personality and Social Psychology, 73,* 1246–1256.

Dipboye, R. (1997). Structured selection interviews: Why do they work? Why are they underutilized? In N. Anderson & P. Herriot (Eds.), *International handbook of selection and assessment* (pp. 455–473). Chichester, England: Wiley.

Dunbar, S. B., Koretz, D. M., & Hoover, H. D. (1991). Quality control in the development and use of performance assessments. *Applied Measurement in Education, 4,* 289–303.

Ford, L. A., Knapp, D. J., Campbell, J. P., Campbell, R. C., & Walker, C. B. (2000). *21st Century soldier and noncommissioned officers: Critical predictors of performance* (Tech. Rep. No. 1102). Alexandria, VA: U.S. Army Research Institute for the Behavioral and Social Sciences.

Freeberg, N. E., Rock, D. A., & Pollack, J. (1989). *Analysis of the revised student descriptive questionnaire: Phase II predictive validity of academic self report* (College Board Research Rep. No. 89–8). New York: The College Board.

Gillespie, M., Kim, B., Oswald, F., Ramsay, L., & Schmitt, N. (2002). *Biodata and situational judgment inventories as measures of college success: Developing and pilot testing phases* (Interim Report available from The College Board, New York).

Goldstein, H. W., Zedeck, S., & Goldstein, I. L. (2002). G: Is this your final answer. *Human Performance, 15,* 123–142.

Hezlett, S. A., Kuncel, N., Vey, M. A., Ahart, A. M., Ones, D. S., Campbell, J. P., & Camara, W. J. (2001, April). *The effectiveness of the SAT in predicting success early and late in college: A comprehensive meta-analysis.* Paper presented at the National Council of Measurement in Education, Seattle, WA.

Hough, L. M. (1998). Personality at work: Issues and evidence. In M. Hakel (Ed.), *Beyond multiple-choice: Evaluating alternatives to traditional testing for selection* (pp. 131–166). Mahwah, NJ: Lawrence Erlbaum Associates.

Hough, L. M., Oswald, F. L., & Ployhart, R. E. (2001). Determinants, detection and amelioration of adverse impact in personnel selection procedures: Issues, evidence and lessons learned. *International Journal of Selection and Assessment, 9,* 152–194.

Hunter, J. E., & Hunter, R. F. (1984). Validity and utility of alternative predictors of job performance. *Psychological Bulletin, 96,* 72–98.

Judge, T. A., Higgins, C. A., Thorensen, C. J., & Barrick, M. R. (1999). The Big Five personality traits, general mental ability and career success cross the life span. *Personnel Psychology, 52*, 621–652.

Kluger, A. N., Reilly, R. R., & Russell, C. J. (1991). Faking biodata tests: Are option-keyed instruments more resistant? *Journal of Applied Psychology, 76*, 889–896.

Kobrin, J. L., Camara, W. J., & Milewski, G. (2002). *The utility of the SAT I and SAT II for admissions decisions in California and the nation* (College Board Research Rep. No. 2002–6). New York: The College Board.

Kobrin, J. L., Milewski, G. B., Everson, H., & Zhou, Y. (2003, April). *An investigation of school-level factors for students with discrepant high school GPA and SAT scores.* Paper presented at the Annual Meeting of the National Council on Measurement in Education, Chicago, IL.

Linn, R. L., Baker, E. L., & Dunbar, S. B. (1991). Complex performance-based assessment: Expectations and validity criteria. *Educational Researcher, 20*, 15–21.

Lounsbury, J. W., Lovejoy, J. M., Sundstrom, E. D., Gibson, L. W., Drost, A. W., & Hamrick, F. L. (in press). An investigation of personality traits in relation to career satisfaction. *Journal of Career Assessment.*

Maxey, J. (2001). *Selected trends in ACT-Tested Students.* Unpublished manuscript. Iowa City, IA: ACT, Inc.

McHenry, J. J., Hough, L. M., Toquam, J. L., Hanson, M. A., & Ashworth, S. (1990). Project A validity results: The relationship between predictor and criterion domains. *Personnel Psychology, 42*, 335–354.

Mitchell, T. W. (1994). The utility of biodata. In G. S. Stokes, M. D. Mumford, & W. A. Owens (Eds.), *Biodata handbook* (pp. 486–516). Palo Alto, CA: Consulting Psychologists Press.

Mosel, J. N., & Goheen, H. W. (1959). The employment recommendation questionnaire: Validity of different types of references. *Personnel Psychology, 12*, 469–477.

Mount, M. K., Witt, L. A., & Barrick, M. R. (2000). Incremental validity of empirically keyed biodata scales over GMA and the five factor personality constructs. *Personnel Psychology, 53*, 299–323.

Muchinsky, P. M. (2003). Predictors: Psychology assessments. In P. M. Muchinsky (Ed.), *Psychology applied to work* (7th ed., pp. 89–135). Belmont, CA: Wadsworth Publishing/Thomson Learning.

Noble, J., & Sawyer, R. (2002). *Predicting different levels of academic success in college using high school GPA and ACT composite score* (ACT Research Rep. No. 2002–4). Iowa City, IA: ACT, Inc.

Ones, D. S., Viswesvaran, C., & Schmidt, F. S. (1993). Comprehensive meta-analysis of integrity test validities: Findings and implications from personnel selection and theories of job performance. *Journal of Applied Psychology, 78*, 679–703.

Paunonen, S. V., & Nicol, A. M. (2001). The personality hierarchy and the prediction of work behaviors. In B. W. Roberts & R. Hogan (Eds.), *Personality psychology in the workplace* (pp. 161–191). Washington, DC: American Psychological Association.

Powers, D. E., & Fowles, M. E. (1997). The personal statement as an indicator of writing skill: A cautionary note. *Educational Assessment, 4*, 75–87.

Pulakos, E. D., & Schmitt, N. (1996). An evaluation of two strategies for reducing adverse impact and their effects on criterion-related validity. *Human Performance, 9*, 241–258.

Ramist, L., Lewis, C., & McCamley-Jenkins, L. (1993). *Student group differences in predicting college grades: Sex, language and ethnic groups* (College Board Research Rep. No. 93–01). New York: The College Board.

Rigol, G. (2003). *Admissions decision-making models: How U.S. institutions of higher education select undergraduate students.* New York: The College Board.

Ryan, A. M., Ployhart, R. E., & Friedel, L. A. (1998). Using personality testing to reduce adverse impact: A cautionary note. *Journal of Applied Psychology, 83*, 298–307.

Sackett, P., Schmitt, N., Ellingson, J. E., & Kabin, M. B. (2001). High-stakes testing in employment, credentialing and higher education: Prospects in a post-affirmative action world. *American Psychologist, 56*, 302–318.

Sackett, P. R., & Wilk, S. L. (1994). Within-group norming and other forms of score adjustment in pre-employment testing. *American Psychologist, 49*, 929–954.

Schmidt, F. L., & Hunter, J. E. (1998). The validity and utility of selection methods in personnel psychology: Practical and theoretical implications of 85 years of research findings. *Psychological Bulletin, 124*, 262–274.

Schmitt, N., Jennings, D., & Toney, R. (1999). Can we develop measures of hypothetical constructs? *Human Resources Management Review, 9*, 169–184.

Schmitt, N., & Kunce, C. (2002). The effects of required elaboration of answers to noncognitive measures. *Personnel Psychology, 55*, 569–577.

Schmitt, N., Rogers, W., Chan, D., Sheppard, L., & Jennings, D. (1997). Adverse impact and predictive efficiency of various predictor combinations. *Journal of Applied Psychology, 82*, 719–730.

Sedlacek, W. E. (1996). An empirical method of determining nontraditional group status. *Measurement and Evaluation in Counseling and Development, 28*, 200–210.

Sedlacek, W. E. (1998). Admissions in higher education: Measuring cognitive and noncognitive variables. In D. J. Wilds & R. Wilson (Eds.), *Minorities in higher education 1997–98. Sixteenth annual status report* (pp. 47–71). Washington, DC: American Council on Education,.

Steiner, D. D., & Gilliland, S. W. (1996). Fairness reactions to personnel selection techniques in France and the United States. *Journal of Applied Psychology, 81*, 134–141.

Sternberg, R. J., & Rainbow Collaborators. (2003). *The rainbow project: Enhancing the SAT through assessments of analytical, practical and creative skills.* (Final Report available from The College Board, New York).

Stricker, L. J. (1993). *Usefulness of noncognitive measures in the College Board's Admissions Testing Program.* Unpublished manuscript.

Stricker, L. J., Rock, D. A., & Bennett, R. E. (2001). Sex and ethnic differences on accomplishments measures. *Applied Measurement in Education, 14*, 205–218.

White, L. A., Young, M. C., & Rumsey, M. G. (2001). ABLE Implementation issues and related research. In J. P. Campbell & D. J. Knapp (Eds.), *Exploring the limits in personnel selection and classification* (pp. 525–558). Mahwah, NJ: Lawrence Erlbaum Associates.

Whitney, D. R. (1989). Educational admissions and placement. In R. L. Linn (Ed.), *Educational measurement* (3rd ed., pp. 515–525). New York: Macmillan.

Wickenden, J. W. (1982). Open letter to college students applying to competitive colleges. In H. C. Hegener (Ed.), *The competitive colleges: Who are they? Where are they? What are they like?* (ix–xvii). Princeton, NJ: Peterson's Guides.

Willingham, W. W. (1985). *Success in college: The role of personal qualities and academic ability.* New York: The College Board.

Willingham, W. W. (1998, December). *Validity in college selection: Context and evidence.* Prepared for a workshop on the role of tests in higher education admissions sponsored by the National Research Council, Washington, DC.

Willingham, W. W., & Breland, H. M. (1982). *Personal qualities and college admissions.* New York: The College Board.

Zwick, R. (2002). *Fair game: The use of standardized admissions tests in higher education.* New York: Routledge-Falmer.

II

Improving Current Practice

6

The Performance–
Diversity Tradeoff
in Admission Testing

Paul R. Sackett
University of Minnesota

I write this chapter as a researcher whose work has examined issues of validity and diversity in the context of pre-employment testing. I note that there are many commonalities between the educational admissions, employment testing, and professional licensure and certification domains, and believe that research findings from each of these domains are useful for the other.

As noted by Sackett, Schmitt, Ellingson, and Kabin (2001), the use of standardized tests in the knowledge, skill, ability, and achievement domains for the purpose of high-stakes decision making in employment, credentialing, and educational admissions has a history characterized by three dominant features. First, extensive research has demonstrated that well-developed tests in these domains are valid for their intended purpose. They are useful, albeit imperfect, descriptors of the current level of knowledge, skill, ability, or achievement. Thus, they are meaningful contributors to credentialing decisions and useful predictors of future performance in employment and academic settings (Mehrens, 1999; Neisser et al., 1996; Schmidt & Hunter, 1998; Wightman, 1997; Wilson, 1981).

Second, racial group differences are consistently observed in scores on standardized knowledge, skill, ability, and achievement tests. In education, employment, and credentialing contexts, test score distributions typically reveal significant mean differences by race (e.g., Bobko, Roth, & Potosky, 1999; Hartigan & Wigdor, 1989; Jensen, 1980; Lynn, 1996; Neisser et al., 1996; Scarr, 1981; Schmidt, 1988; Schmitt, Clause, & Pulakos, 1996; Wightman, 1997; Wilson, 1981). African Americans tend to score approximately one standard deviation lower than Whites, and Hispanics score approximately two thirds of a standard deviation lower than Whites. Asian Americans typically score higher than Whites on measures of mathematical and/or quantitative ability and lower than Whites on measures of verbal ability and comprehension. These mean differences in test scores can translate into large adverse impact against protected groups when test scores are used in selection and credentialing decision making. As subgroup mean differences in test scores increase, it becomes more likely that a smaller proportion of the lower scoring subgroup will be selected or granted a credential (Sackett & Wilk, 1994).

Third, the presence of subgroup differences leads to questions regarding whether the observed differences bias the resulting decisions. An extensive body of research in both the employment and education contexts has demonstrated that these tests generally do not exhibit predictive bias. In other words, standardized tests do not underpredict the performance of minority group members (e.g., American Educational Research Association, American Psychological Association, & National Council of Measurement in Education, 1999; Cole, 1981; Jensen, 1980; Neisser et al., 1996; O'Conner, 1989; Sackett & Wilk, 1994; Wightman, 1997; Wilson, 1981).

These features of traditional tests cause considerable tension for many organizations and institutions of higher learning. Most value that which is gained through the use of tests valid for their intended purpose (e.g., a higher performing workforce, a higher achieving student body, a cadre of credentialed teachers who meet knowledge, skill, and achievement standards). Yet, most also value racial/ethnic diversity in the workforce or student body, with rationales ranging from a desire to mirror the composition of the community, to a belief that academic experiences or workplace effectiveness are enhanced by exposure to diverse perspectives. What quickly becomes clear is that these two values—performance and diversity—come into conflict. Increasing emphasis on the use of tests in the interest of gaining enhanced performance has predictable negative consequences for the selection of African Americans and Hispanics. Conversely, decreasing emphasis on the use of tests in the interest of achieving a diverse group of selectees often results in a substantial reduction in the performance gains that can be recognized through test use (e.g., Schmidt, Mack, & Hunter, 1984; Schmitt et al., 1996).

This chapter examines three options that have been suggested as approaches to reducing group mean differences in test scores. The first is to modify current tests. This would include modifications to test content (e.g., identify and remove biased test items) or modifications to test administration procedures (e.g., change time limits or provide coaching programs). Research examining this option is generally based on the premise that the constructs that existing tests are intended to measure are useful ones. The concern is the possibility that observed scores are contaminated by some biasing factors, and that these biasing factors contribute to subgroup differences. The second option is to replace the current tests entirely. The hope is that, with a fresh start, a different set of tests can be constructed that result in smaller subgroup differences. The third option is to supplement the current tests with additional measures. This position acknowledges the predictive power of current tests, but argues that current tests measure only a subset of the attributes important for success. Attributes from the personality, values, and motivation domains are not tapped by current tests in the ability and achievement domains, and their inclusion in admissions testing could conceivably simultaneously increase validity and reduce subgroup differences. The prospects for each of these three alternatives will be considered in turn.

OPTION 1: MODIFY TEST CONTENT OR TEST ADMINISTRATION PROCEDURES

Discussion of research on modifying test content and test administration procedures summarizes a recent review by Sackett, Schmitt, Ellingson, and Kabin (2001); that review can be consulted for a more thorough treatment.

Identify and Remove Biased Items

One strategy pursued in an attempt to resolve the performance versus diversity dilemma involves investigating the possibility that certain types of test items are biased. The traditional focus of studies examining differential item functioning (DIF) has been on the identification of items that function differently for minority versus majority test takers (Berk, 1982). Conceivably, such items would contribute to misleading test scores for members of a particular subgroup. Statistically, DIF seeks items that vary in difficulty for members of subgroups who are actually evenly matched on the measured construct. That is, an attempt is made to identify characteristics of items that lead to poorer performance for minority group test takers than for equally able majority group test takers. The recent review by Sackett et al. (2001) concluded that although DIF may be detected for a variety of test items, it is often the case that the magnitude of the DIF effect is very small. Furthermore, there does not appear to be a consistent pattern of items favoring one group versus another. Results do not indicate that removing these items would have a large impact on overall test scores. Thus biased items do not appear to be a significant contributor to subgroup differences.

Alter Test-Taking Motivation

Steele and colleagues (Steele, 1997; Steele & Aronson, 1995) proposed a provocative theory of stereotype threat that suggests that the way in which a test is presented to examinees can affect examinee performance. They hypothesized that when a person enters a situation in which a stereotype of a group to which the person belongs becomes salient, concerns about being judged according to that stereotype arise and inhibit performance. Although this phenomenon can affect performance in many domains, one area that has been the focus of much research is the applicability of stereotype threat in the context of cognitive ability testing. According to the theory, when members of racial minority groups encounter tests, their awareness of the common finding that members of some minority groups tend to score lower on average on tests leads to concern that they may do poorly on the test and thus confirm the stereotype. This concern detracts from their ability to focus all of their attention on the test, and results in poorer test performance.

To test these ideas, Steele and Aronson (1995) induced stereotype threat in a sample of high-achieving majority and minority students statistically equated in terms of their prior performance on the SAT. In the stereotype threat condition, participants were told that they would be given a test of intelligence; in the nonthreat condition, they were told they would be given a problem-solving task. In fact, all participants receive the same test. Steele found a larger majority–minority difference in the threat condition than the nonthreat condition, a finding supportive of the idea that the presence of stereotype threat inhibits minority group performance. In the nonthreat condition, they found no difference between the majority and minority groups, after controlling for prior SAT scores.

This research is commonly misinterpreted as showing that African Americans and Whites score the same on tests when the stereotype threat is removed.

Such misinterpretations are made in 14 of 16 popular press depictions of Steele's work, and in 10 of 11 depictions in the scientific literature (Sackett, Hardison, & Cullen, 2004). The misinterpretation results from ignoring the fact that Steele studied samples of African American and White students who had been statistically equated on the basis of SAT scores. Thus, rather than eliminating the large score gap, the research actually showed something very different. Absent stereotype threat, the African American versus White difference was just what one would expect (i.e., zero), as the two groups had been equated on the basis of SAT scores. However, in the presence of stereotype threat, the African American versus White difference was larger than would be expected, given that the two groups were equated.

Thus, although Steele's work is important in calling attention to issues linked to test-taker motivation, it would be a serious mistake to conclude that the research shows that the test score gap between majority and minority students is an artifact of the way a test is presented to examinees.

Use Coaching Programs

Another strategy for reducing subgroup differences is the use of coaching or orientation programs. Sackett et al.'s (2001) review concluded that the majority of studies on coaching and orientation programs indicate that these programs have little positive impact on the size of subgroup differences. These programs do benefit minority and nonminority examinees slightly, but they do not appear to reduce subgroup differences.

Provide More Generous Time Limits

A final option available for addressing group differences in test scores is the strategy of increasing the amount of time allotted to complete a test. Unless speed of work is part of the construct in question, it can be argued that time limits may bias test scores. Tests that limit administration time may be biased against minority groups in that certain groups may be provided too little time to complete the test. Sackett et al.'s (2001) review, however, indicated that although relaxed time limits will likely result in higher test scores for all examinees, there does not appear to be a differential benefit favoring minority subgroups. In fact, it is more common that extending the time provided to examinees to complete a test increases subgroup differences, sometimes substantially.

In sum, none of the options reviewed here appear to offer much promise for substantially reducing subgroup differences. Thus the next section considers replacing existing tests.

OPTION 2: REPLACE CURRENT TESTS
WITH NEW TESTS

One set of options receiving considerable attention involves replacing currently used admissions tests with alternative tests. I offer a number of observations about doing so.

First, research shows that replacing a current measure (e.g., the SAT I) with another measure squarely in the cognitive domain (e.g., achievement: SAT II) can be expected to produce comparable results in terms of subgroup differences. The recent University of California report comparing the SAT I with a SAT II composite (Geiser & Studley, 2001) is a good illustration of this. The two measures do not differ much in either subgroup differences or in validity in predicting subsequent academic performance. There may be reasons to prefer the SAT II to the SAT I, but those will be reasons other than validity or diversity.

Second, many, though not all, advocates of replacing currently used admissions tests assert that traditional measures are of limited value. The assertion is that they predict first-year grades and nothing more. This is clearly false. Recent meta-analyses of the SAT and GRE reveal substantial correlations with academic performance throughout the course of one's education, and smaller, but meaningful, correlations with degree attainment (Hezlett et al., 2001; Kuncel, Hezlett, & Ones, 2001).

Other work suggests that cognitively loaded tests are linked to at least some indicators of life success beyond college. Johnson and Neal (1998) summarized data about links between cognitive tests and earnings in a national longitudinal sample following individuals into their mid-30s. They reported links between cognitive test scores and wages, even after controlling for educational attainment.

Third, another feature clouding the waters in terms of the value of currently used admissions tests is the common practice of using degree completion as the criterion in examining the validity of admissions tests. A well-known principle of psychometrics is that the possible value of a correlation drops radically when a dichotomous criterion with an extreme split is used. In settings where the degree completion rate is high (e.g., 90% in the study of elite colleges reported in Vars & Bowen, 1998) one might mistakenly conclude that there is something wrong with the test, because there are large majority–minority differences on the test, but small differences in the rate of degree completion. A very different pattern emerges when one looks at a more sensitive criterion, such as grade-point average. In the Vars and Bowen (1998, Table 13A-1) study of elite colleges, a .50 GPA difference between African Americans and Whites was found (3.3 vs. 2.8); with a *SD* of .44, this results in a standardized mean difference (*d*) value of 1.14. Thus the argument that existing tests are flawed because there are group mean differences on the test but not on the criterion is not supported.

Fourth, it is useful to consider some conclusions that follow logically from the aforementioned. If measures in the cognitive domain show a predictable and persistent pattern of subgroup mean differences, then the types of instruments that could conceivably replace existing tests must be measures from different domains. Without specifying what those domains might be, one definitional characteristic for classifying any replacement measure as coming from a different domain would be that it would have a low correlation with existing tests. For such a test to be useful, it would also have to be predictive of criteria of interest. However, the fact that the proposed replacement test has a low correlation with existing tests means that it achieves its predictive power by predicting a different portion of criterion variance than existing tests. It therefore follows that validity in predicting criteria of interest must be higher if the proposed replacement test were used in conjunction with existing tests rather than alone. Thus advocating replacement of existing tests implies accepting lower predictive power than would be obtained by using proposed new tests as a supplement to, rather than as a replacement for, existing tests.

Thus traditional cognitive measures have considerable validity for predicting both academic performance and later earnings. Any proposal for replacement should be clear and explicit about the consequences for predictive validity of any proposed alternative. And although discussions are often framed in terms of the consequences of replacing a traditional measure with an alternative, one cannot ignore the question of the degree of validity that would be achieved if the alternative were used in conjunction with the traditional test. Thus the next section shifts attention to the issue of supplementing existing tests with new measures.

OPTION 3: SUPPLEMENT EXISTING TESTS WITH NEW MEASURES

I offer a number of observation about the prospects for reducing subgroup differences by supplementing currently used admission tests with new measures. This discussion does not discuss any specific measures. Rather, the focus is on a conceptual understanding of the degree to which supplementing existing measures can reduce group differences. I believe that the psychometric theory of composites offers some very useful insights into this issue. There are a set of useful psychometric formulas that shed light on what happens when two or more measures are combined. This chapter examines the consequence for group differences of forming a composite of an existing measure, like an SAT I, and one or more proposed new measures. The psychometric theory of composites can be applied if we know the subgroup differences on each of the individual measures and the correlations between the measures.

To start, let us look at the relationship between subgroup differences and the proportion selected from each group. Subgroup differences are expressed as "d," the standardized mean difference between two groups. A d value of .0 means that the means for the two groups are the same; a d of 1.0 means that one group's M is one SD higher than the other. A 1.0 SD M difference is roughly the average African American–White d value for tests commonly used for admissions. Now consider Table 6.1, which shows the relationship between subgroup differences and majority and minority group selection ratios. Here three majority group selection ratios are presented: 10%, representing a highly selective admissions program; 50%, presenting a moderately selective admissions program; and 90% representing a minimally selective admissions program. The table addresses the question, "If a test cutoff were used that resulting in screening in the top 10% (or 50%, or 90%) of members of the majority group, and if the majority–minority d were of a given value, what would be the resulting minority group selection ratio?"

Table 6.1 shows that the majority–minority gap differs with the value of d. In any given majority group selection ratio, the discrepancy between majority and minority group selection ratios increases as d increases. The table also

TABLE 6.1

Minority Group Selection Ratio
When Majority Group Selection Ratio is .10, .50, and .90
as Standardized M Difference Between Groups (d) Varies

	Majority Group Selection Ratio		
d	.10	.50	.90
.0	.10	.50	.90
.2	.07	.42	.86
.4	.05	.35	.81
.6	.03	.27	.75
.8	.02	.21	.68
1.0	.01	.16	.61

Note. Extracted from Table 1 of Sackett and Ellingson, 1997.

TABLE 6.2

Four Fifths Ratio
When Majority Group Selection Ratio is .10, .50, and .90
as Standardized M Difference Between Groups (d) Varies

d	Majority Group Selection Ratio		
	.10	.50	.90
.0	1.00	1.00	1.00
.2	.69	.84	.98
.4	.46	.69	.90
.6	.30	.55	.84
.8	.19	.42	.72
1.0	.11	.32	.68

Note. Extracted from Table 2 of Sackett and Ellingson, 1997.

shows that the gap is much more pronounced at low selection ratios. Table 6.1 illustrates that the use of a measure with a d of about 1.0, which is typical of the African American–White d for admissions tests, will have more impact for selective institutions.

Table 6.2 transforms this same information, tabling the ratio of minority to majority group selection ratios as a function of d and the majority selection rate. This reflects the commonly used "$4/5$ rule" used in employment discrimination settings, where a value of this ratio of minority to majority selection rate less than 80% triggers scrutiny under government antidiscrimination guidelines.

This is useful for identifying a target value for d: How low would d have to be in order to achieve a given level of the ratio of minority to majority group selection ratio? Note that at high levels of selectivity (e.g. 10%), even a d as small as .2 produces a substantial discrepancy between the two-group selection ratios. At more modest levels of selectivity (e.g. 50%), a d of .2 produces a value (.84) within the $4/5$ rule of thumb. With Table 6.2 as background, I now turn to the question of what can be achieved via the use of composites. Specifically, what level of d will result when two or more equally weighted predictors are combined to form a composite? To set the stage, I encourage you to take the following quiz. Assume:

Predictor A produces a d of 1.0.
Predictor B produces a d of 0.0.
A and B are uncorrelated, and both are in z-score form.
Question: What is the d for the unit-weighted composite A + B?
    (a) 1.00 (b) .71 (c) .50 (d) .0

Sackett and Ellingson (1997) presented the following formula for determining the degree of group differences present when two predictors are combined to form a composite is obtained:

$$d = \frac{d_1 + d_2}{\sqrt{2 + 2r_{12}}}$$

where d_1 indicates the d value of the first predictor, d_2 indicates the d value of the second predictor, and r_{12} indicates the correlation between the two predictors. A more general form of the equation for any number of predictors is:

$$d = \frac{\sum\limits_{i=1}^{k} d_i}{\sqrt{k + k(k-1)r_{ii}}}$$

where d_i indicates the d value for each predictor included in the composite, k indicates the number of predictors combined to form the composite, and r_{ii} indicates the average correlation between the predictors included in the composite.

Some very useful, though sobering, principles emerge from a study of these formulas. First, in discussions about the issue of supplementing an existing test with a new predictor, we find that the intuition of many of our colleagues is that the d for a composite of two predictors will be approximated by "splitting the difference" between the d values for the two predictors (e.g., a composite of a predictor with a d of 1.0 and another with a d of .0 will have a d of .5). Particularly when the correlation between the predictors is low, this intuition will severely underestimate the composite d (e.g., in the previous example, with two uncorrelated predictors, the composite d will actually be .71). Thus the degree to which group differences and, subsequently, adverse impact can be reduced by supplementing a predictor with a large d with a second predictor with a small d may be commonly overestimated.

Second, try another quiz. Assume a state bar exam produces $d = 1.0$. There is a proposal to reduce d by using law school grades as a component of the bar examination process. It is observed that law school grades produce $d = .8$, and correlate .5 with bar exam scores. Given this fact pattern, what will be the d if a unit-weighted composite of bar exam and grades is used?

(a) 1.0   (b) .9   (c) .8   (d) 1.04

Applying the formula above produces 1.04 as the answer. Thus in certain contexts, supplementing a predictor with a large d with another predictor with a smaller d actually produce a composite with a larger d than either of the individual predictors. This can occur when the supplemental predictor is correlated with the existing predictor. For example, in the bar exam example, the formation of a composite including both the bar exam and law school grades will only reduce the level of group differences observed when the two measures correlate at $r \geq .70$. When the correlation between the two predictors is less then .70, use of both predictors actually results in greater differences between groups than would the use of the bar exam alone. Thus adding a supplemental predictor can actually increase d, rather than decrease it.

Third, although these examples focus on adding a single supplemental predictor, it is useful to consider the effects on composite d of adding additional predictors. Using these equations, it becomes clear that adding additional predictors results in diminishing returns. If the existing test has a d of 1.0, and additional uncorrelated tests, each with a d of .0, are included in a composite, the composite d for a 2, 3, 4, and 5 predictor composite is .71, .58, .50, and .45, respectively.

Fourth, up to this point all variables combined in a composite have been equally weighted. The formulas above can be extended to the setting where differing weights can be applied to each predictor:

$$d = \frac{\sum\limits_{i=1}^{k} w_i d_i}{\sqrt{\sum\limits_{i=1}^{k} w_i^2 + 2 \sum\limits_{i=1}^{k-1} \sum\limits_{j=i+1}^{k} w_i w_j r_{ij}}}$$

where w_i and w_j are the weights of each predictor included in the composite, d_i indicates the d value for each predictor included in the composite, k indicates the number of predictors combined to form the composite, and r_{ij} indicates each of the correlations between predictors included in the composite.

Table 6.3 uses this formula to examine the setting where an existing predictor with $d = 1.0$ is combined with an uncorrelated supplemental predictor with $d = 0$. The table examines the outcomes both when the high-d predictor is given the higher weight and when the low-d predictor is given higher weight. Table 6.3 shows that the high-d predictor must be given a very small weight relative to the low-d predictor if one hopes to reduce composite d to a very small value. If the low-d predictor is given smaller weight, the effectiveness of adding a supplemental predictor as a strategy for reducing composite d is quite limited. This a critical point, as the weights to be given to different predictors are generally a function of their relative value in predicting the criterion of interest. A supplemental predictor that makes a small, but useful, incremental contribution to predicting academic performance would be given a relatively small weight, and consequently would have a relatively small effect on composite d.

TABLE 6.3

d Resulting From Forming a Differentially Weighted Composite
of a Cognitive Measure With $d = 1.0$ With an Additional
Uncorrelated Predictor with $d = 0.0$

Weight for High d Predictor	Weight for Low d Predictor	Composite d
.1	1.0	.10
.3	1.0	.29
.5	1.0	.45
.7	1.0	.57
1.0	1.0	.71
1.0	0.7	.82
1.0	0.5	.89
1.0	0.3	.96
1.0	0.1	1.0

Note. Extracted from Table 5 of Sackett and Ellingson, 1997.

In sum, the theory of composites offers four key messages. First, adding a supplemental predictor has a smaller effect on composite d (and, consequently, on minority selection) than many people expect. Second, there are diminishing returns for adding each additional supplemental predictor. Third, supplemental predictors would have to receive very high weight relative to existing predictors to reduce composite d to a small level. Fourth, depending on the level of correlation between an existing predictor and a supplemental predictor, it is possible to add a supplemental predictor with a smaller d than the existing predictor and yet produce a higher composite d than the existing predictor. All of this is not meant to argue against searching for supplemental predictors. Such supplemental predictors could affect the validity with which the criterion of interest is predicted. What this discussion does is to help clarify the limits on the degree to which a supplemental predictor that enhances prediction will also reduce subgroup differences.

OPERATIONAL ISSUES
WITH SUPPLEMENTAL PREDICTORS

In the testing field, the common tradition is to first engage in extensive research on the validity of a proposed test for its intended purpose. Only after collecting strong and persuasive validity evidence does the perspective shift to a consideration of the operational issues involved in test use. In considering new measures to supplement current admissions tests, I believe that this sequence may not be the most productive way to proceed. I suggest that a preferable strategy may be to identify a set of conditions that any proposed measure must meet for operational use is the admissions testing environment. I assert that, for many types of measures, one can conclude prior to any validation research that there are insurmountable obstacles to operational use. If one reaches this conclusion, the merit of proceeding with validation research is unclear.

As a starting point, here are two conditions that I believe must be met for a proposed new measure to merit further consideration. First, one must be able to develop an inexhaustible supply of parallel forms of the measure. As with current admissions tests, test content is compromised after one administration, requiring the availability of a new parallel measure for each subsequent administration. The second consideration follows from the fact that the content of the first form of the measure is public knowledge after initial administration, either via a policy of public release after administration, or by the capturing of content by motivated parties, such as those with an interest in preparing applicants to take the test. In some small-scale testing applications, there may be limited opportunity for an applicant to obtain information about test content. For example, applicants for employment in a particular small firm may have no ready basis for identifying other prior applicants and thus gaining information about test content. However, given the high degree of attention given to admissions testing, it is not plausible to believe that any new measures could be implemented without considerable public scrutiny. Thus, if one assumes that the content of the first form of a measure is in the public domain after the first administration, knowledge of the first form of the test must not have a marked effect on applicant performance on subsequent forms.

Consider, for example, a type of measure that is being investigated by several contributors to this volume (Schmitt, Oswald, & Gillespie, chap. 11, this volume; Sternberg, chap. 9, this volume), namely the situational judgment test. Such measures present a scenario to the applicant, along with multiple possible courses of action. (Example: "In the library, you observe heated argument between two students whom you do not know. This argument is disrupting those trying to study. The best thing to do is: (a) try to ignore it; (b) intervene, asking them to take the argument outside; (c) ask a library staff member to intervene." In this example, applicants are asked to identify the best course of action; in some applications they are asked to identify the course of action they personally would chose.

The questions of interest here are whether multiple parallel forms of such instruments can be created, and whether knowledge of the keyed response to the initial form of the instrument would permit identification of the keyed responses to subsequent forms. At the extreme, response strategies might be learned that would reduce variance to negligible levels, negating the value of the measure. At the other extreme, it may prove to be the case that knowledge of prior forms has a negligible effect on performance on subsequent forms.

As another example, consider some of the innovative new measures investigated by Sternberg (chap. 9, this volume). One example in the creativity domain involves presenting examinees with cartoons with the caption removed; the examinees' task is to generate a humorous and creative caption. It is likely that this task is totally new for participants in the initial research study. It is unclear whether the task would function in the same way in an operational setting once the task was no longer novel. Imagine students practicing writing captions for hundreds of cartoons, or attending courses on responding effectively to this task.

With both the situational judgment test and the cartoon task, it is not clear in advance what the outcomes would be of these types of measures moving into the public spotlight. The point here is that susceptibility to coaching may profitably be examined relatively early in the test development and validation process. The outcomes of such research may aid decisions into whether to engage in expensive large-scale validation efforts.

CONCLUSION

This chapter explored several aspects of what may be termed the performance–diversity tradeoff. The tradeoff results from the fact that tests widely used in the educational admissions process show mean differences between various racial and ethnic groups. The result is the possibility of competing motivations: a desire to give considerable weight to these tests as a result of their documented value in predicting academic performance versus a desire to give higher weight to other factors (and hence less weight to tests) in the interests of greater diversity in the student population. In an attempt to reconcile these competing motivations, there is considerable interest in creating tests that achieve comparable or greater predictive power relative to existing tests and that simultaneously reduce or eliminate subgroup mean differences.

This chapter first considered prospects for reducing subgroup differences by modifying test content or test administration conditions. Removing differentially functioning items, increasing testing time, providing coaching and test preparation, and interventions aimed at test-taker motivation were examined. Although some of these may have value for other reasons (e.g., applicant perceptions of fairness), findings to date do not suggest that change in these domains will prove to be effective routes to reducing subgroup differences. The chapter then considered prospects for eliminating existing tests and replacing them with completely new tests. This was rejected on the basis that existing tests are clearly useful in predicting academic performance. New tests may improve prediction by predicting additional variance in academic performance, but using new tests instead of existing tests would result in losing the predictive power of existing tests. Thus I argued for considering supplementing existing tests with new measures, rather than considering the elimination of existing measures.

In considering supplementing existing tests with new measures, a number of general principles emerged from a careful examination of a set of formulas that reveal the degree to which group differences can be reduced by combining existing measures with new ones. The overarching message is that although supplemental predictors can indeed reduce group differences, the reduction in differences is likely to be less than many might expect. In addition, there are a number of important operational concerns, such as susceptibility to coaching, that must be taken into account when considering supplemental predictor. There is no readily available or complete solution to the performance–diversity tradeoff; the hope is that this chapter will contribute to a clearer picture of what can and cannot be achieved through the use of various proposed methods.

REFERENCES

American Educational Research Association, American Psychological Association, & National Council on Measurement in Education. (1999). *Standards for educational and psychological testing.* Washington, DC: American Psychological Association.

Berk, R. A. (1982). *Handbook of methods for detecting test bias.* Baltimore: Johns Hopkins University Press.

Bobko, P., Roth, P. L., & Potosky, D. (1999). Derivation and implications of a meta-analytic matrix incorporating cognitive ability, alternative predictors, and job performance. *Personnel Psychology, 52,* 561–590

Cole, N. S. (1981). Bias in testing. *American Psychologist, 36,* 1067–1077.

Geiser, S., & Studley, R. (2001). *UC and the SAT: Predictive validity and differential impact of the SAT I and SAT II at the University of California.* Oakland: University of California, Office of the President.

Hartigan, J. A., & Wigdor, A. K. (1989). *Fairness in employment testing.* Washington, DC: National Academy Press.

Hezlett, S., Kuncel, N., Vey, M., Ones, D., Campbell, J., & Camara, W. (2001, April). *The effectiveness of the SAT in predicting success early and late in college: A comprehensive meta-analysis.* Paper presented at the annual meeting of the National Council of Measurement in Education, Seattle, WA.

Jensen, A. R. (1980). *Bias in mental testing*. New York: The Free Press.

Johnson, W. R., & Neal, D. (1998). Basic skills and the Black–White earnings gap. In C. Jencks & M. Phillips (Eds.), *The Black-White score gap* (pp. 480–497). Washington, DC: The Brookings Institute.

Kuncel, N. R., Hezlett, S. A., & Ones, D. S. (2001). A comprehensive meta-analysis of the predictive validity of the graduate record examinations. *Psychological Bulletin, 127,* 161–181.

Lynn, R. (1996). Racial and ethnic differences in intelligence in the U.S. on the Differential Ability Scale. *Personality and Individual Differences, 20,* 271–273.

Mehrens, W. A. (1999). The CBEST saga: Implications for licensure and employment testing. *The Bar Examiner, 68,* 23–32.

Neisser, U., Boodoo, G., Bouchard, T. J., Jr., Boykin, A. W., Brody, N., Ceci, S. J., Halpern, D. F., Loehlin, J. C., Perloff, R., Sternberg, R. J., & Urbina, S. (1996). Intelligence: Knowns and unknowns. *American Psychologist, 51,* 77–101.

O'Connor, M. C. (1989). Aspects of differential performance by minorities on standardized tests: Linguistic and sociocultural factors. In B. R. Gifford (Ed.), *Test policy and test performance: Education, language, and culture* (pp. 129–181). Boston: Kluwer.

Sackett, P. R., & Ellingson, J. E. (1997). The effects of forming multi-predictor composites on group differences and adverse impact. *Personnel Psychology, 50,* 707–722.

Sackett, P. R., Hardison, C. M., & Cullen, M.J. (2004). On interpreting stereotype threat as accounting for Black–White differences on cognitive tests. *American Psychologist, 59,* 7–13.

Sackett, P. R., Schmitt, N., Ellingson, J. E., and Kabin, M. B. (2001). High stakes testing in employment, credentialing, and higher education: Prospects in a post-affirmative action world. *American Psychologist, 56,* 302–318.

Sackett, P. R., & Wilk, S. L. (1994). Within-group norming and other forms of score adjustment in preemployment testing. *American Psychologist, 49,* 929–954.

Scarr, S. (1981). *Race, social class, and individual differences in I.Q.* Hillsdale, NJ: Lawrence Erlbaum Associates.

Schmidt, F. L. (1988). The problem of group differences in ability test scores in employment selection. *Journal of Vocational Behavior, 33,* 272–292.

Schmidt, F. L., & Hunter, J. E. (1998). The validity and utility of selection methods in personnel psychology: Practical and theoretical implications of 85 years of research findings. *Psychological Bulletin, 124,* 262–274.

Schmidt, F. L., & Mack, M. J., & Hunter, J. E. (1984). Selection utility in the occupation of U.S. park ranger for three modes of test use. *Journal of Applied Psychology, 69,* 490–497.

Schmitt, N., Clause, C. S., & Pulakos, E. D. (1996). Subgroup differences associated with different measures of some job-relevant constructs. In C. R. Cooper & I. T. Robertson (Eds.), *International review of industrial and organizational psychology* (Vol. 11, pp. 115–140). New York: Wiley.

Steele, C. M. (1997). A threat in the air: How stereotypes shape intellectual identity and performance. *American Psychologist, 52,* 613–629.

Steele, C. M., & Aronson, J. (1995). Stereotype threat and the intellectual test performance of African Americans. *Journal of Personality and Social Psychology, 69,*
797–811.

Vars, F. E., & Bowen, W. G. (1998). Scholastic aptitude test scores, race, and aca-
demic performance in selective colleges and universities. In C. Jencks & M. Phillips
(Eds.), *The Black–White score gap* (pp. 457–479). Washington, DC: The Brookings
Institute.

Wightman, L. F. (1997). The threat to diversity in legal education: An empirical analysis of the consequences of abandoning race as a factor in law school admission decisions. *New York University Law Review, 72,* 1–53.

Wilson, K. M. (1981). Analyzing the long-term performance of minority and nonminority students: A tale of two studies. *Research in Higher Education, 15,* 351–
375.

7

Prospects for Improving Grades for Use in Admissions

Warren W. Willingham

Distinguished Research Scientist, Retired
Educational Testing Service, Princeton, NJ

Classroom grading is time-honored because grades offer obvious benefits to education. When teaching and grading work well, grades serve as a direct connection between learning goals and learning outcomes and provide immediate feedback on the results of student effort. Although grading may have more value to schooling than we are inclined to credit, the value is often poorly realized. Routine complaints about the shortcomings of grading are familiar enough: the unintended negative effects on learning, the difficulty of focusing instruction and grading on important educational outcomes, the challenge of maintaining fair standards, and the threat of capricious or biased judgment in assigning grades (Milton, Pollio, & Eison, 1986; Terwilliger, 1989). For centuries, educators have cited such problems and argued over the very purpose of grades and how they are used (Cureton, 1971).

Let me distinguish the particular use of grades that we are considering. Teachers use grades to help clarify learning goals and evaluate student performance in individual classes. Later, those grades serve administrative purposes like granting diplomas or admitting a college class. In such subsequent use, grades take on a high-stakes function much broader than the teacher's original assessment. Because it is this subsequent administrative use with which we are presently concerned, it is important to recognize at the outset that high-stakes grades should be subject to the same standards of validity and fairness that we expect of high-stakes tests (American Psychological Association, American Educational Research Association, National Council on Measurement in Education, 1999). We improve grades by better application of those widely accepted standards of good measurement practice.

That is a worthy but daunting objective. The authors of other chapters in this volume have examined many aspects of measurement principles as they apply to tests. For this brief discussion devoted primarily to grades, it may be useful to consider how grades and tests are different. By tests, I mean external tests, not classroom tests developed by individual teachers. If based on similar material, grades and external test scores should presumably reflect much the same performance, but we know that these two measures often give somewhat different results. If we can identify and demonstrate some reasons why they differ, perhaps those differences can give added perspective regarding possible ways to improve grades—either by lessening their more troublesome weaknesses or building on their special strengths.

MAJOR DIFFERENCES BETWEEN GRADES AND TEST SCORES

There are three major factors that make grades different from tests. These factors come from a study recently completed with two colleagues that is referred to here as Grades and Test Scores (Willingham, Pollack, & Lewis, 2000, 2002). The study was based on extensive data for 8,454 high school students in the National Education Longitudinal Study of 1988 (NELS; Ingels et al., 1994). Our purpose was to see to what extent we could account for observed differences in the grades and test scores that students earn.

For this large group of students, the original correlation between total NELS test score and 4-year high-school average was .62. By applying appropriate statistical corrections and taking into account relevant information about the students, it was possible to examine the relationship between grade performance and test performance under more nearly comparable conditions than normally obtain in actual practice. So adjusted, the correlation between grades and test scores increased to .90. The average differential prediction of grade performance for eight subgroups (women, three ethnic groups, and four school programs) was reduced to .02 of a letter grade (Willingham et al., 2002, Tables 2 & 5).

Thus, both individual differences and group differences between grade performance and test performance were substantially reduced. Some of this reduction was attributable to adjusting for the unreliability of grades and test scores and some to adjusting the grade average and the test score so that each covered, as nearly as possible, the same subject areas. Both unreliability and discrepancies in the subjects covered will cause observed grades and test scores to differ, but neither of these two sources of difference need concern us here because neither suggests any intrinsic distinction in the character of the two measures.

Much of the increase in correlation between grade average and test scores, as well as the reduction in differential prediction of grade performance across groups, resulted from taking into account three other factors. Each of the three factors was a major source of observed discrepancies between grade performance and test performance, and each factor suggested an intrinsic difference between the two measures. Table 7.1 proposes a way of contrasting critical qualities of classroom grades and external tests.

The first two columns of Table 7.1 list the three factors along with a common assessment objective to which each factor is particularly relevant. Factor 1, Grading Variations, refers to differences in grading standards from one group of students to another. Factor 2, which we called Scholastic Engagement, was based on nine student characteristics—all especially related to differences in grade performance and test performance. Factor 3, Teacher Judgment, was based on ratings of student behavior collected by NELS during the second year

TABLE 7.1

Potential Strengths of Grades and Test Scores in High-Stakes Assessment

		Special Strengths of:	
Added Factor in Grades	Relevant Assessment Objective	Grades (Local Contract)	Test Scores (External Standard)
1. Grading variations	To assess fairly	Local standards	Common yardstick
2. Scholastic engagement	To evaluate important skills	Conative skills	Cognitive skills
3. Teacher judgment	To motivate teaching and learning	Individual assessment	Standards-based assessment

Note. Adapted from Willingham et al., 2002.

of high school. Each of these factors can be viewed as an added feature or additional component of grades. Factors 1 and 3 are found only in grades; Factor 2 is more directly represented in grades than in test scores.

The last two columns of Table 7.1 suggest ways in which these factors are manifested as special strengths, or better, special features of grades and tests. As we see, they are not strengths in all assessment situations. The strengths of grades and test scores differ here for two reasons: First, as noted, the three factors influence grades either exclusively or more strongly than they do test scores. For example, the "common yardstick" is a special strength of tests precisely because test scores do *not* include Factor 1, Grading Variations.

A second reason that grades and test scores have different strengths is that the two measures have a different genesis. Grades represent performance on the implicit local contract between a teacher and a student; that is, how well the student has done according to the teacher's standard. High-stakes tests represent an external standard; that is, how well teachers and students have done on standards that apply across an educational system. Even under the best of circumstances, teacher standards and system standards are unlikely to be precisely the same.

In considering possible implications of these factors for improving grades, I refer mainly to the use of grades for high-stakes admissions decisions—more specifically, for undergraduate admissions, although similar implications would apply at other educational levels as well. Improving grades must mean improving validity and fairness in some broad sense. Note, however, that improving grades for use in high-stakes decisions will not necessarily improve grades for use in the classroom, or vice versa. Consider each factor in turn.

GRADING VARIATIONS

Grading standards vary when some students are assessed more leniently, others more strictly. Statistical evidence of such grading variation is normally a difference in average grade earned by two groups of similar tested ability or by the same group in different classes. Public concern about grading standards is often directed to overly lenient grading—so-called grade inflation. Inflated grading can pose a measurement problem, especially if it becomes widespread and extreme. Rather than drift inexorably downward as we might imagine, grading standards tend to vary from place to place, and nationally, grades have shown inflation and deflation at different times over the past 50 years (Webb, 1959; Willingham & Cole, 1997; Ziomek & Svec, 1995). Furthermore, during a given time period, evidence suggests that grading levels rise in some institutions and fall in others (Willingham & Lewis, 1990).

Factor 1 is concerned with variation in grading standards from class to class and school to school at a given time. In secondary schools and colleges, it is such situational variations that are likely to have the most persistent and serious effect on the usefulness of grades for high-stakes decisions. If a high-stakes measure needs to be comparable from student to student, as in making admissions decisions, then Factor 1 represents error. When grading standards vary from one situation to another, both the predictive validity and the fairness of those grades are thereby diminished. There is a substantial history of research demonstrating the nature of variation in grading standards and its effect on the quality of grades as a selection measure or as a criterion of educational outcomes (Elliott & Strenta, 1988; Willingham et al., 2000).

Teachers are not likely to be concerned about the predictive validity of grades they assign, but grading fairly is always an important objective. Some local variations in grading standards may be deliberate. Because American schools do not follow a standard curriculum, the ability to adapt standards to local educational purposes and circumstances can be a strength of grades. But in high-stakes decisions, like college selection, variation in grading standards clearly poses a problem. College selection decisions involve applicants from many different schools, and individual students take different courses of study. A special strength of an admissions test is to provide a common yardstick. In Grades and Test Scores, we confirmed again that school and classroom grading standards vary widely (Linn, 1966; Ramist, Lewis, & McCamley, 1990; Starch & Elliott, 1912). Reducing that source of error is one way to improve grades for use in selective admissions.

Can grading variations be adjusted statistically? To some extent, if correctly done, but useful adjustments are probably impractical in most situations for several reasons. For one thing, an accurate and fair adjustment would likely require a common anchor test in all schools. If an anchor test is already available—an admissions test, for example—an adjustment for school grading variations typically does not improve a college grade prediction that is based on the available grades and test scores (Linn, 1966; Willingham, 1963). Variation in course grading is another stumbling block. Patterns of course-grading differences apparently vary substantially from one school to another, independent of the overall grading standard typical of the school (Willingham et al., 2002). But the most serious problem would likely be public resistance and legal challenge to what some would perceive as statistical "monkeying" with the grades a student has earned.

One way to improve grading would be to give it the attention it deserves. If teachers and administrators had better information about grades assigned, unintentional inequities across groups might be self-corrective to some degree. Currently, there is remarkably little data about the fairness of grading for different groups of students in different educational situations. Accountability in student assessment requires that educators should know more about how grading levels vary—for comparable performance—from school to school and course to course.

Grading is and should be the teacher's prerogative, but practices vary, as do standards. Is that always bad? Not necessarily, but variation in practices that can favor one student over another raises an important issue: What freedom and what discipline are appropriate when teachers assign grades? Developing and promoting local principles of good grading practice might help to reduce arbitrary differences in grading levels. Improved practices notwithstanding, local grading variations are always likely to lessen the validity and fairness of grades to some degree. That is a problem in using grades alone for high-stakes decisions. Using a valid test with grades helps to moderate inconsistencies in grading. It is a good example of two measures being better than one.

As we know, computing a grade average is not the only way to make use of grades in admissions. Some colleges have long used class rank in lieu of grade average in evaluating applicants for admission. Higher education institutions in some states give admission priority to a set proportion of each school's highest ranking students (e.g., the top 10% of the graduating class). Class percentile rank is seemingly a common scale, but the meaning of the scale varies to the extent that actual student performance varies from school to school. The intention and likely outcome of automatically accepting the highest ranking students is not to improve college-grade prediction. This particular use of class rank addresses other aspects of validity and fairness in selection; that is, issues such as local entitlement, opportunity to learn, and fostering diversity. From this perspective, *local excellence* is self-validating, because it is sufficient in its own right as a consideration in selective admission. That argument can carry weight regardless of whether local excellence is always comparable from school to school.

In a local excellence model, any variation in typical student performance from school to school is ignored, but the resulting variation in a college's selection standards can not correctly be assumed to be random error. In fact, such variation in selection standards is likely to be associated with, if not produced by, other social characteristics of communities like economic condition and parents' education. Thus, in a local excellence model, such community characteristics become an active element in admissions policy. Different observers will have different views regarding the values brought into play by rewarding local excellence. It appears to be an evolving admissions strategy, still under review. Finally, note that the practice in many colleges of using class rank rather than grade average in selection should have a similar but less pronounced effect.

SCHOLASTIC ENGAGEMENT

In Grades and Test Scores, we found that certain behavioral characteristics were especially related to grades earned in school. Scholastic Engagement was defined on the basis of nine such characteristics. These characteristics reflected a pattern of constructive behaviors that help to develop skills important in school—behaviors like taking serious courses, doing the work assigned, and avoiding competing activities. Scholastic Engagement was correlated with both test scores and grade average, but more highly with the latter (.41 vs. 57; see Table 6 in Willingham et al., 2002).

A strength of tests lies in the possibility of focusing a measure of learning outcomes on cognitive skills that are vital to educational objectives. The pattern of student behavior just described involves somewhat different strengths. Scholastic Engagement implies *conative skills* like volition, habits of inquiry, and self-regulation. These broadly useful skills arise from and also strengthen intrinsic motivation. Conative skills are an important aspect of schooling because they facilitate learning and performance (Snow, 1989). Recall the earlier caution against using grades alone. The conative feature of school performance, especially as reflected in grades, complements the cognitive emphasis of tests. This pairing illustrates a weakness in using tests alone when making high-stakes decisions about individual students. It seems clear enough that scholastic engagement enhances academic effort; no doubt such engagement fosters useful adult skills as well. How can we improve this conative feature of grades?

One approach is to focus more deliberately on what types of skills deserve recognition—in assessment and in schooling. Many teachers give extra grade credit when students show effort or other evidence of engagement in their schooling (Public Agenda, 2000; Robinson & Craver, 1989). That is one reason that Scholastic Engagement is more highly correlated with grades than with test scores. Conative skills also influence grades because motivated students are likely to learn more. We use grades as a sanctioned and official measure of a person's educational performance. What role should conative skills play in grading and instruction? More attention to that question would likely improve the validity of grades as a measure of educational outcome as well as a basis for admissions to further, more demanding programs.

Another approach is for admissions officers not to depend on grades and tests alone for evidence that a student is promising and serious. An applicant's record can be supplemented with additional indicators of scholastic engagement; that is, other information that may reflect commitment, energy, and coping skills more directly than does grade average. Students' track records contain quite public evidence of taking school seriously—evidence like coming to school, taking tough courses, doing the work, or being successfully involved in school activities that have some significant scholastic connection.

It was public evidence of that type that was used to develop the measure that we call Scholastic Engagement. There is a long and continuing history of research showing that such student behavior predicts later achievements that colleges value (Adelman, 1999; Richards, Holland, & Lutz, 1967; Willingham, 1985). A prudent concern is the possibility of negative side effects from more extensive use of evidence other than grades and test scores in selective admissions. If stakes are high, there is danger that the evidence may be misrepresented or the activities themselves may become distorted. These problems are real. They can possibly be mitigated by emphasizing reliable information about student performance that is already available through existing educational records and publicly sanctioned programs. The official school transcript and recognized youth activities, in and out of school, can be prime sources if carefully evaluated. Both deserve further study.

TEACHER JUDGMENT

One objective of assessment is to motivate learning; that is, to direct the effort and reward the result. With external tests, the intention often is to motivate the educational process—to hold teachers and schools accountable. With teacher grading, we hope to motivate students. The teacher's judgment of the particular character of each student's performance is reflected in grades, but not in test scores. That judgment is a strength of grades for several reasons.

Grades can cover a broader range of knowledge, skills, and performance than is practical with any test. Even with established common standards as to subject matter and objectives, instruction and outcomes will vary somewhat among schools and among students. Students have different interests and passions. Individual assessment by the teacher can be based more closely on the specific material that each student has studied and what each has learned than is possible with a standards-based test. Furthermore, individual students can achieve common standards in differing ways that may require a somewhat different assessment.

For all these reasons, valid teacher judgment promises to complement a standards-based test. Note this distinction: The word *standard* is often used, and was previously used here, in reference to grading difficulty—as in the grading standard or the grading level that is typical of a course or a school. In this discussion of Teacher Judgment, I use *standard* mainly in reference to the particular knowledge and skills on which teachers base their assessments; that is, the substance of the learning rather than the calibration of the scale.

How can we improve this judgmental feature of grades? One approach is to bring more rigor and expertise to classroom assessment. Recently, writers like Shepard (2000) and Stiggins (2001) have shown how difficult that task is and how much benefit can accrue from good assessment. Evaluating a student's complex performance or imaginative solutions requires a trained and disciplined judgment—without personal preference or bias. Effective grading should reinforce effective learning. In this manner, good grading has good consequences—for students and for teachers, even though there may be individual and situational differences in the way effective learning is defined.

Another approach is to capitalize on individual differences in abilities, interests, and style. The standards-based movement improves our focus on significant educational objectives—for instruction and assessment (Baker & Linn, 1997). With individualized grading, it is also possible to recognize and nurture unique capabilities. Better means of doing that can help to encourage students and make more effective use of diverse skills. Remarkably, we are still somewhat in the dark as to how grading can best enhance intrinsic motivation for learning (Deci, Koestner, & Ryan, 2001).

In college admissions, there is a familiar method of realizing additional benefit of teacher judgment; that is, to seek directly the teacher's assessment of a student's notable cognitive and conative skills rather than rely only on grades. Issues of privacy and disclosure do compromise candid recommendations, but graduate schools still rely on references. And we know that school recommendations can help in selecting students who are successful in college (Willingham, 1985). Our data in Grades and Test Scores indicate that there is a wealth of information in teacher judgments, even though those judgments are also subject to variation in standards. It may be worth the effort to seek legal and ethical ways to solicit teacher judgments more systematically.

THE PROSPECTS

Overall, how should we view the possibilities for improving grades for use in admissions? There is no grand solution to improving grades, because valid and fair grading entails a complex set of issues and considerations. Correcting for disparate grading standards from class to class or school to school seems technically and politically doubtful for the reasons cited. The local excellence model addresses such variations in grading in a different manner and deserves further study. Improvement in the quality of the grade itself (as opposed to adjusting for differences in grading level) depends largely on the people who assign grades, not researchers or admissions officers. That is because improving the substance of grades does not merely mean improving the use or technology of grading. It also means improving education.

With that thought, consider that grades and tests not only have complementary strengths; to some degree they represent different pedagogies. The motivational and judgmental features of grades are more student centered (J. Dewey & E. Dewey, 1915/1962); the cognitive and standards-based emphasis of tests are more centered on the academic-curriculum (Ravitch, 2000). These two philosophies have competed for many decades. Improving the rigor and effectiveness of the student-centered features of classroom grading is clearly a goal worth pursuing, but history suggests that it will not happen easily or quickly (Wraga, 2001).

Meanwhile, a reasonable alternative is to use additional information that gets at the student-centered features of grading—particularly evidence that is more precise or more direct regarding educationally relevant student skills and dispositions. I still have an old-fashioned attraction to teacher references, but a student's public record is richer and probably a more direct and practical source of such additional information. Studies continue to suggest that more can be gleaned from the student's transcript and experience in school than we do at present (Adelman, 1999; Willingham et al., 2000).

Finding better ways to assess and encourage scholastic engagement seems a promising avenue. But does the use of such additional information just create more hurdles in the admissions process? I prefer to think that it would give applicants more choice of hurdles—and perhaps soften the edges of a selection process that may be unduly mechanical for some students. It is reasonable to caution, however, that broadening and detailing the basis of high-stakes decisions may well inspire new negative influences on the educational experience in secondary school. Obvious among the possibilities are even more intensive coaching efforts and admissions gamesmanship than students already face. However, those effects may befall students just as readily as a consequence of defining the particulars of a standards-based test as from emphasizing the specifics of meritorious engagement in school.

As Gardner (1961) argued years ago, there are multiple forms of excellence. Placing more priority on the special strengths of grades should help to enhance diversity in standards of admission and student bodies so admitted. Correspondingly, we can make better use of grades if grading fosters common educational objectives but also recognizes unique skills and accomplishments that can further enhance individual development and opportunity. Our most valued educational outcomes are not likely to be fully plumbed or realized without professional judgment regarding the development of individual students.

Finally, I discussed the use of grades in admissions only as a selection measure. College selection measures are routinely and too narrowly evaluated on the basis of their correlation with college GPA. In the best interests of the institution and of society generally, colleges might well give equal consideration to what skills and characteristics, on their merits, deserve representation in a freshman class. That distinction prompts a question seldom examined. How good is the college GPA as a measure of success in college—and in adult life? It is wise to remember that the adequacy of the criteria of success is just as important—and no less problematic—as the adequacy of admissions criteria.

REFERENCES

Adelman, C. (1999). *Answers in the tool box: Academic intensity, attendance patterns, and bachelor's degree attainment.* Washington, DC: U.S. Department of Education, Office of Educational Research and Improvement.

American Psychological Association, American Educational Research Association, & National Council on Measurement in Education. (1999). *Standards for educational and psychological testing.* Washington, DC: American Educational Research Association.

Baker, E. L., & Linn, R. L. (1997). *Emerging educational standards of performance in the United States* (CSE Tech. Rep. No. 437). Los Angeles: National Center for Research on Evaluation, Standards, and Student Testing.

Cureton, L. W. (1971). The history of grading practices. *Measurement in Education, 2*(4), 1–8.

Deci, E. L., Koestner, R., & Ryan, R. M. (2001). Extrinsic rewards and intrinsic motivation in education: Reconsidered once again. *Review of Educational Research, 71*(1), 1–27.

Dewey, J., & Dewey, E. (1962). *Schools of tomorrow.* New York: Dutton. (Original work published 1915)

Elliott, R., & Strenta, A. C. (1988). Effects of improving the reliability of the GPA on prediction generally and on comparative predictions for gender and race particularly. *Journal of Educational Measurement, 25*(4), 333–347.

Gardner, J. W. (1961). *Excellence: Can we be equal and excellent too?* New York: Harper & Row.

Ingels, S. J., Dowd, K. L., Baldridge, J. D., Stipe, J. L., Bartot, V. H., & Frankel, M. R. (1994). *Second follow-up: Student component data file user's manual* (NCES 94-374). Washington, DC: National Center for Education Statistics, U.S. Department of Education.

Linn, R. L. (1966). Grade adjustments for prediction of academic performance: A review. *Journal of Educational Measurement, 3* (4), 313–329.

Milton, O., Pollio, H. R., & Eison, J. A. (1986). *Making sense of college grades.* San Francisco: Jossey-Bass.

Public Agenda (2000, February 16). Reality check 2000 [Special rep.]. *Education Week,* pp. S1–S8.

Ramist, L., Lewis, C., & McCamley, L. (1990). Implications of using freshman GPA as the criterion for the predictive validity of the SAT. In W. W. Willingham, C. Lewis, R. Morgan, & L. Ramist (Eds.), *Predicting college grades: An analysis of institutional trends over two decades* (pp. 253–288). Princeton, NJ: Educational Testing Service.

Ravitch, D. (2000). *Left back: A century of failed school reforms.* New York: Simon & Schuster.

Richards, J. M., Jr., Holland, J. L., & Lutz, S. W. (1967). Prediction of student accomplishment in college. *Journal of Educational Psychology, 58* (6), 343–355.

Robinson, G. E., & Craver, J. M. (1989). *Assessing and grading student achievement.* Arlington, VA: Educational Research Service.

Shepard, L. A. (2000). *The role of classroom assessment in teaching and learning* (CSE Tech. Rep. No. 517). Los Angeles: National Center for Research on Evaluation, Standards, and Student Testing.

Snow, R. E. (1989). Toward assessment of cognitive and conative structures in learning. *Educational Researcher, 18* (9), 8–14.

Starch, D., & Elliott, E. C. (1912). Reliability of the grading of high-school work in English. *School Review, 20,* 442–457.

Stiggins, R. J. (2001). The unfulfilled promise of classroom assessment. *Educational Measurement: Issues and Practice, 20* (3), 5–15.

Terwilliger, J. S. (1989). Classroom standard setting and grading practices. *Educational Measurement: Issues and Practices, 8* (2), 15–19.

Webb, S. (1959). Measured changes in college grading standards. *College Board Review, 39,* 27–30.

Willingham, W. W. (1963). Adjusting college predictions on the basis of academic origins. In M. Katz (Ed.), *The twentieth yearbook of the National Council on Measurement in Education* (pp. 1–6). East Lansing, MI: National Council on Measurement in Education.

Willingham, W. W. (1985). *Success in college: The role of personal qualities and academic ability.* New York: College Entrance Examination Board.

Willingham, W. W., & Cole, N. S. (1997). *Gender and fair assessment.* Mahwah, NJ: Lawrence Erlbaum Associates.

Willingham, W. W., & Lewis, C. (1990). Institutional differences in prediction trends. In W. W. Willingham, C. Lewis, R. Morgan, & L. Ramist (Eds.), *Predicting college grades: An analysis of institutional trends over two decades* (pp. 141–158). Princeton, NJ: Educational Testing Service.

Willingham, W. W., Pollack, J., & Lewis C. (2000). *Grades and test scores: Accounting for observed differences* (ETS RR-00-15). Princeton, NJ: Educational Testing Service.

Willingham, W. W., Pollack, J., & Lewis, C. (2002). Grades and test scores: Accounting for observed differences. *Journal of Educational Measurement, 39* (1), 1–37.

Wraga, W. G. (2001). Left out: The villainization of progressive education in the United States. *Educational Researcher, 30* (7), 34–39.

Ziomek, R. L., & Svec, J. C. (1995). *High school grades and achievement: Evidence of grade inflation* (ACT Research Rep. No. Series 95–3). Iowa City, IA: American College Testing Program.

8

Evaluating
College Applicants:
Some Alternatives

Robert L. Linn
University of Colorado at Boulder

The subject of college admissions initially brings to mind the image of a highly selective college or university that faces the task of deciding who will be included among the small fraction of its applicants offered admission. In fact, of course, most colleges are not very selective. Indeed, many colleges will accept any high school graduate. These colleges have to work harder to recruit enough students to fill their freshman classes than to choose which of their applicants they will admit. Nonetheless, public perceptions of and debates about college admissions are shaped by the practices of the highly selective institutions, particularly the most prestigious private colleges and public universities that receive many more applicants than they have spaces in the freshman class.

Attention to the practices of highly selective colleges and universities is understandable in light of the substantial benefits that Bowen and Bok (1998) demonstrated those institutions bestow on their graduates. Bowen and Bok have also noted, "[t]he AIMS and VALUES of an educational institution are often revealed most vividly by the choices it makes in selecting its students"

(p. 15). For these reasons, the admissions practices of highly prestigious colleges and universities deserve close scrutiny and public debate.

HIGH SCHOOL RECORDS

In a society that values hard work and individual achievement, it is to be expected that past accomplishments as reflected in a student's high-school record (courses completed and GPA or rank in class) play a prominent role in admissions. There is ample evidence that high-school rank in class (HSR) or high school GPA (HSGPA) is a good, often the best, predictor of future academic success in college (e.g., ACT, 1988; Bridgeman, McCamley-Jenkins, & Ervin, 2000; Camara & Echternacht, 2000; Donlon, 1984; Willingham, Lewis, Morgan, & Ramist, 1990). That the HSR or HSGPA is a good predictor of either freshman or 4-year college GPA is rather remarkable in light of the wide variation in grading standards that exists from school to school and from course to course within a school.

Prediction can be improved by accounting for some of the variation in grading standards. For example, the use of a GPA based solely on academic courses instead of overall HSGPA or HSR generally results in better prediction. Improvements can also be achieved by making adjustments for school-to-school differences in grading standards (e.g., Linn, 1966). The precision of the predictions made from HSGPA or HSR can be improved also by taking into account known sources of variation in the criterion measure, college GPA, by predicting separately by college major or by adjusting for differential grading standards of different clusters of college courses (e.g., Elliott & Strenta, 1988; Pennock-Roman, 1994).

There is little doubt about the utility of high-school records in the college admissions process, nor is there much controversy about their use for this purpose. On the other hand, the use of other information, whether in the form of personal characteristics or the results of standardized tests, can engender considerable debate and controversy.

STANDARDIZED TESTS

Tests have played a prominent and often controversial role in admissions to selective colleges in the United States throughout the 20th century. The nature of the tests and the test-related issues that have led to the greatest controversy has changed over the years. At times, the focus of controversy has been on issues of presumed bias against students from lower socioeconomic backgrounds, against racial and/or ethnic minority students, or against women. At other times the debate has been about the presumed effects of the tests on schools or on issues related to coaching for the tests.

Prior to the creation of the College Entrance Examination Board at the start of the 20th century, colleges relied on their own testing procedures. Not surprisingly, the specific admissions requirements of individual colleges were varied enough to cause major problems for secondary schools seeking to prepare students for a variety of colleges.

The College Entrance Examination Board was created as a means of bringing coherence and uniformity to the examinations used in college admissions. Curriculum standards were a central concern in the formation of the College Board (Valentine, 1987). In today's terminology, the Board addressed voluntary content standards and assessments while leaving it to each college to determine its own performance standards for admission. As stated in the First Annual Report of the Secretary in 1901, the goal was to "set a fair standard based upon normal secondary school instruction; this standard to be set, and to be administered in cooperation with other colleges and schools" (College Entrance Examination Board, 1925, p. 84). That is, the aim was the establishment of "uniformity of definitions, topic by topic, with a uniform test uniformly administered." Each college, however, was expected to "fix its own standards for admission" (College Entrance Examination Board, 1925, p. 84).

The early College Board tests were, of course, essay exams. More relevant to current discussions stimulated by Atkinson's (2001) call for the University of California to use achievement tests in place of the SAT I, the early College Board tests were examinations in specific subject areas such as Latin, mathematics, or physics.

Although the number of test takers was tiny by today's standards (4,952 candidates in 1915), the influence of the College Board tests on the curriculum of both private and public secondary schools increased as the number of colleges participating increased (see chap. 2 in Valentine, 1987). The influence over the secondary school curriculum contributed to the movement away from specific subject-matter examinations to tests that were intended to be more curriculum neutral—an idea that is today, once again, a controversial one.

The subject-specific examinations gave way to more curriculum-neutral "comprehensive" examinations, which, in turn, gave way to the Scholastic Aptitude Test (SAT) in 1926. The essay exams continued as the dominant format of admissions testing, however, until the exigencies of World War II created a climate that favored the machine-scored SAT.

The close linkages between the SAT and conceptions of intelligence tests and notions of fixed abilities that were in vogue at the time the SAT was introduced is an unfortunate legacy that clouds discussions of admissions testing even today (e.g., Gladwell, 2001). Although scholastic aptitude is more modest in scope than intelligence, the popular connotation of aptitude being a fixed capacity has proved hard to dispel despite repeated efforts to describe the SAT as a measure of developed ability that is influenced by experiences both in and out of school (e.g., Messick & Jungeblut, 1981).

A fixed-capacity interpretation undermines reforms that would use tests and assessments to encourage greater effort. Concerns about such unintended connotations of the word "aptitude" led to the decision of the College Board to change the name of the SAT from Scholastic Aptitude Test to Scholastic Assessment Test and then simply to the SAT I.

The College Board Web site recently provided the following description of what the SAT I measures for potential test takers. "The SAT I measures verbal and mathematical skills that you develop over time through the work you do in school and on your own" (College Board, 2002a). This description clearly attempts to tie the SAT I to work done in school, but does so at a very general level rather than to any particular courses of study.

Based on the fact that some form of standardized test has been used as part of the college admissions process throughout the past 100 years, it seems clear that standardized tests are perceived to serve a useful role in the admissions process. The question is not so much whether standardized tests will be part of the process, as it is what type of tests should be used and what principles should drive the choice of tests.

The most fundamental question for any test use is, of course, validity. But the concept of *validity* is quite broad. Several different aspects of validity must be considered if appeals to validity are going to help guide the choice of tests to be used for a specific purpose such as college admissions.

Willingham et al. (1990) suggested that there are four major aspects of validity that should be considered in evaluating a test for use in college admissions. These categories are concerned with test content, prediction, fairness, and consequences of test use. Questions about these four aspects of validity touch on central aspects of the current debate about the types of tests that should be used in college admissions.

Appropriateness of Content

Willingham et al. (1990) argued that the first category of questions is concerned with the test content. "Is the content of the test appropriate? Does it measure educationally important knowledge, skills, and developed abilities? Is there alternative content that would serve better?" (p. 7).

It is significant that questions regarding content are first on the list. It makes it clear that "dust-bowl" empiricism that would support any test that had desired empirical properties, such as good prediction of subsequent performance, is not a sufficient basis for defending the use of a test in college admissions. The test must measure knowledge, skills, and developed abilities that are judged to be educationally important. Although judges will surely differ in what is considered educationally important, raising the question of appropriate content would seem to make it harder to defend, if not rule out completely, certain types of test tasks such as digit span or progressive matrices. The question of the appropriateness of content is likely to privilege content that is more closely aligned to educational goals or standards. Judges will differ, however, in the priority that they would give to tests such as the SAT I that measure developed verbal and mathematical reasoning abilities that are not tied to any particular curriculum or course of study versus achievement tests in specific content areas that are closely linked to content standards or courses of study in high school.

The College Board makes a case for the appropriateness of the content of the SAT I in a document entitled "What Does the SAT Measure and Why Does it Matter?" (College Board, 2002c). In that document, it is argued that the SAT verbal test measures "critical reading" skills that "have gained importance for success in high school" (p. 4). The SAT math test is said to measure "problem solving" and it is noted that "[t]he emphasis on problem solving mirrors the higher academic standards that are in effect in virtually every state" (p. 4). The focus on critical reading and problem solving is further justified as follows: "The reason that both the standards and the SAT focus on critical reading and problem solving is that these are the very skills required for full access to academic life in college" (p. 4).

Not surprisingly, the argument for the content appropriateness of the ACT assessment takes a somewhat different form. The following description is provided on the ACT Web site. "The ACT Assessment tests are curriculum based. The ACT Assessment is not an aptitude or an IQ test. Instead, the questions on the ACT are directly related to what you have learned in your high school courses in English, mathematics, and science. Because the ACT tests are based on what is taught in the high school curriculum, students are generally more comfortable with the ACT than they are with the traditional aptitude tests or tests with narrower content" (ACT, Inc., 2002).

The SAT II subject tests are designed to be even closer to the intended content of high-school courses. They are linked more directly to specific high-school courses, such as biology, chemistry, U.S. history, or Spanish, than either the SAT I or the ACT. According to the College Board, the stated purpose of the SAT II subject tests is to "measure knowledge or skills in a particular subject and [the test taker's] ability to apply that knowledge" (College Board, 2002b, p. 1).

Although the appeal to different audiences will vary, it is clearly possible to make a coherent argument supporting the appropriateness of the content of the SAT I, the ACT, and the SAT II for use in college admissions. Defensible arguments regarding the appropriateness of content could also be made for some state high-school testing systems (e.g., the New York Regents examinations or the Virginia end-of-course tests). The challenge for colleges and universities choosing a test in terms of content is to answer the last content question suggested by Willingham et al. (1990), that is, to decide which test has the content that will best serve the goal of measuring "educationally important knowledge, skills, and developed abilities" (p. 7).

Prediction

The second category of questions identified by Willingham et al. (1990) deals with prediction. Some questions about prediction for a potential admissions test are as follows: "Is the test effective in predicting academic performance? Would other measures work better or prove to be useful supplements? Does the test add useful information to measures already available?" (Willingham et al., 1990, p. 7).

Although the vast majority of research concerning college admissions tests has been focused on evaluating the degree to which tests predict performance in college—most commonly defined as the freshman GPA (FGPA)—and the degree to which tests have incremental predictive power beyond high-school grades or rank in class, prediction is the second question for Willingham and his colleagues.

Considerations of predictive power do relatively little to distinguish among the different types of standardized tests that have been used or have been proposed for use in college admissions. Small differences in predictive accuracy or incremental validity of the SAT I, the ACT, and the SAT II are sometimes found. Geiser and Studley (2001), for example, recently found that a combination of three SAT II subject tests provides slightly better prediction and has somewhat greater incremental validity than the SAT I for predicting grades at the University of California campuses. They also found that the SAT I does not have incremental predictive value beyond HSGPA and the SAT II. Generally, however, the SAT I, the ACT, or a combination of three SAT II achievement tests provide reasonably similar levels of predictive accuracy either by themselves or in combination with HSR or HSGPA in predicting college GPA. Furthermore, the predictive value of the three test batteries is largely redundant, that is, adding a second test battery does not markedly improve the predictive accuracy beyond what can be achieved with HSR or HSGPA and one of the test batteries (see, e.g., Bridgeman, Burton, & Cline, 2001, 2004; Kobrin, Camara, & Milewski, 2004).

Moreover, using data from 10 selective colleges, Bridgeman et al. (2001, 2004) found that the students who would be selected using high-school grades and the SAT II test average would be mostly the same as those who would be selected using high-school grades and the SAT I. One exception to this broad general finding is that more Mexican American and other Latino students would be selected with the SAT II subject test average, particularly if they were allowed to include the Spanish test. The latter finding for the SAT II subject test average that includes the Spanish test is consistent with the results obtained by Geiser and Studley (2001) for the University of California system. Overall, however, prediction does not provide a strong basis for preferring one test to another.

Fairness

"Is the test fair to subgroups? Does it fairly represent their educational achievement and their likely success in college? Is the balance of content as fair as possible to diverse groups? Would alternative content or measures be fairer overall?" (Willingham et al., 1990, p. 7). Such questions represent the third category of validity concerns.

Standardization used to be almost synonymous with test fairness when the latter "was viewed mainly as the administration of objective tests under standard and secure conditions to protect individuals from prejudiced or capricious high-stakes decisions" (Willingham & Cole, 1997, p. 6). As Willingham and Cole noted, however, the concept of test fairness has evolved. They argued that the concept of test fairness was made more complicated by the addition of requirements that the test be unbiased and that the uses of test results be equitable and just. They went on to make the case that "fairness is an important aspect of validity" and that "[a]nything that reduces fairness also reduces validity" (p. 6). They concluded that "test fairness is best conceived as comparability in assessment; more specifically comparable validity for all individuals and groups" (pp. 6–7).

There is considerable evidence that validity coefficients vary as a function of gender and race and/or ethnicity. Correlations of test scores with

FGPA are generally lower for men than for women. Some reviews (e.g., Linn, 1982a; Ramist, Lewis, & McCamley-Jenkins, 1993; Young, 2004) have also found that test validities tend to be slightly lower for African American and Hispanic students than for White students. Because of the somewhat lower validity coefficients for African American and Hispanic students than for White students, Young (in press) suggested that less weight might reasonably be given to test scores for African American and Hispanic students than for White or Asian American students. It should be noted, however, that the slightly lower validity finding is not universal. Other meta-analyses have found that validities are as high or even higher for African American and Hispanic students than they are for White students (e.g., Bridgeman et al., 2000). Furthermore, even when the validities are slightly lower correlations between test scores and freshman grades, the incremental contribution of test scores to a combined prediction equation involving high-school grades and test scores is generally as large or larger for African American and Hispanic students as it is for White students (Kobrin et al., in press; Ramist, Lewis, & McCamley-Jenkins, 1993).

Systematic differences in regression equations for subgroups are more rel-evant to questions of fair selection than are differences in validities. That is so because different regression lines can result in systematic over- or underpre-diction of the actual performance of members of a subgroup. When subgroup regression equations are compared, it is commonly found that the actual FGPAs of women are slightly underpredicted by test scores alone or test scores in com-bination with high-school grades. FGPAs of African American and Hispanic students, on the other hand, tend to be slightly overpredicted from test scores alone or in combination with high-school grades (see, e.g., Burton & Ramist, 2001; Linn, 1982a; Noble, 2004; Ramist et al., 1993; Young, 2004). Differ-ences in validities for men and women and the underprediction for women are attributable, in part, but not entirely, to differences in course-taking pat-terns (e.g., Pennock-Roman, 1994; Young, 2004). Explanations of differences in validities for different racial and/or ethic groups and the tendency for the actual performance of African American and Hispanic student to be slightly overpredicted are not so apparent.

Equating test fairness with comparable validity for all individuals and groups places some constraints on the concept that may not be compatible with certain views of equity or justice. The formulation by Willingham and Cole (1997), however, provides a useful lens for analyzing quite a range of fairness issues. Test fairness defined as comparable validity has serious implications for the ways in which evidence can be brought to bear on fairness questions and challenges some older ways of thinking about fairness.

Although popular discussions often speak of validity as if it were an all-or-nothing characteristic of a test, there is broad professional consensus that validity is neither a property of the instrument nor an all-or-nothing characteristic. Inferences and actions based on test scores are validated—not the test itself. Validity is always a matter of degree. The same could be said of fairness. Conceptualizing fairness as a matter of degree rather than as an all-or-nothing characteristic, however, may be even farther removed from common usage than in the case of validity. It may also be even more foreign to think of fairness as residing not in the test but in the inferences or decisions based on test scores.

Evidence about construct underrepresentation and construct-irrelevant difficulty (Messick, 1989) is especially important to an evaluation of the fairness of a test because groups may differ in a wide variety of attitudes, experiences, and capabilities that are not explicitly a part of the intended focus of measurement. The test would have reduced validity and be less fair to the degree that those ancillary skills and characteristics affect performance on the test. It should be noted that skills that are considered ancillary or sources of construct-irrelevant difficulty for one interpretation or use of test results may be relevant for a different intended use and interpretation.

It is certainly reasonable to ask whether the SAT I reasoning tests, the SAT II subject tests, the ACT general achievement tests, or some other set of tests, for example, a state-sponsored set of end-of-course tests such as those in use in Virginia or a set of standards-based general achievement tests such as the New York Regents examinations, is best when judged in terms of fairness. Not surprisingly, however, the answer is complicated. The answer depends on considerations of differential student access to high-quality instruction in school and to learning experiences outside of school. Course specific examinations, for example, may be considered fair if there is reasonably uniform access, across identifiable subgroups of students, to courses that provide an adequate opportunity to learn the material that is tested. More generalized achievement tests such as the ACT or the SAT I reasoning tests may be considered fairer when there is substantial variation in the specific courses that are available for students as well as in the content coverage of those courses.

Geiser and Studley's (2001) analyses for the University of California system reveal some small comparative advantages of using two or three SAT II subject tests rather than using the SAT I. This analysis was based on subgroups of students classified by their high school's quintiles on an achievement index based on the California state assessment program. Standardized differences in the means between racial and/or ethnic groups and all students were slightly smaller for underrepresented minority groups on the SAT II than the SAT I.

There also was a small advantage for the SAT II over the SAT I when predictions were made within racial and/or ethnic groups.

Consequences of Test Use

The fourth and last category of questions proposed by Willingham et al. (1990) is concerned with the consequences of test use. Although there has been some disagreement in the field regarding the desirability of including the consequences of test use as a part of validity, there is a broad consensus that investigations of the consequences of test use are an important part of the overall evaluation of particular interpretations and uses of test results.

For the evaluation of tests for use in college admissions, Willingham et al. (1990) suggested that the questions regarding consequences should include the following. "Are the consequences of test use—including costs, benefits, practical considerations, and side effects—positive overall? If there were no test—or another type of test—would the effects on students, schools, colleges, and the educational system be better or worse?" (p. 7).

The *perceived* consequences of using different types of tests in college admissions elicit the clearest distinctions and the sharpest debate. Atkinson's (2001) speech at the Annual Meeting of the American Council on Education relied on presumed consequences on high schools and on college-intending students as the primary rationale for his suggestion that the University of California phase out the SAT I in favor of the SAT II or other achievement tests that have a more direct connection to desired instruction and learning in high school. Specifically, Atkinson (2001) reasoned that

> the use of tests that assess mastery of specific subject areas . . . will help strengthen high school curricula and pedagogy, create a stronger connection between what students accomplish in high school and their likelihood of being admitted to UC, and focus student attention on mastery of subject matter rather than test preparation. (p. 1)

The College Board has argued that an SAT I requirement does not discourage high schools from offering challenging courses because the evidence shows that, increasingly, students who take the SAT I have been taking more challenging academic courses in high schools over the past 10 years. But, it might be noted that this correlation does not necessarily imply that the SAT I requirement is reinforcing the teaching of demanding courses in various subject areas. The possibly stronger argument in favor of the SAT I is the claim that it can identify promising students who have not been adequately challenged by their schools.

Twenty years ago, I made a similar argument, noting that one of the advantages of a test like the SAT is that it provided a second chance to students who may not have had access to good preparation in high school or who may not have applied themselves in high school to show that they were capable (Linn, 1982b). Unfortunately, that argument, as well as the ones advanced by Atkinson and by the College Board, depends almost entirely on armchair analyses. There is a paucity of hard evidence to support any of these arguments. There is, however, a lingering concern for the SAT I that stems from its legacy; no matter how often recanted, there remains a commonly held view that the SAT I measures native ability. This interpretation undermines the message to students that effort is important. To the extent that the native ability view is believed, it has a negative consequence.

PERSONAL CHARACTERISTICS

College admissions procedures often include consideration of a variety of personal characteristics. High-school athletic accomplishments obviously loom large in recruiting college athletes, but many other factors can also influence the likelihood of admissions to selective colleges and universities. Involvement in leadership activities in high school, in volunteer activities, and accomplishments in art or music can all influence the probability of admissions above and beyond high-school grades and test scores. Preference for children of alumni is also evident at many institutions. The state of residence of applicants is, in some cases, a major consideration.

At the most selective 20% of colleges and universities, the probability of admissions also depends on an applicant's racial and/or ethnic status (Kane, 1998). It has been more than 20 years since the Supreme Court ruled in the Bakke case (*Regents of the University of California v. Bakke*, 1978) that race could be considered as one factor in admissions decisions. Despite strong arguments for the benefits of diversity and for the importance of considering race in admissions to achieve a diverse student body (e.g., Bowen & Bok, 1998), affirmative action practices by public universities have been undermined by executive and legislative actions, referenda, and court decisions in recent years in some of the most populous states (e.g., California, Texas, Florida, and Michigan). Two related decisions by the U.S. Supreme Court in June 2003 involving undergraduate (*Gratz v. Bollinger*) and law school admissions (*Grutter v. Bollinger*) at the University of Michigan, however, have held that race can be considered in admissions but not in a formulaic way as was being done at the undergraduate level.

Challenges to race-based admissions polices have led public universities to seek other means of achieving diversity. The use of correlates of race and/or ethnicity such as socioeconomic status, however, have been shown to fall far short of accomplishing what was achieved by direct consideration of race and/or ethnicity (Kane, 1998). Moving to $x\%$ rules, where the top $x\%$ of each high-school graduating class is eligible for or offered admissions, such as the policies implemented in California, Texas, and Florida, comes closer to achieving the level of diversity that was in effect before requirements for race-neutral admissions were put in place. Because of the lower probability of students from high schools with high proportions of African American or Hispanic students both applying and meeting other admissions requirements (such as course or test requirements), the $x\%$ rules still falls short of achieving the diversity that selective universities in California had when race and/or ethnicity was explicitly considered as one factor in admissions (Koretz, Russell, Shin, Shasby, & Horn, 2001).

There is a compelling case for the benefits of diversity to institutions, the larger society, and to both the majority and minority group students attending selective colleges and universities. Students and graduates attest to the benefits of diversity. The case is quite strong that racial and/or ethnic minorities, educated at selective institutions, make contributions to the professions they enter and to the wider society (Bowen & Bok, 1998). The value does not derive from better aggregate academic performance, but from richer experiences for all students. Although there are strong pressures to curtail the direct use of race as a factor in admissions, there is also considerable evidence that selective colleges and universities will find ways achieving the desired degree of diversity of their student bodies in other ways. They may do this by using $x\%$ rules, or by moving, as Atkinson (2001) urged, away from "narrowly quantitative formulas and instead adopt procedures that look at applicants in a comprehensive, holistic way" (p. 1).

CONCLUSION

The basis on which colleges and universities make admissions decisions is indicative of the values of the institution and has major implications, not only for the make-up of their student bodies, but for the prestige of the institutions. Achievement in high school, as reflected in courses completed and high-school grades earned, are the most widely used and most readily accepted academic measures used in making admissions decisions. They provide good, usually the single best, prediction of academic achievement in college.

Standardized tests, although subject to a considerably greater degree of controversy than are grades, have also been used by a substantial majority of selective colleges and universities in making admissions decisions throughout the 20th century. A useful set of questions for evaluating the use of standardized tests in college admissions has been proposed by Willingham et al. (1990). Those questions fall into four categories: the appropriateness of content, prediction, fairness, and consequences of test use. Although some distinctions can be made among the major test competitors, (i.e., the ACT, the SAT I, and the SAT II) in terms of prediction and fairness, the major distinctions among these tests are in terms of the perceived appropriateness of the content of the different tests in the putative consequences of using the different tests.

The SAT I, the ACT, and the SAT II differ in the degree to which their content is tied to the materials intended to be covered in the high-school curriculum. The SAT I is farthest removed from specific content of high-school courses, but an argument can be made that it measures the broad process skills, for example, critical reading and problem solving, that are emphasized in the content standards adopted by a number of states. The ACT has a closer correspondence to the subject matter content taught in high schools than does the SAT I, but is not aligned to specific courses of study such as physics, American history, or Spanish to the same degree as the SAT II.

When consequences of test use are considered, arguments in favor of the SAT I rely heavily on the idea of offering a second chance to students who may not have achieved up to their ability in high school. Arguments in favor of the ACT or SAT II, on the other hand, rely on the notion that those tests will reinforce content standards and curriculum expectations and encourage greater effort on the part of students. Unfortunately, there is a paucity of evidence to support claims regarding the consequences of using the different tests.

Although high-school grades and standardized tests are the two dominant factors in selection among students who apply, they are frequently not decisive. Personal characteristics of students such as athletic skills, alumni status of parents, and personal accomplishments beyond grades can have a major impact on the probability of admissions. Race and ethnicity can also alter the probability of admission, especially at the most selective colleges and universities. Rationales for affirmative action and for explicitly considering race and/or ethnicity as a factor in admissions include the benefits of a diverse student body and the contributions of racial and/or ethnic minorities to the professions and society. Nonetheless, affirmative action is under siege from executive orders, legislative actions, referenda, and court decisions. It seems clear that when the most selective colleges and universities are denied the ability to take race and/or ethnicity into account explicitly as one factor in the admissions process, they will make a concerted effort to meet the goals of diversity in other ways.

REFERENCES

ACT, Inc. (2002). *ACT assessment: Frequently asked questions.* Retrieved November 5, 2002, from www.act.org/aap/faq/general.html

American College Testing Program. (1988). *ACT assessment program technical manual.* Iowa City: Author.

Atkinson, R. C. (2001, February 18). *Standardized tests and access to American universities.* The 2001 Robert H. Atwell Distinguished Lecture, delivered at the 83rd Annual Meeting of the American Council on Education, Washington, DC.

Bowen, W. G., & Bok, D. (1998). *The shape of the river: Long-term consequences of considering race in college and university admissions.* Princeton, NJ: Princeton University Press.

Bridgeman, B., Burton, N., & Cline, F. (2001). *Substituting SAT II: Subject tests for SAT I: Reasoning test: Impact on admitted class composition and quality* (Research Rep. No. 2001–3). New York: The College Board.

Bridgeman, B., Burton, N., & Cline, F. (2004). Replacing reasoning tests with achievement tests in university admissions: Does it make a difference? In R. Zwick (Ed.), *Rethinking the SAT: The future of standardized admissions testing* (pp. 277–288). New York: RoutledgeFalmer.

Bridgeman, B., McCamley-Jenkins, L., & Ervin, N. (2000). *Predictions of freshman grade-point average from the revised and recentered SAT I: Reasoning Test* (Research Rep. No. 2000–1). New York: The College Board.

Burton, N., & Ramist, L. (2001). *Predicting success in college: SAT studies of classes graduating since 1980* (Research Rep. No. 2001–2). New York: The College Board.

Camara, W. J., & Echternacht, G. (2000, July). *The SAT-I and high school grades: Utility in predicting success in college* (Research Notes No. RN-10). New York: The College Board.

College Board. (2002a). *Q & A: Nearly everything you want to know about the SAT.* Retrieved October 29, 2002, from http://www.collegeboard.com

College Board. (2002b). *SAT II learning center: Meet the SAT II: Subject tests.* Retrieved November 5, 2002 from http://www.collegeboard.com/sat/center2/meet.html

College Board. (2002c). *What does the SAT measure and why does it matter?* Retrieved November 5, 2002, from http:// www.collegeboard.org/html/pdf/sat_measure.pdf

College Entrance Examination Board. (1925). *Twenty-fifth annual report of the Secretary.* New York: Author.

Donlon, T. (Ed.). (1984). *The College Board technical handbook for the Scholastic Aptitude Test and Achievement Tests.* New York: College Entrance Examination Board.

Elliott, R., & Strenta, A. C. (1988). Effects of improving the reliability of GPA on prediction generally and on comparative predictions for gender and race particularly. *Journal of Educational Measurement, 25,* 333–347.

Geiser, S., & Studley, R. (2001). *UC and the SAT: Predictive validity and differential impact of the SAT I vs. the SAT II achievement tests at the University of California.* Oakland: University of California, Office of the President.

Gladwell, M. (2001, December 17). Examined life: What Stanley Kaplan taught us about the SAT. *The New Yorker.*

Gratz v. Bollinger, 123 S. Ct. (2003).

Grutter v. Bollinger, 123 S. Ct. (2003).

Kane, T. J. (1998). Racial and ethnic preferences in college admissions. In C. Jencks & M. Phillips (Eds.), *The Black–White test score gap* (pp. 431–456). Washington, DC: The Brookings Institute.

Kobrin, J. L., Camara, W. J., & Milewski, G. G. (2004). The utility of the SAT I and SAT II for admissions decisions in California and the nation. In R. Zwick (Ed.), *Rethinking the SAT: The future of standardized admissions testing* (pp. 251–276). New York: RoutledgeFalmer.

Koretz, D., Russell, M., Shin, D., Shasby, K., & Horn, C. (2001). *Testing and diversity in postsecondary education: The case of California* (Tech. Rep.). Newton, MA: Boston College.

Linn, R. L. (1966). Grade adjustment for prediction of academic performance: A review. *Journal of Educational Measurement, 3,* 313–329.

Linn, R. L. (1982a). Ability testing: Individual differences, prediction and differential prediction. In A. K. Wigdor & W. R. Garner (Eds.), *Ability testing: Uses, consequences and controversies* (pp. 335–388). Washington, DC: National Academy Press.

Linn, R. L. (1982b). Admissions testing on trial. *American Psychologist, 37,* 279–291.

Messick, S. (1989). Validity. In R. L. Linn (Ed.), *Educational measurement* (3rd ed., pp. 13–103). New York: Macmillan.

Messick, S., & Jungeblut, A. (1981). Time and method in coaching for the SAT. *Psychological Bulletin, 89,* 191–216.

Noble, J. (2004). The effects of using ACT composite scores and high school averages on college admissions decisions for ethnic groups. In R. Zwick (Ed.), *Rethinking the SAT: The future of standardized admissions testing* (pp. 303–319). New York: RoutledgeFalmer.

Pennock-Roman, M. (1994). *College major and gender differences in prediction of college grades* (College Board Rep. No. 94–2) New York: The College Board.

Ramist, L., Lewis, C., & McCamley-Jenkins, L. (1993). *Student group differences in predicting college grades: Sex, language, and ethnic groups* (College Board Rep. No. 93–1). New York: The College Board.

Regents of the University of Cal. v. Bakke, 438 U.S. 265 (1978).

Valentine, J. A. (1987). *The College Board and the school curriculum.* New York: College Entrance Examination Board.

Willingham, W. W., & Cole, N. S. (1997). *Gender and fair assessment.* Mahwah, NJ: Lawrence Erlbaum Associates.

Willingham, W. W., Lewis, C., Morgan, R., & Ramist, L. (1990). *Predicting college grades: An analysis of institutional trends over two decades.* New York: College Entrance Examination Board.

Young, J. W. (2004). Differential validity and prediction: Race and sex differences in college admissions testing. In R. Zwick (Ed.), *Rethinking the SAT: The future of standardized admissions testing* (pp. 289–301). New York: RoutledgeFalmer.

III

New Constructs
and New Measures

9

Augmenting the SAT Through Assessments of Analytical, Practical, and Creative Skills

Robert J. Sternberg
Yale University

The Rainbow Project Collaborators[1]

Standardized tests are used rather frequently in the United States as well as abroad as one basis for making high-stakes decisions about educational opportunities, placements, and diagnoses. One of the most widely used tests for these purposes is the SAT. Many colleges and universities in the United States use the SAT, usually taken during the high-school years, as a predictor of success in postsecondary education.

[1]The Rainbow Project Collaborators are Damian Birney, Brent Bridgeman, Wayne Camara, Anna Cianciolo, Michael Drebot, Sarah Duman, Richard Duran, Howard Everson, Ann Ewing, Edward Friedman, Elena L. Grigorenko, Diane Halpern, P. J. Henry, Charles Huffman, Linda Jarvin, Smaragda Kazi, Donna Macomber, Laura Maitland, Jack McArdle, Carol Rashotte, Jerry Rudmann, Amy Schmidt, Karen Schmidt, Brent Slife, Mary Spilis, Steven Stemler, Robert J. Sternberg, Carlos Torre, and Richard Wagner. The research described in this article was supported by the College Board.

The SAT I, the main focus of this chapter, is a 3-hour examination currently measuring verbal comprehension and mathematical thinking skills. A writing component is to be added in the near future. A wide variety of studies have shown the usefulness of the SAT as a predictor of college success (Bridgeman, McCamley-Jenkins, & Ervin, 2000; Ramist, Lewis, & McCamley-Jenkins, 1993). The SAT II is a set of subject-specific tests that measures achievement in designated areas such as mathematics, several foreign languages, various sciences, and so forth. An applicant typically takes three subjects.

A recent meta-analysis of the predictive validity of the SAT, encompassing roughly 3,000 studies and over 1 million students, suggested that the SAT is a valid predictor of early college academic performance (as measured by first-year GPA), with validity coefficients generally in the range of .44 to .62 (Hezlett et al., 2001). The validity coefficients for later college performance were somewhat lower but still substantial—generally ranging from the mid-.30s to the mid-.40s. Ramist et al. (1993) found that the validity of the SAT I at 39 colleges was better than that of high-school GPA (HSGPA) for predicting individual course grades, but that HSGPA was a better predictor of overall first-year GPA. The correlations (corrected for shrinkage, restriction of range, and criterion unreliability) were .60 for SAT I, .62 for SAT II, and .63 for HSGPA. The fully corrected multiple correlation of SAT I and SAT II with freshman GPA was .63, and the multiple correlation of HSGPA and SAT I with freshman grades was .71. Correlations for females were generally higher than for males. Correlations of the SAT II differed somewhat for different ethnic groups.

Kobrin, Camara, and Milewski (2002) examined the validity of the SAT for college-admissions decisions in California and elsewhere in the United States among a sample of students in 1995. They too found a substantial relationship between the SAT and performance in college. The correlations (corrected for range restriction and shrinkage) between freshman GPA and the combined SAT I and SAT II scores ranged across different ethnic groups from .35 to .48. However, they also found that in California, SAT I and SAT II both showed moderate correlations with family income (in the range of .25 to .55 for SAT I). Correlations with parental education ranged from .28 to .58. These findings indicate that SAT scores may be a function, in part, of social class. Predictive effectiveness of the SAT was similar for different ethnic groups; however, there were important mean differences on the SAT for the several ethnic groups (see also Bridgeman, Burton, & Cline, 2001). The group differences between the mean score for each group and White students' mean are reported in standard deviation units. On average, African American students scored about one full standard deviation below White students on both the verbal and mathematics tests. Latino students scored about three fourths of a standard deviation lower than the White students, and Native Americans scored about one half of a standard deviation lower than White students on the two tests. Asian students scored higher than White students on the math test by about one third of a standard deviation but were about one third lower on the verbal test.

Altogether, these results suggest good predictive validity for the SAT in predicting college performance. But as is always the case for a single test or type of test, there is room for improvement. The theory of successful intelligence (Sternberg, 1997, 1999) provides one basis for improving prediction and possibly for establishing greater equity. It suggests that broadening the range of skills tested beyond analytical skills, to include practical and creative skills as well, might significantly enhance the prediction of college performance beyond current levels. Thus, the theory does not suggest replacing, but rather, augmenting the SAT in the college-admissions process. A collaborative team of investigators sought to study how successful such augmentation could be.

THE THEORY OF SUCCESSFUL INTELLIGENCE

Successful intelligence is defined in terms of the ability to achieve success in life in terms of one's personal standards, within one's sociocultural context. One's ability to achieve success depends on capitalizing on one's strengths and correcting or compensating for one's weaknesses. Success is attained through using a balance of three aspects of intelligence: analytical, practical, and creative skills. More details on the definition and the theory can be found in Sternberg (1980, 1984, 1985, 1990, 1997, 1999).

Analytical intelligence is involved when skills are used to analyze, evaluate, judge, or compare and contrast. It typically is involved when processing components are applied to relatively familiar kinds of problems where the judgments to be made are of a fairly abstract nature.

Practical intelligence is involved when skills are utilized, implemented, applied, or put into practice in real-world contexts. It involves individuals applying their abilities to the kinds of problems that confront them in daily life, such as on the job or in the home. Practical intelligence involves applying the components of intelligence to one's experience so as to adapt to, shape, and select environments. *Adaptation* is involved when one changes oneself to suit the environment. *Shaping* is involved when one changes the environment to suit oneself. And *selection* is involved when one decides to seek out another environment that is a better match to one's needs, abilities, and desires. People differ in their balance of adaptation, shaping, and selection, and in the competence with which they balance among the three possible courses of action.

Creative intelligence is involved when skills are used to create, invent, discover, imagine, suppose, or hypothesize. Tests of creative intelligence go beyond tests of analytical intelligence in measuring performance on tasks that require individuals to deal with relatively novel situations. Sternberg and his colleagues have shown that when certain types of unconventional tests of intelligence are used, one starts to tap sources of individual differences measured little or not at all by the traditional tests (Sternberg, 1985). Thus it is important to include in a battery of tests problems that are relatively novel in nature. These problems can be either convergent or divergent in nature.

The current study applied the theory of successful intelligence in the creation of tests that capture analytical, practical, and creative skills. This battery, referred to as the Rainbow Measures, was administered to 1,013 students at a variety of institutions across the country, and was used to predict success in school as measured by GPA. The hypotheses were twofold: First, we expected that the battery of tests based on the theory of successful intelligence would predict a substantial proportion of variance in GPA above and beyond that captured by the SAT. Second, we expected that this battery of tests would reduce ethnic differences in scores that result from current standardized college entrance exams such as the SAT.

WHAT WE DID

In this section, we outline the basic methodology used to test the aforementioned hypotheses. First, we describe the institutions that participated in data collection and the participants themselves. We then describe in detail the measures used in the study, including baseline measures and the Rainbow Measures we are introducing as candidates for supplementing the SAT. These measures include three multiple-choice measures from the Sternberg Triarchic Abilities Test (STAT; Sternberg, 1993), three practical performance tasks, and three creativity performance tasks. Finally, we finish the Methods section with a discussion of the study design and procedure.

Participating Institutions

Data were collected at 15 schools across the United States, including 8 4-year colleges, 5 community colleges, and 2 high schools.[2] Most of the data were

---

[2] Participating institutions included Brigham Young University; Florida State University; James Madison University; California State University, San Bernardino; University of California, Santa Barbara; Southern Connecticut State University; Stevens Institute of Technology; Yale University; Mesa Community College; Coastline Community College; Irvine Valley Community

collected from mid-April 2001 through June 2001, although some institutions extended their data collection somewhat further into the summer. All institutions were supportive in their efforts toward collection of the data; when technical problems did occur, they tended to be with the online administration of the measures. Such technical difficulties were, perhaps, to be expected, given the fact that online data collection using these new tests of analytical, practical, and creative skills had not been done before.[3]

Participants were recruited on a volunteer basis, through fliers distributed on campus and through psychology courses at the university and college level, and through psychology classes at the high-school level. Participants either received course credit or were paid $20 for their participation. The participants were 1,013 students predominantly in their first year of college or their final year of high school. Six participants were removed from the analyses due to procedural errors, leaving 1,007 participants.

In this report, we include analyses only for college students, except where otherwise noted. Although the data from the high-school students have their own usefulness, we analyze in detail only data from the college students because we were interested in the extent to which our new measures predict success in college, not success in high school. The final number of participants included in these analyses was 777.

Baseline measures of standardized test scores and HSGPA were collected to evaluate the predictive validity of current tools used for college admission criteria, and to provide a contrast for our current measures. Students' scores on standardized college entrance exams, as well as their self-reported HSGPA, were obtained from the College Board. For most students, we accessed performance on the SAT (math and verbal sections separately, SAT-M and SAT-V), and when these scores were not available, PSAT or ACT scores were obtained. In a small number of instances where students had ACT but not SAT data, the ACT scores were transformed to match the scaling of SAT scores via the algorithm described in Dorans (1999).

There is a potential concern about restriction of range in scores using the SAT when considering students from a select sample of universities.

College; Orange Coast Community College; Saddleback Community College; Mepham High School; and Northview High School.

[3] A few procedural techniques were noted that seemed to facilitate data collection at these institutions. First, when one or two proctors were generally responsible for all data collection for that institution, confusion and administration problems tended to be attenuated. Second, when communication with Yale University was channeled through one spokesperson rather than several people from the same institution, and when that spokesperson was in good contact with the technical support staff from their institution, the data collection ran more smoothly.

However, our sample was taken from institutions that varied widely in selectivity—from community colleges through highly selective 4-year institutions. Additionally, the standard deviation of the SAT scores (for the college sample, $SD_{SAT\ Verbal} = 118.2$, and $SD_{SAT\ Math} = 117.5$) was comparable to the standard deviation of the SAT tests in the broader population. If anything, a chi-squared test suggests that the variance for the sample for these items is statistically larger than for the typical population of SAT examinees. For these reasons, the concern of a restriction of range in the SAT scores is reduced.

The Rainbow Measures

The STAT was developed as a means of capturing analytical, practical, and creative skills using multiple-choice questions (Sternberg & Clinkenbeard, 1995; Sternberg, Ferrari, Clinkenbeard, & Grigorenko, 1996). Level H of the test (Sternberg, 1993) was designed to measure cognitive skills among secondary school and college students, and was used in this study. The STAT briefly measures each of the triarchic skills with three types of item content: verbal, quantitative, and figural. As a result, the STAT scale is composed of nine subscales: analytical–verbal, analytical–quantitative, analytical–figural, practical–verbal, practical–quantitative, practical–figural, creative–verbal, creative–quantitative, and creative–figural. Essay items from the STAT were not used. Each subscale included five multiple-choice items, for a total of 45 items. Nine of those items were new to the STAT. The particular contents of the items that comprise these scales have been described elsewhere (e.g., Sternberg et al., 1996). Each multiple-choice item in the STAT had four different response options from which the correct response is to be selected. A scoring key was used for computing the STAT scores for participants who completed the tests in paper-and-pencil format. In this format, participants circled their response. The responses on the computer-administered tests were automatically entered into a computer file. Ability scores were then computed by combining the responses to the subscales, using item response theory (IRT) to create three final scales representing analytical, practical, and creative skills ($STAT_{Analytical}$, $STAT_{Creative}$, and $STAT_{Practical}$).

Creative Skills—Performance Tasks

In addition to the creative skills measured by the STAT, other such skills were assessed using open-ended measures. Because open-ended measures require more spontaneous and free-form responses, these performance tasks were expected to tap an important part of creativity that might not be measured using multiple-choice items alone.

For each of the tasks, participants were given a choice of topic or stimuli for creating their creative stories or cartoon captions. Although these different topics or stimuli varied in terms of their difficulty for inventing creative stories and captions, these differences are accounted for in the derivation of IRT ability estimates. The data from this portion of the assessment were analyzed using the Facets program (Linacre, 1998). This program generates Rasch ability estimates that have been corrected for differences in: (a) difficulty level of the items; (b) difficulty level of the tasks (e.g., humor, originality); and (c) severity of the judges rating the items.

Each of the creativity performance tasks were rated on criteria that were determined a priori as indicators of creativity.

- *Cartoons.* Participants were given five cartoons purchased from the archives of the *New Yorker,* but with the captions removed. The participants' task was to choose three cartoons, and to provide a caption for each cartoon. Two trained judges rated all the cartoons for cleverness, humor, originality, and task appropriateness on 5-point scales. A combined creativity score was formed as a faceted ability estimate that was adjusted for rater severity, item difficulty, and task difficulty.

- *Written Stories.* Participants were asked to write two stories, spending about 15 min on each, choosing from the following titles: "A Fifth Chance," "2,983," "Beyond the Edge," "The Octopus's Sneakers," "It's Moving Backwards," and "Not Enough Time" (Lubart & Sternberg, 1995; Sternberg & Lubart, 1995). A team of six judges was trained to rate the stories. Each judge rated the stories for originality, complexity, emotional evocativeness, and descriptiveness on 5-point scales. For purposes of efficiency, 64.7% of the stories were rated by one of the six judges.

- *Oral Stories.* Participants were presented with five sheets of paper, each containing a set of 11 to 13 images linked by a common theme (e.g., keys, money, travel, animals playing music, and humans playing music). There were no restrictions on the minimum or maximum number of images that needed to be incorporated into the stories. After choosing one of the pages, the participant was given 15 min to formulate a short story and dictate it into a cassette recorder, which was timed by the proctor for the paper assessments and by the internal computer clock for the computer assessments. In the paper-and-pencil administration of the test, participants simply pressed the "record" button on a cassette recorder to begin dictation of their stories, and pressed "stop" when they were completed. For the computer administration, participants dictated their story into a computer microphone that translated the stories into a *.wav* file that was automatically saved onto the computer. In both cases, the actual dictation period for each story was not to be more than 5 min long. The process was then repeated with another sheet of images so that each participant dictated a total of two oral stories. Six judges were trained to rate the stories. As with the written stories, each judge rated the stories for originality, complexity, emotional evocativeness, and descriptiveness on 5-point scales. For purposes of efficiency, 48.4% of the stories were rated by one of the six judges.

Practical Skills—Performance Tasks

As outlined in Sternberg (1997; Sternberg et al., 2000), *practical skills* include the ability to acquire useful knowledge from experience, including "tacit knowledge," which is not explicitly taught and is often difficult to articulate, and to apply this knowledge to solving complex everyday problems. Complex everyday problems are distinguished from academic problems in that they are practical, they must be solved with incomplete information, and they often do not have a single correct answer. In addition to the practical skills measured by the STAT, practical skill was assessed using three situational-judgment inventories: the Everyday Situational Judgment Inventory (Movies), the Common Sense Questionnaire, and the College Life Questionnaire, each of which tapped different types of tacit knowledge. The general format of tacit-knowledge inventories has been described in detail elsewhere (Sternberg et al., 2000), so only the content of the inventories used in this study is described here.

Unlike the creativity performance tasks, in these tasks the participants were not given a choice of scenarios to rate. For each task, participants were told that there was no "right" answer, and that the options described in each scenario represented variations on how different people approach different situations. That no single correct answer could be determined in our assessment scenarios is consistent with the kind of everyday problems that individuals with practical skills handle successfully. Even "experts," when asked to determine the quality of various solutions to a complex problem, show a great deal of variability in their problem-solving strategies. The uncertainty surrounding solutions to ill-defined problem situations and surrounding the link between a particular response and resulting outcomes represents a qualitative difference between traditional cognitive testing and testing for practical skill (see Legree, 1995).

- *Everyday Situational Judgment Inventory (Movies)*. This video-based inventory presented participants with seven brief vignettes that captured problems encountered in general, everyday life, such as determining what to do when one is asked to write a letter of recommendation for someone one does not know particularly well. Each scenario was accompanied by six written options for how one might handle the situation. For each option, participants were asked to rate how appropriate each option was for resolving the problem, on a scale from 1 (*a very bad course of action*) to 7 (*an extremely good course of action*).

• *Common-Sense Questionnaire.* This written inventory presented participants with 15 vignettes that capture problems encountered in general business-related situations, such as managing tedious tasks or handling a competitive work situation. Each scenario was accompanied by eight written options for how one might handle the situation. Like the movies task just described, each option was rated on its quality for resolving the problem, on a scale from 1 (*extremely bad*) to 7 (*extremely good*).

• *College-Life Questionnaire.* This written inventory presented participants with 15 vignettes that capture problems encountered in general college-related situations, such as handling trips to the bursar's office or dealing with a difficult roommate. Each scenario was accompanied by several written options (with the number of options varying depending on the situation) for how one might handle the situation. The participant indicated how characteristic each option was for him or her or how good the option was, as a means of handling the situations described, on a scale from 1 (e.g., *not at all characteristic, not a very good choice*) to 7 (e.g., *extremely characteristic, a very good choice*).

School Performance

School performance was measured using CGPA as obtained from school transcripts. For high school students, this measure was HSGPA, assessed during their senior year. For college students, this measure was freshman GPA, assessed at the end of their first year.

All materials were administered either in paper-and-pencil format (41%) or on the computer via the World Wide Web (59%).[4] Participants were either tested individually or in small groups. During the oral stories section, participants who were tested in the group situation either wore headphones or were directed into a separate room so as not to disturb the other participants during the oral dictation of the stories.

---

[4] The type of administration, whether paper-based or computer-based, typically depended on the institution. Because of this confound, it is difficult to determine whether there are important differences between the pencil-based versus computer-based methodologies.

TABLE 9.1
Exploratory Factor Analysis of Triarchic Measures

Estimated Correlations[a]

	1	2	3	4	5	6	7	8	F1	F2	F3
1. Oral Stories	1.00								.31	.03	.07
2. Written Stories	.14	1.00							.37	.18	.18
3. Cartoons	.16	.21	1.00						.49	.04	.15
4. STAT-creative	.17	.30	.28	1.00					.37	.28	.59
5. STAT-analytic	.11	.23	.21	.59	1.00				.16	.12	.85
6. STAT-practical	.17	.29	.29	.58	.65	1.00			.37	.19	.67
7. Movies	.09	.21	.14	.31	.18	.25	1.00		.21	.65	.08
8. College Life	.06	.21	.08	.36	.25	.29	.58	1.00	.06	.86	.16
9. Common Sense	.06	.21	.09	.38	.28	.31	.56	.77	.06	.82	.21

Note. 62.4% of variation explained.
[a]correlations estimated using FIML, Nominal $N = 776$.

There were two discrete sessions, conducted one directly after the other, for each participant. The order of test administration was the same for all participants. No strict time limits were set for completing the tests, although the instructors were given rough guidelines of about 70 min per session. The time taken to complete the battery of tests ranged from 2 to 4 hours.

As a result of the lengthy nature of the complete battery of assessments, participants were administered parts of the battery using an intentional incomplete overlapping design, as described in McArdle and Hamagami (1992; also see McArdle, 1994). The participants were randomly assigned to the test sections they were to complete. All missing data in the sample were managed using the full information maximum likelihood (FIML) estimation technique.

WHAT WE FOUND

Factor Structure of the Triarchic Measures

An exploratory factor analysis with Varimax rotation was conducted to explore the factor structure underlying the triarchic measures. The results of these analyses are reported in Table 9.1. Three factors were extracted with Eigenvalues greater than 1 and these accounted for 62.4% of the variation between the measures.

The results suggest that evidence for a unidimensional latent creativity factor is mixed. The practical ability measures clearly define a latent factor, again consistent with the analyses just reported. The fact that the STAT variables define a latent factor suggests that methodology (multiple-choice) and, to some extent, content (numerical, figural, verbal) is common across the analytical, practical, and creative items. It would seem that in this sample, the common methodological factor might overwhelm the unique creative, practical, and analytical contribution offered by the different multiple-choice STAT subtests.

Hierarchical Regressions

In order to test the incremental validity provided by triarchic measures above and beyond the SAT in predicting GPA, a series of hierarchical regressions was conducted that included the analytical, creative, and practical abilities, as well as HSGPA. The correlation matrix on which these analyses are based

TABLE 9.2

Intercorrelations Between Rainbow Measures, GPA, and SAT

	Mean	1	2	3	4	5	6	7	8	9	10	11	12
1. College GPA[a]	-.01	1.00											
2. Everyday Situational Judgment	-.94	.15	1.00										
3. College Life Questionnaire	-.97	.17	.59	1.00									
4. Common Sense Questionnaire	-.95	.26	.54	.32	1.00								
5. SAT-math[a]	-.10	.28	.26	.24	.28	1.00							
6. SAT-verbal[a]	-.11	.26	.29	.23	.26	.75	1.00						
7. Oral Stories	-.20	.29	.15	.02	.17	.23	.23	1.00					
8. Written Stories	-.43	.12	.23	.14	.30	.29	.38	.11	1.00				
9. Cartoon	.02	.07	.13	.12	.04	.26	.37	.14	.23	1.00			
10. STAT-Creative	1.04	.35	.29	.38	.38	.59	.53	.10	.26	.28	1.00		
11. STAT-Practical	.47	.24	.26	.29	.30	.56	.53	.17	.30	.28	.60	1.00	
12. STAT-Analytic	1.48	.24	.17	.24	.25	.61	.52	.14	.23	.22	.58	.64	1.00
13. High School GPA[a]	-.02	.37	.18	.22	.21	.55	.48	.08	.18	.20	.46	.40	.41

Note. The estimation of correlations in FIML is partially dependent on the variables included in the model. Nominal $N = 777$; FIML used to estimate statistics.
[a]z-score transformation applied.

is provided in Table 9.2. A latent practical variable combining the Everyday Situational Judgment Questionnaire, the College Life Questionnaire, and the Common Sense Questionnaire was entered. The creativity measures were entered separately because these items did not include enough common variance to define a latent variable. The hierarchical regressions that include all three dimensions of the triarchic model are shown in Table 9.3.

• *Success in College.* As shown in Table 9.3A, SAT-V, SAT-M, and HSGPA were included in the first step of the regression because these are the standard measures used today to predict college performance. Only HSGPA contributed uniquely to R^2. In Step 2 we added the analytic subtest of the STAT, because this test is closest conceptually to the SAT tests. The inclusion of the analytical subtest of the STAT did not increase the R^2. In Step 3, the measures of practical ability were added, resulting in a small increase in R^2. Notably, the latent variable representing the common variance among the practical performance measures and HSGPA were the only variables to significantly account for variance in college GPA in Step 3. The inclusion of the creative measures in the final step of this regression indicates that, by supplementing the SAT and HSGPA with measures of analytical, practical, and creative abilities, a total of 24.4% of the variance in GPA can be accounted for. Inclusion of the triarchic measures in Steps 2, 3, and 4 represents an increase of about 8.0% (from .164 to .244) in the variance accounted for over and above the typical predictors of college GPA. Table 9.3B reports the same analyses as Table 9.3A but without HSGPA.

Additional hierarchical regressions were run in which the order of entry of the variables is such that SAT and HSGPA are entered in the last steps. Importantly, the set of regressions show that SAT does not add significant incremental validity above and beyond the triarchic measures in the penultimate step, although HSGPA does in the final step. Approximately 18.8% of the variance in college GPA can be accounted for by using triarchic measures alone. With the addition of HSGPA in the last step, three of the four creative measures significantly contribute to the incremental prediction of college GPA above and beyond HSGPA and the SAT. These three variables include oral stories ($p < .05$), written stories ($p < .05$), and the creative portion of the STAT ($p < .01$). In addition, the latent practical-ability measure underlying performance on the three tacit knowledge tests is marginally significant ($p < .10$).

The multiple regression analyses pose some concern because of the large number of measures used representing each of analytic, creative, and practical skills. This risks a great deal of construct overlap. To account for this problem, a final multiple regression analysis was conducted that included only HSGPA,

TABLE 9.3

Incremental Prediction of College GPA Using the Triarchic Abilities, (A) Above and Beyond the SAT and HSGPA, and (B) Above and Beyond SAT

A.	Step 1	Step 2	Step 3	Step 4
SAT/HSGPA				
Verbal[a]	.080	.065	.047	.030
Math[a]	.083	.013	.002	−.081
HSGPA[a]	.300*	.293*	.283*	.283*
Analytical				
Analytic STAT		.103	.060	.016
Practical				
Performance Latent			.128*	.063
Practical STAT			.011	−.047
Creative				
Written				.128
Oral				.174*
Cartoons				−.089*
Creative STAT				.259*
R^2	.164	.158	.166	.244

B.	Step 1	Step 2	Step 3	Step 4
SAT				
Verbal[a]	.124	.105	.076	.056
Math[a]	.205*	.121	.096	.015
Analytical				
Analytic STAT		.129*	.076	.021
Practical				
Performance Latent			.148*	.072
Practical STAT			.036	−.034
Creative				
Written				.117
Oral				.153*
Cartoons				−.080
Creative STAT				.300*
R^2	.096	.095	.108	.188

Note. Entries are standardized beta coefficients. *$p < .05$. $N = 777$.
[a]z-score transformation applied.

SAT, and one measure from each of analytic (Analytic STAT), creative (Oral Stories), and practical (performance latent) skills. Two of the creative measures maintained a statistically significant beta coefficient.

• *Group Differences*. These were the second focal point of this study. An important goal involved developing measures that might reduce ethnic group differences in the mean levels for the predictor variables. Table 9.4 reveals the extent of our success in achieving this goal.

We conducted a series of one-way ANOVAs considering differences in mean performance levels among the six ethnic and racial groups reported, that is, Caucasian, Asian, Pacific Islander, Latino, African American, and Native American. We considered differences among these groups for the following measures: the baseline measures (SAT-V and SAT-M), the STAT ability scales, the creativity performance tasks, and the practical ability performance tasks. We include here the size of omega-squared (ω^2) as a measure of the effect size of race on each variable, which indicates the amount of variance in the variables that is accounted for by the socially defined ethnicity of the participant. The F-statistic for each ANOVA, its significance, the N on which

TABLE 9.4
Amount of Variance in Each Assessment
Accounted for by Ethnicity

Measure	F	p	N	ω^2
SAT				
Verbal	35.8	<.001	341	.09
Math	15.2	<.001	341	.04
Total (combined)	28.2	<.001	340	.07
STAT				
Analytical	.5	ns	370	.00
Practical	12.8	<.001	374	.03
Creative	6.7	<.01	369	.02
Practical Performance				
EDSJ (Movies)	5.9	<.05	493	.01
Common Sense	2.6	ns	273	.01
College Life	8.4	<.01	298	.02
Creative Performance				
Cartoon Captions	14.0	<.001	569	.02
Oral Stories	6.0	<.05	152	.03
Written Stories	3.1	ns	329	.01

each analysis was based, and the ω^2 for each analysis are presented in Table 9.4. These results indicate that triarchic tests not only predict school performance (as indicated in the analyses just described) but also reduce race and ethnicity differences relative to traditional assessments of abilities like the SAT. This finding has important implications for reducing adverse impact in college admissions.

WHAT IT MEANS

The theory of successful intelligence appears to provide a strong theoretical basis for an augmented assessment of the skills needed for college success. There is evidence to indicate that it has good incremental predictive power, and serves to increase equity. Thus, the new Rainbow Measures meet our goals for improving prediction of performance and increasing equity. As teaching improves and college teachers give greater emphasis to the creative and prac-tical skills needed for success in school and life, the predictive power of the test may increase. Cosmetic changes in testing over the last 100 years have made relatively little difference to the construct validity of assessment proce-dures. The theory of successful intelligence could provide a new opportunity to increase construct validity.

Phase 2 of the Rainbow Project, currently underway, involves a thorough revision of the Rainbow assessment as well as testing 5 to 10 times as many students as were tested in Phase 1. So far, three universities have agreed to pro-vide large numbers of students. In Phase 2, we use a broader range of outcome (dependent) variables than in Phase 1, and also follow students longitudinally. Our hope is to show on a larger scale that the Rainbow assessment can provide reliable and valid information that increases prediction of college success at the same time that it increases equity in the admissions process.

REFERENCES

Bridgeman, B., Burton, N., & Cline, F. (2001). *Substituting SAT II: Subject Tests for SAT I: Reasoning Test: Impact on admitted class composition and quality* (College Board Rep. No. 2001-3). New York: College Entrance Examination Board.

Bridgeman, B., McCamley-Jenkins, L., & Ervin, N. (2000). *Predictions of freshman grade-point average from the revised and recentered SAT I: Reasoning test* (College Board Rep. No. 2000-1). New York: College Entrance Examination Board.

Dorans, N. J. (1999). *Correspondences between ACT and SAT I scores* (College Board Rep. No. 99–1; ETS Research Rep. RR., No. 99–2). New York: College Entrance Examination Board.

Hezlett, S., Kuncel, N., Vey, A., Ones, D., Campbell, J., & Camara, W. J. (2001, April). *The effectiveness of the SAT in predicting success early and late in college: A comprehensive meta-analysis.* Paper presented at the annual meeting of the National Council of Measurement in Education, Seattle, WA.

Kobrin, J. L., Camara, W. J., Milewski, G. B. (2002). *The utility of the SAT I and SAT II for admissions decisions in California and the nation* (College Board Rep. No. 2002–6). New York: College Entrance Examination Board.

Legree, P. J. (1995). Evidence for an oblique social intelligence factor established with a Likert-based testing procedure. *Intelligence, 21,* 247–266.

Linacre, J. M. (1998). *Facets user's guide.* Chicago: MESA Press.

Lubart, T. I., & Sternberg, R. J. (1995). An investment approach to creativity: Theory and data. In S. M. Smith, T. B. Ward, & R. A. Finke (Eds.), *The creative cognition approach* (pp. 269–302). Cambridge, MA: MIT Press.

McArdle, J. J. (1994). Structural factor analysis experiments with incomplete data. *Multivariate Behavioral Research, 29*(4), 409–454.

McArdle, J. J., & Hamagami, F. (1992). Modeling incomplete longitudinal and cross-sectional data using latent growth structural models. *Experimental Aging Research, 18*(3), 145–166.

Ramist, L., Lewis, C., & McCamley-Jenkins, L. (1993). *Student group differences in predicting college grades: Sex, language and ethnic groups* (College Board Rep. No. 2001–5). New York: College Entrance Examination Board.

Sternberg, R. J. (1980). Sketch of a componential subtheory of human intelligence. *Behavioral and Brain Sciences, 3,* 573–584.

Sternberg, R. J. (1984). Toward a triarchic theory of human intelligence. *Behavioral and Brain Sciences, 7,* 269–287.

Sternberg, R. J. (1985). *Beyond IQ: A triarchic theory of human intelligence.* New York: Cambridge University Press.

Sternberg, R. J. (1990). *Metaphors of mind: Conceptions of the nature of intelligence.* New York: Cambridge University Press.

Sternberg, R. J. (1993). *Sternberg Triarchic Abilities Test.* Unpublished test.

Sternberg. R. J. (1997). *Successful intelligence.* New York: Plume.

Sternberg, R. J. (1999). The theory of successful intelligence. *Review of General Psychology, 3,* 292–316.

Sternberg, R. J., & Clinkenbeard, P. R. (1995). A triarchic model applied to identifying, teaching, and assessing gifted children. *Roeper Review, 17*(4), 255–260.

Sternberg, R. J., Ferrari, M., Clinkenbeard, P. R., & Grigorenko, E. L. (1996). Identification, instruction, and assessment of gifted children: A construct validation of a triarchic model. *Gifted Child Quarterly, 40*(3), 129–137.

Sternberg, R. J., Forsythe, G. B., Hedlund, J., Horvath, J., Snook, S., Williams, W. M.,

Wagner, R. K., & Grigorenko, E. L. (2000). *Practical intelligence in everyday life*. New York: Cambridge University Press.

Sternberg, R. J., & Lubart, T. I. (1995). *Defying the crowd: Cultivating creativity in a culture of conformity*. New York: Free Press.

10

The Case for
Noncognitive Measures

William E. Sedlacek
University of Maryland

We appear to have forgotten why tests were created in the first place. Although they were always considered to be useful in evaluating candidates, they were also considered to be more equitable than using prior grades because of the variation in quality among preparatory schools. The College Board has long felt that the SAT was limited in what it measured and should not be relied upon as the only tool to judge applicants (Angoff, 1971). The College Board gave advice in 1926 as it developed the first SAT that is as relevant today as it was then:

> The present state of all efforts of men [sic] to measure or in any way estimate the worth of other men, or to evaluate the results of their nurture, or to reckon their potential possibilities does not warrant any certainty of prediction. This additional test now made available through the instrumentality of the College Entrance Examination Board may resolve a few perplexing problems, but it should be regarded merely as a supplementary record. To place too great emphasis on test scores is as dangerous as the failure properly to evaluate any score or rank in conjunction with other measures and estimates which it supplements. (Brigham, 1926, pp. 44–45)

In 1993, the verbal and mathematical reasoning sections of the SAT were lengthened and the multiple-choice Test of Standard Written English was dropped. The name was changed from Scholastic Aptitude Test to Scholastic Assessment Tests, while retaining the SAT initials. Currently it is just called the SAT I. In 2003, the College Board announced that an essay would be added and the analogies type item removed as of 2005. Despite various changes and versions over the years, the SAT in essence measures what it did in 1926, verbal and math ability; it is basically still a general intelligence test (Sedlacek, 2003, 2004).

However, we have come to the point where the "big test" has become the focal point in our schools (Lemann, 2000). It has become the standard by which we judge ourselves and others. Many assume that if an individual has high SAT scores, or if a school has high mean SAT scores, the students must be learning something, and the school must be good. To cite that common metaphor, "The tail is wagging the dog."

Test results should be useful to educators, student service workers, and administrators, by providing the basis to help students learn better and to analyze their needs. As currently designed, tests do not accomplish these objectives. Many teachers tend to teach to get the highest test scores for their students, student service workers may ignore the tests, and too many administrators are satisfied if the average test scores rise in their school. We need some things from our tests that currently we are not getting. We need tests that are fair to all and provide a good assessment of the developmental and learning needs of students, while being useful in selecting outstanding applicants. Our current tests do not accomplish that.

KEEPING UP WITH CHANGE

The world is much different than it was when the SAT and other tests were developed in the last century. Women, people of color, gays, lesbians and bisexuals, among others, are participating in higher education in more extensive and varied ways (Harvey, 2002; Knapp, Kelly, Whitmore, Wu, & Gallego, 2002; McTighe, Musil, et al., 1999; Mohr & Sedlacek, 2000). Commonly employed tests have not kept up with these changes (Sedlacek, 2003, 2004).

Additional questions about tests range from their legality (Harvey & Hurtado, 1994), the validity of their scores (Williams, 1997), methodology in developing tests (Sedlacek, 1986, 1994, 2003, 2004), and restriction of range problems (Darlington, 1998).

A Fresh Approach

We need a fresh approach. It is not good enough to feel constrained by the limitations of our current ways of conceiving tests. Instead of asking; "How can we make the SAT and other such tests better?" we need to ask, "What kinds of measures will meet our needs now and in the future?" The purpose of this chapter is to present the underlying logic and research supporting a method that yields such measures. We do not need to ignore our current tests, we need to add some new measures that expand the potential we can derive from assessment.

The Three Musketeers Problem

The rallying cry of "all for one and one for all" is one that is used often in developing what is thought of as fair and equitable measures (Sedlacek,1994). Commonly, the interpretation of how to handle diversity is to hone and fine-tune tests so they are equally fair for everyone. However, if different groups have different experiences and different ways of presenting their attributes and abilities, it is unlikely that one could develop a single measure, test item, and so on, that could yield equally valid scores for all. If we concentrate on results rather than intentions, we could conclude that it is important to do an equally good job of selection for each group, not that we need to use the same measures for all to accomplish that goal. Equality of results, not process, is most important.

Therefore, we should seek to retain the variance due to culture, race, gender, and other aspects of nontraditionality that may exist across diverse groups in our measures, rather than attempt to eliminate this variance (Sedlacek, 2003, 2004). Sedlacek (2004) defined *nontraditional persons* as those with cultural experiences different from those of White, middle-class males of European descent; those with less power to control their lives; and those who experience discrimination in the United States.

NONCOGNITIVE VARIABLES

Although the term *noncognitive* appears to be precise and scientific sounding, it has been used to describe a wide variety of attributes. Willingham (1985) studied high-school honors, high-school follow through, personal statements, and references, and concluded that they added to prediction of college success. Other researchers have included student involvement (Astin, 1993), academic and social integration (Milem & Berger, 1997), study skills (Nisbet, Ruble, & Schurr, 1982), and socioeconomic background, institutional, and environmental variables (Ting & Robinson, 1998) in their conceptions of non-cognitive variables related to student success. Throughout this chapter, *success* refers to grades, retention, or graduation, unless otherwise noted.

Noncognitive is used here to refer to variables relating to adjustment, motivation, and student perceptions, rather than the traditional verbal and quantitative (often called cognitive) areas typically measured by standardized tests. Noncognitive variables appear to be in Sternberg's (1996) experiential and contextual domains, whereas standardized tests tend to reflect the componential domain. Although noncognitive variables are useful for all students, they are particularly critical for nontraditional students, because standardized tests and prior grades may provide only a limited view of their potential. The following is a discussion of the eight variables recommended to be included in admissions assessment systems (see Table 10.1).

Positive Self-Concept

There is evidence that the way students feel about themselves is related to their adjustment and success in college (Sedlacek, 2003, 2004). A strong self-concept is particularly important for students of color (Neville, Heppner, & Wang, 1997), students with disabilities (Patterson, Sedlacek, & Scales, 1988), and women returning to school (Adelstein, Sedlacek, & Martinez, 1983).

A number of studies have shown that a positive self-concept correlates with college grades, retention, and graduation, particularly the later two, for regularly admitted African American students (McNairy, 1996; Milem & Berger, 1997; Tracey & Sedlacek, 1984a, 1984b, 1985, 1987, 1988, 1989). O'Callaghan and Bryant (1990) found self-concept important for the success of Black students at the U.S. Air Force Academy.

Fuertes, Sedlacek, and Liu (1994) demonstrated the importance of a strong self-concept for Asian and Pacific Islander university students. Bennett and Okinaka (1990) found that Asian Americans often had feelings of social isolation and dissatisfaction on campus. Chung and Sedlacek (1999) also noted that Asian Americans had lower career and social self-appraisals than students of other races.

Fuertes and Sedlacek (1995) noted the importance of a Latino self-concept, and Longerbeam, Sedlacek, and Alatorre (in press) found that Latinos were more likely to feel they lacked academic ability than other racial groups. Also, Latinos have been found to be more likely than other groups to be uncomfort-

TABLE 10.1
Description of Noncognitive Variables

Variable No.	Variable Name
1	*Positive Self-Concept* • Demonstrates confidence, strength of character, determination, and independence.
2	*Realistic Self-Appraisal* • Recognizes and accepts any strengths and deficiencies, especially academic, and works hard at self-development. Recognizes need to broaden his or her individuality.
3	*Understands and Knows How to Handle Racism (the System)* • Exhibits a realistic view of the system based upon personal experience of racism. Committed to improving the existing system. Takes an assertive approach to dealing with existing wrongs, but is not hostile to society, nor is a "cop-out." Able to handle racist system.
4	*Prefers Long-Range to Short-Term or Immediate Needs* • Able to respond to deferred gratification, plans ahead and sets goals.
5	*Availability of Strong Support Person* • Seeks and takes advantage of a strong support network or has someone to turn to in a crisis or for encouragement.
6	*Successful Leadership Experience* • Demonstrates strong leadership in any area of his or her background (e.g., church, sports, noneducational groups, gang leader, etc.).
7	*Demonstrated Community Service* • Participates and is involved in his or her community.
8	*Knowledge Acquired in or About a Field* • Acquires knowledge in a sustained and/or culturally related ways in any field.

able on a campus stressing diversity issues (Ancis, Sedlacek, & Mohr, 2000; Helm, Sedlacek, & Prieto, 1998).

Boyer and Sedlacek (1988) found self-concept to be predictive of grades and retention for international students, whereas Sedlacek and Adams-Gaston (1992) found self-concept related to grades for student athletes. Betz and Fitzgerald (1987) as well as Ancis and Sedlacek (1997) provided evidence that women's self-concept related to their academic success. White and Sedlacek (1986) found self-concept to be predictive of success for students in special programs.

In summary, a positive self-concept is predictive of success in higher education for all students. Although having a good self-concept is important for any student, it becomes even more important for those with nontraditional experiences because of the added complexity of dealing with a system that was not designed for them.

Realistic Self-Appraisal

Realistic self-appraisal is the ability to assess one's strengths and weaknesses and allows for self-development. Realism in self-appraisal by nontraditional persons does not connote cultural, racial, or gender deficiency or inferiority.

White students may do well pursuing their own interests (internal control) in a society designed to meet their needs, whereas students of color need to also be aware of the external control on their lives that requires them to negotiate the racism in the system (Sedlacek, 1995, 1996, 2003, 2004; Sedlacek & Brooks, 1976). Perrone, Sedlacek, and Alexander (2001) found that White and Asian American students perceived intrinsic interest in a field as the major barrier to achieving their career goals, whereas African Americans, Latinos, and Native Americans cited personal finances as their major barrier.

Tracey and Sedlacek (1984a, 1984b, 1985, 1987, 1988, 1989) found realistic self-appraisal to correlate with college grades, retention, and graduation for students of all races, but the relationships were particularly strong for African Americans. Women who are able to make realistic self-appraisals have been shown to get higher grades in a university than those who have difficulty with such assessments (Ancis & Sedlacek, 1997).

In summary, students of color and women of all races who are able to make realistic assessments of their abilities, despite any obstacles to making those assessments, do better in school than those less able to make those judgments. Realistic self-appraisal is also a predictor of success for traditional students.

Understands and Deals With Racism

The successful nontraditional student is a realist based on a personal experience with discrimination, is committed to fighting to improve the existing system, and is able to handle a racist system. *Institutional racism* is defined as the negative consequences that accrue to a member of a given group because of the way a system or subsystem operates in the society (e.g., college admissions) regardless of any other attributes of the individual (Sedlacek, 1995, 2003, 2004; Sedlacek & Brooks, 1976). Racism can take many forms and is used here to cover all types of "isms" (e.g., sexism, ageism, athletism). Although racism can be "individual" rather than institutional, the primary concern here is for dealing with the policies procedures and barriers, intentional or not, that interfere with the development of people.

For traditional students, the variable takes the form of handling the system without the addition of racism (Sedlacek,1996, 2003, 2004; Tracey & Sedlacek, 1984a, 1984b). How a person learns to handle the circumstances with which he or she is confronted tells us much about an individual's ability and potential.

Steele's (1997) work on "stereotype threat" supports the importance of the psychological set with which examinees approach a test. If African Americans are told that they do not usually do well on a test, they do less well than if a more positive set is given. It is documented in the professional and popular literature that African Americans do not do as well as Whites on standardized tests (Lemann, 2000; Sedlacek, 1998a, 1998b, 2003, 2004). Therefore, for African Americans, the act of taking a test probably involves dealing with the racism that may have been involved in helping to create a stereotype threat in the first place. Hence, part of the variance that is being measured when an African American takes the SAT is likely to relate to how that person handles racism. If nontraditional individuals, as defined here, can approach an evaluation with a feeling of empowerment, or expected success, they may be employing a noncognitive skill that would give a more accurate prediction of their potential. This skill should be measured directly rather than inferred from other measures.

Prefers Long-Range Goals

Having long-range goals will predict success in college for students. Because role models often are more difficult to find, and the reinforcement system has been relatively random for them, many nontraditional students have difficulty understanding the relationship between current efforts and the ultimate practice of their professions (Sedlacek, 2003, 2004).

In other words, because students of color tend to face a greater culture shock than White students in adjusting to a White student-oriented campus culture, students of color may not be as predictable in their academic performance in their first year as are traditional students (Farver, Sedlacek, & Brooks, 1975). However, by the time of their second year, students of color are about as predictable as others.

Boyer and Sedlacek (1988) found a significant relationship between setting long-range goals and grades and retention for international students. Moore (1995) concluded that for international community college students, having long-range goals correlated with persistence in school. Hence, students who show evidence of having long-range goals do better in college than those without such goals.

Availability of a Strong Support Person

Students who have done well in school tend to have a person of strong influence who provides advice to them, particularly in times of crisis (e.g., Sedlacek, 2003, 2004). This individual may be in the education system, but for nontraditional students it is often a relative or a community worker.

Having a strong support person has been shown to be a significant correlate of grades, retention and/or graduation for African Americans (Tracey & Sedlacek, 1984a, 1984b, 1985, 1987, 1988, 1989), women (Ancis & Sedlacek, 1997), athletes of all races (Sedlacek & Adams-Gaston, 1992), international students (Boyer & Sedlacek, 1988), and students in special support programs including Asian Americans, African Americans, and Whites (Ting, 1997; White & Sedlacek, 1986).

Because of inconsistent reinforcement of the relationship between individual effort and positive outcome, it may take relatively little to make a student of color drop out or fail school (Mallinckrodt, 1988). If a White student drops out, there may be many forces in the society to bring him or her back into the educational system, but the student of color may leave and never be heard from again.

Successful Leadership Experience

Students who are most successful in higher education have shown an ability to organize and influence others. The key here is that nontraditional students may show evidence of leadership in different ways than their White counterparts, such as working in their communities, through their places of worship, or even as street gang leaders. Application forms and interviews are slanted typically in directions likely to yield less useful information about the backgrounds of nontraditional students.

It is important to pursue the culture and gender-relevant activities of the applicants rather than to treat them as if they come from a homogeneous environment. For example, Liu and Sedlacek (1999) found that Asian American students had unique and culturally related ways of expressing their leadership. If an applicant succeeds in his or her culture and is now ready to "take on" college, there is evidence that the student has the potential to succeed.

Assertiveness is likely to be an important component in leadership as a predictor of success (Sedlacek, 2003, 2004). A passive operational style for students of color will deny them many opportunities in a system that is not optimally designed for them. Seeking out resources, human and environmental, is correlated with success for students of color.

Tracey and Sedlacek (1984a, 1984b, 1985, 1987, 1988, 1989) and White and Shelley (1996) showed evidence of the value of leadership in the retention of Latinos and Native Americans. They also found leadership to be predictive of success in school for African American undergraduate students. Webb et al. (1997) found a similar relationship for female African American medical students. White and Shelley (1996) also found evidence of the value of leadership in the retention of Latinos and Native Americans. Ancis and Sedlacek (1997) and Betz and Fitzgerald (1987) identified leadership as a correlate of success for women in college, and Boyer and Sedlacek (1988) found a similar relationship for female and male international students. Ting (1997) and White and Sedlacek (1986) found that leadership correlated with academic success for students in special support programs.

In summary, students of color and women who show evidence of leadership prior to matriculation in college, often in race or gender-related forms, are more likely to be successful in college than those who do not have leadership experiences. Leadership ability is important for any student, but it may take different forms for students with less traditional experiences.

Community

Having a community with which students can identify, and from which they can receive support, is critical to their academic success. For White students, there tends to be a number of opportunities to find a community, in or out of school. The community for nontraditional students often is based on racial, cultural, or gender-related variables. Students of color, women, and other persons with nontraditional experiences who are active in a community learn how to handle the system, exhibit leadership, and develop their self-concepts in such groups. For example, Mallinckrodt and Sedlacek (1987) found that African American students who used campus athletic facilities and certain student union programs were more likely to stay in school than those who did not.

Fuertes et al. (1994) found identification with a community important for Asian American success in school, as did Sedlacek and Adams-Gaston (1992) for male and female athletes of all races. White and Shelley (1996) indicated the importance of community in retaining Latino and Native American students. Bennett (2002) concluded that having a race-based community correlated with college graduation for "underrepresented minorities" in a teacher training program. Ancis and Sedlacek (1997) found community to be a correlate of success for undergraduate women as did Ting (1997) for White students in special programs. Boyer and Sedlacek (1988) and Moore (1995) also found community involvement to be important for the academic success of international students. Therefore, those who have been involved in a community, often based on race and/or gender, are more successful in college than those not so involved.

Nontraditional Knowledge Acquired

The ability of someone to learn from experiences outside the classroom correlates with their success in school. Persons of color are more apt to learn and develop using methods that are less traditional and are outside the education system. The methods may be culture or gender-related and the field itself may be nontraditional. A range of studies (Ancis & Sedlacek, 1997, for women; Boyer & Sedlacek, 1988, for international students; Fuertes & Sedlacek, 1995, for Latinos; Ting, 1997, for special program students; Tracey & Sedlacek, 1984a, 1984b, 1985, 1987, 1988, 1989, for African Americans) have shown the predictive value of nontraditional learning for the academic success of those groups.

MEASURING NONCOGNITIVE VARIABLES

The noncognitive variables shown in Table 10.1 can be assessed in a number of ways including questionnaires, short-answer questions, essays, interviews, portfolios, and application reviews (Sedlacek, 2003, 2004).

The Noncognitive Questionnaire (NCQ)

NCQ was designed to assess the eight noncognitive variables just discussed and shown in Table 10.1. Tracey and Sedlacek (1984a, 1984b), Woods and Sedlacek (1988), and Ting and Sedlacek (2000) provided construct validity evidence for scores on the eight dimensions measured by the NCQ for African American and White samples. Woods and Sedlacek (1988) also showed evidence that the NCQ correlates with a measure of stress. Warmsley (1998) found that first-year grades for African American students at the City University of New York were significantly better predicted by the NCQ than by the SAT. Faubert (1992) showed that the NCQ was related to the success of 9th- and 10th-grade African American rural students.

Several forms of the NCQ have been developed and employed in different selection contexts (Sedlacek, 2003, 2004). The questionnaire can be administered online. Tracey and Sedlacek (1984a) reported 2-week test–retest reliability estimates on NCQ scores ranging from .74 to .94, with a median of .85

for the NCQ items with different samples. Interrater reliability on scores from the three open-ended NCQ items ranged from .73 to 1.00.

Alternate forms of the NCQ have shown test-retest reliability estimates in the .80s and relationships of alternate form scores (median $r = .79$) with scores from the basic NCQ (Sedlacek, 2003, 2004). Tracey and Sedlacek (1989) provided some reliability and validity evidence, with different samples, for scores on a revised version of the NCQ containing more items but no open-ended items, with a somewhat revised factor structure. Lockett (1980) reported validity and reliability data for scores from a modified version of the NCQ for Black students at a large Midwestern university. Ting and Sedlacek (2000) provided information on the validity and reliability of scores from a revised NCQ in predicting retention for White students at a large Southeastern university.

Another version of the NCQ was shown to correlate with college grades of traditional and nontraditional students in health programs at a western state community college (Noonan, Sedlacek, & Suthakaran, 2001). Also, Webb et al. (1997) found that a version of the NCQ predicted success for students of color at two medical schools on examinations offered by the National Board of Medical Examiners.

CONCLUSIONS AND RECOMMENDATIONS

There appears to be enough evidence to give noncognitive variables a try in higher education admissions. Measures have been shown to yield reliable and valid scores, and they are available at no cost (Sedlacek, 2004). It is recommended that noncognitive measures be added to current measures, such as the SAT, ACT, or GPA, in an admissions program rather than to replace existing measures. The Three Musketeers Problem previously discussed regarding tests, could then be avoided. If this were done, diversity within an entering class could be achieved without directly focusing on selecting members of a specific group. This is accomplished because a broader range of attributes would be assessed on which many nontraditional applicants would score well.

Some have felt that simply eliminating the use of cognitive measures would result in improved admission procedures. Unless there is a focus on different sources of variance, one could be attempting to measure cognitive abilities in a way that is less efficient than that achieved with current tests.

Because noncognitive variables have yet to be employed widely in admissions, problems of restriction of range may not be present to the same extent as using cognitive measures. For example, scores on over 16,000 applicants to the

Gates Millennium Scholars Program, which employs the noncognitive variables shown in Table 10.1 in selecting scholarship recipients, showed a nearly perfectly normal distribution (Sedlacek, 2004). Also, because a variety of measurement methods can be employed to obtain noncognitive scores, there may be less likelihood of sample bias than with cognitive measures.

Noncognitive variables appear to be positively related to retention and graduation criteria. The nature of the noncognitive variables is such that they can be employed in postmatriculation situations. They can be used in counseling, advising, teaching, and student service programs in ways that traditional test scores probably are not useful (Sedlacek, 2003, 2004). We might seek to develop students on the noncognitive dimensions after they start college, but we would not likely try to improve their SAT scores.

The use of noncognitive variables in admissions has been supported in court. The University of Maryland Medical School employed interviews to assess applicants on the noncognitive variables shown in Table 10.1. It has defended their use in an ongoing lawsuit that has challenged their fairness (*Farmer v. Ramsay et al.*, 1998). The court has ruled in favor of allowing the University to employ noncognitive variables in admitting students and an appeal was denied. In *Castañeda et al. v. The University of California* (1999), a number of civil rights groups have filed a suit against the University of California, Berkeley. The plaintiffs charged that the current admissions procedures are unfair to applicants of color, and have petitioned for inclusion of the noncognitive variables shown in Table 10.1. In settling the case, every applicant to the University is evaluated on the basis of his or her entire applicant file, including personal statements and extracurricular activities as well as grades and test scores.

Two cases decided by the Supreme Court of the United States are relevant to this discussion. The cases involved the University of Michigan's policies to consider race in admissions in its undergraduate program and law school. In *Gratz and Hamacher v. Bollinger* (2002), the Court ruled that the University could not assign a specific weight to an applicant solely because of his or her race. For example, Michigan awarded 20 points to each "underrepresented minority," which was one fifth of the points necessary to guarantee admission.

However, in *Grutter v. Bollinger* (2002), the Court ruled that the Law School could consider race as one of many factors in admitting students. This logic is similar to that used by Justice Powell in his dissenting opinion in the Bakke case (*Regents of the University of California v. Bakke*, 1978).

While I supported the efforts of the University of Michigan to consider race directly in its admissions policies, I believe there is a better way to proceed.

If the University were to use the noncognitive variable proposed here in its admissions systems, it would achieve diversity in its classes by virtue of considering variables that reflect race, culture, gender, and the other aspects of nontraditionality discussed previously. Thus, by not directly selecting on aspects of diversity, a school can achieve increased diversity in a more sophisticated way, based on the research evidence available. The noncognitive variable method yields important attributes that correlate with student success that appear to be legal and fair to all applicants.

It is also recommended that research on improving admissions measures move beyond attempts to better measure verbal and math ability. It does not appear to be a fruitful area for investigation. The variance that reflects important cultural, racial, gender variables, and other aspects of nontraditionality appears to exist elsewhere.

REFERENCES

Adelstein, S. M., Sedlacek, W. E., & Martinez, A. C. (1983). Dimensions underlying the characteristics and needs of returning women students. *Journal of the National Association for Women Deans, Administrators, and Counselors, 46* (4), 32–37.

Ancis, J. R., & Sedlacek, W. E. (1997). Predicting the academic achievement of female students using the SAT and noncognitive variables. *College and University, 72* (3), 1–8.

Ancis, J. R., Sedlacek, W. E., & Mohr, J. J. (2000). Student perceptions of the campus cultural climate by race. *Journal of Counseling and Development, 78* (2), 180–185.

Angoff, W. H. (1971). *The College Board admissions testing program.* New York: College Entrance Examination Board.

Astin, A.W. (1993). *What matters in college?: Four critical years revisited.* San Francisco: Jossey-Bass.

Bennett, C. I. (2002). Enhancing ethnic diversity at a Big Ten university through project TEAM: A case study in teacher education. *Educational Researcher, 31,* 21–29.

Bennett, C., & Okinaka, A. M. (1990). Factors related to persistence among Asian, Black, Hispanic, and White undergraduates at a predominantly White university: Comparison between first and fourth year cohorts. *Urban Review, 22,* 33–60.

Betz, N. E., & Fitzgerald, L. F. (1987). *The career psychology of women.* San Diego: Academic.

Boyer, S. P., & Sedlacek, W. E. (1988). Noncognitive predictors of academic success for international students: A longitudinal study. *Journal of College Student Development, 29,* 218–222.

Brigham, C. C. (1926). The Scholastic Aptitude Test of the College Entrance Examination Board. In T. S. Fiske (Ed.), *The work of the College Entrance Examination Board, 1901–1925* (pp. 45–46). New York: Ginn.

Castañeda, et al. v. The Regents of the University of California. (1999). U.S. District Court for the Northern District of California, Civil Action No. C. 99–0525.

Chung, B. Y., & Sedlacek, W. E. (1999). Ethnic differences in career, academic, and social self-appraisals among college freshmen. *Journal of College Counseling, 2* (1), 14–24.

Darlington, R. B. (1998) Range restriction and the Graduate Record Examination. *American Psychologist, 53,* 572–573.

Farmer v. Ramsay, et al. (1998). U.S. District Court for the District of Maryland, Case No. L-98–1585.

Farver, A. S., Sedlacek, W. E., & Brooks, G. C., Jr. (1975). Longitudinal predictions of university grades for Blacks and Whites. *Measurement and Evaluation in Guidance, 7,* 243–250.

Faubert, M. (1992). *Cognitive and ego development of successful African American rural youth: Deliberate psychological education.* Unpublished doctoral dissertation, North Carolina State University.

Fuertes, J. N., & Sedlacek, W. E. (1995). Using noncognitive variables to predict the grades and retention of Hispanic students. *College Student Affairs Journal, 14,* 30–36.

Fuertes, J. N., Sedlacek, W. E, & Liu, W. (1994). Using the SAT and noncognitive variables to predict the grades and retention of Asian American university students. *Measurement and Evaluation in Counseling and Development, 27,* 74–84.

Gratz & Hamacher v. Bollinger et al. (2002). U.S. Court of Appeals for the Sixth Circuit. No. 02-516.

Grutter v. Bollinger et al. (2002). U.S. Court of Appeals for the Sixth Circuit. No. 02 241.

Harvey, C., & Hurtado, A. (1994). The jurisprudence of race and meritocracy: Standardized testing and "race neutral" racism, in the workplace. *Law and Human Behavior, 18,* 223–248.

Harvey, W. B. (2002). *Minorities in higher education 2001–2002: Nineteenth annual status report.* Washington, DC: American Council on Education.

Helm, E. G., Sedlacek, W. E., & Prieto, D. O. (1998). The relationship between attitudes toward diversity and overall satisfaction of university students by race. *Journal of College Counseling, 1,* 111–120.

Knapp, L. G., Kelly, J. E., Whitmore, R. W., Wu, S., & Gallego, L. M. (2002). Enrollment in postsecondary institutions, fall 2000 and financial statistics, fiscal year 2000 (NCES 2002–212). Washington, DC: National Center for Education Statistics.

Lemann, N. (2000). *The big test: The secret history of the American meritocracy.* New York: Farrar, Straus & Giroux.

Liu, W. M., & Sedlacek, W. E. (1999). Differences in leadership and co-curricular perception among male and female Asian Pacific American college students. *Journal of the Freshmen Year Experience, 11,* 93–114.

Lockett, G. C. (1980). *A study of traditional measures and nontraditional measures used to predict the success of Black college students.* Unpublished doctoral dissertation, University of Missouri–Columbia.

Longerbeam, S. L., Sedlacek, W. E., & Alatorre, H. A. (in press). In their own voices:

Latino student retention. *National Association of Student Personnel Administrators Journal.*

Mallinckrodt, B. (1988). Student retention, social support, and dropout retention: Comparison of Black and White students. *Journal of College Student Development, 29,* 60–64.

Mallinckrodt, B., & Sedlacek, W. E. (1987). Student retention and the use of campus facilities by race. *National Association of Student Personnel Administrators Journal, 24*(3), 28–32.

McNairy, F. G. (1996). The challenge for higher education: Retaining students of color. In I. H. Johnson & A. J. Ottens (Eds.), *Leveling the playing field: Promoting academic success for students of color* (pp. 3–14). San Francisco: Jossey-Bass.

McTighe Musil, C., García, M., Hudgins, C. A., Nettles, M. T., Sedlacek, W. E., & Smith, D. G. (1999). *To form a more perfect union: Campus diversity initiatives.* Washington, DC: Association of American Colleges and Universities.

Milem, J. F., & Berger, J. B. (1997). A modified model of college student persistence: Exploring the relationship between Astin's theory of involvement and Tinto's theory of student departure. *Journal of College Student Development, 38,* 387–400.

Mohr, J. J., & Sedlacek, W. E. (2000). Perceived barriers to friendship with lesbians and gay men among university students. *Journal of College Student Development, 41,* 70–79.

Moore, S. K. (1995). *Indicators of academic success and the student characteristics of international students at Santa Monica College.* Unpublished doctoral dissertation, Pepperdine University, Los Angeles, CA.

Neville, H. A., Heppner, P., & Wang, L. (1997). Relations among racial identity attitudes, perceived stressors, and coping styles in African American college students. *Journal of Counseling and Development, 75,* 303–311.

Nisbet, J., Ruble, V. E., & Schurr, K. T. (1982). Predictors of academic success with high risk college students. *Journal of College Student Personnel, 23,* 227–235.

Noonan, B., Sedlacek, W. E., & Suthakaran, V. (2001). *Predicting the success of community college students using noncognitive variables* (Counseling Center Research Report No. 5–01). College Park: University of Maryland.

O'Callaghan, K. W., & Bryant, C. (1990). Noncognitive variables: A key to Black American academic success at a military academy. *Journal of College Student Development, 31,* 121–126.

Patterson, A., Sedlacek, W. E., & Scales, W. R. (1988). The other minority: Disabled student backgrounds and attitudes toward their university and its services. *Journal of Postsecondary Education and Disability, 6,* 86–94.

Perrone, K. M., Sedlacek, W. E., & Alexander, C. M. (2001). Gender and ethnic differences in career goal attainment. *Career Development Quarterly, 50,* 168–178.

Regents of the University of California v. Bakke, 438 U.S. 265 (1978).

Sedlacek, W. E. (1986). Sources of method bias in test bias research. In *Measures in the college admissions process* (pp. 86–92). New York: College Entrance Examination Board.

Sedlacek, W. E. (1994). Issues in advancing diversity through assessment. *Journal of Counseling and Development, 72,* 549–553.

Sedlacek, W. E. (1995). Using research to reduce racism at a university. *Journal of Humanistic Education and Development, 33,* 131–140.

Sedlacek, W. E. (1996). An empirical method of determining nontraditional group status. *Measurement and Evaluation in Counseling and Development, 28,* 200–210.

Sedlacek, W. E. (1998a). Admissions in higher education: Measuring cognitive and noncognitive variables. In D. J. Wilds & R. Wilson (Eds.), *Minorities in higher education 1997–98: Sixteenth annual status report* (pp. 47–71). Washington, DC: American Council on Education.

Sedlacek, W. E. (1998b, Winter). Multiple choices for standardized tests. *Priorities, 10,* 1–16.

Sedlacek, W. E. (2003). Alternative measures in admissions and scholarship selection. *Measurement and Evaluation in Counseling and Development, 35,* 263–272.

Sedlacek, W. E. (2004). *Beyond the big test: Noncognitive assessment in higher education.* San Francisco: Jossey-Bass.

Sedlacek, W. E., & Adams-Gaston, J. (1992). Predicting the academic success of student-athletes using SAT and noncognitive variables. *Journal of Counseling and Development, 70* (6), 724–727.

Sedlacek, W. E., & Brooks, G. C., Jr. (1976). *Racism in American education: A model for change.* Chicago: Nelson-Hall.

Steele, C. M. (1997). A threat in the air: How stereotypes shape intellectual identity and performance. *American Psychologist, 52,* 613–629.

Sternberg, R. J. (1996). *Successful intelligence.* New York: Plume.

Ting, S. R. (1997). Estimating academic success in the first year of college for specially admitted White students: A model combining cognitive and psychosocial predictors. *Journal of College Student Development, 38,* 401–409.

Ting, S. R., & Robinson, T. L. (1998). First-year academic success: A prediction combining cognitive and psychosocial variables for White and African American students. *Journal of College Student Development, 39,* 599–610.

Ting, S. R., & Sedlacek, W. E. (2000). *Validity of the Noncognitive Questionnaire–Revised 2 in predicting the academic success of university freshmen* (Counseling Center Research Report No. 1–00). College Park: University of Maryland.

Tracey, T. J., & Sedlacek, W. E. (1984a). Noncognitive variables in predicting academic success by race. *Measurement and Evaluation in Guidance, 16,* 172–178.

Tracey, T. J., & Sedlacek, W. E. (1984b). Using ridge regression with noncognitive variables by race in admissions. *College and University, 50,* 345–350.

Tracey, T. J., & Sedlacek, W. E. (1985). The relationship of noncognitive variables to academic success: A longitudinal comparison by race. *Journal of College Student Personnel, 26,* 405–410.

Tracey, T. J., & Sedlacek, W. E. (1987). Prediction of college graduation using noncognitive variables by race. *Measurement and Evaluation in Counseling and Development, 19,* 177–184.

Tracey, T. J., & Sedlacek, W. E. (1988). A comparison of White and Black student academic success using noncognitive variables: A LISREL analysis. *Research in Higher Education, 27*, 333–348.

Tracey, T. J., & Sedlacek, W. E. (1989). Factor structure of the Noncognitive Questionnaire-Revised across samples of Black and White college students. *Educational and Psychological Measurement, 49*, 637–648.

Warmsley, D. (1998, October). *Incorporating noncognitive variables in the scholarship selection process of African American students.* Paper presented at the meeting of the National Association of College Admission Counseling, Indianapolis, IN.

Webb, C. T., Sedlacek, W. E., Cohen, D., Shields, P., Gracely, E., Hawkins, M., & Nieman, L. (1997). The impact of nonacademic variables on performance at two medical schools. *Journal of the National Medical Association, 89* (3), 173–180.

White, C. J., & Shelley, C. (1996). Telling stories: Students and administrators talk about retention. In I. H. Johnson & A. J. Ottens (Eds.), *Leveling the playing field: Promoting academic success for students of color* (pp. 15–34). San Francisco: Jossey-Bass.

White, T. J., & Sedlacek, W. E. (1986). Noncognitive predictors of grades and retention for specially admitted students. *Journal of College Admissions, 3*, 20–23.

Williams, W. M. (1997, October 10). Reliance on test scores is a conspiracy of lethargy. *Chronicle of Higher Education,* p. A60.

Willingham, W. W. (1985). *Success in college: The role of personal qualities and academic ability.* New York: College Entrance Examination Board.

Woods, P. A., & Sedlacek, W. E. (1988). *Construct and congruent validity of the Noncognitive Questionnaire (NCQ)* (Counseling Center Research Report No. 6–88). College Park: University of Maryland.

11

Broadening the Performance Domain in the Prediction of Academic Success

Neal Schmitt
Frederick L. Oswald
Michael A. Gillespie
Michigan State University

Academic institutions have long claimed in their mission statements that students benefit from a college education along multiple dimensions. Certainly knowledge within one's disciplinary focus and knowledge about future employability are important, but most advocates of the college experience also cite important development in areas such as leadership, citizenship, community involvement, personal values, and character (Taber & Hackman, 1976; Willingham, 1985). Despite the explicit statements of these multiple objectives, today's institutions continue to evaluate or account for the outcomes of the college experience on relatively narrow criteria such as GPA and graduation. In addition, efforts to validate college admissions procedures often rely solely on GPA and, very often, only freshman GPA.

In this chapter, we argue that the usual practice of paying primary or sole attention to GPA or graduation as criteria of college success results in what is termed *criterion deficiency* by industrial/organizational psychologists interested in employee selection. In other words, if educators take seriously their attempt to define and develop the various nonacademic dimensions of their undergraduate students, then in turn, it is appropriate to measure the development of their students and the effectiveness of their institutions on these dimensions, as well as on college GPA or graduation rates. The situation is as depicted at the top of Fig. 11.1. The ultimate criterion or goal of college education includes academic success, but also informed and involved citizenship, leadership, health, integrity, and other dimensions. Traditionally, the actual criterion of success is almost always college GPA or successful graduation. The degree to which the circle representing the ultimate criterion overlaps with the actual criterion represents the relevance of the outcomes we consider in most existing research on academic success. The portion of the actual criterion that does not overlap with the ultimate criterion represents *criterion contamination* including such possibilities as special learning opportunities to which only a select few have access. In this area, gender, race, and other correlates of GPA unrelated to ultimate success have been of considerable and continuing concern. The portion of the ultimate criterion that is not related to the actual criterion is referred to as *criterion deficiency* and, as already stated, represents those organizational and individual outcomes that are not part of an actual measure of success. Arguably, criterion deficiency exists when we consider only GPA in evaluating student success. The focus of this chapter is on criterion deficiency and the description of some research designed to minimize this problem.

The bottom half of Fig. 11.1 depicts how the sole use of college GPA as the outcome of interest in studies of the validity of academic admissions procedures is likely to provide an inadequate view of the entire phenomena of interest. The relationship of the actual and ultimate criterion is depicted in the same manner as in the top half of the figure. In addition, we introduce circles that represent different possible predictors. The usual college admissions tools, the SAT, ACT, and/or HSGPA, are represented by the circle on the bottom left. It overlaps significantly with the usual actual outcome measures (i.e., college GPA or graduation). It also overlaps with the ultimate criterion reflecting the fact that one important goal of a college education is academic success. However, the SAT, ACT, and HSGPA may not relate all that well to the remainder of the ultimate criterion that includes many nonacademic objectives that are among the stated goals of most higher education institutions. If we introduce other noncognitive or motivational predictors into this system, it

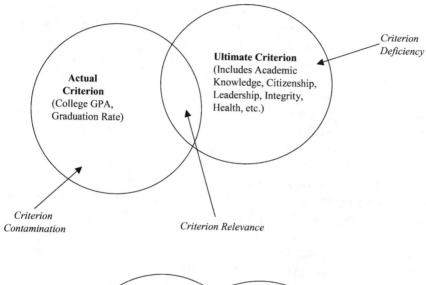

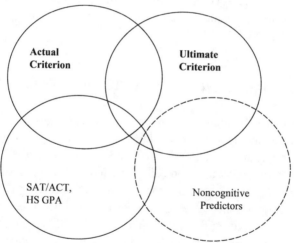

FIG. 11.1. Relationship between actual criterion, ultimate criterion, and various predictors.

is our hypothesis that those predictors are most likely to relate to the portion of the ultimate criterion that is frequently neglected in most empirical studies. So, the typical study of the validity of academic prediction is inadequate on two counts. First, the outcomes considered in these studies are deficient. Second, because the actual criterion usually considered does not include the full domain, predictors that may be related to a more complete consideration of college success will not display good empirical validity.

Serious attention to noncognitive predictors is also relevant and potentially beneficial to concerns about the impact of academic prediction on members of some minority groups as well as females. Unlike the SAT or ACT on which we find large subgroup differences favoring Whites over African Americans and Hispanic Americans, and smaller differences usually favoring males over females (Bowen & Bok, 1998; Jencks & Phillips, 1998; Ramist, Lewis, & McCamley-Jenkins, 1994; Willingham & Cole, 1997), subgroup differences on noncognitive predictors are often small, nonexistent, or on occasion favor women and minorities (Hough, Oswald, & Ployhart, 2001).

Our position in this chapter is that we are unlikely to improve the prediction of academic performance as traditionally conceptualized given the relatively high criterion-related validity usually reported for a combination of SAT/ACT scores and HSGPA (Hetzlett et al., 2001; Willingham, 1985). To improve validity, and at the same time reduce the adverse impact of traditional academic predictors on minorities and women, we must broaden our conceptualization of college success. Along with this change in the outcome space, we must develop and validate predictors that are conceptually related to this broadened domain.

EXPANDING THE CRITERION DOMAIN

If we accept that the marketing materials of U.S. colleges and the statements by various stakeholders in the academic enterprise (e.g., college presidents, state legislators, parents, the students themselves) accurately reflects the broad development we expect to see in college students, then we must acknowledge that college student success is a broader domain than is reflected by traditional criteria of academic success. As just indicated, traditional criteria for college student success have tended to fall under the broad category of *task performance* (e.g., grades on specific assignments, GPA, receiving a college degree). The criteria we discuss in this chapter also include dimensions that fall under the broad category of *contextual performance*, dimensions such as social responsibility (cf. Borman & Motowidlo, 1993) and adaptability and life skills (cf. Pulakos, Arad, Donovan, & Plamondon, 2000). This distinction between task performance and contextual performance has been useful in understanding and modeling job performance (Borman & Motowidlo, 1997; Campbell, Gasser, & Oswald, 1996).

Conceptualizing and evaluating successful development as a college student depends on the multiple outcomes desired by students and the school administration (Willingham, 1985). In an early attempt to discern dimensions of college performance, Taber and Hackman (1976) found 17 dimensions, academic and nonacademic, to be important in classifying successful and unsuccessful college students. Furthermore, college students actively involved in numerous domains tend to achieve greater success in their overall college experience as reflected in their involvement, accumulated achievement record, or their graduation (Astin, 1984; Willingham, 1985). High-school honors, school references, personal statements, and a measure of persistence or follow-through have predicted scholarship, leadership, nonacademic accomplishments, and overall success ratings, above and beyond high school rank and SAT score (Willingham, 1985). In related work, Ra (1989) found that measures of high school leadership, athletic success, persistence in extracurricular activities, honors, personal statements, and references predicted college GPA, but not perceived success or leadership experience. More recently, Cress, Astin, Zimmer-Oster, and Burkhardt (2001) found that those who participated in leadership education and training showed development in personal and societal values, civic responsibility, multicultural awareness, leadership skills, and understanding of leadership theories.

Our attempt to determine the nature and number of dimensions of college student success was guided by two considerations. First, the number of dimensions should not be so large that the information is unwieldy yet not be so limited that the domain of college success is not appropriately represented. Second, we wanted to understand how a variety of stakeholders, invested in the process of college education, defined college student success. Relying on one source alone could lead to inadequate definitions of college student success, or at the very least would not reveal how different sources converge and diverge in the dimensions of student success they identify and the importance they ascribe to those dimensions.

In identifying our criterion dimensions, we first examined the Web pages of colleges and universities, including both public and private institutions. We examined the mission statements and the stated educational objectives of programs of 35 colleges and universities. These institutions varied on characteristics such as their public and/or private funding base and size. From this search, we identified 174 separate goal statements. The authors independently sorted the statements into as many or as few clusters as they felt necessary. They then discussed and agreed on 12 major dimensions of college student performance as reasonably describing the various university statements. We also analyzed University Residence Life materials at Michigan State University and conducted an interview with a lead administrator in the residence halls to

TABLE 11.1

Dimensions of College Performance

Knowledge, Learning, Mastery of General Principles
Gaining knowledge and mastering facts, ideas, and theories and how they interrelate, and understanding the relevant contexts in which knowledge is developed and applied. Grades or GPA can indicate, but not guarantee, success on this dimension.

Continuous Learning, Intellectual Interest, and Curiosity
Being intellectually curious and interested in continuous learning. Actively seeking new ideas and new skills, both in core areas of study as well as in peripheral or novel areas.

Artistic Cultural Appreciation and Curiosity
Appreciating art and culture, either at an expert level or simply at the level of one who is interested.

Multicultural Tolerance and Appreciation
Showing openness, tolerance, and interest in a diversity of individuals (e.g., by culture, ethnicity, or gender). Actively participating in, contributing to, and influencing a multicultural environment.

Leadership
Demonstrating skills in a group, such as motivating others, coordinating groups and tasks, serving as a representative for the group, or otherwise performing a managing role in a group.

Interpersonal Skills
Communicating and dealing well with others, whether in informal social situations or more formal school-related situations. Being aware of the social dynamics of a situation and responding appropriately.

Social Responsibility, Citizenship, and Involvement
Being responsible to society and the community, and demonstrating good citizenship. Being actively involved in the events in one's surrounding community, which can be at the neighborhood, town/city, state, national, or college/university level. Activities may include volunteer work for the community, attending city council meetings, and voting.

Physical and Psychological Health
Possessing the physical and psychological health required to engage actively in a scholastic environment. This would include participating in healthy behaviors, such as eating properly, exercising regularly, and maintaining healthy personal and academic relations with others, as well as avoiding unhealthy behaviors, such as alcohol/drug abuse, unprotected sex, and ineffective or counterproductive coping behaviors.

Career Orientation
Having a clear sense of the career one aspires to enter into, which may happen before entry into college, or at any time while in college. Establishing, prioritizing, and following a set of general and specific career-related goals.

Adaptability and Life Skills
Adapting to a changing environment (at school or home), dealing well with gradual or sudden and expected or unexpected changes. Being effective in planning one's everyday activities and dealing with novel problems and challenges in life.

(Continued)

TABLE 11.1 (*continued*)

Perseverance

  Committing oneself to goals and priorities set, regardless of the difficulties that stand in the way. Goals range from long-term goals (e.g., graduating from college) to short-term goals (e.g., showing up for class every day even when the class is not interesting).

Ethics and Integrity

  Having a well-developed set of values, and behaving in ways consistent with those values. In everyday life, this probably means being honest, not cheating (on exams or in committed relationships), and having respect for others.

---

gain a better understanding of the characteristics and skills valued in residence life at the university. Dimensions identified at this level included academics, social development (e.g., roommate and romantic relationships), personal development (e.g., substance abuse, leisure time, time management), ethical and character development (e.g., challenge to values, maintaining community standards), and multicultural competence (e.g., seeking out other cultures and lifestyles). For other sources of potentially salient dimensions of college performance, we gathered information from the published educational research literature and national educational reports. This latter information was used to refine further the definitions of the 12 dimensions of college success. The final list is presented in Table 11.1 and includes knowledge, learning, and mastery of general principles; continuous learning, intellectual interest, and curiosity; artistic cultural appreciation; multicultural tolerance and appreciation; leadership; interpersonal skills; social responsibility, citizenship, and involvement; physical and psychological health; career orientation; adaptability and life skills; perseverance; and ethics and integrity.

To measure the 12 dimensions, behaviorally anchored rating scales (BARS) were constructed to reflect each of the 12 dimensions. These BARS clearly described each dimension of interest and provided examples of different degrees of successful behavior for each dimension. To ensure the appropriateness of the examples and anchors, examples were adapted from original college-related critical incidents that had been provided by students. A sample BARS item is presented in Fig 11.2.

These twelve dimensions were also operationalized in a checklist of college experiences thought to reflect student activity on the same dimensions. A sample of the checklist items for three dimensions is presented in Table 11.2.

Using this broadened conceptualization of student success and the operationalization of these dimensions in the form of BARS and an activity checklist, we proceeded to develop predictors that reflected these dimensions.

Artistic cultural appreciation and curiosity.

Definition: Appreciating art and culture, either at an expert level or simply at the level of one who is interested.

Unsatisfactory			Fulfills Expectations			Exceptional
1	2	3	4	5	6	7

Before you make your rating, please read these two examples:

Example 1

Your roommate's class is going on an outing to an art gallery. You are not registered for the class, but think the trip sounds interesting.
What do you expect you would do?

Unsatisfactory	Fulfills Expectations	Exceptional
You don't go on the outing.	You discuss the outing after your roommate went, and then go to the art gallery on your own time.	You make a special arrangement to go with the class, participate fully in the trip, and have fun at the art gallery.

Example 2

You have set ideas about what music is pleasing to the ear, and friends are pushing you to join them at a concert that they think you would enjoy. The band would be playing music that you prefer to avoid. What do you expect you would do?

Unsatisfactory	Fulfills Expectations	Exceptional
You would not go, but would decline as politely as possible.	You go to the concert planning to enjoy only a few pieces.	You go to the concert with an open mind, looking forward to trying something new, especially since it came with a recommendation.

FIG. 11.2. Example BARS item.

TABLE 11.2

Artistic Cultural Appreciation and Curiosity
College Experience Checklist Items

Participants indicated whether or not they had engaged in this list of activities or if the
event listed had occurred to them at least once during college.

Participants marked items:
  a = *Yes*
  b = *No*

Artistic Cultural Appreciation and Curiosity
  Learned to play an instrument.
  Participated in a play/musical (as an actor, building props, in the orchestra, etc.).
  Learned a new type of dance (e.g., ballroom dancing, break dancing).
  Visited a public or school museum.
  Attended a cultural event in the last 6 months, (e.g., art exhibit, play, musical, dance
    performance).
  Am a member of an orchestra/band/choir.
  Am a member of an art (e.g., painting, photography, music) club.
  Am a member of a private band, musical, or vocal group.
  Am a member in a band (school or private) or in a vocal group.

Multicultural Tolerance and Appreciation
  Learned (or significantly improved in) a foreign language.
  Visited a foreign country for at least a week.
  Am a member of a multicultural organization.

Leadership
  Am the head/president of an organization to which I belong.
  Have been the team captain for an official school or club sports team.
  Started a new club, organization, or official group.

PREDICTOR DEVELOPMENT

In attempting to predict the noncognitive attributes alreday mentioned, we
used two different types of measures: a situational judgment inventory and a
biographical data measure.

Situational judgment inventories (SJIs) are multiple-choice tests that generate
a more realistic appraisal of how an applicant (for a job, or in this case for college) might react in different relevant contexts (Motowidlo & Tippins, 1993).
Typically, respondents choose or rate possible actions in response to hypothetical situations or problems, usually in a paper-and-pencil format. In the employment context, the use of SJIs usually reduces adverse impact for minorities
relative to that of cognitive tests (Pulakos & Schmitt, 1996; Sackett, Schmitt,
Ellingson, & Kabin, 2001), and the SJI produces favorable test-taker reactions

(Hedlund et al., 2001) as well as high perceptions of face validity (Clevenger, Pereira, Wiechmann, Schmitt, & Harvey-Schmidt, 2001; McDaniel, Bruhn-Finnegan, Morgeson, Campion, & Braverman, 2001). Such support for SJIs in employment settings suggests that they may be a viable supplement or alternative to traditional cognitive ability testing in college admissions, though we are aware of only one previous application in academic prediction: Hedlund et al. (2001) found an SJI to have rather small incremental validity above Graduate Management Admission Test (GMAT) scores for MBA students ($\Delta R^2 = .03$).

More importantly, both structured biographical data, usually called "biodata," and SJIs are broadly applicable to a variety of circumstances. They have the potential to increase criterion-related validity over traditional measures because item content can be tailored to specific dimensions of college success as well as to the goals of a particular college and college-admissions process. Biodata and SJIs also have increased practical utility over typical subjective evaluations, such as essays or reference letters, because they require less time, labor, and cost to score and because they provide a fair and standardized process for obtaining information about the broad range of prior educational and social experiences of applicants.

A search of existing situational judgment inventory measures produced item stems that fit many of the aforementioned 12 dimensions. We recruited and paid undergraduate students at our home institution to participate in developing further our SJI. This development process consisted of three separate data-collection phases that were also instrumental to developing the BARS described previously. First, students generated critical incidents for use as additional item stems for dimensions underrepresented by existing SJI items. Second, an independent set of students created multiple response options for each item stem. Third, ratings of the favorability of each response option and judgments regarding the best and worst options were collected from an advanced undergraduate psychology course. Students were all junior and senior college undergraduates, who completed the instrument as part of a project for a psychological measurement class. Forty-two respondents provided usable data for use in developing the SJI scoring key. Procedures developed and reported in Motowidlo Dunnette, and Carter (1990) and Motowidlo, Russell, Carter, and Dunnette (1988) resulted in a key that could yield item scores from −2 to +2. Three to six items (57 total) for each of the 12 scales survived the item review and score development process. An example of two situational judgment items is presented in Table 11.3.

Structured biographical data (biodata) measures provide a systematic method for collecting and scoring information on an individual's background and life history. Despite the informal use of similar information in college

TABLE 11.3

Examples of Two Situational Judgment Items
Written to Measure Ethics/Integrity and Leadership

Ethics/Integrity
You know that a group of students in your class cheats on exams by putting formulas into scientific calculators or into cell phones. The professor has clearly warned against such activity, but you are not sure what she or he would do if she or he knew what these students were doing.
    What action would you take?
    a. Try doing the same thing until people start getting caught.
    b. Study the way you know best, do not cheat, but do not turn in the other students either.
    c. You would do nothing: it is none of your business.
    d. You would mention it to the professor so she can deal with the problems in the class.
    e. Don't tell the professor, but make it clear you are not involved in case the students get caught.
    f. Send the professor an anonymous message about what is going on.

Leadership
You are assigned to a group to work on a particular project. When you sit down together as a group, no one says anything.
    What would you do?
    a. Look at them until someone eventually says something.
    b. Start the conversation yourself by introducing yourself.
    c. Get to know everyone first and see what they are thinking about the project to make sure the project's goals are clear to everyone.
    d. Try to start working on the project by asking everyone's opinion about the nature of the project.
    e. You would take the leadership role by assigning people to do things or ask questions to get things rolling.

---

applications (e.g., extracurricular activity lists and resumes), we undertook the development of a biodata inventory with standard multiple-choice responses to questions about one's previous experiences, similar to tests used in employee selection processes.

Multiple sources were searched for pre-existing biodata items that would fit as many of the 12 performance dimensions (see Table 11.1) as possible. When necessary, item stems were modified for appropriateness to the college context. We generated additional items for those dimensions that lacked a sufficient number of items. Using the help of six paid college students who supplied open-ended responses, we also created or adapted the response options to make them applicable to a college student population. Using these responses, we modified item responses to reflect an appropriate range

TABLE 11.4

Examples of Two Biodata Items Designed to Measure Leadership

The number of high-school clubs and organized activities (such as band, sports, newspapers, etc.) in which I took a leadership role was:

    a. 4 or more
    b. 3
    c. 2
    d. 1
    e. I did not take a leadership role in these activities

How often do you talk your friends into doing what you want to do during the evening?

    a. most of the time
    b. sometimes (about half the time)
    c. occasionally (about as often as others in the group)
    d. seldom or infrequently
    e. never

---

and dropped items showing little variance. Some items were also dropped because they were near duplicates of other items. The final biodata inventory consisted of 115 items representing the 12 dimensions and scored on a 4- or 5-point scale. Additional detail regarding the development, dimensionality, and psychometric adequacy of both the SJI and the biodata measures is provided in two reports (Gillespie, Kim, Oswald, Ramsay, & Schmitt, 2002; Oswald, Schmitt, Ramsay, Kim, & Gillespie, 2003). Examples of two biodata items are presented in Table 11.4.

In the following section, we describe a data collection effort designed to assess the degree to which the broader conceptualization of student performance provides unique information. In addition, we evaluate the degree to which noncognitive instruments designed to reflect these broader dimensions do indeed relate to student performance on those dimensions as well as on GPA and student attendance at class.

SAMPLE AND DATA COLLECTION

Six hundred and fifty four first-year undergraduate students at a large Midwestern university volunteered for this study and received $40 for their participation. Of these, 644 provided usable data after screening for careless responses. Mean age was 18.5 years ($SD = .69$); 72% were female; 77.3% were White, 9.8% Black/African American, 5.4% Asian, 1.9% Hispanic American, and 4.9% other.

In addition to self-ratings on the BARS, the checklist, biodata, and SJI measures, the students were asked to provide a self-report of their absenteeism from class in the previous 6 months using a 5-point scale ranging from *less than five* to *more than 30*. Authorization was also obtained from the students to obtain their college GPA from the university registrar's office and their SAT/ACT scores from the admissions office. Finally, peer ratings on the 12 dimensions were obtained for 154 of the students by e-mail correspondence with a person nominated by the student. Peers were paid $5 for their participation.

Results

Confirmatory and exploratory factor analyses of the peer ratings and self ratings indicated that a composite of the 12 dimensions was the best representation of these performance ratings. A composite was therefore created for both sets of ratings by summing scores obtained for the 12 dimensions. Alpha coefficients for these composites were .83 and .80 for peer and self-ratings, respectively. The alpha coefficient associated with a summed composite of the checklist items was .76. Consequently, we computed the correlations shown in Table 11.5 between college GPA, absenteeism, self-rated BARS, peer-rated BARS, and the composite activity checklist to examine relationships within our broadened definition of student performance.

Correlations of these same five outcome measures with the SJI, biodata, and composite SAT/ACT are presented in Table 11.6 as evidence of the validity of our experimental predictors and a typical standardized admissions test.

As can be seen in Table 11.5, the correlations between the five outcome variables are not very large, the highest being the −.42 between absenteeism

TABLE 11.5

Means, Standard Deviations, and Intercorrelations
of Student Outcome Variables

Variable	M	SD	1	2	3	4	5
Freshman GPA (1)	3.02	.69	1.00				
Times absent (2)	1.98	1.08	−.42	1.00			
Self-ratings (3)	4.88	.71	.12	−.19	1.00		
Checklist composite (4)	.38	.10	.06	−.13	.23	1.00	
Peer ratings (5)	4.96	.80	.31	−.15	.08	.08	1.00

Note. N = 619 to 640 with the exception of Peer Ratings for which N = 147. GPA was based on a 0–4.0 scale, Times Absent M equaled a response of 5–10 classes, Self and Peer ratings were averages of ratings on 12 dimensions on 7-point scales, and the Checklist Composite was a M of Yes–No responses to 65 items.

TABLE 11.6

Predictor–Outcome Correlations

			Outcomes		
Predictors	GPA	Absenteeism	Self-Rating BARS	Checklist	Peer-Rating BARS
Biodata					
Knowledge	.22	−.18	.46	.24	.21
Continuous learning	.05	.00	.40	.36	.06
Artistic appreciation	.01	.07	.37	.29	.09
Multicultural tolerance	.07	.02	.37	.31	.10
Leadership	.14	−.03	.41	.36	.20
Interpersonal skills	.04	−.09	.25	.13	.21
Community involvement	.08	−.09	.38	.42	.22
Health	.23	−.23	.21	.20	.11
Career orientation	−.02	−.06	.18	.14	−.01
Adaptability	.21	−.15	.23	.10	−.13
Perseverance	.15	−.20	.46	.31	.21
Ethics/integrity	.14	−.31	.35	.10	.02
Situational Judgment					
Knowledge	.15	−.38	.31	.10	.08
Continuous learning	.16	−.12	.27	.03	.23
Artistic appreciation	.00	−.08	.38	.12	.12
Multicultural tolerance	.06	−.07	.39	.14	.08
Leadership	.02	−.10	.37	.19	.11
Interpersonal skills	.10	−.08	.27	.08	.15
Community involvement	.00	−.12	.28	.17	.03
Health	.13	−.22	.29	.11	.11
Career orientation	.11	−.16	.19	.06	.11
Adaptability	.08	−.14	.32	.13	.07
Perseverance	.08	−.22	.31	.12	.08
Ethics/integrity	.23	−.18	.30	.06	−.02
SAT/ACT composite	.33	.11	.00	−.11	.09

Note. Correlations with peer ratings in excess of .16 were statistically significant, $p < .05$. Correlations in excess of .07 were significant ($p < .05$) for the other four outcomes.

and GPA, indicating that students who are absent more frequently tend to get lower grades. Peer ratings and GPA also correlated .31. Peer ratings are correlated only .08 with self ratings, indicating that individuals see themselves very differently than do their peers. The major conclusion here, given the pattern of correlations, is that student performance is multidimensional.

A second question addressed in this data collection was the degree to which experimental biodata and SJI items as well as traditional admissions tests were correlated with this set of outcomes. The data in Table 11.6 indicate that, as expected, the best predictor of GPA is the composite SAT/ACT measure ($r = .33$). However, GPA is also moderately related to several of the biodata and SJI measures, most notably Health, Adaptability, and Knowledge biodata indices and the Ethics/Integrity, Knowledge, and Continuous Learning SJI measures. Absenteeism, which is relatively uncorrelated ($r = .11$) with the SAT/ACT composite, has a relatively strong relationship with the biodata measures of Health, Perseverance, and Ethics/Integrity as well as with the Perseverance, Health, Knowledge, and Ethics/Integrity SJI measures. Self-ratings and checklist indices, which are self-reported measures indexed to the 12 major performance outcomes, have relatively high correlations with virtually all the biodata dimensions. Self-reported behaviorally anchored ratings of performance were also relatively highly related to the SJI measures, but only weakly related to the checklist measure. Correlations of peer ratings of the same 12 performance outcomes with the biodata and SJI measures are not affected by the same source "bias" of self-report instruments and are correspondingly lower than similar correlations with the self-ratings and checklist outcomes. Even so, biodata measures of Knowledge, Leadership, Interpersonal Skills, Community Involvement, and Perseverance are correlated above .20 with the peer rating outcome measure. Only the situational judgment measure of Continuous Learning was correlated significantly ($r = .23$) with the peer rating composite. The SAT/ACT composite was correlated .00, $-.11$, and .09 with the self-rating, checklist, and peer-rating composites, respectively.

Results of hierarchical regression analyses presented elsewhere (Oswald et al., in press) indicate that even in predicting freshman college GPA, biodata and SJI predictors added incremental validity above that afforded by the SAT/ACT and personality variables (extraversion, conscientiousness, agreeableness, emotional stability, and openness to experience). The latter two sets of measures were used as controls since SAT/ACT test scores are the current standard in academic prediction, and biodata and SJI measures are sometimes found to be highly related to personality measures and performance. For all other outcomes, the biodata and SJI measures were the most predictive. Adjusted Multiple Rs for this complete set of predictors were .50, .47, .67, .48, and .49 for GPA, absenteeism, and the self-rating, checklist, and peer-rating composites, respectively.

DISCUSSION

In this chapter, we argued for a model of college student performance that includes outcomes in addition to the usual GPA measure. Accordingly, we examined what various universities viewed as desirable student outcomes and constructed measures of these outcomes. Our multidimensional view of student performance was supported by the relatively weak correlations among peer ratings of performance on the 12 outcomes, checklist indictors of student activity, and GPA. As might be expected, there was a relatively strong relationship between absenteeism and GPA.

We also constructed experimental SJI and biodata predictors of these outcomes. These experimental predictors added to the predictability of GPA beyond an SAT/ACT composite and were the major predictors of absenteeism and the other measures directly constructed to mirror the major performance dimensions in our model of student performance.

These results are encouraging, but there is certainly a need for additional research in these areas prior to any operational use of biodata and SJIs. One major concern is the degree to which these measures will be coachable or fakable. Previous research on similar measures suggests this is a important concern (Hough, Eaton, Dunnette, Kamp, & McCloy, 1990; Lautenshlager, 1994; Paulhus, 1991). We are experimenting with various ways to assess the degree of fakability and its impact on examinee scores and test validity (Schmitt et al., 2003). This concern, as well as other possible motivational issues, will require research in which the student participants are responding as actual applicants and the research design is predictive rather than concurrent as was the case in the research described in this chapter.

The sample, in this instance, included only students from a single university. We were also unable to obtain the HSGPA for this sample. HSGPA has proven to be a substantial predictor of college GPA in other studies (e.g., Hezlett et al., 2001; Willingham, 1985). HSGPA, unlike the SAT/ACT scores, is likely affected by motivation as well as ability. Because some of the SJI and biodata items and scales are also motivational in nature, it is likely that these measures may not provide as much incremental prediction when HSGPA is part of the prediction equation. This may not be a serious concern, however, because in addition to including SAT/ACT scores as a measure of cognitive ability, we also included personality variables (e.g., conscientiousness) that may relate to college GPA in a way similar to the motivational component of HSGPA.

In addition, subgroup differences should be explored; Gillespie et al. (2002) reported trends in subgroup mean differences for several minority groups and men and women, but the subgroup sample sizes are relatively small. Although we were unable to look for differences across different individual majors, again due to small subgroup sample sizes, we were able to divide our sample into "hard" sciences and "soft" sciences. We then computed predictor-outcome correlations for male and female samples within each of these broad disciplinary groups. Tests of the significance of the differences in these correlations across all subgroup pairs for all criteria except for the peer-rating composite revealed fewer significant differences than expected by chance ($p < .05$) For the peer-rating criterion, some noteworthy patterns of differences were observed for the biodata scales of Knowledge, Continuous Learning, Artistic Appreciation, Multicultural Appreciation, and Leadership and the SJI scales of Continuous Learning, Multicultural Appreciation, and Ethics and Integrity. The general trend was that validities for males in the hard sciences ($N = 18$) and females in the soft sciences ($N = 62$) were moderately positive (.2 to .5) whereas validities for males in the soft sciences ($N = 12$) and females in the hard sciences ($N = 43$) were slightly negative (.0 to $-.4$). These groups are very small, but the results suggest that further inquiry into the prediction of peer-rating criteria across gender and disciplinary subgroups may be warranted. It is possible that predictors are differently related to peers' perceptions of student performance when the students' interests or major are nontraditional.

Additional attention should also be directed to the psychometric development of biodata and SJI scales. One application of biodata and SJI might be in the career-guidance domain. However, if differential decisions are to be made on the basis of subscale scores, the subscales must be highly reliable and there must be discriminant validity. There was some evidence that this goal was possible for the biodata subscales, but there was disappointing evidence for the hypothesized dimensionality of the SJI.

REFERENCES

Astin, A. W. (1984). Student involvement: A developmental theory for higher education. *Journal of College Student Personnel, 25,* 297–308.

Borman, W. C., & Motowidlo, S. J. (1993). Expanding the criterion domain to include the elements of contextual performance. In N. Schmitt & W. C. Borman (Eds.), *Personnel selection in organizations* (pp. 71–98). San Francisco: Jossey-Bass.

Borman, W. C., & Motowidlo, S. J. (1997). Task performance and contextual performance: The meaning for personnel selection research. *Human Performance, 10,* 99–109.

Bowen, W. G., & Bok, D. (1998). *The shape of the river: Long-term consequences of considering race in college and university admissions.* Princeton, NJ: Princeton University Press.

Campbell, J. P., Gasser, M. B., & Oswald, F. L. (1996). The substantive nature of job performance variability. In K. R. Murphy (Ed.), *Individual differences and behavior in organizations* (pp. 258–299). San Francisco: Jossey-Bass.

Clevenger, J., Pereira, G. M., Wiechmann, D., Schmitt, N., & Harvey-Schmidt, V. (2001). Incremental validity of situational judgment tests. *Journal of Applied Psychology, 86,* 410–417.

Cress, C. M., Astin, H. S., Zimmer-Oster, K., & Burkardt, J. (2001). Developmental outcomes of college students' involvement in leadership activities. *Journal of College Student Development, 42,* 15–27.

Gillespie, M. A., Kim, B. H., Oswald, F. L., Ramsay, L. J., & Schmitt, N. (2002). *Biodata and situational judgment inventories as measures of college success: Development and pilot testing phases.* Report submitted to the College Board.

Hedlund, J., Plamondon, K., Wilt, J., Nebel, K., Ashford, S., & Sternberg, R. J. (2001, April). Practical intelligence for business: Going beyond the GMAT. Paper presented in J. Cortina (Chair), *Out with the old, in with the new: Looking above and beyond what we know about cognitive predictors.* Symposium presented at the 16th Annual Convention of the Society for Industrial and Organizational Psychology, San Diego, CA.

Hetzlett, S. A., Kuncel, N. R., Vey, M. A., Ahart, A. M., Ones, D. S., Campbell, J. P., & Camara, W. (2001, April). The predictive validity of the SAT: A meta-analysis. Paper presented in D. Ones & S. Hetzlett (Chairs), *Predicting performance: The interface of I-O psychology and educational research.* Symposium presented at the 16th Annual Conference of the Society for Industrial and Organizational Psychology, San Diego, CA.

Hough, L. M., Eaton, N. K., Dunnette, M. D., Kamp, J. D., & McCloy, R. A. (1990). Criterion-related validities of personality constructs and the effect of response distortion on those validities. *Journal of Applied Psychology, 75,* 581–595.

Hough, L. M., Oswald, F. L., & Ployhart, R. E. (2001). Determinants, detection, and amelioration of adverse impact in personnel selection procedures: Issues, evidence, and lessons learned. *International Journal of Selection and Assessment, 9,* 152–194.

Jencks, C., & Phillips, M. (Eds.). (1998). *The Black-White test score gap.* Washington, DC: The Brookings Institute Press.

Lautenschlager, G. J. (1994). Accuracy and faking of background data. In G. S. Stokes, M. D. Mumford, & W. A. Owens (Eds.), *Biodata handbook: Theory, research, and use of biographical information in selection and performance prediction* (pp. 391–420). Palo Alto, CA: Consulting Psychologists Press.

McDaniel, M. A., Bruhn-Finnegan, E. B., Morgeson, F. P., Campion, M. A., & Braverman, E. P. (2001). Predicting job performance using situational judgment tests. *Journal of Applied Psychology, 86* (4), 730–740.

Motowidlo, S. J., Dunnette, M. D., & Carter, G. W. (1990). An alternative selection procedure: The low-fidelity simulation. *Journal of Applied Psychology, 75,* 640–647.

Motowidlo, S. J., Russell, T. L., Carter, G. W., & Dunnette, M. D. (1988). *Revision of the Management Selection Interview: Final report.* Minneapolis, MN: Personnel Decisions Research Institute.

Motowidlo, S. J., & Tippins, N. (1993). Further studies of the low-fidelity simulation in the form of a situational inventory. *Journal of Occupational and Organizational Psychology, 66*, 337–344.

Oswald, F. L., Schmitt, N., Ramsay, L. J., Kim, B. H., & Gillespie, M. A. (in press). Noncognitive predictors of college student success. *Journal of Applied Psychology.*

Paulhus, D. L. (1991). Measurement and control of response bias. In J. P. Robinson, P. R. Shaver, & L. S. Wrightsman (Eds.), *Measures of personality and social psychological attitudes* (pp. 17–59). New York: Academic.

Pulakos, E. D., Arad, S., Donovan, M. A., & Plamondon, K. E. (2000). Adaptability in the workplace: Development of a taxonomy of adaptive performance. *Journal of Applied Psychology, 84*, 612–624.

Pulakos, E. D., & Schmitt, N. (1996). An evaluation of two strategies for reducing adverse impact and their effects on criterion-related validity. *Human Performance, 9*, 241–258.

Ra, J. B. (1989). Validity of a new evaluative scale to aid admissions decisions. *Evaluation and Program Planning, 12*, 195–204.

Ramist, L., Lewis, C., & McCamley-Jenkins, L. (1994). *Student group differences in predicting college grades: Sex, language, and ethnic groups* (College Board Rep. No. 93–1, ETS Research Rep. no. RR–94–27. New York: College Entrance Examination Board.

Sackett, P. R., Schmitt, N., Ellingson, J. E., & Kabin, M. B. (2001). High-stakes testing in employment, credentialing, and higher education: Prospects in a post-affirmative action world. *American Psychologist, 56*, 302–318.

Schmitt, N., Oswald, F. L., Kim, B. H., Gillespie, M. A., Ramsay, L. J., & Yoo, T. (2003). Impact of elaboration on socially desirable responding and the validity of biodata. *Journal of Applied Psychology, 88*, 979–988.

Taber, T. D., & Hackman, J. D. (1976). Dimensions of undergraduate college performance. *Journal of Applied Psychology, 61*, 546–558.

Willingham, W. W. (1985). *Success in college: The role of personal qualities and academic ability.* New York: College Entrance Examination Board.

Willingham, W., & Cole, N. (1997). *Gender and fair assessment.* Mahwah, NJ: Lawrence Erlbaum Associates.

12

Assessing the Personal Characteristics of Premedical Students

Patricia M. Etienne
Ellen R. Julian
Association of American Medical Colleges, Washington, DC

The Association of American Medical Colleges (AAMC) has begun to develop tests of personal characteristics as an additional component of the Medical College Admission Test (MCAT®).[1] The MCAT currently consists of four sections: Biological Sciences, Physical Sciences, Verbal Reasoning, and the Writing Sample, administered in a 7-hour test day. Scores on these test components, used in conjunction with other preadmissions data, especially undergraduate school GPAs, have been established as useful tools in the medical school admission process. In short, the test is already long enough and already does a good job as an admission tool. What then is the rationale for adding new components to the MCAT, and why personal characteristics? Why not use traditional measures of personality? This chapter provides some background information on AAMC's interest in these new measures, a brief review of some of the literature on the relationship between personality variables and

---

[1] MCAT® is a registered trademark of the Association of American Medical Colleges.

success in medical school and practice, and a description of the current test development effort, to explain why new measures of personal characteristics are being developed.

WHY NEW COMPONENTS?

Used in combination with other preadmissions indicators, MCAT scores continue to be an important tool of medical school admissions committees in the United States and Canada, helping them make decisions about who should be admitted into medical school. MCAT scores substantially supplement the ability of undergraduate GPAs to predict success in medical school (Julian, 2000a; Wiley & Koenig, 1996). As predictors of success in medical school, undergraduate GPAs alone explain approximately 29% of the variance in students' grades in the first 2 years of medical college. Undergraduate GPAs also account for about 13% of the variance in medical school clerkship grades. When MCAT scores are combined with undergraduate GPAs, an additional 21% of the variance in grades in the first 2 years of medical school is explained, and the percentage of variance in the clerkship grades that is accounted for by the predictors more than doubles. MCAT scores alone are almost as effective in the prediction of United States Medical Licensure Examination scores as is the combination of MCAT scores and undergraduate GPAs.

If the MCAT does such a fine job at helping to predict performance in medical school, what exactly is the rationale for creating new measures? The goal in developing measures of personal characteristics for the MCAT is to provide medical school admissions committees with additional, nonacademic information that will help to inform decisions about who should enter medical school. From its earliest interest in developing measures of personal characteristics, AAMC has pointed out that the potential new measures, ". . . reflect a desire to concentrate on those qualities which admissions officers have been addressing in a less than adequate way and which they feel would be more relevant to their task of selecting future physicians" (AAMC, 1976, p. 10).

These new measures might also increase the validity of the MCAT as a predictor of medical school performance and/or contribute to the prediction of areas of medical school performance not yet addressed by MCAT predictive validity research studies. The new measures may also be beneficial to applicants who might tend to be overlooked by admissions committees when only their MCAT score and undergraduate GPA are considered. The new measures may influence students' preparation for the MCAT by raising an awareness of the need for good personal characteristics among prospective physicians. In addition, the new measures will help to address concerns about what has been referred to as the status of the social contract between society and the medical profession (Sabalis, 2002).

MCAT Test Length

How then might the benefits of new measures for the MCAT be realized in the context of an already long test? MCAT researchers have studied five alternative MCAT configurations to determine the extent to which changing the number of test sections, reducing the test length, or changing the proportions of items per section might affect the effectiveness of the MCAT in predicting performance in medical school (Searcy, Oppler, & Chen, 2001).

The predictive validity of the MCAT was highly consistent across different criteria and samples for each of the five alternative configurations. Current MCAT scores, alone, and when combined with undergraduate variables, resulted in the highest predictive validity in almost all cases. Although the current MCAT produced the highest validity coefficient, none of the alternatives caused the validity to drop appreciably, even when the overall test length was reduced by as much as 15%. These results suggest that, as the AAMC contemplates various changes to the MCAT, test developers may have considerable flexibility in modifying test length to accommodate new test specifications.

Background

Some background information might help explain AAMC's current interest in modifying the MCAT specifications by introducing measures of personal characteristics. AAMC's interest in measuring personal characteristics goes back to the 1960s when the AAMC made the commitment to conduct research into and develop instruments designed to measure nonintellectual characteristics of medical college applicants. Toward that end, an advisory committee was created

> to study and make recommendations concerning the possible uses of personality measurement in medical education, specifically in admissions, medical specialty choice, professional adjustment, individualized instructional strategy development, and personal counseling of students. (Haley, D'Costa, & Schafer, 1971, p. 3)

That advisory committee reported on the results of A Survey of Non-cognitive Tests Used in Medical Schools (D'Costa & Schafer, 1972). The purposes of the survey were to find out which noncognitive instruments were being used by medical schools and to encourage collaborative efforts in noncognitive research nationally. The survey sought information about standard instruments being used, as well as nonstandard instruments that individual schools might have developed according to their particular interests. The advisory committee was particularly interested in finding out how these instruments were being used with entering students. Survey responses revealed the need for standardization of instrumentation and usage. The committee recommended that "Perhaps AAMC could serve as a non-cognitive test bank or clearinghouse for medical schools and facilitate . . . national team efforts [to develop and standardize instruments]" (D'Costa & Schafer, 1972, p. 3).

Morris (1973) pointed out the discrepancy between the approach used to measure noncognitive variables among medical school applicants and the approach used to measure cognitive variables among these applicants. He noted that although input from various committees and stakeholders had resulted in the strengthening and general improvement of the MCAT (the cognitive measure), the measurement of noncognitive variables had been undertaken

> in quite a different way, and with quite different results. Mainly what has been done over the years has been to try to adapt already existing personality tests and methods to purposes for which they were never intended. (Note: we did not do this in the case of the assessment of intellectual variables, although there were many tests available at the time which might have been used in this way.) In the non-cognitive domain perhaps one of the most striking examples . . . is the Minnesota Multiphasic Personality Inventory which was originally designed to be of assistance in the diagnosis of psychiatric patients. (Morris, 1973, p. 28)

Morris (1973) proposed, therefore, that "using the best features of existing inventories, we develop an instrument or instruments designed as precisely as possible to accomplish the purpose we have in mind and then standardize it or them on medical school applicant populations" (p. 29).

In the mid-1970s a subcommittee of the advisory committee identified eight noncognitive characteristics that should be the focus of research at the AAMC: concern for human and societal needs; ethical behavior; interpersonal relations; coping capabilities; sensitivity in interpersonal relations; decision-making skills; staying power—physical and motivational; and orientation toward lifelong learning.

Of the noncognitive instrument to be developed, the subcommittee noted:

> The likelihood . . . exists that any non-cognitive battery can be "faked" by a test taker who perceives he knows the characteristics which a medical school is seeking. The non-cognitive profile may suggest certain characteristics but these findings must be assessed in conjunction with observations made on personal

interview and from letters of reference. Thus, the non-cognitive instrument must be viewed simply as an adjunct in the overall evaluation of the non-cognitive characteristics in much the same way that the MCAT has been viewed as an adjunct in the evaluation of the cognitive characteristics of a candidate.[2]

The list was later reduced to seven by dropping "ethical behavior," and the subcommittee decided that the focus of instrument development would be on biographical data and situational tests. In the early 1980s, however, the AAMC's plans to measure noncognitive characteristics were put on hold, mainly because the project developers were unable to secure funding to proceed with further development.

CURRENT INTEREST

Despite earlier disappointments, the AAMC has maintained an interest in developing instrumentation to measure characteristics of medical school applicants other than the cognitive abilities that the MCAT now measures. This interest has been kept alive, in part, by the medical profession's continued expressed concern that the concept of *professionalism* among physicians not be limited to academic knowledge and skills, but also be understood to included attitudes and behaviors related to patient care, particularly interpersonal communication skills (*Contemporary Issues in Medicine: Communication in Medicine,* 1999, p. 4). More recently, the AAMC has expressed renewed interest in measuring noncognitive characteristics among entering medical school students and has identified altruism, communication skills, compassion, empathy, and integrity as characteristics of interest to the medical profession (Julian, 2000b). The inclusion of communication skills among the list of desired characteristics suggests that the term *noncognitive* might not be the best way to describe the characteristics of interest. The term *personal characteristics* has, therefore, recently been adopted to describe the characteristics for the new test development effort. One of the first steps in this effort was the investigation of traditional measures of personality. It quickly became clear from these investigations that the observations of earlier committees regarding the inappropriateness of traditional personality measures were still valid despite more recent research on the use of personality scores as indicators of academic and professional success.

[2]*Report to the Committee on Medical School Admissions Assessment on Development of a Non-Cognitive Instrument.* Taken from minutes of a meeting of the AAMC Committee on Admissions Assessment, March 4, 1975.

WHY NOT USE EXISTING MEASURES
OF PERSONALITY?

Studies based, primarily, on existing standardized measures of personality have found that scores on personality tests predict performance in the clinical years (Hojat, Erdmann, Robeson, Damjanov, & Glaser, 1994). These existing measures generally can be categorized as personality questionnaires, projective techniques, and objective tests. Although many of these measures have good reliability, evidence of their validity for selection of medical students is often tenuous or lacking. In other words, although most of these measures tend to measure characteristics with consistency, it is not always clear just what characteristics are being measured, or how those characteristics might be relevant to the success of medical students or physicians.

These tests, unlike the MCAT, are generally single-form tests, intended for use in low-stakes situations where there is only one examinee or a very small group of examinees, such as in personnel testing or in clinical or counseling psychology settings. In the latter two settings, issues of test fakability and test coachability are usually not relevant because examinees are seeking insights into themselves and thus tend to give truthful information about themselves. Examinees in these therapeutic settings are generally not trying to "game the system" because the emphasis is on diagnosis and not selection. In personnel selection, the examinee usually has no prior knowledge of the measurement instrument that will be used. Personnel selection tests are generally of interest to relatively small populations of test takers and, as such, are not popular among test-prep programs that coach the examinee on how to score well. Under such circumstances, test fakability is not a big concern.

"If instructed to do so, can individuals fake? What is the magnitude of such response distortions under instruction?" Viswesvaran and Ones (1999) posed these questions in a meta-analysis of the literature on faking in personality measurement. The researchers were also interested in determining whether some personality traits are more fakable than others. Because a large part of the fakability research literature included social desirability scales, the researchers include this variable in their analysis as well as the "Big Five"[3] dimensions of personality: agreeableness, conscientiousness, emotional stabil-

---

[3] In personality psychology, The Big Five is a taxonomy of traits that is sometimes used to describe personality differences among individuals: I—*extraversion versus introversion*, II—*agreeableness versus antagonism*, III—*conscientiousness versus undirectedness*, IV—*neuroticism versus emotional stability*, V—*openness to experience versus not open to experience* (Romney & Bynner, 1992, pp. 52–55).

ity, extraversion, and openness to experience. Viswesvaran and Ones (1999) based their analysis on studies in which subjects were instructed to "fake good" and to "fake bad." The researchers found that across 51 studies, fakability did not vary by personality dimension and concluded that all of the Big Five factors were equally fakable. Social desirability scales, however, were twice as sensitive to faking than were scales for the Big Five personality factors. The scores of "fake good" subjects were about half of a standard deviation higher than their nonfaking scores. The researchers found that the effects of faking bad were higher than for faking good. That is, subjects appeared to do better at faking bad than at faking good on personality measures. Viswesvaran and Ones (1999) concluded that, indeed, individuals can fake if instructed to do so.

A personality test intended for large-scale, high-stakes testing should be such that alternative forms can be created for different test administrations. Alternative forms would minimize item-response faking by examinees who have been coached to give "correct" responses. The MCAT Project, therefore, proposes to depart from the procedure by which existing standard personality measures were developed. Rather, the AAMC will develop a test plan that supports the development of alternative forms. The research literature on the relationship between personality characteristics and academic and professional success within the medical field supports the need for valid and reliable measures of the personal characteristics of interest to the AAMC.

PERSONALITY VARIABLES AND SUCCESS IN MEDICAL SCHOOL AND PRACTICE

Our brief review of the literature related to personal characteristics included studies that examined the relationship between personality variables and academic or professional success. In a 1968 study, Solkoff examined the relationship between academic performance and scores on a battery of personality, attitude and aptitude tests among high and low performing first- and second-year law and medical students. Solkoff's battery consisted of the Minnesota Multiphasic Personality Inventory (MMPI), three attitude scales, and the Otis Self-Administering Test of Intelligence. Although Solkoff found several significant differences between the test battery scores of the high performers and the low performers, he concluded that his results were not sufficiently reliable to justify the routine administration of these instruments as part of the admission process (Solkoff, 1968).

Haley, Juan, and Paiva (1971) compared the performance of high-, mid-, and low-MCAT scorers on selected personality measures. Personality measures used were the Survey of Interpersonal Values, the Allport-Vernon-Lindzey Study of Values, and Rokeach's Form E Dogmatism Scale. The researchers found that high MCAT scorers scored higher than low MCAT scorers on Independence and Aesthetic value scales, whereas low MCAT scorers scored higher on Conformity. High-, mid-, and low-MCAT scorers performed similarly on Support, Benevolence, and Leadership scales. Haley et al. (1971) concluded that MCAT scores are somehow related to personality variables although they make no definitive statement about the nature of that relationship. In a later study, researchers sought to determine whether measures of personality enhanced the relationship between predictor and criterion measures of student performance in medical school (Hojat et al., 1993). These researchers concluded that scores on personality tests contributed uniquely and significantly to the power of predictive measures and should, therefore, be used in the admissions process.

Other studies, such as that by Newton et al. (2000), examined the relationship between personality characteristics and choice of medical profession. Their findings suggest a link between medical students' degree of empathy and their choice of medical specialty. The researchers administered the Balanced Emotional Empathy Scale to medical students at different stages of their academic careers. They found that the students who chose core specialties such as family medicine and pediatrics tended to have higher scores on the empathy scale than students who chose noncore specialties such as radiology and pathology.

The literature also included research aimed at identifying predictors of humanistic qualities among students preparing to enter the medical profession. In a longitudinal study of medical school students, Rogers and Coutts (2000) posed the question of whether students' attitudes during their preclinical years predicted their humanism as clerkship students. The researchers administered attitude questionnaires to students during their preclinical and clerkship years. In their third year, students also completed a clinical performance examination in which they were rated on their humanism. The researchers found a consistent relationship between the scores on the attitude scale and the humanism scale. Although pointing out some important limitations of their study and recommending further instrument development, they concluded that scores on attitude scales in the preclinical years can serve as a good predictor of students' humanism in their clerkship years. In an earlier related study, Hojat et al. (1999) concluded that understanding the qualities of successful physicians could be helpful in career counseling of medical students and young physicians.

AAMC RESEARCH

Some of AAMC's own recent research on measuring personal characteristics has focused on identifying categories of behaviors associated with successful and unsuccessful performance in medical school and residency (Etienne & Julian, 2001). This research, conducted in the context of a critical incidents study, included documented incidents of successful and unsuccessful behaviors among students and residents. Approximately 170 faculty members, residents, and students from 21 medical schools in seven cities across the four AAMC geographical regions were recruited for the study by the medical schools involved. The researchers determined that key aspects of performance for medical students and residents could be best described by the following 10 categories of behavior:[4]

1. *Shaping the learning experience (students only)*. This dimension centers on whether students take an active or a passive role in their own learning and knowledge acquisition. Students who take an active role tend to show initiative and demonstrate effort for the purpose of enhancing their educational experience or to correct situations that obstruct their progress or education. Proactive behavior is demonstrated by such things as conducting research (e.g., online literature searches) solely for the purpose of broadening one's own knowledge base, and/or requesting extra responsibilities that become opportunities to learn new techniques. Active students also tend to seek feedback when negative evaluations are received and tend to be appropriately assertive (e.g., such as requesting grade changes). Students who are passive about their own learning tend not to use negative feedback as a diagnostic tool to help correct deficiencies and do not seek out opportunities to develop their technical skills. Students high on this dimension know how to navigate through the environment successfully (e.g., getting oneself into right situations and out of wrong and/or abusive situations).

2. *Extra effort and motivation (students and residents)*. The positive pole of this dimension involves actions that entail being motivated and conscientious. Such behaviors could include taking the initiative in assisting a doctor with a diagnosis, conscientiously staying late to complete patient care, conducting Internet searches for doctors, and taking on extra responsibility. In contrast,

---

[4]The list and description of behavioral categories were compiled by the research staff at the American Institutes for Research in Washington, DC (Adams, Goodwin, Searcy, Norris, & Oppler, 2001, Appendix B & Appendix C).

the negative pole of this dimension is anchored by behaviors that demonstrate a lack of motivation, such as social loafing, shirking assigned work, taking time off without permission, being late for shifts, skipping rounds, and not completing mandatory paperwork.

3. *Technical knowledge and skill (students and residents)*. This dimension involves the demonstration of an understanding of medical knowledge and skills appropriate to medical students and residents. Positive behaviors that demonstrate adequate technical knowledge involves answering questions posed by doctors, presenting technical knowledge to peers, using knowledge to assist doctors with patient diagnoses and treatment plans through information gathering, and knowing when to request assistance with unfamiliar procedures (e.g., knowing limitations). Similarly, an adequate understanding of medical skills allows students to perform certain techniques (e.g., intubations, IVs, CPR, giving injections, drawing blood, suturing) on patients under the supervision of a doctor. Students should be able to perform detailed histories and physicals, actions that involve good information gathering and assessing skills, and should be able to recognize when patients need immediate assistance. Behaviors at the negative pole of this dimension indicate a lack of appropriate knowledge or inadequately developed skills in treating patients.

4. *Self-management and coping skills (students only)*. The positive pole of this dimension involves behaviors such as prioritizing to-be-learned information and then focusing on the most critical information, understanding limitations and strengths, utilizing review sessions, being disciplined, balancing school and personal life, adopting effective time management techniques, using the best study strategy and technique for the situation (e.g., knowing when to use group versus individual study) and learning efficient and effective study techniques and strategies. Creating a system to manage learning large amounts of information, forming study groups, and dividing labor among classmates are also effective study strategies. This dimension includes the ability of students to prioritize work and/or school tasks, to set limits appropriately, and to know when to request assistance from professors or other students. In contrast, the negative pole of this dimension involves failing to recognize that a study strategy is not working and needs to be changed, not knowing when to ask for help and/or tutoring, and not being organized.

5. *Interpersonal skills and professionalism (students and residents)*. The positive pole of this dimension incorporates respecting peers and authority figures, refraining from making inappropriate comments, exhibiting cultural and gender sensitivity, sharing knowledge appropriately, adopting a professional appearance, and handling uncomfortable or stressful situations appropriately. In addition, sharing professional opinions with tact and respect, handling

offensive comments professionally, refraining from making offensive comments, exhibiting respectful classroom behavior, and acting maturely would define the positive pole of this dimension. The negative pole for this dimension includes behaviors such as confronting others in a harsh manner, telling inappropriate jokes, losing one's composure, arguing with doctors, being defiant, inappropriately using humor in uncomfortable situations, speaking in a defensive or argumentative tone, and excessively disrupting class.

6. *Ethical behavior (students and residents)*. This dimension incorporates positive behaviors such as being honest, exhibiting integrity, maintaining patient confidentiality, maintaining appropriate interpersonal relationships with patients, adhering to the ethical norms of the profession (e.g., no drug use), and reporting unethical behavior on the part of others. The negative pole is marked by unethical behaviors such as lying about duties performed, blaming others for personal mistakes, performing procedures that one is clearly not qualified to perform, "making up" patient information rather than gathering the correct information, and failing to accept responsibility for mistakes made.

7. *Interacting with patients and families (students and residents)*. This dimension centers on empathic and communication-oriented behaviors. Positive behaviors include good communication skills, providing sensitivity and compassion to patients and family members, dispensing needed information to patients and family, interpreting tests, explaining diagnoses and treatment alternatives, and being sensitive to patients' emotional states. In addition, behaviors such as developing patient and family rapport, handing difficult patients with compassion and tact, explaining disease progression, convincing patients to adhere to prescribed treatment, cultural and gender sensitivity, overcoming communication barriers, and dealing with the death of a patient with the patient's family would be included in this dimension. The negative pole includes behaviors that demonstrate insensitivity to patient and family concerns and failure to adequately communicate the implications of a diagnosis or the treatment alternatives.

8. *Fostering a team environment (students only)*. The positive pole of this dimension encompasses behaviors such as fostering a cooperative work environment and working as a team, helping others rather than exhibiting competitive and self-centered behaviors, demonstrating extra effort to assist other students and/or team members, keeping team members informed, showing sportsmanship, sharing class notes and exams, and communicating with team members. In addition, matching the level of effort of other team members, helping other students with questions, sharing class material, translating for doctors and students when needed (e.g., when a language barrier exists), filling

in for other student's shifts, orienting new students, posting class material and/ or notes on the Web, helping other students through difficult times, holding review sessions for other students in areas where knowledgeable, and tutoring other students are all examples of behaviors that would define the positive pole of this dimension. In contrast, attempting to look good at the expense of others (e.g., withholding information and trying to make others look bad), overstepping bounds by taking on work assigned to other students or "overdoing" an assignment, and gathering information regarding other students' patients and then not sharing that information with the other students are behaviors that define the negative pole of this dimension.

9. *Mentoring and educating medical students (residents only)*. This dimension involves training and instructing others and coordinating the work of students. At times, the education of medical students requires extra effort on the part of the residents. Behavioral examples of the positive pole of this dimension include providing students with structured learning experiences by recognizing and taking advantage of teaching opportunities, suggesting readings to help students excel, taking the time and effort to demonstrate techniques and procedures to students, being patient and/or supportive with and showing concern for students, responding to questions in a constructive manner, providing guidance to students regarding their educational process, and providing performance feedback to students. A negative example would be yelling at students for poor performance rather than providing constructive feedback and training.

10. *Maintaining calm under pressure (residents only)*. This dimension is focused on maintaining ones' composure during stressful situations, especially those occurring when performing medical procedures. An emotional outburst or inability to focus on the patient and required procedure would mark the negative pole.

Together, the behavioral categories for students and residents provide a model that spans the medical education process. The overlap between the two groups' behavioral categories suggests that there is a core set of behaviors that become relevant early in medical school and continue to remain important throughout residency. The consistency of the categories developed by the two independent groups of researchers supports the conclusion that the behavioral categories identified capture important aspects of performance and are generally stable across geographic regions and medical schools in the United States. Measures based on these categories of behavior may be useful to medical school admissions committees as they try to determine which related undergraduate student behaviors might be relevant to the admission process.

CURRENT DEVELOPMENT OF MEASURES
OF PERSONAL CHARACTERISTICS

The AAMC has recently used these research findings as the basis for defining assessment objectives for the development of measures of personal characteristics. Among the five recently identified personal characteristics—altruism, empathy, integrity, compassion, and communication skills—AAMC has selected communication skills for the initial development and has begun the development of a test of listening skills. This test may become one part of a communication skills component that would also include the current Writing Sample and Verbal Reasoning MCAT sections and an oral communication section.

An MCAT Test Development Advisory Committee (TDAC) has been established to advise on the development of the listening skills test. The eight-member committee includes representatives of various communities served by the MCAT: admissions officers, medical school faculty, medical students and residents, practicing physicians, nurses, psychometricians, and undergraduate health professions advisors. TDAC's role is to:

- Help to identify relevant observable behaviors;
- help to define specific test objectives;
- participate in developing scenarios for situational tests of communication;
- serve as resource persons for item writers;
- participate in refining the test.

In defining the assessment objectives for the listening skills test, TDAC gained some insight from the findings of the critical incidents research just described.

Based on the assessment objectives defined by TDAC, AAMC, in consultation with Educational Testing Service, is using a video format in the development of scenarios and test items for the planned listening skills test.

The assessment objectives suggest that the listening test will measure listening skills in the context of overall interpersonal communication and will target skills such as the ability to process, extract, and respond to information. The assessment objectives emphasize what Cassell (1985) refers to as the ability to "separate the observation (what was said and how) from the interpretation (what does the speaker mean)" (p. 10). The MCAT listening skills test will, therefore, require that test takers pay attention to nonverbal communication, such as facial expression and other body language, as well as to the paralinguistic features such as pause, pitch, speech rate, volume, and intonation. These skills will include such components as the ability to:

- Recognize others' emotions and feelings;
- respond to others' emotions and feelings;
- recognize nonverbal cues such as facial expression, intonation, volume;
- extract the most pertinent information in a multimessage situation;
- clarify unclear communication;
- receive evaluative feedback nondefensively;
- respond nondefensively to verbal attack;
- follow directions.

Four different item types have been developed, all based on scenarios set in different medical contexts The items do not, however, require the test taker to have any medical knowledge. The scenarios are based on some of the incidents reported in the AAMC critical incidents research study. The four item types are based on scenarios that present different behaviors involving listening and require test takers to:

- Use a Likert-type scale to rate the quality of the different behaviors (situational judgment);
- rank order the appropriateness of each of the different behaviors (ordering);
- select the most appropriate behaviors from a list of possible reactions to a situation (classifying); and
- select the one most appropriate behavior from a list of possible reactions to a situation (multiple choice).

In one of the prototype scenarios, the wife of a hospitalized patient becomes upset after she learns that the hospital staff acted contrary to her husband's Living Will. In the scenario, it becomes clear that this situation has arisen partly because of communication problems between the junior physician and the senior physician and also between the junior physician and the patient's wife. The items based on this scenario emphasize that understanding the feelings as well as the words is important in listening situations (Halley, 1997).

Correct responses to the items were determined based on the consensus of a panel of judges who discussed the scenarios and items at length. The panel included persons representative of physicians, nurses, medical school faculty, researchers, and communication specialists from diverse ethnic and cultural backgrounds. These prototypes will serve as the basis for developing additional test material for a pilot administration of the MCAT listening skills test.

The degree of subjectivity associated with responses to items in a test of listening skills such as that proposed for the MCAT will pose substantial psychometric challenges. The possibility that cultural differences will have an impact on the responses must also be recognized. AAMC is determined, however, to overcome these challenges. In the context of the psychometric community's current interest in new measures and constructs, AAMC is encouraged by the face validity to be gained from using the video format for a test that is more akin to what has been described as empathetic or responsive listening than it is to the comprehensive or critical listening skills that traditionally have been the focus of listening tests (Arnett & Nakagawa, 1983). The successful development of this listening test will provide medical college admissions committees with an additional tool for evaluating whether candidates have an important personal quality that is linked to the development of well-prepared physicians.

REFERENCES

Association of American Medical Colleges. (1976). *Development of a non-cognitive assessment system for evaluation of applicants to medical school.* Unpublished report. Washington, DC: Author.

Adams, K., Goodwin, G., Searcy, C., Norris, D., & Oppler, S. (2001). *Development of a performance model of the medical education process.* Washington, DC: The American Institutes for Research.

Arnett, R., & Nakagawa, G. (1983). The assumptive roots of empathic listening: A critique. *Communication Education, 32,* 368–378.

Cassell, E. (1985). *Talking with patients: Vol. 1. The theory of doctor–patient communication.* Cambridge, MA: MIT Press.

Contemporary Issues in Medicine: Communication in Medicine. (1999). Washington, DC: Association of American Medical Colleges.

D'Costa, A., & Schafer, A. (1972). *Results of a survey of non-cognitive tests used in medical school.* Washington, DC: Association of American Medical Colleges.

Etienne, P., & Julian, E. (2001). Identifying behaviors of successful medical students and residents. *Analysis in Brief, 1,* 4.

Haley, H., D'Costa, A., & Schafer, A. (Eds.). (1971). *Proceedings of a Conference on Personality Measurement in Medical Education.* Washington, DC: Association of American Medical Colleges.

Haley, H., Juan, I., & Paiva, R. (1971). MCAT scores in relation to personality measures and biographical variables. *Journal of Medical Education, 46,* 947–958.

Halley, R. (1997). *And then I was surprised by what you said. The impact of love and listening on community.* Columbia, MO: Kaia Publishing.

Hojat, M., Erdmann, J., Robeson, M., Damjanov, I., & Glaser, K. (1994). A study of psychometric characteristics of abridged versions of selected psychological measures given to medical school students for the purpose of predicting their clinical competence. *Interdisciplinaria, 11,* 129–148.

Hojat, M., Nasca, T., Magee, M., Freeney, K., Pascaul, R., Urbano, F., & Gonnella, J. (1999). A comparison of the personality profiles of internal medicine residents, physician role models, and the general population. *Academic Medicine, 74,* 1327–1333.

Hojat, M., Robeson, M., Damjanov, I., Veloski, J., Glaser, K., & Gonnella, J. (1993). Students' psychological characteristics as predictors of academic performance in medical school. *Academic Medicine, 68,* 635–637.

Julian, E. (2000a). The predictive validity of the Medical College Admission Test. *Contemporary Issues in Medical Education, 3,* 2.

Julian, E. (2000b). *A request for the Committee on Admissions input on a proposal for Regional Initial Interview and Personality Characteristic Assessment Centers.* Unpublished manuscript.

Morris, W. (1973). On the assessment of non-cognitive aspects of medical school applicants. *Position papers for the AAMC Regional Conferences, as part of the Medical College Admission Assessment Study.* Washington, DC: Association of American Medical Colleges

Newton, B., Savidge, M., Barber, L., Cleveland, E., Clardy, J., Beeman, G., & Hart, T. (2000). Differences in medical students' empathy. *Academic Medicine, 75,* 1215.

Rogers, J., & Coutts, L. (2000). Do students' attitudes during pre-clinical years predict their humanism as clerkship students? *Academic Medicine, 75,* S74-S77.

Romney, D., & Bynner, J. (1992). *The structure of personal characteristics.* Westport: Praeger.

Sabalis, R. (2002, June). *Allopathic medicine report to the National Association of Advisors for the Health Professions 15th National Meeting Las Vegas, Nevada.* Washington, DC: Association of American Medical Colleges.

Searcy, C., Oppler, S., & Chen, W. (2001). *Evaluating five alternative configurations of the multiple-choice test components of the current MCAT.* Washington, DC: The American Institutes for Research.

Solkoff, N. (1968). The use of personality and attitude tests in predicting the academic success of medical and law students. *Journal of Medical Education, 43,* 1250–1253.

Viswesvaran, C., & Ones, D. (1999). Meta-analysis of fakability estimates: Implications for personality measurement. *Educational and Psychological Measurement, 59,* 197–210.

Wiley, A., & Koenig, J. A. (1996). The validity of the Medical College Admission Test for predicting performance in the first two years of medical school. *Academic Medicine 1996, 71,* 83S–85S.

13

Access and Diversity in Law School Admissions

Peter J. Pashley
Andrea E. Thornton
Jennifer R. Duffy
Law School Admission Council, Newtown, PA

The Law School Admission Council (LSAC®) has expended a considerable amount of resources researching and advocating appropriate test use and admission practices that promote access and diversity. Although these efforts have primarily focused on the LSAC's Law School Admission Test (LSAT®) and admission to law school, many of the results and ideas can be applied to a wider array of higher education settings.

This chapter begins by reviewing the LSAC's commitment to diversity. It then turns to the impact of the LSAT on admissions and the efforts to promote good admission practices. Research on a novel approach to the selection process is described before a consideration of future directions for the LSAC.

Many involved with the LSAC, volunteers and employees alike, continuously walk a fine line between standing proudly behind our products and cautioning users against employing some of them inappropriately or to excess. For example, in a 1997 article titled "The LSAT: Good—But Not That Good,"

Philip Shelton, the LSAC President and Executive Director, illustrated both the potential usefulness and limitations of the LSAT as a law school admission tool. The intent of this chapter is to highlight many of the LSAC's services, products, and research aimed at improving admissions, along with the LSAC's commitment to ensure that none of its products, services, or research results are used inappropriately or to excess.

THE LSAC AND ITS COMMITMENT TO DIVERSITY

The LSAC is a nonprofit corporation headquartered in Newtown, Pennsylvania. Established in 1947, the voting membership of the Council is comprised of all law schools approved by the American Bar Association and Canadian law schools granting degrees in accordance with standards approved by the Federation of Law Societies of Canada. The current membership totals 202 law schools. Volunteer member representatives, composed of law school admission professionals, legal educators, and deans, are relied on by the Council to govern and guide its activities.

The LSAC is best known for administering the LSAT; other services provided to law schools and law school candidates include:

- *Law School Data Assembly Service (LSDAS):* Provides law schools with individual applicant reports containing standardized summaries of biographical and academic information.
- *Candidate Referral Service (CRS):* Brings potential law school applicants together with schools that may be interested in them.
- *Admission Communication and Exchange System (ACES):* This software application has become the primary mode of contact between law school admission offices and the LSAC, allowing for timely access to fully integrated data collection, retrieval, and exchange services.
- *Correlation Studies:* These annual reports provide each participating law school with information detailing the relationships among LSAT scores, undergraduate GPAs, and law school grades for its first-year matriculants.

Beyond helping to facilitate law school admissions in general, the Council has a long history of promoting diversity in all its forms. A recent and significant indication of this commitment was made in December 2000 when the LSAC Board of Trustees adopted the following resolution (see LSAC, 2001b):

The United States will have no majority racial/ethnic group by the middle of the century. If the legal profession does not more proportionately reflect the make-up of society, the justice system and legal profession will be in jeopardy. Therefore, the greatest challenge to the legal profession and legal education is to increase the number of underrepresented minorities who become lawyers.

Access to legal education is a critical component of this challenge. The Law School Admission Council recognizes that the LSAT is viewed, and justifiably so, by law schools as an important and valuable criterion in determining who shall have access to legal education. At the same time, the Council is concerned that legal education may be placing too much emphasis on the LSAT, and by doing so may be overlooking important additional admission criteria that could aid legal education in achieving its diversity goals.

Because of this concern regarding undue emphasis on the LSAT, the Law School Admission Council commits the expenditure of up to $10 million over the next five years to:

- Study, and encourage change where warranted, the culture and attitudes of legal educators, lawyers, judges, law students, prospective law students, prelaw advisors, journalists, and the public regarding the use of the LSAT;
- Promote appropriate use of the LSAT among all test-score users and test takers; and
- Develop and implement new approaches to law school admissions that further the diversity goals of legal education.

These funds will support various activities, projects, research, and publications designed to achieve this purpose. Existing activities that serve as examples of efforts these funds will support include the Alternative Models Implementation Project and the Faculty Outreach Program. (p. 20)

As of February 2003, 14 projects have received approval for funding, totaling over $2 million in committed expenditures.

In addition to the LSAC Board of Trustees, three LSAC standing committees, in particular, actively promote diversity and good admission practices:

- The *Minority Affairs Committee* (MAC) was established to develop, fund, and promote programs designed to increase the representation of minority groups in the legal profession. MAC projects have included academic assistance training workshops, regional minority recruitment workshops, the establishment of a minority advisor database, the development of minority enrollment videos, and outreach efforts to Minority Bar Associations, to name just a few.

- The *Services and Programs (S&P) Committee* has been charged with the responsibility of overseeing the various services the LSAC provides to law schools, as well as the educational programs, tools, and publications targeted toward law school candidates, prelaw advisors, admission professionals, and others involved in legal education. An example of an S&P program that assists law schools and candidates is the series of law school forums, held in major cities across the United States each year, at which prospective law students are given the opportunity to meet representatives of the LSAC-member law schools.

• The *Test Development and Research (TD&R) Committee* has had the responsibility of monitoring the validity and reliability of the LSAT, the level of equity and fairness with which it is being used, and the development and implementation of LSAC-funded research. A project titled *U.S. Minorities and the Process of Becoming a Lawyer: Investigating Factors Underlying Degree Completion, Bar Passage, and Overall Success, Using the National Longitudinal Bar Passage Study* (Clydesdale, 2000) is an example of external research that has recently been approved for LSAC funding.

The LSAC staff (i.e., employees of the LSAC) have also applied their research and legal expertise, both in the support of the LSAC committees and independently, to promote diversity. Two of the resulting publications are *Preserving Access and Diversity in Law School Admissions—An Update* (LSAC, 1998) and *The Road to Law School and Beyond: Examining Challenges to Racial and Ethnic Diversity in the Legal Profession* (Wilder, 2003). The latter research tracked the representation of various racial/ethnic groups among high school graduates, college graduates, those admitted to law school, law school graduates, and law professionals, and identified possible means of increasing minority representation at various points along the way.

THE LSAT AND ITS IMPACT
ON ADMISSIONS

The LSAT is a half-day standardized multiple-choice assessment of acquired verbal and deductive reasoning skills, given at four major administrations each year. Three different item (or question) types are employed in the LSAT: reading comprehension, analytical reasoning, and logical reasoning. These item types are administered within four separately timed 35-minute scored sections—one section each of reading comprehension and analytical reasoning, and two sections of logical reasoning. Test takers are also administered an unscored variable section, which could contain any one of the three LSAT item types. The unscored variable section is used for pretest and equating purposes.

The reading comprehension section contains four item sets, each consisting of a reading passage of approximately 450 words, followed by five to eight related questions. The goal of this item type is to assess a test taker's ability to read, with understanding and insight, materials that are similar in complexity to those that law students routinely encounter. Items may deal with, for example, the main purpose of, ideas that can be inferred from, and the organization of the reading passage.

The analytical reasoning section also contains four item sets, each with a passage describing a structure of relationships, along with five to seven questions that require test takers to draw conclusions about the structure. The purpose of this item type is to simulate the detailed analyses of relationships that law students commonly undertake while solving legal problems. All components of the analytical reasoning items are stated in relatively simple terms, concentrating on assessing deductive reasoning rather than a test taker's ability to read linguistically complex text.

Finally, the two logical reasoning sections each contain between 24 and 26 individual items. These items measure a test taker's ability to understand, analyze, criticize, and complete the types of arguments regularly confronted by law students. Although these items do not presuppose knowledge of formal or symbolic logic, test takers are expected to possess a college-level understanding of informal logic concepts, such as argument, premise, assumption, and conclusion.

At each LSAT administration, test takers are given 30 minutes to complete a writing sample in response to a prompt that establishes a factual context and identifies an audience for the writer, who may then assume a specific position while responding to the topic. Although there are no right or wrong positions, the prompt allows the writer the opportunity to argue a position clearly and succinctly. The writing sample is not scored, but copies of it are sent to the schools to which the writer has applied. A research project is currently underway to investigate the feasibility of adding a scored writing component to the LSAT.

Since its inception in 1947, the LSAT has gone through many changes to improve its validity. A wide variety of item types have been experimented with, including artificial language and data interpretation (Reese & Cotter, 1994). (Note that at no time did the LSAT require knowledge of the law.) A recently completed construct validity study (Luebke, Swygert, McLeod, Dalessandro, & Roussos, 2003) indicates that the current LSAT format, in use since

1991, measures many of the skills critical to success in law school. Predictive validity studies also routinely indicate that the current LSAT does a better job of predicting first-year law school grades than do undergraduate GPAs. The most recent national summary of correlation studies gave a median correlation of .4 between first-year law school averages and LSAT scores, compared to a median correlation of .27 between the same criterion and undergraduate GPAs among the 164 participating law schools (Thornton, Suto, Anthony, & Liu, 2001). The linear combination of LSAT and undergraduate GPA typically provides the best correlation with first-year law school grades, with a median of .5. (Note that these correlations have not been corrected for factors such as restriction of range and unreliability of the criterion.)

Given the high level of construct, content, and predictive validity possessed by the LSAT, it is not surprising that many law schools rely on it heavily to make admission decisions, and law school candidates often use average law school LSAT score credentials to evaluate the selectivity of institutions. Various published law school rankings and the perception that average LSAT scores contribute significantly to a law school's placement in the rankings has placed added pressure on many law schools to attempt to raise their admitted students' LSAT score credentials.

The LSAC, through its cautionary policies and outreach programs, has consistently encouraged users to employ LSAT scores appropriately. This effort has intensified recently as law schools have worked to maintain or enhance racial and ethnic diversity even as affirmative action programs have been the subjects of numerous court challenges. Unfortunately, the LSAT, like most standardized tests, routinely yields disparate average scores across racial and ethnic subgroups. For example, the average difference between scores from African American and White test takers has been approximately one standard deviation (Dalessandro & Stilwell, 2002).

LSAC-funded research (e.g., Wightman, 1997, 1998) has consistently highlighted the dire effect abandoning race and ethnicity as a factor in law school admissions could have on diversity. The actual impact of constraining affirmative action programs can be observed currently, especially in California since the approval of Proposition 209 in 1996. This has given additional impetus to the LSAC's efforts to educate users on the limitations of the LSAT. Although the "practice" of admissions falls within the domain of individual law schools, LSAC resources have been directed toward efforts that may assist law schools that are attempting to maintain academic credentials and diversity at the same time, regardless of the possible constraints on their affirmative action programs that might exist.

RESEARCHING AND PROMOTING
GOOD ADMISSION PRACTICES

For many years, the LSAC has provided those involved in law school admissions with opportunities to learn, exchange ideas, and benefit from the experience of others. These LSAC-sponsored programs include:

- *The LSAC Newcomers Workshop.* For more than 25 years, this annual event has benefited law schools by providing comprehensive training and support to newcomers to the admission field (i.e., admission professionals, legal educators, and deans).
- *The LSAC Annual Meeting and Educational Conference.* Every spring since 1980, the Council has hosted a conference for its membership that provides broad opportunities for professional development and continuing education on a variety of admission-related topics.
- *Faculty Outreach.* In this more recently established endeavor, past and present LSAC volunteer committee members have visited more than 50 law schools to discuss appropriate test use and good admission practices.

An effort to investigate new approaches to admissions was begun with the formation of the LSAC Alternative Models Work Group in 1997. This work group was established to draw on the experience and knowledge of law school admission practitioners in order to document past procedures or develop new admission methodologies that promote diversity. Findings of the work group were incorporated in the report titled "The Art and Science of Law School Admission Decision Making" (LSAC, 2001a). The following are examples of the "best practices" suggestions and guidelines contained in the report:

- Use test scores properly—do not overrely on them or use them as the sole criterion;
- Relate admission criteria to the law school educational mission with respect to the education of students and the training of legal practitioners;
- Give all applicants the opportunity to provide information relative to the admission criteria that your school employs;
- Evaluate all applicants; consider each applicant individually and consistently apply your school's criteria.

Although these suggestions and guidelines appear simple and straightforward, suspicions abound that they are not being applied consistently by all law schools.

An ongoing study called the Alternative Admission Practices Implementation Project is investigating admission factors, beyond LSAT scores and undergraduate GPAs, that could be used by law schools to diversify their incoming classes. Working with the LSAC staff, an advisory committee of law school admission professionals, legal educators, and deans first identified factors that might be included in a broad definition of diversity. These factors included (a) experiences that demonstrated leadership, service, and other personal qualities; (b) obstacles overcome in the pursuit of an education; (c) special skills and accomplishments; and (d) two separate categories of diversity: background and experiential.

Law school applicant files were then reviewed to assess the extent to which evidence of these factors is currently being elicited and collected. This initial investigation suggested that although some related information can be found in current applicant files, law schools are not systematically eliciting evidence of these factors. Also, applicants to individual law schools did not appear to be providing related evidence in a consistent manner.

To address this data problem, a questionnaire was developed to supplement the information that is available in current application files. Two examples of open-ended queries contained in the questionnaire are:

1. Provide information about factors that you believe may have caused your LSAT score(s) and undergraduate performance to underestimate your ability to be a successful law student or attorney.

2. Briefly describe your most significant work experience—paid or unpaid—before, during, or after college, and explain its importance to you.

The supplementary questionnaire was administered online to applicants to three law schools. Questionnaire responses were combined with original applicant files and the resulting augmented files were read and evaluated by trained readers. Two readers evaluated each file. The next steps of this study involve making admit/deny decisions, and then comparing these experimental admission decisions with those actually made by the three law schools participating in this study.

The optimal procedure for combining applicant information to make admit/deny decisions has yet to be determined. A novel approach to this problem, now described, focuses on choosing a class rather than individual students.

CHOOSING A CLASS RATHER THAN
INDIVIDUAL STUDENTS

A UCLA School of Law admissions task force stated the following in its Report to the Faculty and UCLA Community (Admissions Task Force, 1997):

> We also recognize that there is no single dimension of excellence in applicants. Just as there are many different kinds of excellent lawyers—as demonstrated in the diverse replies we received to our informal survey of the faculty—there are many quite distinctive applicants to this law school with demonstrated potential for excellence. We agree with our colleague who responded to the survey with the preface: "There is no 'ideal applicant,' but rather an ideal mix of students in a class." In other words, we believe in a pluralist conception of a great law school. (p. 2)

This sentiment appears to be shared by many law schools, and probably a large number of other institutions of higher education.

To address the goal of admitting an ideal mix of students, Pashley and Thornton (1999) developed a systematic approach to selecting an entering class rather than simply ranking and admitting individual applicants. This *entering-class optimization* approach is briefly reviewed in this section and compared to two other admission methodologies, namely *presumptive admit/deny* and *factor weighting*.

To make this discussion more concrete, consider the following simple admission problem that places constraints or requirements on how the entire entering class is chosen: Law School X obtains 500 applications and must admit 100 applicants to fill its entering-class seats. (In this simple example, it is assumed that all those admitted will matriculate.) Law School X has two goals in mind as it selects among its applicants. First, the entering class should have an average age of at least 24. Second, assuming the first goal is satisfied, the entering class with the highest average LSAT score should be chosen. In other words, of all the possible choices of entering classes with an average age of at least 24, Law School X prefers the one with the highest average LSAT score.

A rationale for the first goal might be that Law School X has found through experience that a class with an average age of at least 24 is more interesting and productive due to the maturity level of the students compared to a younger group of students. The second goal may reflect Law School X's preference (once other goals have been satisfied) for selecting an entering class with highest estimated levels of the skills measured by the LSAT. (To ensure that this is not a completely trivial example, assume that the average age of the highest 100 LSAT scorers is 23. In other words, simply ranking the applicants in terms of LSAT scores and admitting the top 100 will not satisfy both of Law School X's goals.) Although this problem is perhaps too simple to be realistic, it is instructive and exemplifies the types of goals a law school might establish for an entire entering class before any applications are read.

Presumptive Admit/Deny

The first methodology that is discussed and applied to the Law School X admission problem is commonly known as the presumptive admit/deny approach. Various versions of this methodology are employed at many law schools. Generally, the first step in this approach is to divide the applicant pool into three parts based on a rank ordering of applicants' academic credentials. Applicants falling in the top segment are presumptively admitted (i.e., admitted unless a cursory review of the applicant's file reveals a reason why they should be denied, such as a falsified reference) because of their high academic credentials. Applicants falling in the bottom segment of the applicant pool are presumptively denied (i.e., denied unless a cursory review of the applicant's file reveals a reason why they should be admitted, such as possessing a unique skill or experience) due to their low academic credentials. Applicants from the middle segment are admitted or denied, based on more than just their academic credentials, in order to satisfy various admission goals.

Applying the presumptive admit/deny approach to the problem outlined, Law School X might first presumptively admit the 50 highest LSAT scoring applicants and presumptively deny the 250 lowest LSAT scoring applicants. Assuming these presumptive admits and denies hold upon review, 200 applicants would be left from which Law School X would admit 50 in an attempt to satisfy their goal of an average age of 24.

Note that this ad hoc approach does not guarantee optimal results (i.e., the 100 highest scoring individuals with an average age of 24). In fact, the optimal solution to this problem might involve admitting at least one applicant from the presumptive deny segment. More potentially troubling is the amount of influence accorded LSAT score versus age. For instance, in the simple example, applicants to Law School X are initially grouped into three segments, allowing them to be presumptively admitted or denied based solely on their LSAT scores. On the other hand, none of the applicants are presumptively admitted or denied according to their ages. Although the relative importance of age and LSAT score might be justified in the simple problem used here, in more realistic admission settings, some nonacademic factors might be employed that are just as important as academic credentials.

Factor Weighting

A second methodology involves explicitly weighting the admission factors of interest to form a composite score for each applicant. All applicants can then be ranked according to their composite scores and the number needed to fill the entering-class seats can be admitted from the top of the list. So although the presumptive admit/deny approach implicitly attaches added importance to academic factors because they are used first to sort applicants, the factor weighting approach defines the relative importance of all the factors being considered. Normally, the relative weights applied to different factors would be determined beforehand by the admission office. However, for problems involving entire class attributes, the factor weights depend in large part on the characteristics of the applicants who apply, as is illustrated now.

In applying the factor weighting approach to the Law School X admission problem outlined, assume that optimal weights of 63% and 37% are determined for LSAT scores and ages, respectively. Composite scores for each of the 500 applicants to Law School X can then be calculated as sums of their (optimally) weighted LSAT scores and ages. After ranking the applicants according to these composite scores, the top 100 would be admitted. The optimal weights should yield the highest average LSAT score that can be achieved through different weighting combinations among entering classes whose average age is at least 24.

There are a number of statistical approaches that can be employed to obtain optimal factor weights. However, they all depend in part on the goals of the admission process and in part on the attributes of the candidates available. For example, in the Law School X problem, the optimal weights will depend in part on the requirement that the entering class has an average age of 24 and in part on the distribution of ages among the applicants. If the average age of the 500 applicants to Law School X is 22, the optimal age factor weight would need to be greater than what would be required if the average age of the 500 applicants was 26. In other words, if older applicants are a scarce commodity, the weight associated with age will need to be greater to ensure a sufficient number of older applicants are admitted to satisfy the average age constraint.

This means that in situations where requirements for the entire class are established, the weights on the factor weighting approach are not as interpretable as when the admission process focuses on admitting individuals. In the latter case, before any applications are reviewed, the admission office might determine, for example, that maturity, as measured by age, should be given a weight of 20% versus 80% for the reasoning skills measured by the LSAT. This second set of weights might arise from policy discussions and they would be clearly interpretable. As such, factor weighting appears to be more conducive to situations involving the rank ordering of individuals based on a combination of personal attributes than to the challenge of admitting an entering class that, as a whole, possesses certain attributes.

Entering-Class Optimization

Given the drawbacks inherent in the presumptive admit/deny and factor weighting approaches, at least with regard to admitting an entering class with predetermined characteristics, Pashley and Thornton (1999) developed a methodology that specifically addresses group rather than individual attributes. This approach has been applied to admission data from a large number of law schools with very good success. It is also an admission methodology that can be employed to ensure diversity in entering classes.

The situation exemplified by the Law School X admission example is equivalent to the types of problems routinely addressed within the field of operations research. These problems can contain multiple goals and numerous constraints or requirements, and can find optimal results for large numbers of applicants. These problems can be solved by enumerating all feasible solutions (solutions that satisfy the requirements of the admission problem, but are not necessarily optimal solutions) and then identifying the optimal one. However, more efficient approaches are usually employed in practice, typically through the use of computer programs.

In the case of the Law School X problem, a feasible solution would be any group of 100 applicants whose average age was at least 24. If all such feasible solutions were enumerated, the group with the highest average LSAT score would be the optimal solution. With 500 applicants and 100 entering-class seats to be filled, the enumeration of feasible solutions could be impractical. Fortunately, there are readily available computer algorithms or packages that could find the optimal solution to the Law School X problem in milliseconds.

Note that with the entering-class optimization approach, none of the applicants are individually ranked against one another. Rather, individuals are admitted if they contribute to an "ideal mix" of students. In other words, this approach does not deal with individual applicant attributes on a case-by-case basis, but rather, with how combinations of individuals collectively satisfy goals set out for the entering class as a whole.

As noted, the Law School X problem, although instructive, is too simple to be realistic. To address more realistic admission situations, entering-class optimization procedures have been developed to handle:

- Variable yield rates (i.e., the probability that an admitted applicant will matriculate varies from individual to individual);
- Matriculant targets (i.e., schools are most interested in the characteristics of those students that matriculate, as opposed to the group of applicants who are admitted); and
- Rolling admissions (i.e., offers of admission are made before the entire pool of applicants is available).

As mentioned, the computer packages that are designed to efficiently solve these types of problems can accommodate large numbers of goals and constraints imposed on the entering class, as well as large pools of applicants.

As with any new methodology, misconceptions abound concerning the entering-class optimization approach. One of the most common misconceptions is a fear that because this methodology employs a computer algorithm, admission decisions will be made by computers and the "art" involved in admissions work will be lost. In fact, the opposite is true. The entering-class optimization method relies heavily on both the objective and subjective judgments of admission professionals, and may be more labor intensive than some other approaches. Clear goals and objectives related to the characteristics of the admitted class must be operationally defined before any application is considered. All applicant files must be thoroughly read, and multiple factors must be quantified, many requiring difficult-to-make subjective judgments. Although computer programs are employed to produce admission solutions, in practice these solutions will only be viewed as starting points. An admission professional (or committee) would still need to review all decisions and make adjustments where necessary, and also deal with the numerous special cases that inevitably arise.

A second misconception is that the constraints used to define a desirable entering class are quotas—a concept that has certainly fallen out of favor lately. To the contrary, the constraints or requirements employed in the entering-class optimization approach typically refer to an average level of some factor, such as age or LSAT score. If the Law School X problem posed had required that "20 applicants with ages over 25 should be admitted," that would have constituted an example of a quota-like constraint. Instead, an average age of 24 was required, with all applicants having some potential input to that constraint. This is not to say that very reasonable quota-like constraints could not be incorporated into an admission solution. For example, many state institutions have residency requirements, so a constraint requiring that 60% of the admitted entering class be in-state residents might be very reasonable.

Research on implementing the entering-class optimization approach is continuing. Of special interest is the ability to achieve diversity without relying on explicit racial and ethnic indicators while employing this methodology. To date, significant degrees of diversity have been achieved by employing various entering-class constraints or requirements, such as the average levels of minority enrollment at the applicant's undergraduate institution. Modeled results (i.e., those achieved by employing an entering-class optimization approach) have been compared to actual results for law schools that are legally able to explicitly employ racial and ethnic indicators. Comparisons typically show similar levels of diversity, but not necessarily large overlaps between modeled and actual minority admittees (e.g., similar numbers of African American applicants are admitted, though not necessarily the same African American applicants).

FUTURE DIRECTIONS

The LSAC plans to continue to promote access and diversity in law schools through various initiatives, like its *amicus* brief filed in the *Grutter v. Bollinger* case that focused on the proper role of standardized tests in admissions and the consequences of abandoning affirmative action (LSAC, 2003). The investigations of the LSAC Alternative Score Reporting Work Group illustrate some of the new admission research the Council is exploring. This work group has primarily concerned itself with three major areas of interest: subscores, improving score reporting, and school-specific scores. The ideas behind these areas of research and the potential for each to advance the cause of promoting appropriate test use are now discussed.

Subscores

Many large-scale testing programs routinely report subscores, in addition to overall or total scores. With regard to admission decisions, the LSAC has long advocated the consideration of the many dimensions found in applicant files. To provide more of a skill profile and to dissuade applicant file reviewers from overrelying on a single number, the LSAC has been investigating the feasibility of reporting LSAT subscores, instead of the current single LSAT score. These subscores could be viewed as contributing toward a fuller picture of candidates' strengths and weaknesses. They would also better complement an applicant's undergraduate record and evidence of personal factors, such as leadership and perseverance.

Research has suggested that the current LSAT exhibits two major skill dimensions (e.g., Camilli, Wang, & Fesq, 1992; Douglas, Kim, Roussos, Stout, & Zhang, 1999), which have been referred to as *deductive reasoning* and *verbal reasoning*. The analytical reasoning items contribute mainly to the deductive reasoning dimension, whereas reading comprehension and logical reasoning items contribute mainly to the verbal reasoning dimension. Although distinct, these two dimensions are still highly correlated with one another. Given this high level of intercorrelation and the small number of analytical items given per form, reliable and distinct subscore reporting does not appear possible at this time (Chiu, Swygert, Pashley, & Brennan, in press). However, new item types, such as listening comprehension and scored writing (as mentioned earlier) are being field tested for potential inclusion in the future, and these may provide for reliable and distinct subscores. The LSAC is also actively investigating the administration of the LSAT as a computerized adaptive test—a move that could also facilitate the reporting of subscores.

Although the LSAC may expand the LSAT to encompass more skills that are both important in law school and amenable to high-stakes standardized measurement, it is arguable that other skills, accomplishments, and personal qualities are better evaluated by way of documented evidence. Examples of these other admission factors (i.e., beyond LSAT scores and undergraduate GPAs) include work experience, leadership skills, and personal qualities (e.g., tenacity, maturity, and integrity). Evidence of these additional characteristics can already be found in applicant files, for example, in personal statements and references. Other avenues for collecting this data, some of which are more verifiable than others, are also being considered by the LSAC.

Improving Score Reporting

The goal of this research is to develop new methods of presenting scores that promote appropriate score use. As many other testing programs do, the LSAC includes score bands (or confidence intervals) as part of candidates' score reports, in part to remind users that there is a certain amount of error associated with standardized scores. Additional ways of presenting admission data, both graphically and in tabular form, which emphasize the limitations of test scores, are now being researched.

One simple example is given in Fig. 13.1, where the estimated percent probability of an applicant falling at or below three percentiles of a particular law school first-year class, given the applicant's LSAT score, is displayed. (Note that the LSAT score scale ranges from 120 to 180 in increments of one.) This presentation might help score users realize that for a relatively wide range of

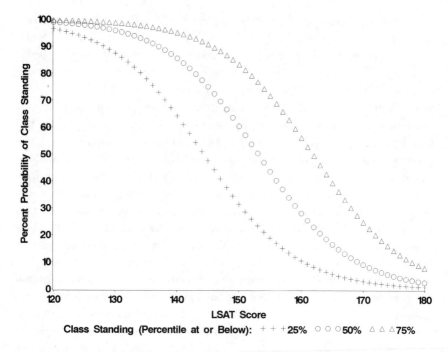

FIG. 13.1.   Three estimated percent probabilities of class standing, given LSAT score, at one law school.

LSAT scores, (i.e., a range that usually covers the majority of the applicants to that law school) differences in estimated class standing are not significant. That is, in the case of the results shown in Fig. 13.1, applicants having an LSAT score close to 155 have similar probabilities of falling in any of the class quartiles. This display reinforces the notion that small differences in LSAT scores should not be overly weighted in admission decisions, and other factors should come into play.

Unfortunately, there are also potential drawbacks to such displays that will require further study. For instance, referring again to Fig. 13.1, users may interpret this graph as indicating applicants below 142 are not worth considering because they are estimated to have more than a 50% probability of falling in the bottom quartile of the class. This interpretation may be made even though the same plot also suggests that they have almost a 50% chance of falling above the bottom quartile. These types of graphs may also tie the LSAT to first-year performance more than is appropriate. For example, the display in Fig. 13.1 may suggest that the LSAT is solely a predictor of first-year law school performance, rather than a measure of some acquired skills that have been shown to be important to success in law school and that should be considered in concert with many other important factors. Finally, on a technical note, because these plots are based on matriculant data, parts of the graph rely heavily on model assumptions rather than actual data. For instance, even though the law school featured in Fig. 13.1 probably had few if any applicants admitted who scored below 140 on the LSAT, extrapolations for those cases are given.

School-Specific Scores

In an effort to encourage law schools to view LSAT scores as one admission factor among many and to downplay its role as a possible indicator of a law school's selectivity, the LSAC is investigating the possibility of reporting school-specific scores. Instead of providing schools with applicants' LSAT scores as reported to individual test takers (i.e., on the current 120 to 180 score scale), each school would receive scores that adhere to that school's customized scale. Details of each law school's customized scale would not be shared across schools.

For example, law schools might receive LSAT scores that have been transformed onto 200 to 800 scales that are individually centered to reflect each school's approximate average applicant score. For instance, a 158 on the LSAT scale might be translated to a 510 and reported as such to one law school, but reported as a 460 at another law school. Reporting LSAT scores as percentiles of an individual law school's (historic) applicant pool is another example of school-specific scores. In either case, within each law school, the scores received would be just as meaningful as LSAT scores that adhere to the current 120 to 180 scale. However, as long as the score-transformation rules remain confidential, comparing scores across law schools would be a meaningless exercise.

Reporting school-specific scores would constitute a large departure from the current norm and requires extensive study to anticipate all of the potential consequences, both positive and negative, of implementing such a methodology. This research does, though, highlight the creativity, effort, and resources the LSAC is directing toward promoting access and diversity in law school. Hopefully, the results of the LSAC's efforts, both past and future, will also benefit the admission processes at other institutions of higher learning.

REFERENCES

Admissions Task Force. (1997). *Report to the faculty and UCLA community: The admissions policies of the UCLA School of Law.* Los Angeles: University of California–Los Angeles.

Camilli, G., Wang, M., & Fesq, J. (1992). *The effects of dimensionality on true score conversion tables for the Law School Admission Test* (LSAC Statistical Rep. No. 92–01). Newtown, PA: Law School Admission Council.

Chiu, C. W. T., Swygert, K. A., Pashley, P. J., & Brennan, R. L. (in press). *On when to use composite scores versus subscores* (LSAC Research Rep. No. 03–01). Newtown, PA: Law School Admission Council.

Clydesdale, T. T. (2000). *U.S. minorities and the process of becoming a lawyer: Investigating factors underlying degree completion, bar passage, and overall success, using the National Longitudinal Bar Passage Study.* (LSAC Research Proposal No. 00–10, unpublished).

Dalessandro, S. P., & Stilwell, L. A. (2002). *LSAT performance with regional, gender, and racial/ethnic breakdowns: 1995–1996 through 2001–2002 testing years* (LSAC Tech. Rep. No. 02–01). Newtown, PA: Law School Admission Council.

Douglas, J., Kim, H. R., Roussos, L., Stout, W., & Zhang, J. (1999). *LSAT dimensionality analysis for the December 1991, June 1992, and October 1992 administrations* (LSAC Statistical Rep. No. 95–05). Newtown, PA: Law School Admission Council.

Law School Admission Council. (1998). *Preserving access and diversity in law school admissions—An update.* Newtown, PA: Author.

Law School Admission Council. (2001a). *The art and science of law school admission decision making.* Newtown, PA: Author.

Law School Admission Council. (2001b). Initiative to advance education on the LSAT. *1999–2000/2000–2001 Law School Admission Council biennial report* (p. 20). Newtown, PA: Author.

Law School Admission Council. (2003, February). *Brief as amicus curiae in* Grutter v. Bollinger, et al., United States Supreme Court, No. 02–241.

Luebke, S. W., Swygert, K. A., McLeod, L. D., Dalessandro, S. P., & Roussos, L. A. (2003). *Final report: LSAC skills analysis law school task survey* (LSAC Computerized Testing Rep. No. 02–02). Newtown, PA: Law School Admission Council.

Pashley, P. J., & Thornton, A. E. (1999). *Crafting an incoming law school class: Preliminary results* (LSAC Research Rep. No. 99–01). Newtown, PA: Law School Admission Council.

Reese, L. M., & Cotter, R. A. (1994). *A compendium of LSAT and LSAC-sponsored item types: 1948–1994* (LSAC Research Rep. No. 94–01). Newtown, PA: Law School Admission Council.

Shelton, P. D. (1997). The LSAT: Good—but not *that* good. *Law Services Report, 97* (5), 2–3.

Thornton, A. E., Suto, D., Anthony, L. C., & Liu, M. (2001). *Predictive validity of the LSAT: A national summary of the 1999–2000 correlation studies* (LSAC Tech. Rep. No. 01–02). Newtown, PA: Law School Admission Council.

Wightman, L. F. (1997). The threat to diversity in legal education: An empirical analysis of the consequences of abandoning race as a factor in law school admission decisions. *New York University Law Review, 72* (1), 1–53.

Wightman, L. F. (1998). Are other things essentially equal? An empirical investigation of the consequences of including race as a factor in law school admission. *Southwestern University Law Review, 28* (1), 1–43.

Wilder, G. Z. (2003). *The road to law school and beyond: Examining challenges to racial and ethnic diversity in the legal profession* (LSAC Research Rep. No. 02–01). Newtown, PA: Law School Admission Council.

14

Toward a Science
of Assessment

Isaac I. Bejar
Educational Testing Service, Princeton, NJ

This chapter briefly reports on recent efforts in developing a *science of assessment*. Referring to a science of assessment does not imply that current assessments are not scientifically based. Rather, it implies that, currently, a clearly articulated and general approach for designing and implementing assessments is lacking. It seems that in the past, assessments started from scratch or reinvented aspects of other assessments that could easily have been reused had we shared a common vision of the assessment design process. A science of assessment would allow us to view specific assessments as instances of well-understood components of any assessment. Such an approach to assessment design can have deep implications for the scientific standing of an assessment instrument but this is not to suggest that instruments designed in this manner would be exempted from the principles that we know as validation. Indeed a turning point in the road toward a science of assessment occurred with the publication of the Cronbach and Meehl (1955) paper on construct validity. They noted, "Construct validity calls for no new scientific approach. Much current research on tests of personality . . . is construct validation, usually without the benefit of *a clear formulation of this process*" (p. 282, italics added).

If *construct validation* can be seen as the execution of a clearly formulated process, it makes sense that the construction of an assessment also follows a clearly formulated process, an assessment design process.

For the most part, a detailed explication of the assessment design process has been missing. A key reason for this omission is that the test development process, the process of producing items, has not been seen as a design process in its own right, it has been seen as an art rather than a science (Bejar, 1991). The notion of test development as a process where items are submitted to statistical analysis after pretesting to see which ones "worked" has a long tradition, even in theoretically driven work. Two of the most successful instruments from the 20th century illustrate the practice. One instrument is the Strong Vocational Inventory Blank (SVIB; Campbell, 1974), a highly successful interest inventory. The basic principle behind its design is that if the pattern of similarity and dissimilarity with respect to the activities you enjoy resemble the pattern of satisfied job incumbents, then you are likely to be satisfied in such a job. There was not, at least originally, a theoretical basis for the inclusion or exclusion of items. The reason it worked is that the items were carefully keyed for each job separately.[1] Empirical keying in the SVIB illustrates an approach to assessment design where the test content is not driven by theory and yet it works for the intended purpose. To this day, as far as I know, there are no explanations for the likes and dislikes of different job groups. Were a theory available to relate behaviors to vocational preferences, it could drive the test development process. Moreover, the administration of an assessment based on that theory would contribute to the validation of the theory, which in turn could lead to improvements in the assessment.

Another example of the independence of the test development process can be found in the history of the SAT. Soon after it became necessary to issue multiple forms per year of the SAT, it became obvious that forms meant to be parallel, that is, psychometrically equivalent, were not, as documented by the following quote (College Board Entrance Examination, 1942):

> It is highly desirable that a given score on the verbal SAT represent approximately the same ability no matter when the test is taken. That is, if a college is to select its incoming class from a group taking the test in April, a group taking it in June, and a group taking it in September, the admissions officer wishes to know whether a candidate receiving a score of 550 in April possesses approximately the same degree of aptitude as another candidate who receives that score in

---

[1] A similar principle is at play in electronic shopping when you are told that "customers like yourself have enjoyed the following items." That is, there is a presumption that if your pattern of purchases matches that of someone else, you might be interested in something they just bought.

June . . . *The increase in the use of the April tests, however, and the consequent shift in the makeup of the group taking the test at any one session, necessitated devising some means for insuring that the scores would continue to have stability of interpretation* [italics added]. The two forms of the verbal test offered in 1940 contained one section of material common to both. Using this common part as a basis, it was possible to equate the scores on those two forms. (p. 34)

Equating methodology is a key development in psychometric theory. Kolen and Brennan (1995) provided an overview of the scope of the methodology. Ironically, equating may have worked so well to solve the problem mentioned in the aforementioned quote that the incentive to study the principles of design that would make it possible to produce forms that are parallel by design, rather than retrospectively adjusting scores, may have been lost. Test developers do their best to assemble a parallel form but with the peace of mind that equating will take care of any lack of parallelism. Today, we take for granted that tests issued in multiple forms must be equated. It is possible, however, to think instead of learning from each administration why forms are more or less equivalent rather than simply equating away the unexpected differences. This would require, among other things, developing a deep understanding of the basis of item difficulty (Mislevy, Sheehan, & Wingersky, 1993). Over time, the need for equating could be reduced to a quality control check. The value in this approach is, of course, that the resulting learning on the part of test developers is not incidental to the construct under measurement. Indeed, over the years, it has become possible to produce SAT forms that are nearly equivalent in terms of difficulty (I. Lawrence, personal communication, March 2003). This is not surprising because the frequency of administration provides more learning opportunities to tighten the specifications and to develop at least an informal understanding of the basis of item difficulty.

The foundational work of Cronbach and Meehl (1955), however, was silent on the question of a theory of item writing in that it dealt with relations among scores (nomothetic span), as was Messick's (1989) considerable expansion of construct validity as an overarching scheme for test-score interpretation. It was in the 1970s, as cognitive psychology regained prevalence, that we could begin to aspire to a scientific approach to the process of producing items. Sternberg's (1977) componential analysis of items was influential, as was Carroll's (1976) "new structure of intellect." Embretson (1983), and subsequent work to expand the concept of construct validity beyond scores to an accounting of variability among items—what Embretson called *construct representation*—brought into focus the idea that items could be subjected to modeling. Corresponding work in psychometrics by Fischer (1973) established that joint modeling of psychometric and content characteristics was feasible. Work on automated scoring brought to the forefront the need for a design perspective (Bennett & Bejar, 1998) by pointing out the dependencies among components of an assessment. Similarly, work on item generation (Bejar, 1993) made it clear that it was possible to conceive and implement item-generation schemes that produced items with reasonably well-predicted item statistics. Thus, by the 1990s, it was possible to think of assessment design as a science comprising scoring, item and task development, and psychometric modeling. But an integrated conception of these processes as pieces of a design puzzle remained to be achieved.

The rest of this chapter outlines the work at ETS to provide that integrated conception and the role of several enabling technologies that moves us closer to a science of assessment.

EVIDENCE-CENTERED DESIGN

A team at ETS led by Robert Mislevy[2] has been developing a conception of assessment design that meets the criteria mentioned earlier—namely, to view specific assessments as realizations of well-articulated design processes (Almond, Steinberg, & Mislevy, 2002; Mislevy, Steinberg, & Almond, 2002). The approach has been called *evidence-centered design* (ECD) and is seen, in part, as a means of cost-effectively undertaking more innovative assessment designs and, also, of building in validity at the design stage. That is, ECD, in addition to providing a conceptual framework, is also a means of producing tangible "design objects" that serve not only the assessment for which they are designed but also future assessments. It is the reusability of these design objects that leads, in principle, to more cost-effective assessments.

Conceptually, ECD formalizes the end product of assessment design as comprising three interrelated models: the *student model*, the *task model*, and the *evidence model*. These three components have counterparts in current assessment development but it is the explication of their interrelationships and dependencies that constitute the key conceptual and practical advance. In addition, the emphasis of evidence has a subtle impact on the assessment development process. In particular, whereas the first instinct when developing a new assessment is to start writing items, the ECD perspective leaves item writing for last. That is, the goals of the assessment are established in sufficient detail to make it possible to specify the evidence that would be necessary to gather to satisfy the goals of the assessment. Then, and only then, is the item development process undertaken.

---

[2] Robert Mislevy is now at the University of Maryland.

Because these components are implemented as software, it becomes possible to exchange information among the models. The modularity of the approach and the connectivity among models allows for a more efficient implementation of subsequent assessments. Each of the ECD models is a set of variables, some of which are in common among models and some of which permit communication among models.

The assessment design process begins (see, e.g., Williamson, Bauer, Steinberg, Mislevy, & Behrens, in press) with the formulation of a student model based on the goals of the assessment and an appropriate construct validation plan. Special consideration needs to be given to the construct representations because they address the mental processes that may underlie responses. The student model is an explication of the variables (and their relationships) that we choose to represent a test taker. The student model can address characterizations of the test taker that are more fine-grained than the score level, such as the postulation of proficiencies or cognitive processes that account for performance in the test. It is this functionality that makes it possible to think of richer characterizations than the "test score" and to implement richer assessments in a manageable way. Ideally, assessments are linked or linkable to instruction and can be seeing as part of the learning process. In contrast to subscores, scores on well-identified proficiencies, designed to be explicitly tapped, can inform the learning process more effectively.

A key component of the methodology is the systematic elicitation and enumeration of what the outcomes of interest are. (It is important to note that this step occurs first, followed by the identification of evidence that would be supportive of the goals of the assessment. Only when this information is at hand does the process of designing tasks and items that will elicit the required evidence move forward.) For example, an assessment inspired by cognitive theory would refer to certain mental processes; an assessment based on content standards in a given jurisdiction would refer to outcomes dictated by those standards. A key aspect of student modeling is the possibility of allowing multiple outcomes and, specifically, the possibility that performance on a given task provides information about multiple outcomes. Because of the flexibility in the student model, diagnostic assessments can be designed from the ground up. In the case of diagnostic assessment, for example, this means explicitly enumerating the types of diagnostic information we seek and designing items and tasks explicitly to elicit that diagnostic information. Items are designed to embody the rationale of the assessment rather than requiring post hoc rationalization.

The second ECD model is the task model. There is no counterpart to this component in existing established practice because item development is "item-centric." That is, the outcome of the process is an item and the item is treated as a self-contained unit. The role of a given item in informing the student model is, at best, tenuous. A pretesting process is used to see if the item functions as intended. Once it is authored, many resource-intensive processes, such as art work, are applied to each item. This occurs before we know whether the item functions well. Because of the item-centric orientation of the process, there is very little opportunity for reusing parts of that item. In fact, on more than one occasion, essentially the same item has been written more than once. Avoiding the possibility of inadvertently writing the same item more than once underscores the savings that may be gained from a task model perspective.

Although there is no counterpart to task models in current practice, task models overlap with work in item generation. Research on item generation in a wide range of domains was reviewed by Bejar (1993). A recent volume (Irvine & Kyllonen, 2002) reported on more recent projects. To generate items, it is necessary to have an item model (Bejar, 1996) or similar structure (Embretson, 1999) from which to generate instances of the item model. For this purpose, item models include the logic to instantiate items. The goal is to generate items such that their psychometric characteristics are known. Psychometric theory to support item generation is emerging (e.g., Johnson & Sinharay, 2003; Sinharay, Johnson, & Williamson, 2003; Wright, 2002).

A task model in ECD is more general than an item model. It could include all the variables in an item model and additional ones that explicitly characterize the task more broadly and connect it to the student model. By contrast, in an item model, broader characterizations are left implied. That is, there is no "metadata" explicitly associated with an item model. Conceptually, a task model is an item model augmented with metadata and instantiation logic and the means of exchanging information with other components of the assessment.

The third model is the evidence model. Strictly speaking, the evidence model is developed before task models because the evidence model contains the information we need to elicit from test takers to update the student model. The eliciting is done by means of the tasks presented to the test taker and, in that sense, the evidence we are seeking is a design specification for the task models. Therefore, the information in the evidence model directly impacts the design of the task models. Of the three models, the evidence model has the most direct counterparts to existing practice. However, to find those counterparts, we need to step outside of the multiple-choice format that characterizes most existing tests.

The evidence model contains the "evidence rules" for scoring test performance. In a multiple-choice format, the rules appear simple because scoring is a matter of comparing the selected choice to a key. In reality, significant effort is devoted to crafting the distractors. Considerable planning is required in determining how to assign a score when responses are more complex, such as written or spoken responses, or complex work products. The typical approach is to use judges, in which case the evidence rules are equivalent to the scoring rubrics typically used in scoring of open-ended responses. The scoring sheets used by judges are the outcome of the application of evidence rules. When scoring is automated, there is a feature extraction process that computes a series of variables. These variables are in turn converted into a single score by a variety of procedures (see Williamson, Mislevy, & Bejar, 2004, and Yang, Buckendahl, Juszkiewicz, & Bhola, 2002, for examples of automated scoring). The main difference between an automated procedure and one based on judges is that the former makes very explicit the rules for extracting features from a performance as well as the aggregation of feature scores into a single score for a given task. In short, the process we know as scoring, whether by means of judges or automated, corresponds to the subcomponent of the evidence model known as evidence rules.

The second subcomponent of the evidence model, the *measurement model*, also has its direct counterpart in existing practice. It is the means of aggregating information of performances across several tasks into the scores expected by the student model. If the student model calls for a single score and the tasks are scored as right or wrong, existing Item Response Theory (IRT) measurement models are appropriate. However, recently, Bayes nets have been used in lieu of IRT. For example, Bayes nets could be used to deal with the case of polytomous responses that need to be integrated into a multivariate representation of the student (Mislevy, Almond, Yan, & Steinberg, 1999).

In a sense, a model-based approach to scoring, whether automated or through raters, was inevitable. Specifically, research on automated scoring anticipated the connections that must exist among the different parts of the assessment for automated scoring to work (Bennett & Bejar, 1998). That is, scoring cannot be designed in isolation, independent of the goals of the assessment. Moreover, the design of automated scoring—specifically, the evidence identification aspect—must occur in concert with task design. For example, in assessments consisting of complex tasks, a whole range of factors may hinder eliciting the evidence we are seeking. The tasks could be too easy or too hard to effectively elicit evidence. The interface used to deliver a computer-based assessment may get in the way of students demonstrating what they are capable of and, therefore, contribute variance that is irrelevant for the purposes of the assessment. Although research on automated scoring recognized the importance of the connections to the student model, the psychometric infrastructure needed to take advantage of those connections was not present. For

TABLE 14.1

A Comparison of ECD Components Against Current Practice

ECD Model	Current Practice
Student model: A set of variables to represent the student. It is the result of an analysis of the goals of the assessment and is informed up front by relevant theory.	The equivalent of the student model is a score representing the outcome of the assessment. The meaning of the scores is established a posteriori by locating the score within a relevant nomological network.
Task model: An abstract characterization or specification from which it is possible to produce items or tasks. The student model and the evidence model drive the design of task models.	The process known as "test development" is the equivalent. However, the process is "item-centric" and seldom leads to reusability of test content.
Evidence model: Comprises both response modeling, for example using IRT or Bayes nets, and scoring in ways that it becomes possible to serve complex characterizations of the student.	Both response modeling and scoring are used in current practice but the palette of response models is more limited and complex characterizations of students are less easily accomplished.

example, performance on a complex task may elicit information about more than one student variable. Seamlessly updating a multivariate student model from within-task performance is one of the important capabilities of the implementation of evidence-centered design.

In short, an evidence-centered approach to assessment design characterizes the different aspects of the assessment: the student, the tasks, and the evidence by means of variables. Table 14.1 provides a summary of each model and its relationship to existing practice. A subset of these variables is shared by the different components of the assessment and is the means of communications among them. By themselves, these models are conceptually appealing and take us closer to a science of assessment. For existing assessments, the approach serves as mechanism for improving them. In particular, it is possible to enhance existing assessments through the incorporation of principles of item design. In the rest of this chapter, I discuss recent work toward a science of item writing.

MODEL-BASED APPROACH TO ITEM WRITING

The completeness of the ECD model is especially appealing when undertaking new assessments (Williamson, Bauer, Mislevy, & Behrens, 2003). Existing assessments were designed through a different process and yet it is possible to think of them from the perspective of a science of assessment. In particular, item writing is often seen as a craft where each item is written with creativity and ingenuity but the expertise that the writer brings to bear is not captured beyond the existence of a given item. Through task or item models, it is possible to capture that expertise in such a way that other items embodying the same expertise can be produced. Doing so requires several enabling technologies and disciplines. In this section, I describe the role of cognitive science in task and item modeling at ETS as well as the role of two enabling methodologies, computing and natural language processing (NLP).

Cognitive Design

Admission tests often rely on the assessment of reasoning skills. Cognitive science is a primary source of inspiration for modeling responses for such assessments. Specifically, cognitive science plays a critical role in the formulation of difficulty models or, more generally, construct representation. By insuring that the performance at an item level can be attributed to particular validated cognitive variables, we help to insure that the test score—the aggregate of performance across all items—is understood in the same terms. Insuring that cognitive principles are applied systematically to the creation of items is greatly facilitated by computer tools designed for that purpose. Several such tools are under development at ETS. These tools are called Test Creation Assistants (TCA). They can be used to author items the old fashion way but, more importantly, they can be used to author item or task models. As noted earlier, an item model entails both a difficulty model and an instantiation mechanism. These two elements take different forms for different types of items.

The earliest operational TCA was developed for mathematics (Singley & Bennett, 2002). In its current form, a primary use of the Math TCA is to author item models such as those that appear in the Graduate Record Examination (GRE®) Quantitative Reasoning section. The tool is capable of instantiating, that is, producing actual items, or exporting the item model encoded in such a fashion that a separate process can carry out the instantiation. In this case, models are authored with the explicit goal that the items generated from the model be exchangeable. That is, the difficulty and other psychometric parameters of each instance should be held as constant as possible. This is done, in part, because, at the moment, there is not a sufficiently robust and validated difficulty model for all of the item types that appear in the GRE. Although such a difficulty model is under development by Susan Embretson and her colleagues, it is still possible to make use of item models for high-stakes assessments. Bejar et al. (2003) illustrated an approach to adaptive testing where items are generated on-the-fly from item models. Scores on the experimental GRE adaptive test correlated as high with operational GRE scores as the typical retest correlation. This is significant because, even though the item models were calibrated, the generated instances were not. That is, all instances of an item model were assigned the same parameter estimates rather than being explicitly calibrated. This means that the parameter estimates were sufficiently close to make model calibration applicable to all instances of the item model.

Significant progress in the use of cognitive design has also been made in creating reasoning items such as those used in the GRE analytical section. These consist of two item types: analytical reasoning (AR) and logical reasoning (LR). A team of psychologists at Plymouth University in Plymouth, England, are developing a cognitive approach to the AR item type (Dennis, Handley, Bradon, Evans, & Newstead, 2002; Newstead, Bradon, Handley, Evans, & Dennis, 2002b). Cognitive psychology has played a prominent role in their efforts from the start. Their approach has been to identify the basic subtypes of AR problems but to approach them from a common framework they call "model semantics." This has many similarities to the mental-models approach of Johnson-Laird (1983). For example, in one problem type, the task is to order a set n of elements, usually between six and seven. The approach begins by identifying the $n!$ possible orderings. In this problem type, a scenario, such as the seating arrangements around a table, is associated with a set of questions. A scenario typically excludes some possible orderings by restricting who can sit next to whom or in certain positions. The items further limit the subset by imposing further restrictions and pose questions about this restricted subset. The complexity of the restrictions is an obvious difficulty factor in these items. For example, not surprisingly, the use of negatives increases complexity and, therefore, difficulty.

The generation approach used by the Plymouth team can be described as "generate and test." That is, the generation algorithm randomly attempts permutations of the restriction rules and tests to see that a well-formed item is embodied by the application of those rules. They report impressive correlations between linear combinations of predictors of difficulty and estimated difficulties (Newstead et al., 2002a).

The second reasoning item type that has been under investigation is logical reasoning (Yang & Johnson-Laird, 2001). The stem of this item type describes some scientific fact about, for example, the development of smiling in infants. The alternative responses then present competing hypotheses to account for the phenomenon. This subtype is classified as an inference problem. Other

LR item types include identifying a missing premise and identifying weakness in an argument. The theoretical framework used to analyze these item types was mental-model theory (Johnson-Laird, 1983). In this case, the theory had implications for ordering the difficulty of the basic subtypes already mentioned. Yang and Johnson-Laird (2001) provided evidence to that effect. In addition they showed that the nature of the distractors also affects difficulty. Finally, they provided evidence that shows the textual relationship of the stem and the distractors affects difficulty. For example, a distractor that is consistent with the text, although presenting a false conclusion, would attract some test takers and, therefore, increase item difficulty. The work on the LR item type is relatively recent and has concentrated on the sources of difficulty. Incorporating this work into an approach to item creation remains a future goal.

Research in the verbal reasoning domain is also being pursued (e.g., Sheehan & Mislevy, 2001). For example, a major study on verbal analogies (Bejar, Chaffin, & Embretson, 1991) went far toward accounting for item difficulty from a cognitive perspective. The creation of items from those principles, however, was not accomplished because the state of the art in natural language processing was not sufficiently well developed at the time.

More recently, attention has been devoted to the assessment of reading comprehension by means of a set of questions related to a passage. In the interest of authenticity, reading passages for admission tests are extracted from actual sources. The creation of these items requires locating suitable passages (Sheehan et al., in press), which, in turn, requires the characterization of the text. Locating text is a text retrieval operation, which I discuss next. The formulation of item models for reading comprehension is being addressed at ETS. The approach is inspired by Kintsch's (1998) theory of comprehension. Specifically, the approach is to calculate the level of activation of the keys and the distractors and to use that information to derive a difficulty estimate.

The foregoing provides a sample of the current efforts toward model-based item development. Much remains to be done but it seems certain item development will take a very different form in the years ahead. The creativity of item writers will be augmented by a set of tools that will make it possible to produce test content in a much more targeted fashion while maintaining or improving quality and efficiency.

Enabling Technologies: Computing

Cognitive science provides the conceptual underpinnings for task modeling for many assessments. To take maximum advantage of task modeling, however, the computer as a delivery medium is essential. The convergence of conceptual and computing aspects of task modeling is illustrated by a recently completed project (Bejar et al., 2003). In this project, the goal was to extend the implementation of adaptive testing currently in place at ETS to include the actual generation of items on-the-fly. The instantiation of task or item models on-the-fly has many advantages such as protecting the security of test content. The implementation of on-the-fly adaptive testing was accomplished by having the adaptive engine draw from a pool of item models instead of a pool of items. The generation process is essentially choosing at random from the set of possible instances that can be generated by a given item model. The adaptive process itself was unchanged.

This project solved the major challenge of selecting an approach for representing item models so that a separate process could operate on the task model to actually generate items on-the-fly. The solution was to adopt Extensible Markup Language (XML) as the representation scheme. The XML standard is growing in popularity for representing content of all sorts. The adoption of XML has tremendous cost implications. In addition to making it possible to generate items on-the-fly, it allows for the automation of formatting items for different media. That is, XML contains a description of the content; the display of the content is a separate formatting operation. The decoupling of content and format allows, in principle, the display of content in different media. Automating the display itself represents a very large cost savings because, at the moment, formatting is a labor-intensive, manual process.

Enabling Technologies:
Natural Language Processing (NLP)

Another important enabling technology for task modeling is NLP. NLP has implications for both the evidence model and the task model of evidence-centered design. The evidence model is concerned with the scoring of constructed responses. Educators believe that a constructed-response format is more conducive to learning but, in practice, implementing constructed-response items is difficult and expensive because of the complexities of involving graders in the process. NLP also has implications for the instantiations of task models and for assisting test developers in locating suitable stimulus material. We now expand on these applications.

NLP in Evidence Identification (Scoring). The application of NLP to the scoring of essays has a long history at ETS and elsewhere. Several products have reached the market and, by all accounts, they are successful commercially (see

Rudner & Gagne, 2001, for a review of three systems, and Williamson, Mislevy, & Bejar, 2004, for a review of approaches to automated scoring). The next frontier is the scoring of short responses where the evaluation criteria emphasize the content of what is written. A program under development at ETS, *c-rater*, appears to be the sole example of this application of NLP to assessment (Leacock & Chodorow, 2003). Interestingly, the scoring of content responses takes a very different form from the scoring of essays. The approach is, essentially, to specify one or more "canonical responses" that describe the ideal response. The challenge for the scoring engine is to determine whether actual responses are paraphrases of the canonical response. Conceptually the process parallels the scoring process for mathematical responses (e.g., Bennett, Morley, & Quardt, 2000). In particular, robust parsing is needed to assess whether a sentence is a paraphrase of another. In the case of textual responses, ways to efficiently produce a list of synonyms for a given context are also necessary to insure that credit is given for all possible correct responses. In due course, complex responses incorporating mathematical, textual, and figural responses will be feasible.

NLP in the Design of Reading Comprehension Sets. I have already alluded to the application of NLP in locating text for reading-comprehension items, currently a very labor-intensive process. A system called Verbal Test Creation Assistant (VTCA) is under development at ETS to support the modeling of verbal test content. The project consists of two subsystems. One, SourceFinder, is designed to locate appropriate texts; the other, Item Rater, is a collaborative tool for authoring sets. In the case of reading comprehension, unlike mathematics, the present goal is not to produce items automatically but rather, to assist the test developer to construct items with control of their difficulty. The Item Rater subsystem enables the test developer to author an item and get feedback as to its likely difficulty.

Potential sources are fed to a database and assigned general attributes indicative of their suitability. A test developer accesses this database as the first step in the authoring process and, through the Item Rater, builds a set of questions related to the passage. A positive by-product of this approach is that it forces an analysis of what makes textual material suitable by investigating linguistic characterizations of the text augmented by information of the discourse style of different disciplines. Although the work is motivated by the pragmatics of locating texts cost-effectively, in the process we may obtain clearer test specifications than currently exist.

NLP in Item Generation. In addition to scoring and text retrieval, an important application of NLP in assessment design is the generation of items in

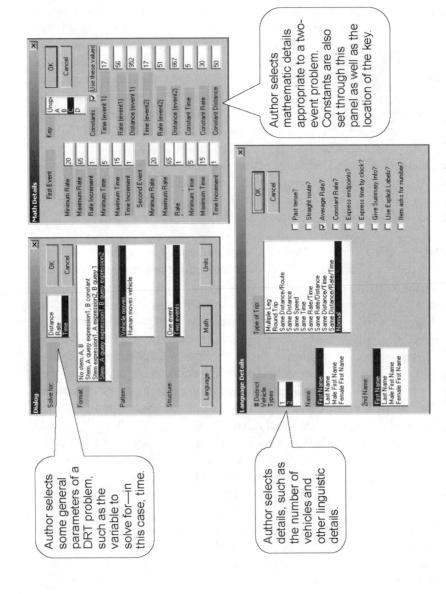

FIG. 14.1. Interface of NLP-based prototype systems for generating mathematics items.

mathematics. Test security is a major consideration in high-stakes tests. Efforts to deal with security revolve around the idea of limiting the exposure of any given item. As noted earlier, task models can be thought of as representing a set of psychometrically interchangeable items. While interchangeable psychometrically, the resulting items can be made sufficiently different to prevent the possibility of recall based on surface characteristics of the items. To achieve that goal efficiently, it is necessary to automate the production of items while maintaining control of linguistic and other attributes. A system under development at ETS (Deane & Sheehan, 2003) does just that.

Figure 14.1 shows aspects of the interface for a common class of problems known as distance-time-rate (DRT) problems where, for example, two vehicles may be traveling in opposite directions and the goal is to determine the point where they meet. The screen labeled *Dialog* allows the author to specify high-level attributes, such as solving for distance, rate, or time. The *Language Details* and *Math Details* windows, as their names imply, allow the author to make decisions concerning linguistic and mathematical details. Underneath the interface there is a powerful linguistic database that, for example, has information about the reasonable speed of different vehicles. The generative power of the system is impressive but does require a significant investment of time in an analysis of the class of problems. Such an analysis is useful in its own right for substantive reasons. Moreover, the linguistic database can be leveraged to render items in languages other than English, albeit with additional effort. The ability to have language as a variable is useful both domestically and internationally. Domestically, several states now require that assessments be available in languages other than English. Internationally, the growing number of surveys argues that an efficient way to handle multiple languages would be welcome. Program for International Student Assessment (PISA), for example, carries out a survey every 3 years to assess 15-year-old students in industrialized countries. The assessment is carried out in as many languages as there are participating countries. Task modeling and the enabling technologies we have discussed here should greatly facilitate the development of such international assessments (Bejar, Fairon, & Williamson, 2002).

SUMMARY

We are making progress toward a science of assessment. A major driver is cost-effectiveness, but a construct validity perspective, the formulation of assessment design principles by means of evidence-centered design, and the application of cognitive science insure that the end result will be more than improved cost-effectiveness. Whereas, traditionally, validation has been seen as postprocessing, the goal of a science of assessment is to deliver assessments that are as valid for their intended purpose as possible. This is not to say that the empirical verification of any validity claim will not be necessary once an assessment is completed. Rather, much of the same "validation" process will need to go on but as a form of quality control.

The advantages of a science of assessment are clear. By viewing assessments as instantiations of well-articulated and connected processes, we begin to see the commonalities among assessments. This, in turn, opens up the possibility of casting components of an assessment as reusable in future assessments. The resulting gains in efficiency release resources that can be put to good use. Similarly, the possibility of more cost-effectively developing new assessments also enhances our ability to manage the risk entailed by the development of a new assessment. For example, serving special populations becomes more feasible (Hansen, Mislevy, & Steinberg, 2003). That is, cost effectiveness is not just about saving expenses but, rather, about enabling us to undertake assessments that otherwise might not be feasible.

ACKNOWLEDGMENTS

I am grateful to Michal Beller, Dan Eignor, Ernie Kimmel, Ida Lawrence, and David Williamson for valuable comments on earlier drafts of this chapter. Special thanks are due to Drew Gitomer who facilitated much of the recent research reported here while he was Senior Vice President for Research and Development at Educational Testing Service.

REFERENCES

Almond, R. G., Steinberg, L. S., & Mislevy, R. J. (2002). Enhancing the design and delivery of assessment systems: A four-process architecture. *Journal of Technology, Learning, and Assessment, 1*(5). Available from JTLA.org

Bejar, I. I. (1991). Item writing—art or science? [A review of constructing test items by S. J. Osterlind]. *Contemporary Psychology, 36,* 310–311.

Bejar, I. I. (1993). A generative approach to psychological and educational measurement. In N. Frederiksen, R. J. Mislevy, & I. I. Bejar (Eds.), *Test theory for a new generation of tests* (pp. 323–359). Hillsdale, NJ: Lawrence Erlbaum Associates.

Bejar, I. I. (1996). *Generative response modeling: Leveraging the computer as a test delivery medium* (RR–96–13). Princeton, NJ: Educational Testing Service.

Bejar, I. I., Chaffin, R. B., & Embretson, S. E. (1991). *Cognitive and psychometric analysis of analogical problem solving.* New York: Springer-Verlag.

Bejar, I. I., Fairon, C., & Williamson, D. M. (2002, June). *Multilingual item modeling as a mechanism for test adaptation: Applications to open-ended and discrete items.* Paper presented at the International Test Commission (ITC) Conference, Winchester, UK.

Bejar, I. I., Lawless, R., Morley, M., Wagner, M., Bennett, R. & Revuelta, J. (2003). A feasibility study of on-the-fly item generation in adaptive testing. *Journal of Technology Learning and Assessment, 2* (3). Available from JTLA.org

Bennett, R. E., & Bejar, I. I. (1998). Validity and automated scoring: It's not only the scoring. *Educational Measurement: Issues and Practice, 17,* 9–16.

Bennett, R. E., Morley, M., & Quardt, D. (2000). Three response types for broadening the conception of mathematical problem solving in computerized tests. *Applied Psychological Measurement, 24,* 294–309.

Campbell, D. P. (1974). *Manual for the Strong–Campbell Interest Inventory T325 (merged form).* Stanford, CA: Stanford University Press.

Carroll, J. B. (1976). Psychometric tests as cognitive tasks: A new structure of intellect. In L. B. Resnick (Ed.), *The nature of intelligence* (pp. 27–56). Hillsdale, NJ: Lawrence Erlbaum Associates.

College Board Entrance Examination. (1942). *Forty-second Annual Report of the Executive Secretary.* New York: Author.

Cronbach, L. J., & Meehl, P. (1955). Construct validity in psychological tests. *Psychological Bulletin, 52,* 281–302. Retrieved February 15, 2003, from http://psychclassics. yorku.ca/Cronbach/construct.htm

Deane, P., & Sheehan, K. (2003, April). *Automatic item generation via frame semantics: Natural language generation of math word problems.* Paper presented at the Annual Meeting of the National Council of Measurement in Education, Chicago.

Dennis, I., Handley, S., Bradon, P., Evans, J., & Newstead, S. (2002). Approaches to modeling item-generative tests. In S. Irvine & P. C. Kyllonen (Eds.), *Generating items from cognitive tests: Theory and practice* (pp. 53–71). Mahwah, NJ: Lawrence Erlbaum Associates.

Embretson, S. E. (1983). Construct validity: Construct representation versus nomothetic span. *Psychological Bulletin, 93,* 179–197.

Embretson, S. E. (1999). Generating items during testing: Psychometric issues and models. *Psychometrika, 64,* 407–433.

Fischer, G. H. (1973). The linear logistic model as an instrument of educational research. *Acta Psychologica, 37,* 359–374.

Hansen, E. G., Mislevy, R. J., & Steinberg, L. S. (2003, April). *Evidence-centered assessment design and individuals with disabilities.* Paper presented at a symposium at the annual meeting of the National Council on Measurement in Education, Chicago. Available from www.ets.org/research/dload/ncme03-hansen.pdf

Irvine, S., & Kyllonen, P. C. (2002). *Generating items from cognitive tests: Theory and practice.* Mahwah, NJ: Lawrence Erlbaum Associates.

Johnson, M., & Sinharay, S. (2003). *Calibration of polytomous item families using Bayesian hierarchical modeling* (ETS RR–03–23). Princeton, NJ: Educational Testing Service.

Johnson-Laird, P. N. (1983). *Mental models: Towards a cognitive science of language, inference, and consciousness.* Cambridge, MA: Harvard University Press.

Kintsch, W. (1998). *Comprehension: A paradigm for cognition.* New York: Cambridge University Press.

Kolen, M. J., & Brennan, R. L. (1995). *Test equating: Methods and practices.* New York: Springer-Verlag.

Leacock, C., & Chodorow, M. (2003). C-rater: Automated scoring of short answer questions. *Computers and the Humanities, 37,* 379–405.

Messick, S. (1989). Validity. In R. L. Linn (Ed.), *Educational measurement* (pp. 13–103). New York: Macmillan.

Mislevy, R. J., Almond, R. G., Yan, D., & Steinberg, L. S. (1999). Bayes nets in educational assessment: Where do the numbers come from? In K. B. Laskey & H. Prade (Eds.), *Proceedings of the Fifteenth Conference on Uncertainty in Artificial Intelligence* (pp. 437–446). San Francisco: Morgan Kaufmann.

Mislevy, R. J., Sheehan, K. M., & Wingersky, M. S. (1993). How to equate tests with little or no data. *Journal of Educational Measurement, 30,* 55–78.

Mislevy, R. J., Steinberg, L. S., & Almond, R. A. (2002). On the structure of educational assessments. *Measurement: Interdisciplinary Research and Perspectives, 1,* 3–67. Retrieved February 15, 2003, from http://www.bc.edu/research/intasc/jtla/journal/v1n5.shtml

Newstead, S., Bradon, P., Handley, S., Evans, J., & Dennis, I. (2002a). *A cognitively based analysis of analytical reasoning item sets with implications for item generation and difficulty prediction.* Unpublished report, Plymouth University, United Kingdom.

Newstead, S., Bradon, P., Handley, S., Evans, J., & Dennis, I. (2002b). Using the psychology of reasoning to predict the difficulty of analytical reasoning problems. In S. Irvine & P. C. Kyllonen (Eds.), *Generating items from cognitive tests: Theory and practice* (pp. 35–51). Mahwah, NJ: Lawrence Erlbaum Associates.

Rudner, L., & Gagne, P. (2001). An overview of three approaches to scoring written essays by computer. *Practical Assessment, Research & Evaluation, 7* (26). Retrieved October 15, 2003 from http://edresearch.org/pare/getvn.asp?v=7&n=26.

Sheehan, K. M., Kostin, I., Deane, P., Futagi, Y., Hemat, R., & Zuckerman, D. (in press). *Inside SourceFinder: Predicting the acceptability status of candidate reading comprehension source documents.* Princeton, NJ: Educational Testing Service.

Sheehan, K. M., & Mislevy, R. J. (2001). *An inquiry into the nature of sentence completion tasks: Implications for item generation* (ETS RR–01–13). Princeton, NJ: Educational Testing Service.

Singley, M. K., & Bennett, R. E. (2002). Item generation and beyond: Applications of schema theory to mathematics assessment. In S. Irvine & P. C. Kyllonen (Eds.), *Generating items from cognitive tests: Theory and practice* (pp. 361–384). Mahwah, NJ: Lawrence Erlbaum Associates.

Sinharay, S., Johnson, M. S., & Williamson, D. M. (2003). *An application of Bayesian hierarchical model for item family calibration*. (RR–03–04). Princeton, NJ: Educational Testing Service.

Sternberg, R. J. (1977). Component processes in analogical reasoning. *Psychological Review, 31*, 356–378.

Williamson, D. M., Bauer, M., Mislevy, R. J., & Behrens, J. T. (2003, April). *An ECD approach to designing for reusability in innovative assessment*. Paper presented at the annual meeting of the American Educational Research Association, Chicago.

Williamson, D. M., Bauer, M., Steinberg, L. S., Mislevy, R. J., & Behrens, J. T. (in press). Design rationale for a complex performance assessment. *International Journal of Testing*.

Williamson, D. M., Mislevy, R. J., & Bejar, I.-I. (2004). *Automatic scoring of complex tasks in computer based testing*. Manuscript in preparation.

Wright, D. (2002). Scoring tests when items have been generated. In S. Irvine & P. C. Kyllonen (Eds.), *Generating items from cognitive tests: Theory and practice* (pp. 277–286). Mahwah, NJ: Lawrence Erlbaum Associates.

Yang, Y. W., Buckendahl, C. W., Juszkiewicz, P. J., & Bhola, D. S. (2002). A review of strategies for validating computer-automated scoring. *Applied Measurement in Education, 15*(4), 391–412.

Yang, Y., & Johnson-Laird, P. N. (2001). Mental models and logical reasoning problems in the GRE. *Journal of Experimental Psychology: Applied, 7*(4), 308–316.

IV

Admission in the Context
of K–16 Reform Efforts

15

The Integration of Secondary and Postsecondary Assessment Systems: Cautionary Concerns

Stanley Rabinowitz
WestEd, San Francisco, CA

The number of assessments and range of purposes for testing in K–16 education in the United States has grown greatly over the past 10 years. As the standards-based accountability movement has driven education reform, states and local districts have added numerous assessments to measure both individual student mastery of key academic content as well as teacher and school effectiveness in supporting student achievement (Olson, 2002). The No Child Left Behind Act (2001), with its various mandated assessments, has fueled an already hard-working assessment machine.

Amid this assessment boom lies a potential for overtesting, most profoundly at the secondary level of the K–16 education system (Ananda & Rabinowitz, 2000). Consider the burden on a typical high school junior. In many states, such students might expect (in addition to regular teacher-developed classroom tests): a high-school graduation test, a nationally developed norm reference test (NRT); multiple state-developed criterion referenced tests (CRTs) linked explicitly to state content standards; state-developed end-of-course examinations in several academic and career subjects; and one or more college entrance examinations (e.g., SAT, ACT).

Research and public opinion question whether the effects of this unprecedented proliferation of testing are all positive. Amrein and Berliner (2002) cited compelling but inconclusive evidence that results of high-stakes assessment programs fail to generalize to other key outcome measures (e.g., SAT and NAEP performance). Jacob (2001) and Rabinowitz, Zimmerman, and Sherman (2001) warned policymakers that assessments based on minimum content levels up through so-called rigorous "world-class" standards may lead to increases in student drop-out rates and other unintended consequences. As the stakes associated with testing increase for students and systems, technical and logistical limitations have resulted in rollbacks in the use of innovative assessment tools in state testing programs (Rabinowitz & Ananda, 2002). Finally, the 1990s growth in assessment was fueled, in part, by the unequaled economic growth found in all sections of the country. As many states now face dire budget deficits, assessment programs that grew unchecked during the good times now compete for limited resources with other vital services, both in education and beyond (e.g., welfare, health care).

Given this state of affairs, policymakers are beginning to search for possible assessment efficiencies. Rather than engaging in the difficult process of setting priorities among the many valuable purposes for testing, some are questioning whether traditionally separate test and assessment functions can be combined. A natural starting point in many states is to examine whether high-school graduation tests can be used for entrance into the state postsecondary education system (Kirst, chap. 16, this volume). This chapter argues that although there is considerable face validity to the idea of integrating these systems, several factors may prevent successful integration of these traditionally separate assessment purposes and programs.

First, we discuss why the option of integrating secondary and postsecondary assessment programs seems so compelling, given the conditions just described. Next, we describe some additional contextual factors that will affect the success of such attempts. We then detail numerous desirable features of high-stakes assessment systems that impact on the potential consolidation of assessment purposes. Finally, we identify a set of specific significant challenges that appear unlikely to be overcome in the near future as states explore the possibility of combining secondary and postsecondary assessment systems to achieve greater time and cost efficiency.

REASONS FOR INTEGRATING
SECONDARY AND POSTSECONDARY
ASSESSMENT PROGRAMS

As many states increase the numbers and types of secondary assessment programs, educators, parents, and students are beginning to question the purpose of each. Policymakers have not been fully effective in describing how the various components fit together to present a comprehensive vision of student achievement and system effectiveness—indeed, many simply added assessments without examining the effect on the whole. Now, as budgets shrink, efficiencies are sought. None seems as natural as integrating high-school testing with college entrance, for the various reasons now described.

• *Growing Number of High-School Graduation Tests.* At the time this chapter was written, 27 states were in the process of developing and implementing high-stakes high-school graduation testing programs. This represents nearly a doubling of such programs over the past 10 years. High-school graduation tests are typically more expensive to develop and support (both logistically and technically) than their lower stakes predecessors (typically off-the-shelf, norm-referenced assessments). This is due both to the greater public and legal scrutiny that accompanies them and to the ethical requirement that such instruments possess adequate technical quality to be used, potentially, to withhold student diplomas. Thus, policymakers and educators, facing budget shortages, look to justify the continued use of these expensive tools by having them serve multiple purposes. A growing hope is that this list of uses may include college admission and placement. This seems especially appealing because the majority of high-school graduates move on to some level of postsecondary education. In addition to cost savings, the use of these tools in the postsecondary arena could reduce some of the overtesting at the secondary level already described.

• *Overlap of Content.* The content standards on which recently developed secondary tests are based, including those used as a requirement for high-school graduation, have become more rigorous, moving the nation well beyond the Minimum Basic Skills roots of graduation testing. It would seem reasonable to assume that such high-level content ought to align with the expectations of college entry. States such as Oregon (Oregon University System, 2003) attempted to align content standards along the full K–16 spectrum. Such efforts have indeed identified significant areas of overlap between secondary and postsecondary knowledge expectations.

• *Temporal Overlap.* No state administers high-stakes high-school testing in Grade 12 for the first time. Although on the surface it would appear that the most valid time to measure whether students have mastered secondary content would be late in their high-school career, certain real-world considerations have shifted the placement of most graduation tests into either spring of Grade 10 or fall of Grade 11. These realities include allowing time for schools to provide targeted remediation in identified problem areas and to provide multiple opportunities for students to retake those sections they have yet to pass. Because most students also take college entrance examinations within this same time frame, consolidation of these programs would seem beneficial to students and taxpayers alike.

• *Facilitate Communication Between K–12 and Postsecondary Systems.* Most states experience a disconnect between policies that affect K–12 students and those affecting state colleges and universities. Often, separate governing boards and administrators oversee these systems. This has led to inefficiencies and complaints that the systems do not reinforce each other's needs. For example, colleges complain that students exit from the K–12 system lacking basic skills needed to succeed at the postsecondary level. Superintendents counter that schools of education are not preparing teachers capable of educating high-risk students. Common standards and assessments are seen as a means of furthering the integration process, creating K–16 systems.

ADDITIONAL CONTEXTUAL FACTORS

Although the factors discussed in the preceding section deal specifically with the desire to combine secondary and postsecondary assessment systems for greater efficiency, other more general assessment trends also influence the potential success of such endeavors.

• *Increased Number of Content Areas for High-Stakes Assessment.* Traditionally, high-stakes state testing programs have focused on English/language arts and mathematics content areas. Other traditional (e.g., science, social studies) and nontraditional (e.g., arts, workplace readiness) subject areas, when included, were used primarily for program evaluation purposes. A growing number of states are now looking to include these additional areas for either student accountability purposes (e.g., Nevada Science High-School Proficiency Examination) or school accountability (e.g., the Kentucky Core Content Test includes assessments in practical living/vocational studies, arts and humanities, in addition to the reading, mathematics, science, social studies, and writing). States that wish to use secondary assessments for postsecondary selection and placement purposes must decide which content to include from the high-school standards and assessments.

• *Item Formats.* As indicated, Rabinowitz and Ananda (2002) reported that state assessment programs have significantly reduced their reliance on innovative assessment formats (e.g., projects, portfolios) as the stakes of such programs have increased. Several factors contribute to this phenomenon, including technical limitations of nontraditional assessment formats, problems with logistics in delivering and supporting innovative programs, unanticipated professional development requirements, and increased costs. Several states (e.g., Utah) are abandoning plans to implement new assessments that include such formats as constructed-response items and multiple-assessment modes; others have significantly reduced the relative weights of these formats to the total test score. As No Child Left Behind (NCLB) reporting provisions kick in, particularly the requirement that assessment results must be reported prior to the commencement of the ensuing school year, reliance on multiple-choice items will grow. Colleges and university admission programs must decide if they wish to accept this retreat from innovation in order to use the results of secondary assessments in the selection and placement process.

• *Additional NCLB Uncertainties.* As described, the No Child Left Behind Act has already affected the format of state assessment programs. Several additional provisions may also influence the potential generalizability of K–12 assessment results for postsecondary applications. Many commentators noted that the major focus of NCLB is on Grades 3–8 programs with little attention to their high-school counterparts (Rabinowitz, 2003). Some fear that this may weaken secondary assessment programs. For example, some states (e.g., West Virginia) are reconsidering plans to develop end-of-course examinations in traditional college-bound courses (e.g., intermediate algebra) to meet NCLB's secondary testing requirements. The pressure on states to limit the number of schools identified as "in need of improvement" has created tensions and motivated some states to lower standards (Paige, 2002) because the Act provides for the states to set performance levels. Some states are considering dropping assessments in grades or content areas (e.g., social studies) that the Act does not require be tested because results in those areas cannot be used to remove schools from sanctions, only add more to the list. Finally, whereas NCLB provides states with resources for development of new assessments, states may not use these funds to supplant current expenditures. If states are already supporting college entrance assessment programs with local revenues, the costs of these programs may be subtracted from state awards if they are replaced with NCLB-supported secondary assessments.

• *Computer-Adaptive Assessments.* Although the previous factors described in this section may serve to inhibit the integration of secondary and post-secondary assessment programs, the use of computer adaptive assessment methodology and technology may increase the odds of successful integration. Such tools allow test content to be tailored more explicitly to the achievement levels of the candidate and purposes of assessment (Rabinowitz & Brandt, 2001). Theoretically, tests of this type can efficiently pinpoint which content a student has mastered and match this level to expected postsecondary entrance requirements. While assessments employing adaptive methodologies are relatively common in postsecondary programs, they remain untested in the K–12 high-stakes arena. In order for these methodologies to become widely accepted, evidence must be gathered regarding (a) comparability to their paper-and-pencil counterparts; and (b) equal access for all segments of the education community, including the most urban and rural communities that often lack basic technology equipment and know-how. Furthermore, supporters must demonstrate that these new technologies will allow students at all achievement levels from all schools to score at all points of the test scale with equal degrees of reliability. In other words, the technology must permit any deserving candidate to qualify for admission from the community college level up through the most elite state university campus.

REQUIRED FEATURES OF STATEWIDE ASSESSMENT SYSTEMS

Certain important features of statewide high-stakes assessment systems will also influence the degree to which secondary and postsecondary assessments can be fully integrated. This section focuses primarily on technical aspects because the ability of an assessment to meet or exceed "industry expectations" (American Educational Research Association/National Council on Measurement in Education/American Psychological Association, 1999) is crucial to its withstanding legal and public scrutiny.

• *Reliability.* Reliability refers to the degree to which an assessment provides scores that are replicable and trustworthy (Feldt & Brennan, 1989). Assessment developers ensure sufficient reliability by employing two primary methods, both of which work against the use of assessments for multiple purposes. First, they increase the numbers of items per content strand. However, because the content standards for high-school graduation and college entrance do not overlap entirely in any state, assessments will face real-time constraints against including all content designated as important for both purposes. Additionally, because the range of content expectation at the postsecondary level varies so widely from community colleges to the various 4-year institutions in many states, the ability of any one test to adequately cover all these purposes is problematic. The practicalities of limiting the length of an assessment will almost certainly lead to limited reliability at various points of the scale.

Second, test developers focus additional test items at those points of the scale corresponding to key decision points (e.g., the passing score) in an effort to increase reliability where it matters most. However, under the "integration" approach, the test scale might need to maximize reliability at as many as three to five such points. High reliability will be needed to attest to the achievement level expected for high-school graduation as well as the level(s) expected for entrance into the various postsecondary institutions found in the state. States will either have to increase the time and cost of assessment to potentially unacceptable levels or risk insufficient reliability at key decision points. As described, computer-adaptive methodology can, in the long term, help to address this issue. However, the limited experience of such approaches in the K–12 arena and remaining issues of comparability and access remain a significant stumbling block.

• *Validity*. Tests are valid to the extent they assess the designated content and provide intended information (Linn, 2001). Psychometricians are quick to point out that no test in itself is valid or invalid—rather, instruments must be judged relative to specific intended uses. The more uses a test is put to, the more difficult and expensive it will be to demonstrate its validity for each of the proposed uses. To the extent that secondary and postsecondary requirements and purposes do not converge in their entirety, a single instrument will be hard pressed to meet content, predictive, and consequential validation requirements (Messick, 1989).

• *Additional Desirable Features*. In addition to reliability and validity, state assessment programs ideally contain various other features, many of which can interfere with the goal of combining secondary and postsecondary assessment systems. For example, K–12 testing programs often include both criterion-referenced and norm-referenced components. The former provides information on how well students are doing relative to state content standards; the latter suggests how well such performance compares with a representative sample of students from across the country. Policymakers and parents typically find both types of information desirable and differentially informative. College admission practices also combine some aspects of criterion- and norm-based information; admission is based on how well a candidate performed in high school and how many other candidates have applied for admission.

Policymakers must decide how to align the information from secondary CRTs and NRTs with postsecondary admission policies. Because states differ both in their use of CRT and NRT programs and in their postsecondary admission policies, multiple models for combining this information must be developed, piloted, and validated across the country.

Other features of high-school assessment programs must also be considered. Only students who fail such tests are expected to retake them. If states begin to use such tests for postsecondary admission or placement, they must develop procedures to control the retake process and develop more complex management information systems to keep track of multiple attempts by much greater numbers of students. Although cheating is a concern of all high-stakes testing programs, increasing the stakes to include college admission will create strains not yet imagined on local oversight practices. Most high-school tests contain a range of content ranging from the mundane to the esoteric. States must decide which content to include and which to omit as they contemplate their use in other arenas. Finally, as already discussed, students at the secondary level face a myriad of assessments at each point along the way. States must decide which ones to count, when to count them, and how much to weight each relative to the others.

ADDITIONAL CAUTIONS

As discussed throughout this chapter, states and programs considering the integration of secondary and postsecondary assessment systems must address several key questions if this approach is to be successful. In this section, we offer several additional cautions that should cause even the most optimistic proponent to re-examine basic assumptions before proceeding along that path.

• *Philosophy.* At the most basic level, states must decide if high-school graduation is equivalent to college admission. Although the majority of high-school graduates do indeed go on to receive postsecondary training, many do not. And although numerous studies report that success in later life is enhanced by life-long learning, many successful citizens manage to achieve high levels of career and family satisfaction without the benefit of college attendance. Before linking high-school graduation with college admission via a testing system, states must fully explain the assumptions that allow them to do so. Although this is not an unreasonable expectation and the process might, in fact, be quite illuminating, policymakers may be surprised to discover that the road from high-school graduation to successful citizenship may not always lead through the state's institutions of higher learning.

• *Which Postsecondary Institution?* States allow a wide range of student achievement across their postsecondary institutions. From the east coast (New York's Community College system ⇒ State College System [SUCO] ⇒ State University system [SUNY]) to the west coast (California's Community College system ⇒ California State University System [CSU] ⇒ University of California system [UC]), opportunities are provided to students with varied backgrounds, interests, resources, and academic achievement levels. This diversity of opportunities (which exists among private institutions, as well) is a hallmark of the American postsecondary education system. Although this richness of options is of great benefit to students and society, it creates havoc for test developers having to accommodate the needs and expectations of such widely differing clients. Developing a single assessment instrument to meet the admissions needs of all these institutions is nearly impossible, given current time and fiscal constraints and the state of computer-adaptive assessments.

• *Student Diversity.* All postsecondary institutions struggle to attract and support a diverse student population. It is no secret among policymakers, educators, and the general public that the results of state K–12 assessment programs are marked by significant achievement gaps along gender, racial, ethnic, and disability lines. The use of such instruments in the postsecondary admissions process should not be expected to improve such institutions' ability to meet student diversity goals. Colleges need to expand the admissions process, not rely more fully on limited measures transferred from other arenas.

• *Student Mobility and Choice.* Significant numbers of students cross state lines as they move from high school to postsecondary education (Morgan, 2002). Many such students attend state-supported colleges and universities. If high-school graduation tests assume greater importance in the postsecondary admissions process, additional procedures must be developed and validated to ensure fairness in the selection process for out-of-state students because not all states administer tests for graduation and the content and difficulty of state tests vary greatly. Many students choose between public and private postsecondary options. Admissions policies and practice around the use of public school secondary assessments in nonpublic, postsecondary institutions need to be addressed or students will experience no lessening of their high-school assessment load.

• *Technical.* This section began at the philosophical level but ends with a reminder of potential technical limitations facing those attempting to integrate secondary and postsecondary assessment systems. This approach parallels the process that should be followed to develop any reliable and valid assessment system. Although there is an admirable desire for efficiency throughout the K–16 education system, responsible policymaking must separate the desirable from the attainable. Current test-development methodology will be hard-pressed to satisfy the many masters that will be brought together to integrate secondary and postsecondary assessment systems. Although the future holds great possibilities, present-day realities rule.

Policymakers interested in creating efficiencies across all levels of statewide K–16 assessment programs should focus on two important sets of activities if they wish to advance this goal for future implementation. First, they should carefully review current assessment practices and requirements to ensure all are equally valid and necessary; those judged desirable but not essential are prime candidates to be dropped entirely or shifted to local responsibility (Rabinowitz & Ananda, 2001). This approach may require (and will certainly benefit from) the type of philosophical review process discussed earlier in this section. Carefully designed reliability and validity studies can help determine when and if the desired integration of testing purposes is feasible. Perhaps high-school graduation tests, used among the various other admissions indicators, may result in incremental validity for the overall admissions decision. States must decide if this potential gain is worth the various negative consequences described.

Next, policymakers must invest in research on future assessment methodologies, be they types of testing formats or systems of delivery, particularly those employing computer-adaptive approaches. The future does hold great possibility for advancements in assessment power and efficiency but only if important questions of comparability, access, and fairness are addressed both from an assessment perspective, and more importantly, at the classroom instructional level as well.

REFERENCES

AERA/NCME/APA. (1999). *Standards for educational and psychological testing.* Washington, DC: American Psychological Association.

Amrein, A. L., & Berliner, D. C. (2002). *The impact of high-stakes tests on student academic performance: An analysis of NAEP results in states with high-stakes tests and ACT, SAT, and AP test results in states with high school graduation exams.* Tempe: Arizona State University, Educational Policy Studies Laboratory. Retrieved April 4, 2003, from http://edpolicylab.org

Ananda, S., & Rabinowitz, S. (2000, June). A *model statewide student assessment system to support school accountability.* Paper presented at the Council of Chief State School Officers Annual Large-Scale Assessment Conference, Snowbird, UT.

Feldt, L. S., & Brennan, R. L. (1989). Reliability. In R. L. Linn (Ed.), *Educational measurement* (3rd ed., pp. 105–146). New York: Macmillan.

Jacob, B. A. (2001). Getting tough? The impact of high school graduation exams. *Educational Evaluation and Policy Analysis, 23,* 99–121.

Linn, R. (2001). *The design and evaluation of educational assessment and accountability systems* (CSE Tech. Rep. No. 539). Los Angeles: Center for the Study of Evaluation, National Center for Research on Evaluation, Standards, and Student Testing, University of California, Los Angeles.

Messick, S. (1989). Validity. In R. L. Linn (Ed.), *Educational measurement* (3rd ed., pp. 13–103). New York: Macmillan.

Morgan, F. B. (2002, Spring). Fall enrollment in Title IV degree-granting postsecondary institutions: 1998. *Education Statistics Quarterly, 4,* 2002–2162.

No Child Left Behind Act of 2001, P. L. No. 107-110, 115 Stat. 1425 (2001).

Olson, L. (2002, January 9). Testing systems in most states not ESEA-ready. *Education Week.*

Oregon University System. (2003). *Annotated introduction to PASS.* Retrieved April 2, 2003, from http://www.ous.edu/pass/about/1.2-1_powerpoint.html

Paige, R. (2002). *Dear colleague letter, July 24, 2002.* Washington, DC: U.S. Department of Education. Retrieved April 4, 2003, from http://www.ed.gov/News/Letters/020724.html

Rabinowitz, S. (2003). *NCLB assessment/accountability for secondary schools.* San Francisco: WestEd Knowledge Brief.

Rabinowitz, S., & Ananda, A. (2001). *Balancing local assessment with state testing: Building a program that meets student needs.* San Francisco: WestEd Knowledge Brief.

Rabinowitz, S., & Ananda, A. (2002, April). *The negative correlation of high-stakes assessment and innovation.* Paper presented at the meeting of the National Council on Measurement in Education, New Orleans.

Rabinowitz, S., & Brandt, T. (2001). *Computer-based assessment: Can it deliver on its promise?* San Francisco: WestEd Knowledge Brief.

Rabinowitz, S., Zimmerman, J., & Sherman, S. (2001). *Do high stakes tests drive up student dropout rates: Myths versus reality.* San Francisco: WestEd Knowledge Brief.

16

Rethinking Admission and Placement in an Era of New K–12 Standards

Michael W. Kirst

Stanford University

OVERVIEW OF THE PROBLEM

Education standards have swept across the United States, engulfing almost every state. Forty-six states have created K–12 academic content standards in most academic subjects, and all but Iowa have required statewide K–12 student achievement tests. There is progress in clarifying what students must be able to know and to do in the K–12 grades, and how to align standards, assessments, textbook selection, and accountability measures at the K–12 level. A gaping hole in this state reform strategy, however, is the lack of coherence in content and assessment standards between higher education and K–12. No state included higher education institutions as an integral part of its K–12 standards deliberations. Higher education faculty participated as individuals, but not as representatives of higher education systems or public institutions.

Unless we close this standards gap and better integrate K–16 policies, students and secondary schools will continue to receive a confusing array of signals and will not be able to prepare adequately for higher education. About

80% of high-school graduates who attend postsecondary education go to broad access institutions that are open enrollment or accept all qualified applicants (McCormick, 2001). These are the students most at risk of not completing their postsecondary programs because of the K–16 disjuncture (Adelman, 1999). The current scene is a "Babel" of standards, rather than a coherent strategy across levels of education. Unclear signals, such as the lack of congruence between K–12 assessments and higher education placement exams, result in the need for high levels of postsecondary remediation, and discourage completion of postsecondary degrees.

The roots of this problem go very deep in the history of American education standards policy. The United States created two separate mass-education systems (K–12 and universities and colleges) that rarely collaborated to establish consistent standards across the levels (Stocking, 1985). Often, economically disadvantaged students are overrepresented in nonhonors courses, and do not receive adequate college admissions-related information from school or nonschool sources. About 60% of high-school seniors who plan to get a postsecondary degree fail to get any degree in the next 10 years (Rosenbaum, 2001). Improving the policy signaling process and aligning K–16 policies will benefit all students, but particularly those who go to less or nonselective 4-year or 2-year colleges. For most of these students, placement standards are more important than admissions standards. The U.S. Department of Education found that about 50% of first-year students are in remedial classes (United States Department of Education, 2001). These students have the least information about what they need to know and be able to do for success in postsecondary education (Lavin, 2000; Rosenbaum, 2001). Because of their mission and the need to fill first-year classes, many nonselective institutions do not base their admissions standards on the likelihood of degree completion.

Very few countries have a history of such a wide disconnect between education systems (Clark, 1985). In England, for example, senior secondary education exams and standards were designed solely to prepare and sort out students for university entrance. Now that England sends about the same percentage of students to universities as does the United States, the English system uses two exams that are aligned to K–12 teaching standards. The United States relies on the SAT and the ACT-Assessment®[1] to provide some uniformity, but these admissions assessments were not designed to be linked with new state K–12 content or assessment standards. The situation is even more disjointed in the area of higher education placement tests. In the southeast United States, for example, the Southern Regional Education Board (SREB) found in 1998

---

[1] ACT-Assessment® is a registered trademark of ACT, Inc.

(Abraham, 1992) that there were nearly 125 combinations of 75 different placement tests devised by universities with scant regard to secondary school standards. The only nationally aligned K–16 standards effort is the Advanced Placement Program—a "stalactite" that extends from universities, utilizing a common content syllabus and exam formulated by both levels of education (Lichten, 2000).

The result of this confusion is that K–12 tests and university entrance and placement assessments usually utilize different formats, emphasize different content, and take different amounts of time to complete. For example, Kentucky's K–12 assessment relies heavily on writing examples, but ACT Assessment measures writing skill through multiple-choice items. Massachusetts' statewide K–12 assessment contains performance items that are dissimilar to the closed-end multiple choice format of SAT and ACT. California's Standards Test (CST) includes math that is considerably more advanced and difficult than the math included in SAT I and ACT. The Texas K–12 assessment (TAAS), however, does not include sufficient algebra or geometry to be as challenging as the SAT I.

Some K–12 state assessments permit students to use calculators, but the state university placement exams do not. Texas has a statewide postsecondary placement test (TASP), but many Texas universities also use their own placement exams for decisions. Interviews with students demonstrate that they have no idea about the content of placement standards (Kirst & Venezia, 2003). Many high-school-level state assessments do not go beyond Grade 10, so their articulation with postsecondary placement exams is unlikely. Illinois, however, has a state test given in Grade 11 to every student, and it combines ACT items with others that match Illinois content standards. California, New York, and Pennsylvania all utilize rigorous Grade 11 exams, and many states have end-of-course exams in subjects such as biology, chemistry, and world history that provide useful admissions and placement data.

Universities and colleges offer some good reasons for paying little attention to K–12 standards or assessments. They emphasize that higher education was not involved in the process of creating or refining K–12 standards. Moreover, state K–12 standards keep changing because of political or technical problems. The K–12 assessments are not evaluated to see how well they predict freshman grades (although this is not difficult to do). Universities hope that the SAT and ACT will make adjustments to accommodate these new K–12 standards, and feel comfortable with the two assessments they know and can influence.

These disjunctures will be hard to fix unless there is an institutional center for K–16 reform. Very few states have any policy mechanism that can deal with K–16 standards alignment. As president of the California State Board

TABLE 16.1
Distribution of Topics on Standardized Math Tests

	Algebra 1	Geometry	Data, Probability, Statistics	Number Theory Arithmetic, Combinatorics, Logic	Algebra 2	Trigonometry/ Precalculus
Percentage of Questions Devoted to						
Privately developed high school assessment tests						
TerraNova	14	29	23	21	0	0
Stanford 9 m/c	29	25	25	21	0	0
State high school assessment tests						
Kentucky (CATS)	9	33	17	18	20	0
Massachusetts (MCAS 10)	23	28	13	18	13	5
New York	29	26	9	26	9	3
Texas (TAAS)	12	23	3	53	0	0
College admissions exams						
SAT I	47	23	3	23	3	0
ACT	25	27	5	18	12	8
Privately developed college placement tests						
Compass	14	23	0	19	25	15
Accuplacer al	25	0	0	0	75	0
Accuplacer cl	16	0	0	0	63	21

Note. From Education Trust, 1999, p. 27. Copyright © 1999 by Education Trust. Reprinted with permission. al = algebra. cl = calculus.

of Education for several years, I never met with my university counterparts. Higher education coordinating bodies do not include K–16 standards and policy within their purview. In short, there are few regular opportunities for K–12 educators to discuss educational standards and admission test issues with college and university faculty or policymakers. The professional lives of K–12 and higher education professionals and leaders proceed in separate orbits.

HIGH SCHOOL STUDENTS FACE A "BABEL" OF ASSESSMENTS

High-school students receive confusing messages about the academic knowledge and skills that they need to succeed in college. Consider math proficiency as an example (Education Trust, 2002). In deciding how many years of math to take, high-school students look at their high-school graduation requirements and college admission requirements; the former reflect the content of any statewide Grade 10 through Grade 12 math assessments, and the latter entail mastering the content that appears in the math sections of the SAT I or the ACT. As a recent analysis shows (see Table 16.1), the content of statewide high-school math assessment tests and the content of the math portions of the SAT I and ACT are fairly similar; they tend to emphasize basic algebra, geometry, probability and statistics, and numbers (number theory, arithmetic, combinatorics, and logic) and to ignore content used for first-year placement such as intermediate algebra, trigonometry, and precalculus (Education Trust, 1999).

But the differences between all these tests and the college placement tests are significant. The state Grade 10 exam in Washington includes two original essays that are more challenging than the community college multiple-choice editing test (Shaw, 2002). College placement exams like COMPASS® and Accuplacer®,[2] which are used by community colleges, put considerable emphasis on intermediate algebra and trigonometry. Thus students prepare for and are admitted to college based on one set of skills, but are then given placement tests that cover different and more complex content (Education Trust, 1999).

Some K–12 state assessments, however, are rigorous and their content more closely resembles that of the college placement tests than that of the SAT I. The Massachusetts and Kentucky K–12 assessments include intermediate algebra

---

[2]COMPASS/ESL® is a registered trademark of ACT, Inc. Accuplacer® is a registered trademark of the College Board.

and trigonometry. Then again, many state K–12 tests, including the California Stanford 9®[3] and the Texas TAAS, stress data, probability, and statistics—topics that the college admissions and college placement tests largely ignore.

It is no wonder that high-school seniors are confused. They are focused on high-school graduation (state assessment tests) and college admission (SAT I or ACT)—not on college placement exams, undergraduate general studies, or distribution requirements—and do not realize the importance of taking mathematics in their senior year as part of their preparation for college. Among high-school students interviewed in six states (California, Illinois, Texas, Maryland, Georgia, and Oregon) by researchers from Stanford's Bridge Project (see Appendix), students did not know how content, standards, or scores on state K–12 assessments were related to college admission or placement standards (see Kirst & Venezia, 2003).

The Bridge Project also examined the assessment of writing skills and found substantial differences in the format and content of tests administered to college-bound high school students. Many state 9–12 assessments are based on writing samples. Oregon and Illinois, for example, require students to write an expository and/or analytical piece and a narrative and/or personal essay. New York, Massachusetts, and Kentucky combine reading comprehension and writing by asking students to write responses to questions about passages. In contrast, the ACT Assessment uses multiple-choice writing tasks that ask students to identify the error in a sentence or paragraph. SAT II does require students to write an essay, but the topics are personal and reflective; no expository or analytical writing is required, and the essay portion of the test lasts only 20 min. Even though most of the writing that students do in college involves analysis, reporting, argument, and persuasion, the college admissions process rarely includes any assessment of students' expository writing skills. College placement tests usually do require writing, but Accuplacer and Compass do not include expository or analytical essays.

Looking beyond mathematics and writing, the Bridge Project compiled lists of the various assessments used in each state. In California, for example, the following tests are administered:

State-Administered K–12 Assessments

STAR System
- California Achievement Test—every pupil Grades 2–11 Norm Reference Test

---

[3] Stanford 9® is a registered trademark of Harcourt, Inc.

- California's Standards Test (CST): Every student tested in Grades 2–11. Also includes end-of-course tests, Algebra I and II, Geometry, and so on.
- Total testing time: 580 minutes in 2001 for STAR.

Other Tests
- State graduation test—being developed (high school exit exam).
- Golden State Exam—high school students in top one third, endorsed diploma.
- GED
- California High School Proficiency Exam—early graduation from high school.
- California English Language Development Test (CELDT)

Public College and University Assessments
- Community college placement exams—vary by college/district.
- SAT I—multiple choice
- SAT II—subject matter—mostly multiple choice
- California State University Placement Exam—over half fail either language arts or math.
- University of California Placement Exam—one third fail English/language arts.
- Advanced Placement—subject-matter based—some multiple choice.

All these tests can be an enormous burden for Grade 10 and Grade 11 students and lessen valuable teaching time in high school. An analysis of the content and format of these California assessments, conducted by the Rand Corporation (Le & Hamilton, 2002), traces some of the misalignment between K–12 tests and college admissions and placement exams to "reforms that have taken hold at one level of the educational system, but not another . . . particularly . . . where new [state] tests have been developed to reflect state standards or frameworks that emphasize inquiry-based teaching and open-ended problem solving" (cited in Burr, Kirst, & Fuller, 2000, p. 180). Faced with a roster of tests that measure different sets of skills and fields of knowledge, high-school seniors are not only confused about how to prepare for college, but also uncertain about any possible relationship between the state K–12 tests they take in high school and their academic future. The Appendix presents a content comparison of all major state K–16 tests in Oregon and Texas.

It is also worth noting that the value of standardized tests as a predictor of students' postsecondary academic achievement—measured by their completion of a certificate or degree program—is uncertain. Lavin (2000), for example, compared the placement test performance of freshmen admitted to the City University of New York in 1988 with their graduation rates. As might be expected, students who passed all [three] of the tests were more likely to graduate (by 1996) than those who did not pass all of them. But what one may find surprising is that graduation rates for those who did not pass all of the tests are often substantial. Indeed, Asian students who failed one test were as likely to graduate as those who passed all of the tests, and even among those who failed two, the graduation rate was quite comparable with those who passed all. Among those who failed all three tests, about a quarter had graduated from CUNY after 8 years.

AFFIRMATIVE ACTION AND COLLEGE ADMISSIONS

The growth of state K–12 standards and assessments is coinciding with the reconsideration of admissions standards after some courts or states banned affirmative action criteria for admissions to highly selective public universities. This reconsideration opens the door to the potential use of Grade 10 and Grade 11 state assessments as one factor in a more comprehensive admissions portfolio. Prior to the banning of affirmative action, both the University of Texas and the University of California—like many state university systems— admitted students by calculating indices of high-school performance and SAT/ACT scores. The higher the GPA or high-school class rank, the lower the SAT/ACT scores needed for admission. The same basic calculation was made for minority students, only some were admitted with lower GPAs and SAT scores than nonminority students. Admissions officials considered race and ethnicity in their decisions for students on the borderline of not being admitted. Proposition 209 in California and the federal appellate ruling in the Texas case (*Hopwood v. State of Texas*, 1996) stopped such affirmative-action practices in their tracks. Some universities felt they had no choice but to radically overhaul their admissions criteria, hoping that the newly developed criteria would somehow continue to promote minority admissions while adhering to the law banning the consideration of race. A grand experiment in university admissions began.

The 2003 Supreme Court decision upholding some forms of affirmative action caused some universities to emulate the University of California's "comprehensive" or "wholistic" admissions criteria. For a specific example of new admissions criteria that appear to satisfy the Supreme Court's ruling, we can look at the University of California. Until fall 2001, UC admitted 50% to 75% of their freshman on GPA and SAT/ACT alone. UC has changed that policy and now uses a more comprehensive review (this process is described in detail in chap. 2, this volume) including such factors as out-of-classroom activities, leadership, educational disadvantage, family income, and overcoming hardships. For example, UC campuses consider (a) first-generation university student; (b) attending a high school with a low-socioeconomic student body; (c) demonstrating marked improvement in Grade 11; and (d) demonstrating specific instances of perseverance. Also considered at many California campuses are factors over which the applicant has had little direct control, and which he or she has to be able to surmount. An applicant, for instance, may have been faced with unusual family disruptions, certain medical or emotional problems, an adverse immigrant experience, an environment of drug or alcohol abuse, a lack of academic role models, or the need to learn English. The admission staff at UCLA had to be expanded greatly because UCLA receives 43,000 applications. UC has begun random checks on student-provided information, such as community service (Portner, 2002). With all these listed factors as part of the admissions decision, 10th- and 11th-grade state assessments including end-of-course tests are a logical addition to the UC comprehensive admissions review.

The University of California admits the top 4% to one of the eight general campuses in its system but also specifies the high-school courses that must have been taken. In 2002, Florida universities accepted any student in the top 20% of his or her class. The University of Texas accepts all students in the top 10% of their respective high-school class, regardless of SAT/ACT scores. After accepting the top 10%, the University of Texas considers other applicants based on 18 criteria. Some of these more conventional criteria include a consideration of essays, the number of college units taken, leadership abilities, work experience, and community service. The university also uses other criteria similar to those being used in California. These include being from a low-income or single-parent home, speaking more than one language, and attending a school operating under a court-ordered desegregation plan.

Although the impact on minority enrollment from these policies is unclear, they should help to increase both geographic representation and the numbers of students from high schools with historically low university enrollment rates. Initial studies from the UC indicate that there is a modest effect in terms of racial and/or ethnic students admitted, but not enough to increase the percentages admitted to a higher level than before affirmative action was banned (University of California, Board of Admissions, 2002).

HIGH-SCHOOL CLASS RANK
AND ADMISSIONS

Defining the top of the class such as 10% or 20% appears to be straightforward, but it has proven to be more complex and elusive than originally thought. This new admissions game will produce winners and losers as students, parents, and school districts learn how to play the game better. High grades at one high school are easier to get than in other high schools. What counts is not merely good grades, but better grades than one's peers (see chap. 7, this volume, for an extensive discussion of the use of grades in selection).

A study of six states concluded that some colleges and universities give extra weight to certain academic courses but others do not (Kirst & Venezia, 2003). The policies run the gamut, and inequities are created. For example, for decades Illinois has been using high school class rank (HSCR) as one half of an admissions index, with ACT scores for the other half. But Illinois universities and the Illinois Board of Higher Education have never specified how high schools should compute class rank. Consequently, Illinois high schools use a variety of techniques and weighting systems to determine HSCR. High schools include different courses in their calculations—some schools count college prep courses for the most part, whereas others include electives and vocational classes. Some types of courses are more heavily weighted but some schools compute HSCR in several ways, and then report the ranking that provides local students with the best chance of being admitted (Kirst, Spivey, & Contreras, 2001).

This system does not provide valid and reliable comparisons of HSCR for university admission. At the University of Illinois, for example, disputes about class rank have led to the creation of a group of special review high schools, mostly in high-income, suburban Chicago. These schools contend that their academic achievement is so high that students below the top 10% to 15% are highly qualified for UI admission. If University of Illinois freshman grades from these secondary schools are high enough, class rankings for subsequent applicants are adjusted upward compared to the rest of the graduates of high schools in the state. Because most high schools use the same class rank system for many years, Illinois has worked out most of the problems with its criteria through encouraging high schools to continue to use the same ranking system (whatever it may be) for many years. But the Illinois experiences demonstrate the complexity of the issue.

All public universities in Texas now accept the top 10% from each of the state's high schools but initially there were no course requirements for computing HSCR. Nonacademic electives and vocational courses can be crucial factors in helping students reach the top 10% more easily, but more difficult courses might be more appropriate for admissions purposes. If universities do not think HSCR is valid and reliable, they will need to place more emphasis on ACT, SAT, and statewide high school exam scores. The top 10% policy in Texas could produce classes of freshmen who have taken an extremely diverse range of courses. A U.S. Department of Education study finds that taking specific courses, especially one math course beyond Algebra II, is crucial to university graduation (Adelman, 1999). The goal, after all, should be to graduate students, not simply to admit them.

One thing is certain about the new admissions criteria: They are a lot more difficult for students, parents, and the public to understand than the old GPA and SAT index. Students in California and Texas can no longer simply calculate their chances of admission from a chart using this index now that qualitative factors such as persistence and determination are also being considered. It cannot be assumed, however, that the more complex criteria are necessarily a bad thing. A major drawback of the traditional GPA/SAT indices is their tendency to overlook the more intangible factors that predict success at universities, while at the same time eliminating the very kind of nontraditional students that universities wish to attract. The new criteria—complex as they may be— may signal to minority students that they are welcome at state universities. In any case, the use of the new criteria will require more thorough counseling of high-school students than in the past, partly because of their complexity and partly because they are more likely to change. So far, neither UC nor the University of Texas has increased the percentage of minority students admitted, despite the use of more comprehensive criteria than GPA/SAT. The number of minority students has recovered from the low numbers admitted immediately after Affirmative Action was dropped, but minority percentages are not increasing beyond the Affirmative Action era (Rodriguez & Johnson, 2003; University of California, 2002). Still, there are critics who believe that these new admission policies are a form of back door Affirmative Action.

THE SENIOR YEAR PROBLEM

Students who slack off during their senior year of high school—a condition so common in the United States that it has become known as "senior slump" or "senioritis"—are merely playing the hand that has been dealt them. High-school seniors who take a break from tough academic courses are reacting rationally to a K–12 system and a college admissions process that provide few incentives for students to work hard during their senior year.

In effect, the education standards reform movement has written off the senior year, and so have our colleges and universities. For instance:

- The K–12 accountability movement has no strategy for assessment in the senior year. Only New York's statewide K–12 assessment includes subject matter from the senior year. Most other state assessments extend only to the 10th-grade level. Grade 11 state tests are most useful for postsecondary purposes.
- The college admissions calendar encourages students to take college preparation courses in their sophomore and junior years, but provides scant incentives for them to study hard during their senior year. Yet, students who do not take math in their senior year are more likely to fail placement exams.
- Because the content of K–12 state tests differs significantly from the content of college placement tests, many students learn only after enrolling in college that their senior year in high school did not prepare them adequately for college-level work.

Senior slump appears to be unique to the United States, and is not typical among the industrialized countries. In many other countries, such as England, France, and Germany, students in their senior year of high school must pass crucial final examinations as a key criterion for postsecondary admissions.

WHAT TO DO ABOUT THESE PROBLEMS

This section presents policy implications for college admissions and placement policies. (For a more complete overview of recommendations concerning K–16, see Kirst & Venezia, 2003.)

College Admissions Policies

Colleges should periodically analyze the messages they send to prospective students regarding academic preparation and admissions standards. In particular, colleges should examine the incentives that are offered to students of various abilities and socioeconomic status. For example, do admissions and financial aid policies reward students who do well on external subject matter exams? Colleges and high schools should cooperate in setting formulas for how the high schools are to calculate GPAs and class rankings. (Currently, high schools in some states can elect to include or exclude grades from nonacademic courses in their computations.) Colleges should accord appropriate weight for honors and AP courses, and performance in senior-year academic courses should be an important component in computing class rank.

Colleges should set explicit standards for senior-year performance in all courses and withdraw admissions offers if those standards are not met. Students should be required to take a specific number of academic credits during each semester of their senior year.

Colleges should include information about freshman placement exams in the admissions information packet sent to applicants.

Colleges should require all applicants to take a test that requires a writing sample. The SAT I and ACT are multiple-choice tests; even the SAT II provides only 20 min for writing (the other 40 min test grammar and mechanics). Some statewide K–12 assessments have a writing sample that could be incorporated into the college admissions process.

Colleges that require math proficiency for college graduation should include a senior-year math course in their admissions requirements. (Many states require only 2 years of math for high-school graduation.)

Colleges and universities should request applicants' scores on statewide subject-matter–based assessments and weigh these scores as a significant factor in admissions and freshman placement. States that appear to have developed appropriate subject matter external exams include Maine, New Hampshire, Pennsylvania, California, New York, and Massachusetts. Unlike the SAT I or ACT Assessment, these tests are curriculum-based by discipline and keyed to the content of specific course sequences (Bishop, 1996, 1997). These exams, therefore, measure a student's academic preparation and achievement relative to an external standard, not relative to other students in the classroom or the school, and they focus students' attention on their coursework. State tests that are focused on minimum competency for graduation and do not have a high ceiling will not be very useful for postsecondary decisions or guidance.

Colleges should explore the feasibility of using student portfolios (authentic assessment) for admissions in lieu of current requirements and thereby create a new currency for higher education admission and placement. The Oregon Proficiency–Based Admissions Standard System (PASS) project has created a promising approach: Oregon PASS trains high school teachers to rate students' writing portfolios and provide scores to college and universities (see chap. 17, this volume, for further discussion of proficiency assessment).

Colleges should widely publicize reports about remediation and the freshman performance of students from specific high schools. Such reports are routinely sent to high schools and central district offices, but they should also be publicized by the mass media and publicly reviewed by local school boards.

Freshman Placement Examinations

Colleges should examine the relationship between their freshman placement exams and K–12 state assessments and standards (see Appendix). This would include whether these assessments that are similar or different with respect to structural and procedural features, content, and cognitive demands (Webb, 1997, 1999). The possible consequences for students from assessments discrepancies needs to be understood. Moreover, placement exams designed by colleges and universities should be reviewed for reliability, validity, and authenticity.

Colleges should inform high-school students of the content, standards, and consequences of the placement exams.

Public colleges and universities should allow students to take placement exams in Grades 11 and 12 and allow them to substitute suitable statewide K–12 assessments for university-devised placement exams. In states that have different placement exams for each university or tier of postsecondary education, content differences should be analyzed to determine whether a common exam is feasible (Impara, 2001).

More fundamental reform could be stimulated by reconceptualizing general education as a project spanning the last 2 years of high school and the first 2 years of college (Adelman, 1992; Clark, 1993). Courses could be sequenced for college-bound students during these 4 years (Orrill, 2000).

CONCLUDING THOUGHTS

The national policy discussion needs to give more emphasis to the admissions practices of the nonselective colleges and universities attended by 80% of the students. The vast majority of media attention is focused on highly selective postsecondary education where completion rates are high (Adelman, 2001). Policies need to shift from a sole concern about access to college to a consideration of access to the preparation needed for success in college. Opening the door is not enough if huge numbers of students are academically unprepared. Over 50% of first-year students begin in remedial classes, and completion rates are too low in broad access institutions. Better signals about standards in postsecondary education would help. This can best be accomplished by joint activities and coherent messages across the K–16 systems (Kettlewell, Kaste, & Jones, 2000).

APPENDIX
THE BRIDGE PROJECT: STRENGTHENING
K–16 TRANSITION POLICIES*

A primary purpose of The Bridge Project is to improve opportunities for all students to enter and succeed in postsecondary education by providing analyses and policy recommendations to increase the connections between postsecondary education admissions- and placement-related requirements and K–12 curriculum frameworks, standards, and assessments. The project, housed at the Stanford Institute for Higher Education Research, is a six-year study funded by the Pew Charitable Trusts with additional funds from the U.S. Department of Education. Project researchers studied 1) the content of K–16 student transition policies, such as postsecondary admissions requirements, placement exams, and remediation policies, and statewide high school assessments, and 2) the ways in which these policies are communicated to, and understood by, stakeholders.

Research was conducted in California, Georgia, Illinois, Maryland, Oregon, and Texas. In those six states, researchers interviewed public university and community college faculty and staff; interviewed K–12 educators and staff; surveyed 9th and 11th graders and their parents; and conducted focus groups with 11th graders and community college students. For more information about the project's research design and methodology, please see the final policy report.

Bridge researchers commissioned researchers at RAND to study the extent to which statewide K–12, college admissions, and college course placement tests are similar and to what extent those assessments differ with respect to structural and procedural features, content, and cognitive demands. This type of analysis is called "categorical concurrence," and is one type of assessment alignment study (Impara, 2001; Webb, 1999 and 1997). The RAND study also examined the implications of the misalignments, focusing on the types of signals students may receive.

The objectives of this study were to describe the degree of alignment among different types of tests in five case study states, and to explore the possible consequences of any discrepancies. Researchers compared assessments used

*Copyright © 2002 RAND. (Reprinted with permission). The work reported herein was supported in part by the Educational Research and Development Center program, agreement number R309A60001, CFDA 84.309A, as administered by the Office of Educational Research and Improvement (OERI), U.S. Department of Education. The findings and opinions expressed in the report do not reflect the position or policies of The Pew Charitable Trusts, OERI, or the U.S. Department of Education.

for college admissions, placement, and K–12 system monitoring and account-ability in each state, classifying items along several dimensions. The report, "Alignment Among Secondary and Postsecondary Assessment in Five Case Study States" (Le, V. and L. Hamilton, 2002), contains summaries of the ways in which the assessments are and are not aligned with one another, and dis-cusses possible implications. (Illinois assessments were not included because the tests were in a state of flux and new exams were not ready when these analyses were conducted.)

It is important to note that RAND researchers defined test alignment as whether or not the test content is aligned with its objectives and specifications. Consequently, the report finds that few misalignments exist because the tests have different purposes. Bridge Project researchers, however, define test align-ment as whether, for example, the content of a high school exit-level exam is compatible with the content of a postsecondary education placement exam. An underlying theory throughout the Bridge Project's work is that academic content at the end of high school and the beginning of college should be closely aligned in order to send clear signals to students and ensure that students are well-prepared for college. Therefore, there is a large difference between the Bridge Project's definition of test alignment, and that of RAND's researchers, which has a bearing on the results of these analyses.

Following are tables excerpted from the report, comparing the content of English/Language Arts and mathematics assessments. Please note that the tables reflect assessment information at the time of the Bridge Project's data collection (1998–1999 in most states) and may not reflect the most current information. Assessment policies in some states are in flux.

Project researchers anticipate that this information will be useful to a vari-ety of audiences, including policymakers and administrators. For example, Oregon's State Department of Education is using the information to help more closely align its 10th grade assessment with what is expected upon entry into Oregon's public university.

Research Design

Purposes of Assessments Examined in this Study

Bridge Project researchers asked RAND to examine four types of assess-ments in this study: state achievement, college admissions, college placement, and end-of-course exams. The tests and their goals are:

- State achievement tests provide a broad survey of student proficiency toward state standards in a particular subject like math or reading.

- College admissions exams sort applicants more qualified for college-level work from those less qualified.
- College placement tests determine which course is most appropriate for students. Some college placement tests are used to identify students who may require additional remediation, whereas other college placement exams are used more broadly to determine which course students are eligible to enroll in, given their prior academic preparation.
- End-of-course tests are measures of knowledge of one particular course.

Because of the magnitude of tests available, it was necessary to limit the number of tests examined in this study. RAND focused its analysis on math and English/Language Arts (ELA) measures administered to high school and incoming first-year college students. Bridge researchers chose math and ELA because most remediation decisions at the postsecondary level are based on achievement deficiencies in these areas.

Because the kinds of tests administered may vary by college, it is important to sample exams from a range of institutions. For each of our sites, researchers examined assessments administered by colleges that represented a range from less selective to highly selective. However, the chosen institutions are not a scientific sample.

National College Admissions Tests Used in Each Case Study Site

The first set of tests RAND examined, which includes the SAT I, SAT II, ACT, and AP exams, are used in five of Bridge's case study sites, as well as nationally, to aid in college admissions decisions. For those students applying to a four-year institution, many are required to take either the SAT I or ACT, and, at more selective schools, several SAT II exams as part of the admissions process.

While AP tests are not a requirement, admissions officers are likely to view students with AP experience as better-prepared and more competitive applicants. Also, students with scores of four or five on AP tests are often rewarded with college credit in the subject area.

The SAT I, a three-hour mostly multiple-choice exam, is intended to help admissions officers distinguish applicants more qualified for college-level work from those less qualified. It is not designed to measure knowledge from any specific high school course, but instead measures general mathematical and verbal reasoning.

The SAT II is a series of one-hour, mostly multiple-choice tests that assess in-depth knowledge of a particular subject, and is used by admissions officers as an additional measure with which to evaluate student subject-matter competence. The SAT II is used primarily at the more selective institutions and is taken by far fewer students than is the SAT I. For this study, RAND examined the following SAT II tests: Mathematics Level IC, Mathematics Level IIC, Literature, and Writing. The SAT II Mathematics Level IC test assesses math knowledge commonly taught in three years of college preparatory math courses, whereas the SAT II Mathematics Level IIC test assesses math knowledge in more than three years of college preparatory math courses. The SAT II Literature test assesses students' proficiency in understanding and interpreting reading passages, and the SAT II Writing test assesses students' knowledge of standard written English.

The ACT is an approximately three-hour exam consisting entirely of multiple-choice items. Developed to be an alternative measure to the SAT I in evaluating applicants' chances of success in college, it does not emphasize general reasoning (as does the SAT I) but is instead a curriculum-based exam that assesses achievement in science, reading, language arts, and math. RAND included only the reading, language arts, and math sections for this study. The AP tests are used to measure college-level achievement in several subjects, and to award academic credit to students who demonstrate college-level proficiency. RAND examined the AP Language and Composition exam for this study. (RAND excluded the two AP exams in calculus—Calculus AB and Calculus BC—because they are markedly different from the other studied math tests. For example, they do not include material from any other mathematical content area except calculus, and are the only measures that require a graphing calculator.)

Analyses are not included here. Rather, this document provides data from RAND's analysis for use by policymakers and researchers interested in relationships between assessments.

Technical Characteristics of Oregon English/Language Arts Assessments

Test	Test Function	Material Examined	Time	Number of Items	Purpose	Reading Section	Editing Section	Essay Section
Certificate of Initial Mastery (CIM) Reading Assessment	state achievement	sample form	No time limit	65 multiple choice reading	monitor student achievement toward specified benchmarks	yes	no	no
Certificate of Initial Mastery Writing Assessment	state achievement	sample writing samples	No time limit	1 open-ended writing	monitor student achievement toward specified benchmarks	no	no	
CIM Locator		full sample form	45 minutes	54 multiple choice reading	identify the appropriate form of CIM to be administered	yes	no	no
ACT	college admissions	full sample form	80 minutes (35 minute reading, 45 minute editing)	115 multiple choice (40 reading, 75 editing)	selection of students for higher education	yes	yes	
AP Language and Composition	college admissions	full sample form	180 minutes (60 minute reading, 120 minute writing)	52 multiple choice; 3 open-ended (1 reading, 2 writing)	provide opportunities for high school students to receive college credit and advanced course placement	yes	no	yes

303

Test	Test Function	Material Examined	Time	Number of Items	Purpose	Reading Section	Editing Section	Essay Section
SAT I	college admissions	full sample form	75 minutes	40 multiple choice reading; 38 multiple choice editing	selection of students for higher education			
SAT II-Literature	college admissions	full sample form	60 minutes	60 multiple choice reading	selection of students for higher education			
SAT II-Writing	college admissions	full sample form	60 minutes (40 minute editing; 20 minute writing)	60 multiple choice editing; 1 open-ended writing	selection of students for higher education	no	yes	
Test of Standard Written English	college placement	full sample form	30 minutes	49 multiple choice editing	evaluate student ability in recognizing standard written English	no	yes	no

Structural Characteristics of Oregon Mathematics Assessments

Test	Framework	Materials Examined	Time	Number of Items	Tools	Purpose	Content as Specified in Test Specifications
Certificate of Initial Mastery (CIM) Mathematics Assessment	state achievement	sample items	No time limit; two session, one each for multiple choice and open-ended	55 multiple choice, one open-ended	calculator	monitor student achievement toward specified benchmarks	calculations and estimations, measurement, statistics and probability, algebraic relationships, and geometry
CIM Locator	state achievement	full sample form	40 minutes	24 multiple choice	calculator	identify the appropriate form of CIM to be administered	calculations and estimations, measurement, statistics and probability, algebraic relationships, and geometry
ACT	college admissions	full sample form	60 minutes	60 multiple choice	calculator	selection of students for higher education	pre-algebra (23%), plane geometry (23%), elementary algebra (17%), intermediate algebra (15%), coordinate geometry (15%), and trigonometry (7%)
SAT I	college admissions	full sample form	75 minutes	35 multiple choice; 15 quantitative comparison; 10 grid-in	calculator	selection of students for higher education	arithmetic (13%), algebra (35%), geometry (26%), and other (26%)

Test	Framework	Materials Examined	Time	Number of Items	Tools	Purpose	Content as Specified in Test Specifications
SAT II-Level IC	college admissions	full sample form		50 multiple choice	calculator	selection of students for higher education	elementary and intermediate algebra (30%), geometry 38% (specifically, plane Euclidean (20%), coordinate (12%), and three-dimensional (6%)), trigonometry (8%), functions (12%), statistics and probability (6%), and miscellaneous (6%)
SAT II-Level IIC	college admissions	full sample form		50 multiple choice	calculator	selection of students for higher education	algebra (18%), geometry 20% (specifically, coordinate (12%) and three-dimensional (8%)), trigonometry (20%), functions (24%), statistics and probability (6%), and miscellaneous (12%)
University of Oregon math placement test	college placement	full sample form		40 multiple choice	calculator	Placement of students into appropriate mathematics course	elementary algebra, intermediate algebra, geometry and trigonometry

Structural Characteristics of Texas English Assessments

Test	Test Function	Material Examined	Time	Number of Items	Purpose	Reading Section	Editing Section	Essay Section
End-of-course exam (English II)	state achievement, end-of-course	full sample form	2 hours	36 multiple choice (18 reading, 18 editing); 2 open-ended reading, 1 open-ended writing	monitor student achievement of state based standards	yes	yes	yes
Texas Assessment of Academic Skills	state achievement	full form, 1998 released exam	no time limit	89 multiple choice (49 reading, 40 editing); 1 open-ended writing	monitor student achievement toward Texas standards	yes	yes	yes
Texas Academic Skills Program	state achievement	full sample form	5 hours	82 multiple choice (42 reading, 40 editing); 1 open-ended writing	assess whether students entering Texas public institutions of higher education possess entry level English skills	yes	yes	yes
ACT	college admissions	full sample form	80 minutes (35 minute reading, 45 minute editing)	40 multiple choice reading; 75 multiple choice editing	selection of students for higher education	yes	yes	no

Test	Test Function	Material Examined	Time	Number of Items	Purpose	Reading Section	Editing Section	Essay Section
AP Language and Compositon	college admissions	full sample form	180 minutes (60 minute reading, 120 minute writing)	52 multiple choice reading; 3 open ended (1 reading, 2 writing)	provide opportunities for high school students to receive college credit and advanced course placement	yes	no	yes
SAT I	college admissions	full sample form	75 minutes	78 multiple choice (40 reading, 38 editing)	selection of students for higher education	yes	yes	no
SAT II–literature	college admissions	full sample form	60 minutes	60 multiple choice reading	selection of students for higher education	yes	no	no
SAT II–writing	college admissions	full sample form	60 minutes (40 minute editing, 20 minute writing)	60 multiple choice editing; 1 open-ended writing	selection of students for higher education	no	yes	yes

Structural Characteristics of Texas Mathematics Assessments

Test	Framework	Materials Examined	Time	Number of Items	Tools	Purpose	Content as Specified in Test Specifications
End-of-course exam (algebra I)	state achievement, end-of-course	full sample form	2 hours	39 multiple choice; 1 grid-in	calculator	monitor student achievement of state-based standards	elementary algebra
Texas Assessment of Academic Skills	state achievement	full sample form	no time limit	60 multiple choice	none	monitor student achievement toward Texas standards	fundamental math, algebra, geometric properties, and problem solving
Texas Academic Skills Program	state achievement	full sample form	5 hours total testing time	48 multiple choice	none	assess whether students entering Texas public institutions of higher education possess entry level math skills	fundamental math, algebra, geometric properties, and problem solving
ACT	college admissions	full sample form	60 minutes	60 multiple choice	calculator	selection of students for higher education	pre-algebra (23%), elementary algebra (17%), intermediate algebra (15%), coordinate geometry (15%), plane geometry (23%), and trigonometry (7%)
SAT I	college admissions	full sample form	75 minutes	35 multiple choice; 15 quantitative comparison; 10 grid-in	calculator	selection of students for higher education	arithmetic (13%), algebra (35%), geometry (26%), and other (26%)

Test	Framework	Materials Examined	Time	Number of Items	Tools	Purpose	Content as Specified in Test Specifications
SAT II-level IC	college admissions	full sample form	60 minutes	50 multiple choice	calculator	selection of students for higher education	elementary and intermediate algebra (30%), geometry 38% (specifically, plane Euclidean (20%), coordinate (12%), and three-dimensional (6%)), trigonometry (8%), functions (12%), statistics and probability (6%), and miscellaneous (6%)
SAT II-Level IIC	college admissions	full sample form	60 minutes	50 multiple choice	calculator	selection of students for higher education	algebra (18%), geometry 20% (specifically, coordinate (12%) and three-dimensional (8%)), trigonometry (20%), functions (24%), statistics and probability (6%), and miscellaneous (12%)
Descriptive Tests of Mathematical Skills in Elementary Algebra	College placement	full sample form	30 minutes	35 multiple choice	none	Assess student readiness for geometry	real numbers, algebraic expressions, equations and inequalities, algebraic operations, data interpretation

REFERENCES

Abraham, A. (1992). *College remedial studies.* Atlanta, GA: Southern Regional Education Board.

Adelman, C. (1992). *Tourists in our own land: Cultural literacies and the college curriculum.* Washington, DC: U.S. Department of Education.

Adelman, C. (1999). *Inside the tool box.* Washington, DC: U.S. Department of Education.

Adelman, C. (2001). Putting on the glitz. *New England Journal of Higher Education 15* (3), 24–30.

Bishop, J. (1996). Signaling, incentives, and school organization in France, the Netherlands, Britain, and the United States. In E. Hanushek & D. Jorgenson (Eds.), *Improving America's schools* (pp. 111–145). Washington, DC: National Academy Press.

Bishop, J. (1997, April). *The effect of national standard and curriculum-based exams on achievement.* Paper presented at the American Economic Association Meeting, New Orleans.

Burr, E., Kirst, M., & Fuller, B. (Eds.). (2000). *Crucial issues in California education 2000.* Berkeley, CA: Policy Analysis for California Education.

Clark, B. (1985). *The school and the university.* Berkeley: University of California Press.

Clark, B. (1993). *The problem of complexity in modern higher education.* Cambridge, England: Cambridge University Press.

Education Trust. (1999). Ticket to nowhere: The gap between leaving high school and entering college and high-performance jobs. In *Thinking K–16 Series, 3* (1). Washington, DC: Author.

Hopwood v. State of Texas, 78 F. 3d. 932 (5th Cir. 1996).

Impara, J. C. (2001, April). *Alignment: One element of an assessment's instructional utility.* Paper presented at annual meeting of the National Council on Measurement in Education. Seattle, WA.

Kettlewell, J. S., Kaste, J. A., & Jones, S. A. (2000). Autonomous boards and standards-based teacher development: The Georgia story of P–16 partnerships. In K. S. Gallagher & J. D. Bailey (Eds.), *The politics of teacher education reform: The National Commission on Teaching and America's Future.* Thousand Oaks, CA: Corwin.

Kirst, M., Spivey D., & Contreras, F. (2001). *Admission and placement policies in two Illinois universities: Phase I case study, 1997.* Stanford, CA: The Bridge Project, Stanford Institute for Higher Education Research.

Kirst, M., & Venezia, A. (2003). *Betraying the college dream.* Stanford, CA: Stanford Institute for Higher Education Research.

Lavin, D. E. (2000). Policy change and access to two and four year colleges. *American Behavioral Scientist, 3* (7), 1155.

Le, V., & Hamilton, L. (2002). *Alignment among secondary and postsecondary assessments in five case study states* (MR–1554-Edu). Santa Monica, CA: Rand Corporation.

Lichten, W. (2000). Whither advanced placement? *Education Policy Analysis Archives* 8 (29), June 24, 2000. Retrieved January 7, 2003, from http://epaa.asu.edu/epaa/v8n29.html

McCormick, A. C. (Ed.). (2001). *The Carnegie classification of institutions of higher education, 2000 edition.* Menlo Park, CA: The Carnegie Foundation for the Advancement of Teaching.

Orrill, R. (2000). *Grades 11–14: The heartland or wasteland of American education.* Unpublished paper, Washington, DC, Woodrow Wilson National Fellowship Foundation.

Portner, J. (2002, November 11). UC will check applicant claims. *San Jose Mercury News,* p. 1.

Rodriguez, E., & Johnson, S. (2003, January 24). Report says university enrollment gap grew after law enacted. *Austin American Statesman,* p. 1.

Rosenbaum, J. (2001). *Beyond college for all.* New York: Russell Sage.

Shaw, L. (2002, November 28). 10th grade exam harder than college test? *Seattle Times,* p. 3.

Stocking, C. (1985). The United States. In B. R. Clark (Ed.), *The school and the university* (pp. 185–201). Berkeley: University of California Press.

United States Department of Education. (2001). *Condition of education 2001.* Washington, DC: U.S. Government Printing Office.

University of California, Board of Admissions. (2002). *First-year implementation of comprehensive review in freshmen activities.* Oakland: University of California.

Webb, N. (1997). *Criteria for alignment of expectations and assessments in Mathematics and Science education* [Research Monograph 6]. National Institute for Science Education. Madison: University of Wisconsin.

Webb, N. (1999). *Alignment of science and mathematics standards and assessments in four states* [Research Monograph 18]. National Institute for Science Foundation. Madison: University of Wisconsin.

17

Proficiency-Based Admissions

David T. Conley
University of Oregon

A proficiency-based admissions system determines college readiness by using a set of academic content standards and criteria as a framework for analyzing data from criterion-referenced tests and classroom-based assessments of student work. This approach has the potential to capture more directly student mastery of academic content knowledge and cognitive skills. Students and teachers can identify weaknesses more clearly and direct their time and energy to tasks that prepare students for college success. The potential advantage of this method is that student readiness for postsecondary education can be ascertained with greater accuracy, provided the assessments are based on the knowledge and skills needed to succeed in entry-level college classes. The result is better data for admissions officers and better preparation for college-bound students, leading to better performance in college.

Proficiency-based admissions systems and strategies came into being in response to state-initiated reforms that affected high schools. The primary elements of the reforms were academic content standards and accompanying assessments that specified what students should know and be able to do. The implications of these reforms were not immediately apparent to the higher education community, in part because the reforms were perceived to be directed at workforce preparation (Conley, 1996). The assumption held by many college and university personnel was that college preparation would continue more or less the same and that state reforms would simply mean high-school students would be taking yet another test, one that college-bound students would, in any event, be able to pass.

This assumption was not entirely groundless. At least some research suggests that state high school tests do not result in improved student scores on measures such as the SAT, ACT, or AP tests (Amrein & Berliner, 2002). In a number of states, however, standards and assessments have been set at a higher, more challenging level or the tests are used to determine if schools meet state accountability requirements. High school teachers have responded by focusing their curriculum more on these tests (Firestone, Mayrowetz, & Fairman, 1998; Olson, 2002; Viadero, 2003). Standards and assessments of this type can, and often do, have an effect on high school organization and instruction, including the college preparation portion of the curriculum (Olson, 2001). Conceivably, the scores on at least some state assessments could be of use in the admissions process—*if* the assessments measure the knowledge and skills needed for post-secondary success.

A way is needed to connect the effort and energy devoted to meeting state standards with the tangible goal and reward of college admission. A proficiency-based admission system can provide this connection. Such a system can help ensure that secondary and postsecondary education do not define and measure student success in divergent ways. When students receive clear, consistent signals about what they should be doing in high school to succeed in college, they have more opportunities to prepare appropriately (Venezia, Kirst, & Antonio, 2003).

WHAT IS A PROFICIENCY-BASED
ADMISSION STANDARDS SYSTEM?

A *proficiency-based admissions system* has several key characteristics. First, it identifies the content knowledge students must master in various academic disciplines to be ready to succeed in college. This requires postsecondary educators to take stock of what they are actually requiring in entry-level college courses. What knowledge and skills are really necessary as a prerequisite to success in the first year of college? Developing such a list can be a time-consuming and agonizing process. If the skills are to be incorporated into state high-school standards and tests, the process must occur in partnership with state education departments as well.

Once standards are developed, the difficult task of determining the degree of concurrence that exists between high-school and college expectations begins. Given that the high-school standards have, in every state, been developed and adopted first, the higher education standards are in essence "backward mapped" onto existing high school content standards. Assuming a reasonable alignment is found to exist, the framework for a proficiency-based system is in place.

Alignment may conceivably be facilitated by the work of national organizations that developed content standards in various disciplines. To the degree to which the national content organization standards are consistent with postsecondary expectations, some alignment may already exist, because many states have referenced these standards as they developed their own. Notable examples include the standards developed by the National Council of Teachers of Mathematics (1991), the Project 2061, American Association for the Advancement of Science (1993), the National Council of Teachers of English (1996), and the American Council on the Teaching of Foreign Language (1996).

HOW IS PROFICIENCY ASSESSED?

Standards alone, however, tell nothing about what a student knows. An assessment system is required to yield that information. Thirty-five states had some sort of high school assessment in place at the time the federal No Child Left Behind Act of 2001 was passed (Education Week, 2001). By 2004, all states are required to have a high-school level test in Grade 10, Grade 11, or Grade 12 (U.S. Department of Education, 2001). The nature of state high school tests varies, but most are multiple-choice instruments keyed to the state's standards. Twenty-four are tied to high-school graduation (Education Commission of the States [ECS] Information Clearinghouse, 2000).

A dialog between secondary and postsecondary education regarding the data needed to inform college admission decisions and the best ways to measure potential college performance can lead to better admissions decisions and improvements in state high-school testing systems. For example, end-of-course examinations, in use or development by a dozen states (Olson, 2001), can serve to create a stronger, more direct connection between what is learned in high school and what is expected in college or provide data for college placement decisions.

The degree to which assessment results have real value and meaning will be the degree to which many students take such tests seriously. This is a particularly important consideration in states where test results are used as elements of an accountability system in which a high school could be rewarded or punished based on test score results (Viadero, 2003). Creating real reasons to do well on tests helps motivate students, but it also means tests must connect well with postsecondary education expectations.

A proficiency-based admissions system opens the door for the use of classroom-based assessment data. Up until now, course grades have been the most direct information admissions officers have had on student performance in the classroom. However, teacher grading criteria and practices vary tremendously within schools and across schools (McMillan, 2001), as do the challenge levels of courses. Teachers and admissions officers do not necessarily agree on the meaning of high-school grades (Baron, 2000). Comparisons of students' grades to their performance on standardized tests demonstrates the differences that exist in grading practices, particularly between urban and suburban schools (Office of Educational Research and Improvement, 1994). The inconsistent relationship among performance on the National Assessment of Educational Progress, grade received in class, and school location (urban or suburban) is only one illustration of this phenomenon (Roey et al., 2001). (See chap. 6, this volume, for a discussion of the role of grades.)

Content-based tests, such as AP, potentially offer additional insight into what is learned in classrooms, although teachers vary considerably in terms of the degree to which they actually teach to the test (National Research Council, 2002). A study on the relationship between performance on AP tests and on the SAT provides indirect evidence of the potential value of connecting classroom instruction to assessment. The results of a post-hoc quasi-experimental study that compared the SAT scores of 53 students who were enrolled in at least one AP course at the time of the study with 58 otherwise comparable students who were not, found that students enrolled in the AP courses had significantly higher verbal, quantitative, and composite SAT scores (L. M. Thomas & S. G. Thomas, 2000). If teachers can be encouraged to focus on criteria related to college success and students are tested with instruments closely tied to classroom instruction, students benefit.

The key potential benefit of a proficiency-based admissions system is the ability to utilize collections of evidence derived from student work in the classroom. Class assignments, tests, reports, research papers, and projects are used to demonstrate mastery of specific proficiencies. Within mathematics, for example, students may be required to collect examples of work that demonstrate proficiency on 7 to 10 standards. Some tasks, such as a particularly complex problem solving assignment, can provide evidence on more than one standard.

Teachers employ standardized sets of performance criteria to judge these collections. Student performance is rated on a multipoint scale. The ratings are entered for all proficiency standards to create a profile of college readiness that an admissions officer can then interpret. The 5-point scale employed by Oregon's Proficiency-Based Admission Standards System (PASS; Oregon University System, 2001) is a representative example of such scales. The PASS scale consists of the following levels:

- *Exemplary.* The collection demonstrates exemplary mastery and exhibits exceptional intellectual maturity or unique thinking, methods, or talents.
- *High-level mastery.* The collection demonstrates mastery at a level higher than entry-level college coursework.
- *Meets the standard.* The collection demonstrates that the student is prepared for entry-level college coursework.
- *Working toward the standard.* The collection approaches readiness for entry-level college coursework. The level of performance may be improved by:
    providing data from a broader variety of assessments;
    providing additional evidence that addresses the range of criteria;
    enrolling in more classes that teach to the standard being assessed.
- *Does not meet the standard.* The collection contains evidence that the student is not prepared to do entry-level college coursework.

A scale of this nature differentiates clearly between student performance that is at a level necessary to succeed in college and that which is not. The most important judgment on the rating scale is the distinction between *Meets the standard* and *Working toward the standard.* The pool of students eligible for admission should consist of those who meet or exceed the standard of college readiness on all measures. Those who meet some standards and are working toward others merit a close review. Some postsecondary institutions may opt to convert the scores into numerical ratings, sum the ratings, and set a cut score that a student must exceed. Others may choose to expect students to be proficient on all the standards within disciplinary areas aligned with their proposed major, but allow more latitude in other areas. Students who do not demonstrate proficiency on all standards can be granted conditional admission and then receive remedial assistance or have their access to particular courses or majors limited until they achieved acceptable grades in entry-level university courses.

The higher levels on the scale, *High-level mastery* and *Exemplary,* can be used to place students, waive particular requirements, make merit-based financial-aid decisions, or grant college credit. Because these uses represent higher stakes decisions, such ratings must be verified externally. This means that even though the classroom teacher may score a collection as being *Exemplary,* raters external to the classroom review the teacher's rating and either confirm or modify it. More selective institutions could look for students who exhibit high-level mastery or are exemplary in multiple areas. The proficiency scale is designed with the idea that most students receive the score of *Meets the Standard,* while a very few, perhaps 5%, receive a score of *Exemplary.* The high standards of the *Exemplary* level helps admissions officers at competitive-admissions institutions identify the most talented students.

Proficiency profiles can incorporate student scores on state tests. These are converted into the proficiency system's numeric scale score. An admissions officer can then tell something about a student's proficiency level relative to state standards. This holds true for multiple-choice tests; performance tasks, such as writing assessments; and end-of-course examinations. Scores on other standards-based tests, for example, AP, the International Baccalaureate Diploma Programme®,[1] and SAT II, can also be converted into numeric scores on the proficiency scale.

In this fashion, the profile of proficiency provides scaled information about what students know and are able to do. The ratings are potentially more reliable and consistent than grades because they are based on standards that are common statewide. Teachers and admissions officers agree on their meaning and on the type of student work associated with each proficiency level. This information comes to the admissions office in a manageable form, a profile of ratings, not an unmanageable portfolio of student work. The profile, though, reflects an underlying portfolio—the test scores and collections of evidence—which is not transmitted to the college. The admissions officer gains the advantage of a measure of student performance across a broad range of academic tasks without the disadvantage of trying to evaluate student work directly.

VALIDITY ADVANTAGES, RELIABILITY ISSUES

Validity has been the Achilles heel of standardized testing generally and of aptitude-based college admissions tests specifically. The primary strength of a

---

[1] International Baccalaureate Diploma Programme® is a registered trademark of the International Baccalaureate Organization.

proficiency-based admissions system is its high content validity. The fact that the standards are developed in part or entirely by higher education faculty helps ensure that what is to be measured is important to success in postsecondary education. Validity is also heightened by the more direct connection to the taught curriculum provided by the classroom-based collections of evidence. The proficiency-based assessment system also tends to oversample some key skills for college success, such as writing and problem solving, thereby further heightening validity.

If content validity is high, the potential to increase predictive validity is strengthened. When high school courses consciously develop skills that are critical to college success, it is logical to assume that achievement in such courses will be more predictive of college performance than achievement in classes that may not emphasize as thoroughly the skills needed to do well in postsecondary education. As Adelman (1999) noted, the challenge level of high-school courses is the most important correlate of college success.

How, then, does a system whose strength is validity cope with reliability issues, the most basic of which is whether the reliability of the proficiency judgments are sufficient to make decisions about individuals? The reliability of the teachers' ratings of students' collections of evidence demands close attention, for technical reasons, but also because admissions officers and higher education faculty can be expected to be skeptical of teachers' ability and willingness to score collections accurately. How can teacher ratings be made consistent and how can the pressure to inflate student ratings be held in check?

The necessary prerequisite to reliable ratings is that teachers embed into their teaching and classroom-based assessments the proficiency standards and criteria, which they then rate with common scoring guides, or rubrics. Evidence suggests that concepts and terminology from scoring guides become deeply embedded in classroom instruction, teacher talk, and even student expectations (Hillocks, 2002). Teachers and students develop mental models of the work necessary to meet the standard.

Reliable scoring of student work requires considerable teacher training. Such training can be connected to the type of professional development taking place in many states to enable teachers to interpret state standards accurately (Fuhrman, 2001). At least 12 states have writing assessments that require the scoring of student work (Council of Chief State School Officers, 2001). A similar number utilize performance tasks, such as writing or math problem solving, which are scored against common standards. State standards and assessment training can be designed to include scoring of student work collections. Evidence from trainings conducted by Oregon's PASS suggests teachers can reach very high rating reliability levels after a relatively short period of training (M. Endsley, personal communication, February, 2003). PASS has developed online training and scoring exercises that enable teachers to reach acceptable levels of reliability quickly in a cost-effective fashion and in some cases to use one set of scoring guides for both state assessment and proficiency-based admissions requirements.

A second piece in the reliability puzzle is the moderation panel (Baker, O'Neil, & Linn, 1993; Gipps, 1994). Moderation panels are composed of teachers and postsecondary faculty with particular knowledge and expertise in using proficiency standards to score collections of evidence. Schools submit previously rated collections of evidence as directed by the moderation panels. The panel then re-scores the collections. When scores given by the teacher or teachers submitting the collections and those of the moderation panel members differ too greatly, this suggests the need for additional teacher training, online or with colleagues at the school site. Moderation panels are also called on to review collections of evidence that teachers have rated at the *High-level mastery* and *Exemplary* levels. Moderation of college-bound student work has been employed successfully with high reliability in Victoria and Queensland, Australia, for over 15 years (Masters & McBryde, 1994).

The accuracy of school-level judgments can also be inferred by comparing the average score of school-level ratings of collections to average school performance on state or national standardized tests. If there are significant differences between the average of teacher ratings of collections in a particular school and the average ratings from high schools with similar scores on state and national tests, this suggests that the teachers in that school are not following the standards consistently. This can be confirmed by having teachers from the school in question submit more collections of evidence to moderation panels. Similarly, admissions offices can combine scores on state standards-based tests with scores on student work collections to create an approximation of the AP assessment strategy of merging scores on a multiple-choice test and a student work sample to generate one overall score on a 1–5 scale.

In the final analysis, teacher judgments are unlikely to rival the reliability of standardized tests anytime soon. It is worth bearing in mind, however, that many current measures with high reliability have been used inappropriately. Incremental score differentials on the ACT Assessment and SAT I are known not to represent significant differences in potential to succeed in college, yet in some cases admissions decisions hinge on these small differentials. High reliability in this context does not necessarily serve to improve the quality of the decision made or the student admitted.

HISTORICALLY UNDERREPRESENTED STUDENTS

Can a proficiency-based admission system increase the proportion of students from historically underrepresented groups who are admitted to college? This important question must be answered: "It depends." If a proficiency-based system includes student work collections or if a state test is aligned with college readiness criteria, it is possible to identify students who demonstrate relatively higher mastery of the knowledge and skills associated with college success. Assuming classroom instruction is aligned with the collections of evidence and tests, these students have demonstrated the ability to learn the taught curriculum. Even if their scores are not as high by an absolute measure, the fact that they do well on indicators that are aligned with the taught curriculum in high school suggests they may have a good chance of mastering the taught curriculum at the university level, as well.

Collections of evidence also serve as an alternative means for students who do not perform well on standardized tests to demonstrate their skills and competence. Classroom-based assessments of a range of student work may provide a better indication of a student's skills because they represent multiple measures over time. Students with successful collections of evidence have clearly worked to achieve the proficiency standards. The collections demonstrate attentiveness to what is expected and the ability to follow through to produce a body of work that demonstrates achievement. These are desirable attributes that can help students from underrepresented groups show they have the capacity to succeed in college.

Continuing to rely on inflated GPAs creates its own set of problems for students from underrepresented groups. Many of these students are subjected to grading practices that lead them to believe they are better prepared for college than they actually are. The disparity between what an A means in a suburban high school and what it means in an urban environment can be so great that students from urban schools can find themselves poorly equipped to cope with the more challenging standards, expectations, and grading criteria they encounter in college. A proficiency-based system makes it much clearer to students in high school what is actually expected in college and where a student stands in relation to those expectations.

OPERATIONAL AND POLICY CHALLENGES OF PBA

The preceding sections have examined the components of and rationale for a proficiency-based admissions system. This section considers the important operational and policy challenges involved in implementing such a radically different approach.

A proficiency approach almost certainly must be incorporated into state-level policy. It not reasonable for an individual postsecondary institution to expect students and teachers to produce collections of evidence for that institution alone, nor would an individual college want to create the scales necessary to interpret state and national test results. High-school–college collaboration at a state level is required to develop academic content standards that align across high school and college, to agree on compatible assessment methods, and to set up the means to moderate teacher judgments.

Further complicating the articulation between high school and college are a host of practical and policy issues. Who is to pay for this intersegmental program when funds are generally allocated either to K–12 or to postsecondary budgets? Should K–12 or higher education pay to train high school teachers to score student work for higher education admission purposes? Who organizes, funds, and controls the moderation panels when they are composed of high-school and postsecondary faculty? Should higher education be responsible for paying for the process of adapting state high-school assessments to make them more useful for admissions purposes? Who informs parents about proficiency requirements and procedures?

Collecting, transmitting, and processing proficiency information presents its own set of challenges. The high-school transcript has to be revised to accommodate proficiency scores and state test scores. High schools must determine who is responsible for recording proficiency information when a collection of evidence contains work from several classes. Colleges must determine how proficiency scores are entered into their data tables and what decision rules to use to sort and categorize applicants. At the very least, software must be adapted and staff trained. Privacy laws may severely restrict the use of the common student identification numbers necessary for test score data to be transmitted efficiently from state education departments to postsecondary institutions. For some period of time and perhaps indefinitely, high-school teachers and counselors, as well as admissions officers, will be expected to work with a hybrid system that contains traditional information on courses and grades alongside proficiency information. It takes time to develop the type of familiarity and comfort with proficiency scores and profiles that teachers, counselors, and admissions personnel have with course titles and grades.

It can take from 4 to 8 years to conduct the necessary predictive validity studies to determine the effects of proficiency-based admissions. During that period, many decisions must be made based on inferential data, anecdote, and informed opinion. Although pilot programs and concurrent validity studies can help alleviate some of this uncertainty and unpredictability, nothing can eliminate a period of time during which the proficiency-based system suffers from what Fullan and Stiegelbauer (1991) referred to as the *implementation dip*, that period of time when a new system is less efficient than the one it replaces, regardless of any potential it may have to be better eventually. Weathering this storm requires substantial commitment from policymakers and educational leaders in both secondary and higher education institutions.

A surprising but perhaps not altogether unexpected challenge is the reluctance of high-school teachers to adopt any new method for grading student work. Although proficiency-based systems create a way for teacher judgments to be comparable in importance to state tests and offer a powerful alternative to "teaching to the test," not all teachers perceive this potential benefit. High-school teachers accustomed to making their own decisions about what constitutes adequate performance in their classes may see little to be gained by surrendering their autonomy to serve the higher education system. Many argue that they are not obliged to be involved in making admissions decisions, that this should be left to higher education, and, in any event, not all students in their classes are going on to college. From the perspective of at least some teachers, replacing grades with proficiencies may seem to provide little benefit—and a lot more work.

Admissions directors have their own set of valid concerns. In addition to logistical challenges already discussed, they may simply not believe that the current system is broken, at least not to the point where it needs an overhaul of this magnitude. The incoming freshman class looks better on paper each year. GPAs and college admission test scores have been improving, the proportion of students taking college preparation programs in high school is increasing, and projections of undergraduate enrollment show steady growth ahead (National Center for Education Statistics, 2001). In short, times are relatively good. Why undertake major changes now?

Other practical issues confront the admissions office. Will this system require more personnel to process transcripts? Will college faculty readily consent to the use of proficiency data for placement purposes? Are students admitted via proficiency really any better prepared? How will the institution treat out-of-state applicants, home-schoolers, international students, and others who lack evidence of proficiency? How should GPA and proficiency scores be combined or weighted?

Although many of these challenges may turn out to be manageable, their magnitude is sufficient to discourage many from embarking on what can only be described as systemic change. In light of the complexity and difficulty of changing admissions policy and procedures, it is all the more remarkable that a number of states have already undertaken some form of a proficiency model. The continuum of approaches ranges from a complete statewide model to more limited pilots, to the alignment of state exams with college admissions standards. The next section offers a brief overview of these efforts.

CURRENT EXPERIMENTS IN PROFICIENCY-BASED ADMISSION

At least six states have made a serious attempt to connect high-school standards-based reforms and college admission. These are Wisconsin, Oregon, Georgia, Maryland, Texas, and California. A full treatment of each is beyond the scope of this chapter, and, in any event, the policies and procedures in these states are continuing to evolve. They are presented here more as "proof of concept" than as mature, stable policy models.

Wisconsin

The University of Wisconsin system launched the Competency-Based Admissions program in 1993. University faculty developed a set of competency standards. High-school faculty members at eight pilot sites used the competency standards to rate the academic performance of each student at their school who was applying to a University of Wisconsin campus. Judgments were based on a student's accumulated work, and were made at a specially convened meeting of faculty by academic department. Students received a score of one to four for each competency within each discipline. Scores were recorded on a Competency Profile.

Wisconsin's experiment is particularly noteworthy because the university system agreed to admit students from the pilot high schools on the basis of either grades or competency scores. Over the 3-year period of the pilot, the university system was able to accumulate data on students and to compare those admitted via competency with those admitted on traditional measures.

In 79% of the cases, the decision reached by admissions officials based on the standard transcript plus ACT score was identical to the decision reached from the independent analysis of the Supplemental Reporting Profile (SRP) plus ACT score. In 67% of the cases, the student was admitted by both processes; in 12% of the cases, the student was denied by both processes. The remaining 21% of the students were admitted by one process, but not both: 13% were admitted by transcript alone, 8% by SRP alone (Garb, 1998).

SRP scores correlated more closely with ACT subject scores than did high-school grades in English, science, and on an overall basis. Analysis of the freshman-year performance of the first year's applicants established that competency scores provided by the high-school teachers were as effective in predicting first-semester performance as traditional admission criteria such as high-school grades, rank in class, and ACT score. Second semester data and third semester data found that students admitted via competency were retained at a slightly higher rate and had a slightly higher GPA than those admitted by grades alone. A separate study of the time it took admissions officers to make a decision using a traditional transcript versus the SRP found that admissions officers took twice as long with the SRP the first year and the same amount of time as a traditional transcript the second year (Garb, 1998).

The competency-based option is still available to Wisconsin students, but few high schools have continued to provide student competency scores after funding for the pilot concluded. This illustrates the difficulty of sustaining this type of approach when only higher education is sponsoring it.

Oregon

Oregon's efforts began around the same time as Wisconsin's and followed a somewhat different path. Whereas Wisconsin's program was undertaken in anticipation of standards-based high-school reform, Oregon's was conceived in response to reforms adopted by the state legislature in 1991. Oregon college and high-school faculty jointly developed, in six subject areas, a comprehensive set of proficiencies that incoming students were expected to meet. Proficiency was measured by state test scores; state assessment tasks, such as math problem solving or a writing sample; and collections of student work scored using common criteria statewide. The Oregon PASS grew to include over 50 pilot high schools enrolling 40% of the state's high-school students. As in the case of Wisconsin, when the funds for pilot programs ended, involvement declined. Current plans call for full implementation of proficiency standards in 2005 in concert with the high-school-level Certificate of Advanced Mastery, one of the original elements of the state's school reform program.

Evidence is still being collected on students admitted on the basis of the proficiency assessment. Previous studies compared scores on collections of student work with grades received in class (Conley, 2000). These yielded correlations in the .45 to .54 range. This suggests that proficiency scores are measuring something related to but not the same as grades. The finding that there was very little relationship between teachers' grading practices and their students' proficiency scores reinforces this conclusion.

Correlations between proficiency scores and performance on state multiple-choice tests in reading and math were .21 and .32, respectively. The correlation between test score and the grade received in the English and math classes in which the student was concurrently enrolled was .50 for both tests. Here again, the classroom-based proficiency scores appear to be measuring something somewhat different than the state tests. This raises the possibility that measures of this nature focused on classroom work can identify students who do well when asked to address a clear expectation related to content knowledge, but may do less well on a test or with a grading system that includes many elements not directly related to knowledge of subject matter.

In 2001, the Oregon University System awarded over 300 scholarships to entering freshmen who had demonstrated proficiency while in high school. These students along with 6,000 other Oregon University System students who took state assessments while in high school are currently being tracked through their second year of college. Initial findings suggest scores on state Grade 10 tests correlate at least as well with students' freshman year college performance 2 years later as do SAT or ACT scores (Oregon University System, Oregon Department of Education, and Oregon Department of Community Colleges and Workforce Development, 2003). PASS continues as a voluntary means for students to be admitted to the state's seven public universities in anticipation of fuller implementation of state high school reform programs.

Georgia

Since 1996, Georgia has been developing and piloting Performance Assessment for Colleges and Technical Schools (PACTS) as a standards-based system for admission into participating technical and 2-year colleges and universities (University System of Georgia, 2002). Local P–16 councils developed content and performance standards in six content areas, which were then adapted for college admission purposes by teams composed of high-school teachers, technical school faculty, and representatives from 2-year colleges, universities, and the business community. Students demonstrate proficiency through collections of classroom work, which are scored on a 4-point scale. For scores to count for college admission, a verification committee must rate them independently. The first students eligible were admitted via PACTS standards in fall, 2003. Seventeen Georgia colleges and universities will accept PACTS transcripts that also include traditional measures. The project is being piloted in five high schools.

Maryland

Maryland is representative of states that have adopted end-of-course examinations as high-school graduation requirements. The Maryland exams test student knowledge in English I, government, algebra/data analysis, geometry, and biology. The tests contain multiple-choice questions and items requiring written responses and are based on the content outlined in Maryland's Core Learning Goals (Shapiro & Haeger, 1999). Beginning in early 1990s, Maryland brought together high-school and postsecondary educators to develop the standards for these exams with the goal of using the results for placement purposes, at the least. These exams offer a source of data on student proficiency, although they fall short of a proficiency-based admissions system.

"Bridge Goals" specify the elements of courses that will prepare students to enter credit-bearing college courses. Colleges in the state are committed to taking the end-of-course assessments into consideration when they review applications, but considerable variation exists among postsecondary institutions in terms of how they use test results. Postsecondary faculty also defined what constitutes a C paper at Maryland postsecondary institutions. Such a definition helps secondary schools understand more specifically the level of performance students must demonstrate in college.

California and Texas

Both states have undertaken to develop tests that will simultaneously determine if students meet state standards and contribute information to college admissions and placement decisions. This approach represents a model that may predominate eventually, where one test serves two purposes. Such a test will efficiently align high school and college. This approach does sacrifice teacher judgment, as described in the collection of evidence methodology. The tests also tend to drive the curriculum away from key college success skills, such as research and writing, problem solving, sustained inquiry, and analysis of complex issues. They are, however, efficient and easily incorporated into traditional admissions models.

THE FUTURE OF PROFICIENCY-BASED ADMISSION STANDARDS SYSTEMS

The future of proficiency-based admissions depends in large measure on how state assessment systems develop. The federal No Child Left Behind (NCLB) Act (2001) requires states without a high school-level assessment to introduce one. NCLB regulations push states strongly in the direction of multiple-choice tests. The question is how much influence state high-school assessments will have on the high-school curriculum. If states choose multiple-choice tests that assess basic knowledge and skills, and if these assessments begin to reshape the high-school curriculum, fewer students may end up developing many of the skills needed for college success, such as writing, reasoning, and critical thinking.

The skills for college success have been detailed in a study of over 400 faculty members and administrators from Association of American Universities member institutions (Conley, 2003). The Knowledge and Skills for University Success standards represent the first comprehensive statement of what students must do to succeed in entry-level university courses. These standards can help inform the content of state tests and proficiency-based college admissions systems as well as the focus of the high school curriculum for schools that wish to prepare students better for college success.

THINKING IN TERMS OF ONE SYSTEM

The future of proficiency-based admissions systems will depend in large measure on the degree to which states seek to align secondary and postsecondary education. If states begin to think in terms of one educational system rather than two, the idea of creating a continuous set of learner expectations will be increasingly appealing. At a time when over 65% of today's students go on to some form of postsecondary education directly out of high school and the proportion of students who matriculate continues to increase (National Center for Education Statistics, 2001), the pressure to ensure that the high-school curriculum prepares students for college will likely grow, as well. Whether state standards-based reforms will prepare more students for college will depend to a significant degree on how well the two education systems, secondary and postsecondary, coordinate their expectations and measures of student success. Proficiency-based admissions systems are a means to achieving greater coordination in ways that will likely lead to more students experiencing greater success in postsecondary education.

REFERENCES

Adelman, C. (1999). *Answers in the tool box: Academic intensity, attendance patterns, and bachelor's degree attainment.* Jessup, MD: Education Publishing Center, U.S. Department of Education.

American Council on the Teaching of Foreign Languages. (1996). *Standards for foreign language learning.* Yonkers, NY: Author.

Amrein, A. L., & Berliner, D. C. (2002). *The impact of high-stakes tests on student aca-*

demic performance: An analysis of NAEP results in states with high-stakes tests and ACT, SAT, and AP test results in states with high school graduation exams. Tempe: Arizona State University, Education Policy Research Unit.

Baker, E. L., O'Neil, H. F., & Linn, R. L. (1993). Policy and validity prospects for performance-based assessment. *American Psychologist, 48* (12), 1210–1218.

Baron, P. A. B. (2000, April). *Consequential validity for high school grades: What is the meaning of grades for senders and receivers?* Paper presented at the Annual Meeting of the American Educational Research Association, New Orleans, LA.

Conley, D. T. (1996). Where's Waldo? The conspicuous absence of higher education from school reform and one state's response. *Phi Delta Kappan, 78,* 309–314.

Conley, D. T. (2000, April). *Who is proficient: The relationship between proficiency scores and grades.* Paper presented at the Annual Meeting of the American Educational Research Association, New Orleans, LA.

Conley, D. T. (2003). *Understanding university success.* Eugene: University of Oregon, Center for Educational Policy Research.

Council of Chief State School Officers. (2001). *Annual survey of state student assessment programs.* Washington, DC: Author.

Education Commission of the States (ECS) Information Clearinghouse. (2000). Many states tie high school diploma to exams. *State Education Leader, 18* (3), 1–3.

Education Week. (2001). *Quality counts: A better balance: Standards, tests, and the tools to succeed.* Washington, DC: Author.

Firestone, W. A., Mayrowetz, D., & Fairman, J. (1998). Performance-based assessment and instructional change: The effects of testing in Maine and Maryland. *Educational Evaluation and Policy Analysis, 20* (2), 95.

Fuhrman, S. H. (Ed.). (2001). *From the capitol to the classroom: Standards-based reform in the states.* Chicago: The University of Chicago Press.

Fullan, M., & Stiegelbauer, S. (1991). *The new meaning of educational change* (2nd ed.). New York: Teachers College Press.

Garb, F. (1998). *University of Wisconsin Competency Based Admissions pilot project spring 1998: Final report.* Madison: University of Wisconsin System.

Gipps, C. V. (1994). *Beyond testing: Towards a theory of educational assessment.* London: Falmer.

Hillocks, G., Jr. (2002). *The testing trap: How state writing assessments control learning.* New York: Teachers College Press.

Masters, G. N., & McBryde, B. (1994). *An investigation of the comparability of teachers' assessments of students' folios.* Brisbane, Australia: Tertiary Entrance Procedures Authority.

McMillan, J. H. (2001). Secondary teachers' classroom assessment and grading practices. *Educational Measurement: Issues and Practice, 20,* 20–32.

National Center for Education Statistics. (2001). *Conditions of education 2001.* Washington, DC: U.S. Department of Education.

National Council of Teachers of English. (1996). *Standards for the English language arts.* Urbana, IL: Author.

National Council of Teachers of Mathematics. (1991). *Professional standards for teaching mathematics.* Reston, VA: Author.

National Research Council. (2002). *Learning and understanding: Improving advanced study of mathematics and science in U.S. high schools.* Washington, DC: National Academy Press.

The No Child Left Behind Act of 2001. (2001). P.L. 107-110 (107th Congress).

Office of Educational Research and Improvement. (1994). *What do student grades mean? Differences across schools* (OR 94-3401). Washington, DC: U.S. Department of Education.

Olson, L. (2001, January 11). Finding the right mix. *Education Week,* pp. 12–20.

Olson, L. (2002, April 24). Survey shows state testing alters instructional practices. *Education Week,* p. 14.

Oregon University System. (2001). *An introduction to the Proficiency-based Admission Standards System (PASS).* Eugene, OR: Author.

Oregon University System, Oregon Department of Education, & Oregon Department of Community Colleges and Workforce Development. (2003). *The first year: Student performance on 10th grade benchmark standards and subsequent performance in the first year of college (2001–02).* Eugene, OR: Oregon University System.

Project 2061, American Association for the Advancement of Science. (1993). *Benchmarks for science literacy.* New York: Oxford University Press.

Roey, S., Caldwell, N., Rust, K., Blumstein, E., Krenzke, T., Legum, S., Kuhn, J., & Waksberg, M. (2001). *The 1998 high school transcript study tabulations: Comparative data on credits earned and demographics for 1998, 1994, 1990, 1987, and 1982 high school graduates.* Washington, DC: National Center for Educational Statistics, U.S. Department of Education.

Shapiro, N. S., & Haeger, J. (1999). The K–16 challenge: The Maryland case. *Metropolitan Universities: An International Forum, 10* (2), 25–32.

Thomas, L. M., & Thomas, S. G. (2000). *The impact of Advanced Placement courses on high school students taking the Scholastic Aptitude Test* (ED445-102). College Park, MD: ERIC Clearinghouse on Assessment & Evaluation.

U.S. Department of Education. (2001). *No child left behind.* Washington, DC: Author.

University System of Georgia. (2002, June 19). PACTS: *Performance Assessment for Colleges and Technical Schools.* Retrieved February 6, 2003, from http://www.usg.edu/p16/pacts/

Venezia, A., Kirst, M., & Antonio, A. (2003). *Betraying the college dream: How disconnected K–12 and postsecondary systems undermine student aspirations.* Palo Alto, CA: Stanford Institute on Higher Education Research.

Viadero, D. (2003, February 5). Researchers debate impact of tests. *Education Week,* pp. 1, 12.

Author Index

Subject Index